Luke 6:40 and the Theme of Likeness Education in the New Testament

Luke 6:40 and the
Theme of Likeness Education
in the New Testament

THOMAS W. HUDGINS

With a Foreword by David Alan Black

WIPF & STOCK · Eugene, Oregon

LUKE 6:40 AND THE THEME OF LIKENESS EDUCATION
IN THE NEW TESTAMENT

Wipf & Stock
An Imprint of Wipf and Stock Publishers
199 W. 8th Ave., Suite 3
Eugene, OR 97401

www.wipfandstock.com

ISBN 13: 978-1-62564-290-5

Manufactured in the U.S.A.

For Robert E. Hudgins Jr.
The best dad in the world, and
My best friend

"Christian education is likeness education."

−David Alan Black

Contents

Tables

Foreword

As an educator for some 37 years now, I realize that a particular function of education is that of modeling. Unfortunately, this emphasis is all too often missing. Many teachers restrict their classrooms to raw information. That is to miss the mark.

I have found that committed students are eager to learn and willing to sacrifice time and effort in order to be more useful to their Lord. They desire training in godly living. Sadly, the practical training to which students are exposed today is pathetically small. The Bible is often seen as merely infallible information. This is emphatically not what discipleship is about. The result is that Christians often emerge from their education with a serious gap between knowing and doing. They emerge without any experience of what Christian living is. Teachers need to be recruited who will not only teach but model what they teach.

In a word, education must return to the biblical pattern of modeling. As Thomas Hudgins puts it in this wonderful book, "Christian education is likeness education." It is impossible to exaggerate the importance of this perspective on education. If education is to be any good, it must be "earthed"—that is, it must make a difference in our lives. Teaching is important, but relationships are vital. Students need the calm personal assistance and care of their teachers. I have had the privilege of mentoring a good number of students through the years, including the author of this book. It was well worth the effort! His examination of Luke 6:40 is long overdue. I anticipate there will be massive opposition, not least from within the seminaries. But one thing I can guarantee. People who read this book will be challenged and edified. Likeness education is, after all, the basic principle behind the Incarnation. God did not send a telegram but His Son to live among us. Relationship is the single most crucial principle for teaching others how to follow Christ.

I am still a learner in this matter of trying to communicate the truth of Scripture in a way that impacts real life. I have a long way to go. Reading this book has brought home to me in a fresh way the need to emulate Jesus' method of teaching. My prayer is that many other readers will make their own discovery of Christ in its pages. We owe it to the next generation to begin in earnest now.

David Alan Black
Dr. M. O. Owens Jr. Chair in New Testament
Southeastern Baptist Theological Seminary

Preface

The Great Commission is for everyone. When a person is saved from their sins, that person is saved to serve the God that has forgiven them and given them eternal life. When a person is rescued out of the domain of darkness and placed into the kingdom of God's beloved Son, that person is supposed to be poured into by spiritually mature brothers and sisters. Sadly, the Great Commission has been misunderstood in places as a mission for the few, a mission for the far away, and a mission without a cost. In those places, believers have eternal life, but they hardly have lives that are living for anything eternal.

The main verb in the Great Commission is μαθητεύσατε. The Christian's marching orders are "Make disciples!" The noun form of this word is found in Luke 6:40, one of the most significant verses for Christian education. Jesus says, "A disciple is not above his teacher. But each disciple, after being fully trained, will be like him." What does Jesus mean by all of this? The answer to this question helps us understand the Great Commission better. What exactly are we supposed to be doing? What does it look like to be training up those who are believing in Jesus?

Let me ask you one more question. Who have you become like in your Christian life? Hopefully you are growing daily in the grace and knowledge of the Lord Jesus Christ. If you are like me, though, you can also point to different people that God has put in your life to make an eternal investment. They have recognized that the typical "Sunday" experience is just not enough if we intend to be faithful to what Christ has charged us to do. Paul felt the same way. Did you know that? This is what he wrote to Timothy: "Now you have followed my teaching. . . ." Now that's generally what people think about making disciples. We stop at teaching. We confine discipleship to a classroom. Paul, however, recognized that if he was going to live his eternal life making an eternal impact this side of heaven, he had to do more than just teach. In 2 Tim 3:10–11a,

Paul says Timothy followed him in eight additional areas of his life. Starting over, Paul wrote, "Now you have followed my teaching, my conduct, my purpose, my faithfulness, my patience, my love, my perseverance, my persecutions, and my sufferings." Timothy became like Paul in each of these areas.

Christian education is not less than teaching, but it is certainly more than teaching. According to the New Testament, Jesus and the apostles were intentionally seeking to cultivate each of these areas in the lives of other disciples. Theirs was eternal life, not just because of the life to come; theirs was eternal life because they were living for those things that had eternal significance. They were driven by seeing the gospel advance in breadth and depth. They wanted the gospel to go near and far across this world. And they wanted the gospel to go deep in the lives of people entrusted to their care. If this book even convinces one person to live in such a way and to exert all their strength in truly making disciples, then all the research is well worth it.

Acknowledgments

The research found within this book would have been absolutely impossible without the love and assistance from many co-laborers in the work of the gospel. Lesly, my lovely Honduran wife, is my most faithful co-laborer in every gospel-driven endeavor. There simply are no words to sufficiently express the blessing that she is in my life. She is amazing. Lesly, I love you.

I am extremely appreciative of Dr. Randy Allen for the use of his facilities over the past year, both for teaching New Testament Greek on-line to pastors throughout Latin America and for the solitude needed for researching and writing. "Mr. Allen" has been there since the beginning of my Christian walk. In fact, it was he who shared the gospel with me. Our relationship has grown from a μαθητής-διδάσκαλος relationship into a deep friendship for which I am eternally grateful.

Ricky Beck and Chris Woods are faithful friends, and my friendship with them spanning the last twelve years has cultivated in me a greater awareness of what the gospel-centered life is all about. They have suffered through numerous phone calls throughout my doctoral studies, listening to everything I was learning and offering valuable insights. Thank you, brothers.

It is my opinion that Southeastern Baptist Theological Seminary is the premiere theological institution for training faithful pastors and other Christian servant-leaders. I am extremely thankful for Dr. Daniel Akin, who provided the funding necessary for me to complete this program and offered me constant encouragement throughout the duration of my studies. The statement "Every classroom is a Great-Commission classroom" is more than a slogan; it is a true description of every classroom I have been in at Southeastern, including the Doctor of Education program. Dr. Kenneth Coley is for me an exemplary teacher. My own teaching will forever bear the imprint of the example he gave to me. Dr. Edward Buchanan is priceless. I learned so much in his classes, but I think his greatest impact in my life is the out-of-the-classroom love and counsel he freely offers to his students, which I am very thankful to have been the recipient of. I am also extremely thankful to our Fall 2010 Doctor of Education cohort: Micheal, Cathy, Marcus, Justin, Denise, Merrie, Mike, and Robert. I also wish to thank the Southeastern library staff for all of their assistance.

Finally, I wish to acknowledge and thank Dr. David Alan Black, the Dr. M. O. Owens Jr. Chair in New Testament Studies and Professor of New Testament and Greek. I have the honor of being his first ever Doctor of Education student. He and his wife, who we affectionately call "Mama B," are extremely important to my wife and me. I'm very thankful to the Lord for your investment in my life. I've grown academically, spiritually, and professionally throughout my relationship with you. I'm most thankful for the ways that God has used you in my own walk with Christ. There are many things that you have emphasized, whether in your classes, your books, or in our conversations, that have resonated in my mind and heart. None of them has been more powerful than this—"The way up in the kingdom of God is down."

1

Introduction

Introduction

Studies concerning the Sermon on the Plain (SOP), Luke's complement to Matthew's Sermon on the Mount (SOM), are primarily entangled in source-critical discussions (i.e., which author used which source and for what reason). Because of the amount of attention given to this interpretive method, less attention has been given to other aspects of biblical interpretation in studies dealing with the SOP, such as lexical, syntactical, structural, and rhetorical analyses. One victim of exegetical neglect is Jesus's "proverbial maxim"[1] concerning the teacher-student relationship (Luke 6:40). It is one of the most important New Testament (NT) texts dealing with Christian education, second only to the Great Commission (Matt 28:19–20).

"An apprentice[2] is not above his or her teacher; but each one, after having been fully trained, will be like his or her teacher" (Luke 6:40). This

1. Evans, *Saint Luke*, 337.

2. The translation "apprentice" will not be used in every translation throughout this research. It is important, however, for believers to rethink what discipleship is. "Apprentice" really captures what Jesus means by the word μαθητής. For discussions on this issue, see Chalke and Wyld, *Apprentice*; Humphreys, *Friends*, 35–37; Dodd, *More New Testament Studies*, 39–40; Skreslet, *Picturing Christian Witness*, 39ff.; Hirsch and Ferguson, *On the Verge*; Calhoun, *Spiritual Disciplines Handbook*, 135; Carlson and Lueken, *Renovation of the Church*, 54–56.

The use of gender-inclusive language here is appropriate. There is no doubt that Jesus views women as disciples, regardless of first-century practices (e.g., Luke 8:1–3; 10:38–42; Acts 9:1–2 [τοὺς μαθητὰς . . . ἄνδρας τε καὶ γυναῖκας]). LaCelle-Peterson notes Greek philosophers at times had female students/followers, but Jewish rabbis did not (*Liberating Tradition*, 60). She writes, "Not only are women named disciples, but verse has been quoted, cited, and referenced in vast amounts of Christian education and discipleship literature.[3] Nevertheless, the verse is nearly untouched in exegetical discussions with the exception of source-critical analyses. These discussions are primarily concerned with (1) where the saying originated, (2) whether Luke's or Matthew's form of the saying is original, and (3) how different forms of the saying (see Matt 10:24–25; John 13:16; 15:20) are used in their respective texts.[4] Some have even suggested that this verse lacks cohesion with its context, leaving interpreters dumbfounded as to how it functions in the paragraph- and section-levels of the discourse.[5]

From this verse arises an undeveloped theme in the Gospel of Luke, the theme of likeness education. Jay Adams, commenting on this verse, writes:

> Our teaching must be of the sort that the Lord commanded. And it calls for great care, because as He once said, "When he is fully trained, the disciple will be like his teacher" (Luke 6:40). Please note, Jesus did not merely say "think" like his teacher, but "be" like his teacher. Holistic teaching takes place whether we know it or not, whether we like or not. We cannot avoid it. That is why it is important to be sure that we know what is being taught by our lives, as well as our lips. Any dichotomy between the two is false and unbiblical.[6]

many women are depicted as doing what disciples do. They witness Jesus's ministry, they follow him, and they serve him, which is what discipleship consists of. In the end they also give witness to what they have seen and heard" (*Liberating Tradition*, 61). See also Köstenberger, *Jesus and the Feminists*, 139; Winston and Winston, *Recovering Biblical Ministry*, 268; Borland, "Woman," 113–23; Hays, *Ethics*, 84ff.

The translations used in the book, unless otherwise noted, are the author's own.

3. See, for example, Letterman, "Public Education," 281; Pazmiño, *Foundational Issues*, 44; Baucham Jr., *Family Driven Faith*, 202 and 209; Heywood, *Divine Revelation and Human Learning*, 1; Hooper, *Christian School Teacher*, 138–39; Mithcell, *Leading, Teaching, and Making Disciples*, 405; Kie and Vining, "Disciple Them, Keep Them," 409; Issler, "Philosophy of Education," 113 and 117; Ogden, *Discipleship Essentials*, 11; Closson, "Public, Private, or Home Education," 121; Hughes, "Why Christian Education?," 251; Bolton and Smith, *Creative Bible Learning*, 17; Litfin, *Christian College*, 230; Yount, *Created to Learn*, 272; Hendricks, *Teaching to Change Lives*, 18.

4. See, for example, Adamczewski, *Q or Not Q?*, 289ff.; Neirynck, "John and the Synoptics: 1975–1990," 3–62.

5. For example, Geldenhuys says, "It is extremely difficult to decide what connection exists between these verses and the foregoing portion of the sermon" (*Gospel of Luke*, 213).

6. Adams, *Help People Change*, 53.

Whatever likeness education is, it involves more than mere cognition. Joe Aldrich, referring to the importance of Luke 6:40 in evangelism, echoes Adams's comments: "Notice it doesn't say 'he will know what his teacher knows.' He will be like his teacher—good or bad, beautiful or ugly."[7] The goal in discipleship is not to know what Jesus knows. Instead, as Lawrence O. Richards writes, the goal is "likeness to his person."[8] Transformation into this likeness requires audial and visual instruction in the things that make Jesus who he is—his life, attitude, values, emotion, commitment, etc.[9] Other writers have referred to research in the area of mentoring/modeling, citing Luke 6:40 as one of the foundational texts. For example, Bill Donahue and Greg Bowman say that research in leadership has validated the words of Jesus:

> [Studies] confirm that in about thirty-six months, the people you lead will very closely reflect who you are. A loving teacher will produce loving disciples. A joyful teacher typically has disciples who are filled with joy. The sobering aspect of this principle is that it works whether the values and practices the teacher models are good or bad. Therefore, it is critical that you model the right pattern of living for your leaders.[10]

These statements seem fair and accurate. Nevertheless, an in-depth analysis of the text in its context will ensure accurate application. For example, was Jesus using a general principle and applying it positively or negatively in Luke 6:40? Was it directed only for his disciples, or was he directing such statements at the crowds, or perhaps even the Pharisees? Did this saying have a revealing-concealing nature as Jesus's parables did elsewhere?[11] Or, is Jesus teaching sagaciously, either using a proverb *creatio ex nihilo* or using a maxim common in Greco-Roman/Judaic first-century Palestine?

An analysis of Luke 6:40 is only the place to begin. Like Matthew's Gospel, Luke's Gospel was designed for discipleship, particularly in the regions where Paul had preached and taught the gospel.[12]

---

7. Aldrich, *Lifestyle Evangelism*, 97.

8. Richards, *Christian Education*, 34.

9. Ibid.

10. Donahue and Bowman, *Coaching Small Group Leaders*, 31.

11. See Luke 6:39 (εἶπεν δὲ καὶ παραβολὴν αὐτοῖς).

12. See Black, *Why Four Gospels?*, 53–55.

Statement of the Problem

This study attempts to develop the theme of likeness education in the NT through lexical, syntactical, structural, rhetorical, and theological connections to Luke 6:40 and its immediate context. The aim is to answer the question "What is likeness education according to the New Testament?" The study consists of three concentric areas of investigation: (1) Luke 6:40 and its immediate context, (2) Luke-Acts, and (3) the New Testament corpus. Luke 6:40 serves as the common center in this investigation. The research questions are as follows:

1. What is likeness education according to Luke 6:40 and its immediate context?

2. What is likeness education according to Luke-Acts?

3. What is likeness education according to the New Testament corpus?

Into what likeness, or, better stated, into whose likeness, should a believer's life be made? And what does this sort of discipleship involve through the lenses of Jesus's teachings and actions and the remainder of the New Testament?

Assumptions

This research adopts the traditional belief in Lukan authorship based on internal (#1–4 below)[13] and external evidences (#5 below):

1. The author of the Gospel and Acts are one and the same.[14]

2. The author of Acts utilizes the first-person plural, indicating he was a close traveling companion of the Apostle Paul.[15]

13. The proposal that Luke's lexicography demonstrates his first-hand familiarity with medical language, a knowledge that could not be possessed by someone other than a doctor/physician, has been refuted over the last fifty years and, thus, not included as one of the internal evidences in the list. Juel writes, "Luke's use of medical terminology is paralleled in the writings of other authors and historians. The technical vocabulary tells us more about the care and sophistication of the writer than it does about his occupation" (*Luke-Acts*, 6). See also Twelftree, *People of the Spirit*, 6.

14. The author refers to "the first account" (τὸν πρῶτον λόγον; Acts 1:1), referring to the Gospel. Both are addressed to Theophilus (Luke 1:3; Acts 1:1).

15. See Acts 16:10–17; 20:5–15; 21:1–18; 27:1–9; 28:1–16. The suggestion that the author of Acts chose this as a rhetorical tool remains unproven. Another suggestion is that the author of Acts was editing a travel diary for one of Paul's close associates. That

3.   The author of Luke-Acts shows many similarities to Pauline teaching and theology when the content of the Gospel and Paul's speeches in Acts are compared to Paul's numerous letters.[16]

4.   Paul thrice refers to this individual, Luke, in his letters.[17]

5.   The general testimony of the Early Church[18] (the Muratorian Fragment, Irenaeus, Tertullian, Clement of Alexandria, Eusebius, and Jerome)[19] ascribes the authorship of the Gospel and its sequel to Luke.[20]

---

the author would change the first person to the third throughout the text and not in the places listed above only weakens the credibility of the work, turning Acts into an edited work that was poorly edited. Drane writes:

> "[T]he use of this pronoun clearly implies that the writer was present on these occasions, and therefore was a companion of Paul. Since the style of these passages is the same as that of the book as a whole, it seems likely that the author has used his own travel diary as a source of information, and a careful scrutiny of the narratives shows that Luke is the person who best fits the evidence." (*Introducing the New Testament*, 200–201)

See also Twelftree, *People of the Spirit*, 6.

16. Some do not recognize parallels between Pauline teaching and theology and the writings of Luke. Arens, for example, writes:

> "La relación entre 'Lucas' y Pablo es relativamente fácil de establecer, en función a los escritos de ambos. Si Lucas hubiese sido compañero de Pablo, una comparación de la teología y la cristología de ambos debería mostrar ciertas afinidades, al menos con los elementos centrales de la predicación paulina, cosa que no encontramos." (*Los Evangelios Ayer y Hoy*, 326)

Not only are there parallels in their doctrine, there are strong similarities between their views of discipleship, especially that it is holistic and involves the transference of one's character to that of another (cf. Luke 6:40 with 2 Tim 2:2 and 3:10–17).

17. He refers to him as "Luke, the beloved physician" (Λουκᾶς ὁ ἰατρὸς ὁ ἀγαπητός; Col 4:14), as one of his "co-laborers" (. . . Λουκᾶς, οἱ συνεργοί μου; Phlm 24) along with Mark, Aristarchus, and Demas, and by his name, Λουκᾶς, with no qualifying description since Timothy would have clearly known who Paul was referring to (2 Tim 4:11). Each reference is made by Paul following the Third Missionary Journey and not once in letters pre-dating his arrival in Rome, thus corroborating the "we" passages in Acts.

18. Even Marcion, who was excommunicated in AD 144, identified Luke as the author in the prologue to his canon (c. AD 150).

19. Twelftree adds P75 to the list of texts supporting Lukan authorship (*People of the Spirit*, 6).

20. Parsons's assessment is fair:

This study also adopts the Fourfold-Gospel Hypothesis as outlined in David Alan Black's *Why Four Gospels? The Historical Origins of the Gospels*. Matthew's Gospel was written first sometime prior to the persecution of Herod Agrippa in AD 42 (Stage 1). Paul's missionary travels took him through the regions of southern Galatia and Macedonia bordering the Mediterranean Sea evangelizing both Jewish and Gentile audiences. While Paul was detained in Caesarea, he recruited Luke, one of his disciples who happened to be a Gentile, to research and record a "fuller elucidation of Jesus's ministry and of the place of the Gentiles in the kingdom of God."[21] Matthew's Gospel, which Paul used during his missionary travels, was designed as a disciple-making resource by the apostles for a predominantly Jewish background. As Black points out, "it was unthinkable that it should ever be outmoded or superseded."[22] Nevertheless, Paul's ministry in predominantly Gentile regions made him aware of both the strengths and weaknesses that the Gospel of Matthew possessed "as an instrument for the evangelization of the Gentiles."[23] Luke's work was completed sometime between AD 58–60[24] (Stage 2), and it was finally published for circulation in AD 62.[25]

"If the Third Gospel were attributed to a person named Luke very soon after its publication, then it is reasonable to assume that the first audiences of this Gospel were already associating this document with the Luke known to be a participant in the Pauline mission. . . . By the fourth century, these traditions were well enough established to be summarized by the historian Eusebius. . . ." (*Luke*, 1)

21. Black, *Why Four Gospels?*, 73.

22. Ibid., 54.

23. Ibid.

24. Markan priority creates a conundrum for the date of Luke's Gospel. A later date for Luke's Gospel follows if it is given that Luke used Mark as one of his sources. Such is not the case, however. Considering the earliest and latest possible dates for the book of Acts provides a strong argument against Markan priority. The Gospel required Luke's investigation into eyewitness accounts, something for which Paul's detainment in Caesarea provided time. However, Acts could be written on the basis of Peter's and Paul's testimony, with Luke able to recount his own eyewitness testimony of the "we" passages in Acts. The latest possible date for Acts must be prior to the destruction of Jerusalem (AD 70) and, more likely, prior to Paul's fate in Rome since Acts ends at that point chronologically. Had it taken place in AD 70 or after, one would expect for Luke to have shown how Jesus's words in Luke 21:20 had been fulfilled, especially since "Luke tells us how the prophecy of Agabus about a world-wide famine was fulfilled (Acts 11:28)" (Carson and Moo, *An Introduction to the New Testament*, 207). The early date is necessary, not just a viable option.

25. The remainder of the Fourfold-Gospel Hypothesis is as follows. While in Rome,

It should also be noted that this research affirms the Pauline authorship of Hebrews. This affirmation does not necessarily impact the research. Nevertheless, so that readers are not caught off-guard when they encounter statements like "Paul wrote . . ." in reference to Hebrews, it is better to deal with this up front. Pauline authorship of this letter is heavily doubted in scholarly circles today. In fact, doubt in the Pauline authorship is now the norm. There is a very strong case, based on internal and external evidences, in favor of Paul as the letter's author.[26] Books continually partition out the *Corpus Paulinum* minus Πρὸς Ἑβραίους. A discussion about the Pauline authorship of Hebrews is beyond the scope of this text. Given the convincing evidence and for the sake of making the text read easier, Paul is referred to throughout this text as the author of the letter.

Method

This study employs qualitative content analysis to examine Luke 6:40 and likeness education.[27] In its broadest sense, content analysis is "a way that researchers can study the world through nonliving materials."[28]

Paul presented Peter with a copy of Luke's final draft for Peter's approval and authorization for use in the Gentile-dominant churches where the gospel was being preached and taught. Peter delivered a series of lectures in Rome utilizing both Matthew and Luke, thus giving his own apostolic seal of approval on the work and validating the new discipleship tool. The Gospel of Luke was thus published in AD 62, with Mark's collection of Peter's lectures following four or five years later (Stage 3). The Gospel of John was penned some twenty-nine years later and published in Ephesus (Stage 4).

26. For a discussion on the external evidence, see David Alan Black's "Pauline Authorship of Hebrews (Part 2)," 78–86. For a discussion on the internal evidence, see Black's "Pauline Authorship of Hebrews (Part 1)," 32–51, especially his discussion of the lexical-syntactical similarities between Hebrews and the rest of Paul's letters (e.g., διὰ τοῦτο, σωτηρία [18x], and a whole list of words found in Hebrews that are exclusively used by Paul elsewhere). Also, a short book by Black dealing with both the internal and external evidence is being published by Energion titled *The Authorship of Hebrews: The Case for Paul*. In addition to this, see Jacob Cerone's post "The Use of γράφω."

27. The methodology selected for this study incorporates thematic analysis methodology, a sub-field of qualitative content analysis that specifically "focuses on the themes mentioned in your material" (Schreier, *Qualitative Content Analysis*, 1). As Julien writes, qualitative content analysis involves a "close reading of text to reveal themes in discourse" ("Content Analysis," 120).

28. Hesse-Biber and Leavy, *Practice of Qualitative Research*, 227. Olabuénaga provides another basic definition: "El análisis de Contenido no es otra cosa que una técnica

The following three definitions are more specific and are provided for consideration:

1. Margrit Schreier defines content analysis as "a method for describing the meaning of qualitative material in a systematic way. You do this by assigning successive parts of your material to the categories of your coding frame."[29]

2. Heidi Julien defines content analysis as "the intellectual process of categorizing qualitative textual data into clusters of similar entities, or conceptual categories, to identify consistent patterns and relationships between variables or themes."[30]

3. Carol Grbich defines content analysis as "a systematic coding and categorising approach which you can use to unobtrusively explore large amounts of textual information in order to ascertain the trends and patterns of words used, their frequency, their relationships and the structures and discourses of communication."[31]

Central to these definitions is the idea of organizing material into coding frames or conceptual categories. Once these categories are established, the textual data in consideration is analyzed in light of them. Grbich's definition shows that word frequency is only one part of content analysis, and it is not a mandatory one. Lynn Meadows and Diane M. Dodendorf show that content analysis moves beyond word-analysis, just as Grbich mentions (i.e., "their relationship . . . structures"). Content analysis includes syntactical, semantic, and pragmatic relationships.[32] Juan Báez and Pérez de Tudela identify the basic objectives of qualitative content

---

para leer e interpretar el contenido de toda clase de documentos y, más concretamente (aunque no exclusivamente), de los documentos escritos" (*Investigación Cualitativa*, 192). Similarly, Andersen and Taylor say content analysis is "a way of using cultural artifacts to measure what people write, say, see, and hear. The researcher studies not people but the communications or documents they produce as a way of creating a picture of the society" (*Sociology*, 40). Were it possible to interview Jesus, or even the apostles, to identify the intricacies of likeness education, that would be ideal. However, the only option at this point is to study the texts that remain from them.

29. Schreier, *Qualitative Content Analysis*, 37.

30. Julien, "Content Analysis," 120.

31. Grbich, *Qualitative Data Analysis*, 112.

32. See Meadows and Dodendorf, "Data Management and Interpretation," 200; Navarro and Díaz, "Análisis de Contenido," 180 and 192; Baird, "Content Analysis," 114. Baird's definition is exclusively quantitative, but he points out that the data extends beyond lexical analysis to include syntax and semantics.

analysis as: (1) search for themes, (2) describe their characteristics, (3) establish categories for analysis, and (4) interpret the textual data.[33]

Content analysis is not entirely new to the fields of religious and biblical studies.[34] Schreier mentions how this methodology, albeit in an infancy stage, was utilized in the late seventeenth and early eighteenth centuries:

> Church potentates were worried that non-religious or unortho-dox material might be distributed in the name of the Church. . . . In eighteenth-century Sweden, for instance, a collection of hymns was analysed for the frequency of certain key words (such as God, Kingdom of Heaven) to determine whether these songs were in line with Church teachings.[35]

Dan Lioy provides a content analysis in his research comparing the Decalogue (Exod 20:1–17//Deut 5:6–21) and the SOM (Matthew 5–7).[36] He uses content analysis to identify themes in the Decalogue so that he can compare the relationship that exists between the discourses. Daniel Lee Ray also uses content analysis methodology to analyze Jesus's teaching methods in order to identify if Jesus used differentiated instruction during his earthly ministry.[37] The application of content analysis methodology in NT studies is not common, but it has amazing potential for significant advances in understanding themes and teachings central to Jesus and the apostles for the life of the church.[38]

33. They write: "Planteado en términos de objetivos de investigación resulta obvio decir que el análisis de contenido cualitativo busca temas, describe sus particularidades, establece las categorías de análisis y los interpreta" (Báez and de Tudela, *Investigación Cualitativa*, 290).

34. While it is not new to the field of biblical studies, Griffin points out the rarity of "explicit" applications of such methodology in the field of biblical studies (*The God of the Prophets*, 24). He adds, "[S]ome exegetical, literary, and historical biblical studies border on content analysis, while few make an overt connection with content analysis" (ibid.).

35. Schreier, *Qualitative Content Analysis*, 8.

36. Lioy, *Decalogue*.

37. Ray, "Jesus's Teaching Methods."

38. Griffin identifies three ways in which content analysis can be useful in the analysis of Scripture: (1) "it could illuminate characteristics of any given text, providing a list of what is or is not emphasized by a text"; (2) "it could be accessed by inputting the characteristics in which one is interested; the system would then provide a text or texts which approximate these characteristics"; and (3) it "could be especially useful for comparing different texts, especially in terms of conceptual similarities and differences" (Griffin, *The God of the Prophets*, 22).

Different content analysts provide different steps for the methodology. Some are more expanded than others, while others are more abbreviated. Richard M. Grinnell Jr. and Yvonne A. Unrau provide the following steps: (1) Develop a research question; (2) Select a sample; (3) Select the unit of analysis; (4) Code; (5) Tally; (6) Analyze the data.[39] The steps provided by Báez and de Tudela are: (1) Preparation of material; (2) Reading and pre-analysis; (3) Unit selection; (4) Coding; and (5) Validation of content analysis.[40] Karin Klenke provides the following steps: (1) Read all the texts repeatedly; (2) Re-read all the texts word-for-word; (3) Take notes; (4) Code; and (5) Interpret.[41] Richard E. Boyatzis lists three stages: (1) Choose the sample and design; (2) Develop themes and code; and (3) Apply the code.[42]

Before identifying the steps of investigation for this research study, two comments are necessary. First, this study builds on raw information, not previous theory. Boyatzis thinks working from raw information is beneficial in content analysis because it "enhances appreciation of the information," jettisons "intermediaries as potentially contaminating factors," and allows for greater appreciation of the "gross . . . and intricate aspects" of the research findings.[43] Second, Schreier mentions that content analysis can be linear or cyclical. Thematic characteristics surface as the researcher works through the material recurrently.[44] Julien calls this an "iterative process," in which the researcher returns to previously identified categories over and over to combine, divide, or otherwise modify them.[45] This allows for a more exhaustive and detailed analysis of the data.

The steps of this content analysis are as follows:

39. Grinnell Jr. and Unrau, *Social Work Research*, 381ff.

40. Báez and de Tudela, *Investigación Cualitativa*, 290–92.

41. Klenke, *Qualitative Research in the Study of Leadership*, 92.

42. Boyatzis, *Transforming Qualitative Information*, 29.

43. Ibid., 30. Working with raw information also frees the researcher from having to adopt the assumptions, projections, or biases (if any existed) of another investigator.

44. She writes: "This would mean that you keep on building and revising your coding frame as you include additional cases and collect more data. When you have completed your data collection, you do one last round of revising your coding frame and then apply it to all your material" (Schreier, *Qualitative Content Analysis*, 36). Adding a cyclical aspect to the analysis deepens the analysis and strengthens the reliability/validity of the research.

45. Julien, "Content Analysis," 120.

1. Identify the text to be studied.[46]

2. Identify the order in which the NT letters will be evaluated: (1) the Pauline corpus, (2) the Non-Pauline corpus.[47]

3. Perform an exegetical analysis of Luke 6:40 and its immediate context.

4. Develop a framing code consisting of different concepts based on the exegesis of Luke 6:40 and its immediate context.[48]

5. Summarize the findings.

6. Read the Pauline corpus.

7. Analyze the Pauline passages using the framing code.

8. Highlight new aspects of likeness education not previously identified through the analysis of Luke 6:40 and its context (if necessary) and modify the framing code.

9. Summarize the findings.

10. Read the Non-Pauline corpus.

11. Analyze the Non-Pauline passages using the framing code.

12. Highlight new aspects of likeness education not previously identified through the analysis of Luke 6:40 and its context and the analysis of the Pauline corpus (if any). And modify the framing code.

46. Since the NT is a relatively small corpus, there is no need to use a sample. The entire NT will be analyzed. This does not mean, however, that the research will be exhaustive.

47. Pauline and non-Pauline letters will be evaluated in the order in which they were written.

48. Coffey and Atkinson define coding as the act of "condensing the bulk of our data sets into analyzable units by creating categories with and from our data" (*Making Sense of Qualitative Data*, 26). Coding will be reductive and conceptual. Concerning the former, Schreier writes, "[T]he focus is on grouping together data addressing the same theme, i.e., on creating links between different pieces of data. This type of coding is purely descriptive, and it essentially reduces large amounts of material to a few general terms" (Schreier, *Qualitative Content Analysis*, 38). This can be accomplished by simply reading data and taking notes, thus identifying manifest content, or by doing more in-depth analysis to draw out the latent content (see Wallen and Fraenkel, *Educational Research*, 415; Bernard, *Research Methods in Anthropology*, 493). Conceptual coding refers to how all of this data relates one to another (Schreier, *Qualitative Content Analysis*, 39). The categories will also utilize labels directly connected to the lexemes and ideas found in the data (Julien, "Content Analysis," 120).

13. Summarize the findings.

14. Conclude research with a summary of likeness education and its characteristics.

Summary

The data analysis is based on the texts of the New Testament. I analyze the data using qualitative content analysis methodology and note recurring ideas. From the initial analysis of Luke 6:40 and its context, a pattern emerges, i.e., the theme of likeness education. The features of likeness education are organized into a coding frame. The size of the initial coding frame depends on the results of the exegetical analysis of Luke 6:40 and its context. I apply the features of likeness education found in Luke 6:39–49 to the remainder of Luke and Acts, followed by the entire New Testament. The finding of additional conceptual categories, should any arise, results in the expansion of the coding frame and broadens the understanding of likeness education. The research concludes with a detailed definition of likeness education and an explanation of its characteristics.

2

Likeness Education in
Luke 6:40 and Its Context

Introduction

Jesus uses the imagery of an apprentice's relationship to his or her teacher in the conclusion of the Sermon on the Plain. The second part of the proverb says that each disciple, after being fully trained, will be like his or her teacher (Luke 6:40). This verse has been cited over and over in Christian education literature, and it is obviously a foundational teaching for Christian educators.[1] The following analysis looks into what Jesus means when he shares this proverb. It consists of four parts using a top-down methodology. First is an analysis of the structure of Luke 6:40 and its context from macro- to micro-structure. Second is a lexical analysis of the use of παραβολή in Luke 6:39, which has been the subject of much debate in the conclusion of the SOP and has dumbfounded many as to what it refers. Next, there is an analysis of Luke 6:39b–45 and its four proverbial units followed by an analysis of the final unit in the sermon's conclusion (6:46–49). This analysis concludes with the development of a

---

1. See, for example, Letterman, "Public Education," 281; Pazmiño, *Foundational Issues*, 44; Baucham Jr., *Family Driven Faith*, 202 and 209; Heywood, *Divine Revelation and Human Learning*, 1; Hooper, *Christian School Teacher*, 138–39; Mithcell, *Leading, Teaching, and Making Disciples*, 405; Kie and Vining, "Disciple Them, Keep Them," 409; Issler, "Philosophy of Education," 113 and 117; Ogden, *Discipleship Essentials*, 11; Closson, "Public, Private, or Home Education," 121; Hughes, "Why Christian Education?," 251; Bolton and Smith, *Creative Bible Learning*, 17; Litfin, *Christian College*, 230; Yount, *Created to Learn*, 272; Hendricks, *Teaching to Change Lives*, 18.

semantic frame, by which the rest of the Luke-Acts and the NT will be analyzed looking for relevant material pertaining to likeness education.

The Structure of Luke 6:40 and Its Context

The Structure of the Gospel of Luke

A survey of scholarship on the Gospel of Luke identifies a generally accepted outline, with only moderate variation:[2]

I. Prologue (1:1–4)[3]

II. Infancy Narratives (1:5—2:52)[4]

III. Preparation for the Public Ministry of Jesus (3:1—4:13)[5]

IV. Jesus's Ministry in Galilee (4:14—9:50)[6]

V. Jesus's Journey to Jerusalem (9:51—19:28)[7]

2. This macro-outline is offered by Lea and Black, *The New Testament*, 154–55; Burkett, *An Introduction to the New Testament*, 204; Ringe, *Luke*, v–xi; Rusam, "Das Lukasevangelium," 186; Friedrich, *Das Neue Testament*, 18.

3. Scholars refer to this section in the following ways: preface, formal preface, introduction, dedication, or statement of purpose. Some pair Luke 1–2 together and label them as introductory material (see deSilva, *Introduction to the New Testament*, 311; Hunter, *Introducing the New Testament*, 50; Tiede, *Luke*, 29; Sabourin, *L'Évangile de Luc*, 51).

4. Branick and others join the infancy narratives and preparation sections (Branick, *Understanding the New Testament and Its Message*, 50; Perrin and Duling, *The New Testament*, 310; Rhein, *Analytical Approach to the New Testament*, 115–20; Kümmell, *Introduction to the New Testament*, 125). Klein also includes both, but he extends the section to 4:44 with the heading "Die Anfänge" (*Das Lukasevangelium*, 79). Stott joins both of these with the prologue (*Story of the New Testament*, 56).

5. Spivey and Smith, as well as Allen, join the preparation and the ministry in Galilee sections, i.e., 3:1—9:50 (Spivey and Smith, *Anatomy of the New Testament*, 137–64; Allen, "The Story of Jesus according to 'Luke,'" 187–91). Johnson combines the sections up to 8:56 (*Gospel of Luke*, 63–144). Tannehill extends this section to v. 44, thus including the beginning of Jesus's ministry (*Luke*, 77).

6. Johnson, who ends the third section at 8:56, includes 9:1–50 as its own section, which he identifies as a period of Jesus's ministry preparing leadership for the people (*Gospel of Luke*, 144ff.).

7. Different scholars place 19:28 at the end of the section covering Jesus's journey to Jerusalem; others place it at the beginning of the section on Jesus's ministry in Jerusalem. Morris, Scholz, Talbert, and Flichy extend this section to v. 44 (Morris, *Luke*, 65–71; Scholz, *Jesus*, 105; Talbert, *Reading Luke*, 219; Flichy, *La Obra de Lucas*, 24), while Stott extends it to v. 40 (*Story of the New Testament*, 58). Tenney, on the

VI. Jesus's Ministry in Jerusalem (19:29—24:53)[8]

Luke organizes his material, both the Gospel and Acts, based on the movement of Jesus and his apostles. According to Luke Timothy Johnson, Jerusalem is the deictic center. In the Gospel, all movement is toward Jerusalem, while in Acts the movement is away from Jerusalem.[9] Sections III and IV of the Gospel are centered around Galilee. A shift takes place in Luke 9:51 when Jesus begins his trek to Jerusalem (καὶ αὐτὸς τὸ πρόσωπον ἐστήρισεν τοῦ πορεύεσθαι εἰς Ἰερουσαλήμ, "and he resolutely determined to go to Jerusalem").[10] The last geographical reference before Jesus arrives in Jerusalem is found in Luke 19:1, when Jesus is passing through Jericho. In 19:28, Luke mentions Jesus's final ascent to Jerusalem, a fifteen-mile distance rising some 3,400 feet (about 226 feet per mile). Luke 19:28–44 describes his travel from Jericho to Bethphage and Bethany, then to the Mount of Olives, until he finally arrives at the temple in 19:45. The remainder of the Gospel takes place in Jerusalem and its environs.

---

other hand, shortens the section to 9:51—18:30 with the heading "The Mission of the Savior" (*New Testament Survey*, 181). Hunter and Klein shorten the section to 19:10 (Hunter, *Introducing the New Testament*, 50; Klein, *Das Lukasevangelium*, 357ff.). Kümmell divides the section in two, naming them the third (9:51—13:30) and fourth (13:31—19:27) parts (*Introduction to the New Testament*, 126-27).

8. Powell, Piñero, and others divide this section in two: 19:28—21:38 and 22:1—24:53 (Powell, *Introducing the New Testament*, 148-49; Piñero, *Literatura Judía*, 196-98; Cousar, *Introduction to the New Testament*, 125; Boring and Craddock, *People's New Testament Commentary*, 176). Tenney, who limited the previous section to 18:30, likewise divides the remaining material into two sections, 18:31—23:56 and 24:1–53, partitioning off the resurrection account into its own section (*New Testament Survey*, 181). Rhein, Perkins, Stein, Craddock, and Johnson divide the section into three parts: 19:28—21:38; 22:1—23:56; 24:1–53 (Rhein, *Analytical Approach to the New Testament*, 119-20; Perkins, *Reading the New Testament*, 215; Stein, *Luke*; Craddock, *Luke*, 225ff.; Johnson, *Gospel of Luke*, 295ff.). Perkins differs with Rhein only where she splits 23:56 into two parts, one ending a section and the other beginning the next. Perrin and Duling also divide the section into three parts; the latter two are 22:1—23:49 and 23:50—24:53, splitting the Passion narrative from the section containing Jesus's burial, resurrection, and ascension (Perrin and Duling, *The New Testament*, 310). Alday opts for four divisions: 19:28—21:38, 22:1-38, 22:39-56, and 24:1–53 (*El Evangelio según Lucas*, 30).

9. Johnson, *The Writings of the New Testament*, 205.

10. See Isa 50:7 (ἀλλὰ ἔθηκα τὸ πρόσωπόν μου ὡς στερεὰν πέτραν, LXX).

The Structure of Luke's Fourth Section (4:14—9:50)

The SOP (Luke 6:20–49) is situated near the middle of the fourth section of Luke's Gospel. For the purposes of this content analysis, it is necessary to identify the point in the Gospel of Luke that Jesus delivers this discourse. While the unit and episode divisions are less important, identifying something about them assists in showing the sermon's context in Jesus's ministry leading to the cross. Donald Guthrie points out two units before the SOP and two that follow:

1. *4:14–44.* This section includes Jesus's inaugural message and rejection in Nazareth (4:16–30), Jesus's teaching and authority over demons in Capernaum (4:31–37), and other teaching and healings (4:38–39, 40–41, 42–44).[11]

2. *5:1–6:16.* This section includes Jesus's call of Peter, James, and John (5:1–11) and, later, Levi (also called Matthew; 5:27–32). It concludes with the selection of twelve disciples as apostles (6:12–16).

3. *7:1–8:56.* This section includes teaching and healing episodes around Capernaum.

4. *9:1–50.* This section includes the mission of the Twelve (9:1–6), Peter's confession that Jesus is "the Christ of God" (τὸν Χριστὸν τοῦ θεοῦ; 9:20), two predictions concerning Jesus's approaching death and resurrection (9:22, 44–45), and the Transfiguration (9:28–45).

Robert H. Stein identifies six units, two preceding the SOP and four that follow.[12] The primary difference between Stein's and Guthrie's divisions pertains to Luke 7:1–8:56. Stein provides three divisions in place of Guthrie's single unit: (1) 7:1–50, (2) 8:1–21, and (3) 8:22–56. The first concentrates on who Jesus is, the second his teachings, and the third Jesus's demonstration of his authority over all things. Joel B. Green has two divisions in place of Guthrie's unit: (1) 7:1–50 and (2) 8:1–56.[13] Stein also concludes the second unit at 6:12, a move that has linguistic support.

Fearghus Ó Fearghail divides the unit slightly different: (1) 5:1—6:11; (2) 6:12–49; (3) 7:1–50; (4) 8:1–56; and (5) 9:1–50. He concentrates on Jesus's movements and characteristic ways in which Luke opens and closes units, especially his use of ἐγένετο δέ to identify the author-intended

11. D. Guthrie, *New Testament Introduction*, 133–34.

12. Stein, *Luke*, 151.

13. Green, *Gospel of Luke*, 27.

structure and to mark the openings of pericopes.[14] He views 5:1—9:50 as the major unit. Despite not including 4:14–44, he recognizes the way Luke concludes in 4:44, using the periphrastic imperfect. He says it is "eminently suitable for the conclusion of a major section of Luke's work, given that it has the character of a general summary (cf. 24,53; Acts 28, 30–31) and represents a pause in the narrative."[15] He also notes how Luke tends to conclude pericopes "on a note of climactic opposition mingled with perplexity or the inability to act."[16] In 5:1–2 and 9:51–52, Luke uses ἐγένετο δέ, something Ó Fearghail considers an element "typical of Lucan pericope-openings."[17] In fact, this construction is unique to Luke in the NT, occurring seventeen times in the Gospel and twenty times in Acts.[18] The ἐγένετο δέ construction and Jesus's movement mark the beginning of the SOP discourse unit (6:12), thus connecting the selection of the Twelve after an intense night of prayer with Luke's complement to the Sermon on the Mount.[19] Identifying the end of the SOP is rather obvious given Luke's immediate geographical reference following Jesus's teaching (εἰσῆλθεν εἰς Καφαρναούμ, 7:1).

The Structure of the Sermon on the Plain

The SOP discourse unit is found in Luke 6:12–49. The first eight verses are introductory (6:12–19). Luke 6:12–16 contains the selection of twelve of Jesus's disciples and their naming as apostles (6:13). Luke 6:17–19 sets the stage for Jesus's teaching, which accomplishes three purposes:

1.   It identifies where the teaching takes place (6:17, ἐπὶ τόπου πεδινοῦ of the mountain/hill [τὸ ὄρος] mentioned in 6:12).[20]

14. Ó Fearghail, *The Introduction to Luke-Acts*, 39–66.

15. Ibid., 42.

16. Ibid., 45.

17. Ibid., 42.

18. See Luke 1:8; 2:1, 6; 3:21; 5:1; 6:1, 6, 12; 8:22; 9:28, 37, 51; 11:14, 27; 16:22; 18:35; 22:24; in Acts, see 4:5; 5:7; 8:1, 8; 9:19, 32, 37, 43; 10:10; 11:26; 14:1; 15:39; 16:16; 19:1, 23; 22:6, 17; 23:9, 28:8, and 17. In the LXX, the construction appears primarily in Genesis (48 occurrences).

19. See also Nickle, *Preaching the Gospel of Luke*, 64.

20. Claims of any symbolism intended by Luke's use of τόπου πεδινοῦ and τὸ ὄρος (i.e., that the mountain/hill represents "vertical, divine/human communication" and the level place represents "horizontal human-to-human communication") are unwarranted (Nickle, *Preaching the Gospel of Luke*, 64). Luke's use strictly continues the narrative offering a geographical reference that connects the material to Matthew's Sermon on the Mount.

2. It specifies who is present for the teaching. The audience consists of three groups. The first group is marked by the pronoun αὐτῶν (6:17), whose antecedent is the Twelve (δώδεκα) who Jesus named as apostles (ἀποστόλους). The second group is the larger group of Jesus's disciples (ὄχλος πολὺς μαθητῶν αὐτοῦ). The third group consists of an even greater number of people traveling from Judea in the south and from coastal regions north of Galilee.

3. It explains why the latter group travelled to where Jesus was. The main clause marked by the relative pronoun reveals two reasons: (1) to hear Jesus teach (ἀκοῦσαι αὐτοῦ), and (2) to be healed (ἰαθῆναι) by him.

Following a brief transition (6:20a), Luke's account of Jesus's teaching begins (i.e., the sermon proper). The sermon proper consists of three discourse units.[21] The first unit (6:20b–26) contains Jesus's pronouncement of blessings (μακάριοι) and woes (οὐαί), consisting of four each. The second unit (6:27–38) records Jesus's commands for kingdom-living supplemented with different rhetorical questions. The final unit (6:39–49), marked by the phrase that has puzzled some[22] (εἶπεν δὲ καὶ παραβολὴ αὐτοῖς, 6:39a), consists of a series of sagacious illustrations ultimately followed by Jesus's call for everyone to come to him, hear his words, and

---

21. Kingsbury, *Conflict in Luke*, 113.

22. For example, John Nolland writes, "It is difficult to follow the thread of thought" (*Luke 1–9:20*, 305). Geldenhuys says, "It is extremely difficult to decide what connection exists between these verses and the foregoing portion of the sermon" (*Gospel of Luke*, 213). Tiede, tracing the problem back to the interpretation of παραβολή, writes, "It is not even clear exactly which of the items that follow is the 'parable' Luke had in mind" (Tiede, *Luke*, 145). Concerning vv. 37–42, Harrington writes, "This passage does not have the structural coherence of the previous one; the warning not to pass judgment on others, the parable of the Mote and Beam, and the remaining elements are rather superficially linked—Luke must have found them so joined in his source" (*The Gospel according to St. Luke*, 113). Bruce has this note: "[T]he connection of thought not being apparent" (*The Synoptic Gospels*, 507). Johnson calls Luke's use of the singular παραβολή "a bit puzzling" and favors the translation "'he began to speak parabolically'" (Johnson, *Gospel of Luke*, 114). Finally, Lieu calls the material "less coherent," saying it is "linked more by association of words and ideas than by logical progression" (*Gospel of Luke*, 52). The argument has also been made that this construction is indicative of Luke's use of a source, a sort of citation (McNichol, *Jesus' Directions for the Future*, 144). This argument, however, does not explain why Luke would need to indicate his use of a source here and not elsewhere (since he only uses this construction five times). It is best to understand it as a transition (Nolland, *Luke 1–9:20*, 306).

act on them (6:46–49).[23] That Luke intends a new unit of thought here is clear because of his narrative insertion,[24] the only such insertion in the sermon proper, and, as David L. Tiede points out, the change in "the kind of sayings material."[25] Even though a new unit begins, the content that follows logically flows from Jesus's commands in vv. 35–38:

1. Love, do good, and lend (v. 35).

2. Be merciful (v. 36).

3. Do not judge or condemn, and pardon (v. 37).

4. Give (v. 38).

Michel Gourgues shows how this formula is used to illustrate preceding material when there is no indication of a change in setting or time.[26] The climax of the SOP will specify how someone can carry out Jesus's commands, be children of the Most High (ἔσεσθε υἱοὶ ὑψίστου, 6:35), and be just like (καθώς) their heavenly Father (6:36) by coming to Jesus, hearing his words, and actually doing what he says.

This third and final unit in the sermon proper is best divided into two subunits: (1) 6:39–45, and (2) 6:46–49.[27] Others divide the unit at different points, such as: 6:39–40, 6:41–42, 6:43–45, and 6:46–49.[28] Nev-

---

23. For examples of those who favor this division, see Kingsbury, *Conflict in Luke*, 113; Major et al., *Mission and Message*, 349; Jeffrey, *Luke*, 101; González, *Luke*, 95–96; Nolland, *Luke 1–9:20*, 305; Talbert, *Reading Luke*, 78. Others, such as Johnson and Sabourin, include 6:36–38 in the final unit (Johnson, *Gospel of Luke*, 112; Sabourin, *L'Évangile de Luc*, 178). This division, however, does not adequately accommodate for Luke's narration in 6:39, the only occurrence in the sermon proper, which clearly marks a new unit.

24. See Arndt, *Luke*, 507.

25. Tiede, *Luke*, 145.

26. Commenting on Luke 13:6–9, Gourgues writes:

"Les vv. 6–9 sont introduits simplement par : 'Or, il disait cette parabole'. À cette formule, qui n'indique aucun changement de temps ni de lieux, ne s'ajoute aucune clause introductive comme on en trouve ailleurs chez Luc lorsqu'il s'agit de paraboles sans lien à ce qui précède. A l'inverse, Luc utilise la même formule qu'ici en d'autres endroits où une parabole est mise en relation avec ce qui précède. Ainsi, par exemple, en Lc 5, 36, la parabole sur le neuf et le vieux est liée de la même manière au développement sur le jeune; en 6, 39, la "parabole" des deux aveugles a l'exhortation à ne pas juger (6, 37–38)." (*Luc, de l'Exégèse à la Prédication*, 40)

27. De Gasperis, *Sentieri di Vita*, 174.

28. See, for example, Bock, *Luke: Volume 1 (1:1–9:50)*, 609.

ertheless, the aforementioned division best subdivides the unit. Verses 39, 40, and 41–42 each concentrate on different types of persons and the effect that they have on another. In 6:39 it is the relationship of a blind person with another blind person; in 6:40 it is the relationship of a teacher with his or her student; in 6:41–42, it is the relationship of two brothers, who each have something in their eye. The first two subunits are addressed in the third person. Jesus switches to the second-person singular in 6:41–42 with two questions. The first question asks "why?" (τί) and the second asks "how?" (πῶς). This subunit concludes with four uses of γάρ (6:43–45). The second subdivision is marked by the switch to the first-person singular followed by the clearest material representative of παραβολή in the unit.

The Meaning of Παραβολή in Luke 6:39

The Semantic Range of Παραβολή

Since Luke 6:39 begins the final section of the SOP and since so much confusion about the logical cohesion within the unit surrounds the understanding of παραβολή, it is necessary to determine Luke's intent when he uses it in his narrative commentary. Black writes, "The key to lexical analysis is to remember that a word can have several meanings, only one of which is likely to be its semantic contribution to any particular sentence in which it occurs."[29] The first step in identifying Luke's intended meaning in Luke 6:39 is to identify the semantic range of the word in the Greek language. The next step is to identify how Luke uses the word throughout the Gospel.

Alfred E. Tuggy, Maurice A. Robinson and Mark A. House, and G. Abbott-Smith each list four meanings for παραβολή. Tuggy lists "parable," "comparison," "symbol," and "figure."[30] Maurice A. Robinson and Mark A. House provide "similitude," "allegory," "parable," or "emblematic allusion."[31] G. Abbott-Smith's first three are "juxtaposition," "comparison," and those understandings most closely resembling the use in the

---

29. Black, *Using New Testament Greek in Ministry*, 99.

30. Tuggy, *Léxico Griego-Español*, 719. A simple comparison is clearly intended by Socrates in Plato's *Philebus* 33b where he refers to his comparison of two different lives (ἐν τῇ παραβολῇ τῶν βίων), one that embraces pleasure and the other wisdom.

31. Robinson and House, *Analytical Lexicon of New Testament Greek*, 262.

Synoptic Gospels, i.e., "parable," ("illustration," "analogy," "figure").[32] He mentions a final meaning, parallel to the Heb. מָשָׁל, a "proverb." David L. Turner views all of these glosses as equivalents to the Heb. מָשָׁל. He writes:

> Both words are used to describe a proverb, an enigma, a riddle, a taunt, a simile, or an allegorical story. In all of these nuances, the common denominator is the use of a concrete analogy to illumine or obscure an abstract thought.[33]

Most scholars reserve the glosses "symbol," "type," and "figure" exclusively for Paul's use in Hebrews. Timothy and Barbara Friberg and Neva F. Miller define παραβολή as a "rhetorical figure of speech, setting one thing beside another to form a comparison or illustration."[34] Stein mentions six different rhetorical uses coupled with a biblical example: proverb (Luke 4:23), metaphor (Mark 7:14–17), similitude (Mark 4:30–32), story parable (Luke 14:16–24), example parable (Luke 12:16–21), and allegory (Mark 12:1–11).[35]

Two final definitions shed some light on the meaning of παραβολή. Henry. G. Liddell and Robert Scott define parable as "a fictitious narrative by which some religious or moral lesson is conveyed."[36] In addition, John J. Kilgallen writes:

> Ordinarily, a parable is a fictitious story with at least one element that represents the real world (some scholars would say that the ideal parable has only one point to make). However, in the ancient world of Jesus, the word *parable* can mean other

32. Abbott-Smith, *A Manual Greek Lexicon of the New Testament*, 338. Sider writes, "In its original application to literary language παραβολή evidently denoted analogy: ideas 'laid side by side' for comparison or contrast" ("Proportional Analogy in the Gospel Parables," 1).

33. Turner, *Matthew*, 338. Cole recognizes the restricted use of παραβολή in Classical Greek and believes that the NT usage reflects the Hebrew expansion of it to capture the idea of מָשָׁל. He says it "had a far wider range of meaning than the Greek," and παραβολή "extended its sphere of meaning to cover the wider range of the Hebrew word that it was translating. In classical Greek, its meaning had been much more restricted" (*Mark*, 146–47 n.1).

34. Friberg et. al., *Analytical Lexicon of the Greek New Testament*, 294. Bullinger mentions only the idea of comparison adding "whose proper meaning is not that which is expressed by the words, but which must become clear by the intended application" (*A Critical Lexicon and Concordance*, 569).

35. Stein, *Mark*, 182.

36. Liddell and Scott, *An Intermediate Greek-English Lexicon*, 594.

> than a story; it can refer to any type of comparison by which one uses the fictitious world to make clearer sense of the real world. For instance, such a simple literary device as metaphor falls under the name of parable; it is no story, but a phrase or word which illuminates the real by virtue of the fictitious.[37]

The word παραβολή can mean any of the aforementioned glosses. At its most basic level, it is a comparison between two fictitious persons, objects, or ideas. Kilgallen mentions one subdivision of παραβολή not yet discussed, namely the *exemplum*, in which a fictitious example is provided for hearers to follow (e.g., the Good Samaritan).[38] Nevertheless, distinguishing between the use of παραβολή as proverbs and parables (in the sense of how Christian circles have come to understand them) is only possible by analyzing the Synoptics and the words as they appear in their context.[39] This uncovers a huge shift in the teaching ministry of Jesus, particularly in Matthew 13 and the point in Jesus's life that it narrates.

The Use of Παραβολή in the New Testament

The word παραβολή occurs eighteen times in the Gospel of Luke compared to the seventeen occurrences in the Gospel of Matthew and thirteen in the Gospel of Mark. Outside of the Gospels, the word only occurs twice in the NT, both being found in Hebrews (9:9; 11:19). There are no occurrences in Acts, nor do the apostles say or write anything resembling parabolic discourse as found in the Gospels.[40] The use of παραβολή in Matthew and Mark is somewhat different than in Luke. In Matthew, all uses are subsequent to the rejection of Jesus as the Messiah of Israel (Matt 12:22ff.). It is on the same day (ἐν τῇ ἡμέρᾳ) as his rejection that Jesus begins to speak in parables to those around him, including the Twelve. Mark, likewise, connects the use of parables to the rejection day (Mark

---

37. Kilgallen, *Twenty Parables of Jesus*, 11.

38. Ibid., 14.

39. For example, Meynet writes, "Contrary to what one might think in the first place, it is not easy to determine what may be called a 'parable' in the gospel of Luke. The safest thing to do therefore is to start out from text that Luke himself qualifies to be such" (*Treatise on Biblical Rhetoric*, 299).

40. Given the many parallels between the Gospel of Luke and Acts, especially the life of Christ and the life of Paul, if the apostles did speak in parables, Luke almost certainly would have included such accounts to solidify the parallelism between the two works.

4:35).[41] His use, however, in 3:23 (pl. παραβολαῖς) follows with Jesus giving (1) a rhetorical question, (2) three quick conditional statements, and (3) an answer to his own question. Given the use of the plural and what follows, it is the only Markan occurrence that differs from Matthean usage. The remaining parables given on that day (Mark 4) are parallel to those found in Matthew 13.

In all the occurrences in Matthew and Mark (with the exception of Mark 3:23) Jesus's teachings incorporate stories with characters, action (often plot), objects, etc.[42] They are more narrative than deductive. Ruth Ann Foster and William D. Shiell refer to these as "pure parables . . . as opposed to illustrative stories or similitudes."[43] For example, in Matthew 13 Jesus gives eight parables:

1. The Parable of the Sower (13:3–9)

2. The Parable of the Tares (13:24–30)

3. The Parable of the Mustard Seed (13:31–32)

4. The Parable of the Leaven (13:33–35)

5. The Parable of the Treasure Hidden in the Field (13:44)

6. The Parable of the Merchant Seeking Fine Pearls (13:45–46)

7. The Parable of the Dragnet (13:47–50)

8. The Parable of the Head of a Household (13:52)[44]

Jesus's parables are often introduced formulaically. Maximilian Zerwick writes:

> Parables are often introduced by the formula ὁμοιωθήσεται, ὡμοιώθη, ὅμοιός ἐστιν with a following dative which however does not correspond, or corresponds only inexactly, to the term of the comparison. Thus 'the kingdom of God' is not in reality

41. It is on this day that Jesus withdraws, the first of four times recorded in the Gospel of Mark (4:35; 6:30–31; 7:24; and 8:13). As Mark mentions, from this point forward Jesus exclusively spoke publicly in parables (4:33–34).

42. Some of these are long such as the Parable of the Talents (Matt 25:14–30), Jesus's longest in Matthew, while others are short like the Parable of the Treasure Hidden in the Field (Matt 13:44) and the Parable of the Merchant Seeking Fine Pearls (Matt 13:45–46).

43. Foster and Shiell, "The Parable of the Sower and the Seed in Luke 8:1–10," 259.

44. This final parable does not liken the kingdom to someone or something else. Instead, it is a parable that likens every scribe who becomes a disciple of the kingdom to a head of household, a use of παραβολή similar to Luke 6:46–49.

'like unto a merchant', but is likened to the pearl of great price (Mt 13,45); nor is it 'like unto ten virgins', but to the wedding (Mt 25,1), nor is it like the sower, but like the harvest (Mt 13:24).[45]

All but the first parable in Matthew 13 begins with one of these three formulaic introductions. They are not mandatory markers of parables.[46] In fact, the only such introductions found in the Gospel of Luke are in chapter 13, in the form of two questions and answers (13:18–19, 20–21).

The parables also served a distinct purpose. Once the nation rejects Jesus as the Messiah, Jesus issues a scathing condemnation found in each of the Synoptic Gospels (Matt 13:11–15; Mark 4:11–12; Luke 8:10) involving the use of Isa 6:9–10. From these verses it is evident that the parables were a divine-pedagogical choice that allowed Jesus to simultaneously reveal and conceal information pertaining to the kingdom. Those who understand the meaning of Jesus's teaching can only do so because it has been granted by God (Matt 13:11, ὅτι ὑμῖν δέδοται γνῶναι) for them to understand the secrets of the kingdom. Those who do not understand cannot because a divine hardening has taken place (Matt 13:14ff.).[47]

The Use of Παραβολή in Luke 6:39–49

Luke's use of παραβολή is the same as the Matthean and Markan usage following Luke's parallel material with the day mentioned in Matthew 12–13 and Mark 3–4.[48] There are only three Lukan uses prior to the day

45. Zerwick, *Biblical Greek*, 22.

46. See also Matt 15:11, 15ff. From Jesus's answer to Peter's question, it is clear that the parable is not what is found in 15:14 dealing with "blind guides" (content similar to Luke 6:39). Jesus explains v. 11 only.

47. See Mark's use of ἵνα in 4:12. Frank Stagg writes, "From these words, we can infer that parables are intentionally obscuring, used by the speaker to withhold understanding from 'those outside', lest they repent and be forgiven. Mark's *hina* cannot be dismissed as other than intending purpose" ("Luke's Theological Use of Parables," 217–18). It is important to note that this "intending purpose" does not occur prior to the day detailed in Matthew 12–13.

48. The material in Luke 14:7–24 might appear as an exception, but it is not one. There is a break between the use of παραβολή in Luke 14:7 and the actual parable found in Luke 14:16–24. Perhaps Jesus began delivering the parable but stopped himself after he noticed how the ones who were chosen to attend began choosing for themselves the positions of honor at the dinner table, an act of self-exaltation that Jesus clearly detested (see Luke 11:43). Something similar to the break in Luke 14 is found in Luke 15:1–32. Luke clearly indicates that Jesus told one parable (15:3, τὴν παραβολὴν

of Jesus's rejection as found in each of the Synoptics (4:23, 5:36, and 6:39). In Luke 4:23, Jesus says, "You will definitely say this parable to me: Physician, heal yourself!" (πάντως ἐρεῖτέ μοι τὴν παραβολὴν ταύτην· Ἰατρέ, θεράπευσον σεαυτόν). The problem with translating παραβολή as "parable" (which is really only a transliteration) in this case is it does not bear the characteristics of what is generally understood as parabolic discourse as seen in Matthew 13 or Luke 14–15.[49] It is, instead, a proverb. The material following the use of παραβολή in Luke 5:36–39 also lacks similarity with parabolic discourse found after Matthew 13//Mark 4–5//Luke 8, specifically that there is no story development. Also worth noting is how Matthew and Mark do not identify the material found in Luke 5:36–39 as παραβολή (Matt 9:16–17; Mark 2:21–22). While it may not be a verbatim recitation of a socially-accepted proverb, Jesus's response to the Pharisees and their scribes in Luke 5:36–39 uses two everyday customs sagaciously. In this case he does so most likely to avoid prematurely announcing his coming death and resurrection while not avoiding the question.[50]

The third use is found in Luke 6:39a, εἶπεν δὲ καὶ παραβολὴν αὐτοῖς. There is no lack of discussion about how the use of παραβολή relates to the remainder of the Sermon on the Plain. Sharon H. Ringe believes that "Luke draws together a 'parable' and sayings found in various places in Matthew."[51] Likewise, Justo L. González calls them "sayings" and says they are "more like a series of proverbs or wisdom utterances."[52] Tom Wright translates the word in Luke 6:39 as "riddle."[53] John Nolland simply refers to the content as "various parabolic pieces"[54] like Keith F. Nickle who calls them "four parabolic analogies," or warnings.[55] H. D. A. Major, T. W.

τὴν). The material in Luke 15:4–7, 8–10 is distinct from the narrative parable in Luke 15:11–32. The former includes discourse in the first and second persons, as does Luke 14:8–15. The parable follows this introductory material that reinforces the story of the man who had two sons.

49. In addition to this, nowhere in the Gospel accounts is there found a parable the likes of Matthew 13 directed toward Jesus. He is the instructor about the kingdom. For a discussion on classical and rabbinic parallels to this saying, see Nolland, "Classical and Rabbinic Parallels," 193–209.

50. In Luke 9:21, Jesus clearly reserves this announcement for his closest disciples and commanded them with a warning that they should not share this information with anyone.

51. Ringe, *Luke*, 96.

52. González, *Luke*, 95.

53. Wright, *Luke for Everyone*, 75.

54. Nolland, *Luke 1–9:20*, 305.

55. Nickle, *Preaching the Gospel of Luke*, 69.

Manson, and C. J. Wright refer to what follows as a "series of parables."[56] The major support for those who believe this is a series of parables, despite Luke's use of the singular (παραβολήν), is the usage in Luke 15:1 and what follows. For example, Charles H. Talbert writes:

> Just as in 15:3, where the evangelist says Jesus told a parable (singular) and followed the statement with three parables in the remainder of the chapter, so the singular is followed here by four stories.[57]

However, there is nothing within the text that indicates in any way that the first two stories should be read apart from the parable of the man and his two sons.

Luke's use of παραβολή in 6:39a best refers to the material found in 6:46–49, the section that bears the ὅμοιός ἐστιν construction often found in Jesus's parables. With the distinct, straight-forward content in Luke 6:39b–45 and the fact that Matthew does not refer to the similar content as παραβολή, there is no strong support to view Luke's use as a collective singular. That he intends for his readers to think about vv. 46–49 in light of vv. 39b–45 is clear by his narrative insertion in v. 39a. Luke could have placed the introduction (εἶπεν δὲ καὶ παραβολὴν αὐτοῖς) immediately before 6:46, yet this would not have isolated and marked vv. 39–49 as the conclusion to the Sermon on the Plain. The end of the SOP, therefore, consists of four proverbial units: (1) 6:39b, (2) 6:40, (3) 6:41–42, and (4) 6:43–45.[58] Verses 46–49 contain the climax of the Sermon on the Plain. The parable found in 6:48–49 is a twofold comparison of what someone is like that comes to Jesus (ὁ ἐρχόμενος πρός με), hears his words (ἀκούων μου τῶν λόγων), and acts on

56. Major et. al., *Mission and Message*, 349. See also Kingsbury, *Conflict in Luke*, 113; Talbert, *Reading Luke*, 78; Bock, *Luke: Volume 1 (1:1—9:50)*, 609; Hobbs, *An Exposition of Luke*, 121.

57. Talbert, *Reading Luke*, 78. For a discussion of Luke 15 as three parables, see Chance, "Luke 15," 249–57. Arguments that the setting in Luke 15:1–3 is not original to the material in Luke 15:4–7 are hardly convincing. Such arguments assume that Jesus used illustrations one time only throughout his teaching ministry, which is really unfounded. Is it not possible that Luke, while conducting his own research, met someone who or found some record that told about how Jesus used Luke 15:4–7 as a segway into the parable of the man with two sons?

58. These seven verses constitute the first subdivision (6:39–45) of the SOP's ending. Talbert identifies an ABA' pattern with these verses, the central section being vv. 41–42. Verses 39–40 and 43–45, according to Talbert, "function as the motivations for the central concern for the personal transformation before undertaking to assist others" (Talbert, *Reading Luke*, 78–79).

them (ποιῶν αὐτούς) and someone that does not. The parable is illustrative, designed to reinforce the importance of coming, hearing, and acting. It does not have a concealing-revealing aspect to it like parables following the day Jesus was rejected.

The Meaning of Luke 6:39–45

The First Proverbial Unit (Luke 6:39)

1.1: μήτι δύναται τυφλὸς τυφλὸν ὁδηγεῖν;
1.2: οὐχὶ ἀμφότεροι εἰς βόθυνον ἐμπεσοῦνται;

The first maxim consists of two rhetorical questions, marked as 1.1 and 1.2 above. The first deals with the capacity (δύναται) a blind person lacks to lead (ὁδηγεῖν) another person who is blind. The second focuses on the common-sense outcome of such a scenario—if a blind person even attempted to lead another blind person, both would surely fall into a pit on account of their combined blindness. This maxim is not unique to Jesus, who uses it in more than one setting. It is found in the writings of Xenophon, Horace, Plato, Seneca, and Philo.[59] Marcus J. Borg calls it a "common proverb"[60] while Alan Kirk notes it "occurs frequently in educational settings."[61] Sabourin alone says the proverb was used rarely.[62]

The word τυφλός is the only word used twice in this unit, positioned side-by-side (*anadiplosis*) to make the maxim easy to remember.[63] This rhetorical technique is common in wisdom literature such as the Tractate Avot, which contains rabbinical proverbs.[64] Arthur Quinn and Lyon Rathbun mention that *anadiplosis* "can infuse emotional force into a passage."[65] The idea of blindness is important to the Gospel of Luke and particularly to this section of the Sermon on the Plain. Kirk writes:

---

59. See Plato *Polit.* VIII, 554b; Seneca *Ep.* 50.3; Philo *De virt.* 7; etc. For more examples, see Schrage, "τυφλός, τυφλόω," 275–78.

60. Borg, *Conflict, Holiness, and Politics*, 130.

61. Kirk, *Sayings Source*, 169.

62. Sabourin, *L'Évangile de Luc*, 167.

63. Reich, *Figuring Jesus*, 89.

64. Tropper, *Wisdom, Politics, and Historiography*, 61.

65. Quinn and Rathbun, "Anadiplosis," 9.

> Besides the fact that both 6:39 and 6:41–42a are rhetorical ques-
> tions based on sight-gags, they are correlated through key words
> from the semantic field of "sight"—τυφλός, ὀφθαλμός, βλέπεις,
> κατανοεῖς—with the total blindness of verse 39 gradually giving
> way to the "seeing clearly" (διαβλέψεις) of the final admonition.[66]

Beyond the use of διαβλέψεις in 6:42, there is also a link between the
effects found in 6:39 (ἐμπεσοῦνται) and 6:49 (συνέπεσεν), forming an *inclusio* in the final portion of the Sermon on the Plain.

Direct references to blindness occur eight times in the Gospel of
Luke, two of which are found in 6:39.[67] The first occurrence is Luke 4:18
where Jesus teaches in the synagogue located in Nazareth. The section
in Isaiah (61:1), from which Jesus reads, connects the presence of the
Holy Spirit (πνεῦμα κυρίου ἐπ' ἐμέ) with the life and ministry of Jesus (εὐαγγελίσασθαι πτωχοῖς). It also explains why the Holy Spirit has
anointed Jesus, part of which includes preaching a message that involves
the recovery of sight to those who are blind (κηρύξαι . . . καὶ τυφλοῖς
ἀνάβλεψιν).[68] Jesus tells everyone in the synagogue that the Isaiah passage
is fulfilled in their hearing (ἐν τοῖς ὠσὶν ὑμῶν, 4:21), not their presence

---

66. Kirk, *Sayings Source*, 170.

67. The direct references to blindness in Acts are interesting. The two people who
experience physical blindness in Acts both have their sight when the narratives begin.
In Acts 9 as Saul traveled to Damascus, he is met by the resurrected Jesus. Luke records
that "even though his eyes were opened, he could not see anything" (9:8). This condition lasted for three days until Ananias came to him so that he would regain his sight
and be filled with the Holy Spirit (9:17). Paul, who certainly influenced the composition of the Gospel of Luke, is himself a healed blind man. In his speech before Agrippa,
he mentions this occasion as the day Jesus gave him his ministry orders to open the
eyes of the Gentiles so that they might turn to God and be forgiven (26:16–18). The
second person is Elymas the magician, who was attempting to turn Sergius Paulus
away from the faith (13:6–12). With a ministry completely opposite that of John the
Baptist (Luke 3:4), this false prophet is made blind and told he will not see the sun for
a divinely-determined period of time. In the case of Paul's blindness, the placement
of Ananias's hands upon him is connected to his regaining of sight. In the case of
Elymas's blindness, it is the placement of the Lord's hand (figuratively) upon Elymas
that is connected to the removal of his sight. The final direct reference to blindness in
Acts is Luke's second use of Isa 6:9–10 at the conclusion of the work.

68. The LXX has τυφλοῖς ἀνάβλεψιν. Hartsock, in his chapter "Physiognomy and
Blindness in Luke-Acts," points out the translations of פְּקַח־קוֹחַ, which can carry the
idea someone being set free from a dark prison or the opening of blind eyes. English
translations of the Hebrew generally opt for the former while the Greek (LXX and
Luke) clearly refers to the latter (*Sight and Blindness*, 176–77).

or sight. The next two references to blindness in Luke are found in the *anadiplosis* of 6:39.

Following the SOP, Luke records Jesus's answer to the disciples of John about whether or not he is the one they have been waiting for (ὁ ἐρχόμενος, 7:20). The answer includes a first-hand demonstration of his miraculous power to cure many people from different illnesses (including evil spirits) and to give sight to many who were blind (τυφλοῖς πολλοῖς ἐχαρίσατο βλέπειν, 7:21). The use of χαρίζομαι indicates Jesus's graciousness and highlights the undeserving nature of someone who is blind to be given his or her sight.[69] Chad Hartsock suggests that the concept of blindness receives a mark of importance in the Gospel since:

1. Luke groups the illnesses generically and specifically mentions the healing of the blind (7:21).

2. Luke places the healing of the blind first in the report John's disciples should carry back to him (7:22).[70]

After healing all of these people in the presence of John's disciples, he told them to go and report what they had seen first-hand, referencing passages from Isaiah (35:5–6; 61:1).

The next two direct references to blindness come in Jesus's reaction to the guests at the unnamed Pharisee's home where Jesus was invited to dine (Luke 14:1–24). In the first instance he told guests to be different by inviting those who would normally be classified as unwanted guests— poor, crippled, lame, and blind people (14:13).[71] The second instance falls in the parable about the man giving a big dinner. In the parable, those who are invited refuse the invitation. The host became angry and, therefore, commands his slave to immediately go and bring in all the poor, crippled, blind, and lame that he can find throughout the city (14:21). This parable indicates something about the disposition of the poor, cripple, blind, and lame.

The final direct reference to blindness is found in Luke 18:35–43, the gift of sight to one blind man on the road to Jericho.[72] Hartsock,

69. Navone, *Themes of St. Luke*, 56. This is something different than what is communicated by ἀναβλέπω.

70. Hartsock, *Sight and Blindness*, 180.

71. This command goes beyond mere mercy, as Denaux points out. The act of inviting was a way to honor such persons (*Studies in the Gospel of Luke*, 74).

72. If the inclusion of the blind man's name is original (Mark 10:46), the most likely explanation is that Peter recalled the man's name while delivering his messages

pointing out Luke's first and only narrative about a blind person receiving sight, believes its position so late in the Gospel "pushes us toward the metaphorical level of meaning that blindness carries."[73] In the narrative, the blind man is brought to Jesus, hears him, and ultimately follows him.

In the Gospel of Luke, there are also indirect references to blindness. For example in Luke's account of the day Jesus was rejected, he includes Jesus's reference to Isaiah 6:9–10: "To you it has been granted to know the secrets about the kingdom of God, but to the rest it is in parables, so that (ἵνα) seeing they might not see (βλέποντες μὴ βλέπωσιν) and hearing they might not hear" (Luke 8:10). The best understanding of this phrase is a literal understanding for the first use of βλέπω and a figurative, or spiritual, understanding for the second use. In other words, even though the majority of people present to witness the miracles Jesus performed could see everything taking place, their rejection of him, especially by attributing these works to the power of Satan (Mt. 12:24), resulted in their remaining spiritually blind (see Mark 2:17; John 9:39). C. D. C. Howard writes:

> The Gospels, like elsewhere in biblical literature, frequently use the words *blindness, deafness, eye*, and *ear* in a figurative sense. . . . To see and hear God's revelation fully requires not only physical sensation but spiritual sensitivity.[74]

Having the correct disposition toward God is absolutely necessary to truly receive divine instruction. As mentioned before, however, Jesus's use of parables from this point on serves as a divine judgment actually preventing those who participated in the rejection from being able to understand in a way reminiscent of the hardening of Pharaoh's heart in Exod 9:12. One essayist shows that spiritual blindness is a universal trait, writing, "[B]lindness is congenital for all humans, who inherit the tendency simply by virtue of belonging to the human race."[75] The author goes on to say it is only "reversed by God's miraculous intervention."[76]

---

in Rome and mentions it. The name itself is not significant exegetically or for the purposes of a Gospel narrative. Neither Luke nor Matthew records it.

73. Hartsock, *Sight and Blindness*, 181.

74. Howard, "Blindness and Deafness," 81. See Avalos ("Blindness," 193) who indicates that blindness is used throughout the Bible as a symbol for unbelief, ignorance, and "other moral inadequacies," citing 2 Pet 1:9.

75. Ryken et. al. (eds.), "Blind, Blindness," 99.

76. Ibid.

What occurs in Luke 8 and the parallel Synoptic accounts is a divine decision to exercise no such miraculous intervention. However, for all mankind, a miraculous intervention is necessary whereby God causes men and women to understand his revelation, thus causing the spiritual scales to fall from their eyes.[77]

Jesus's capacity to remove such spiritual blindness is also found at the end of the Gospel of Luke. Two events—the encounter with the two disciples headed to Emmaus and the appearance of Jesus to the disciples in Jerusalem—identify the disciples' incapacity to see, recognize, and understand. The former (Luke 24:13–32) culminates with the two disciples, who had unknowingly been communicating to the resurrected Jesus the things that transpired in Jerusalem, having their eyes opened (αὐτῶν δὲ διηνοίχθησαν οἱ ὀφθαλμοί) and recognizing Jesus. The latter (Luke 24:33–49) finishes with Jesus opening the disciples' minds to understand the Scriptures.

In addition to the aforementioned references to blindness, there exists a semantic relationship between blindness and the failure to recognize or identify someone or something. For example in Luke 19:41–44, Jesus predicts the destruction of Jerusalem. In his reaction to the Pharisees, Jesus attributes the coming destruction to their failure to recognize (εἰ ἔγνως, 19:42; ἀνθ᾽ ὧν οὐκ ἔγνως, 19:44) this period of time as the time God came to save them from their sins. In fact this event is similar to what transpires in Luke 8:9–10. Their failure to recognize what was taking place in and through Jesus Christ, and their rejection of him, resulted in a divine judgment causing the things that make peace (τὰ πρὸς εἰρήνην, 19:42) between God and man to be hidden from their eyes (ἐκρύγη ἀπὸ ὀφθαλμῶν σου, 19:42).[78] Robert C. Tannehill writes, "Although Jesus does not destroy the temple, the temple is destroyed because of the blindness of those who reject Jesus and his witnesses."[79]

---

77. In 2 Corinthians, Paul speaks of the gospel being "veiled to those who are perishing" (ἐν τοῖς ἀπολλυμένοις ἐστὶν κεκαλυμμένον, 2 Cor 4:3). In addition, he refers to this state as one in which Satan "has blinded" (ἐτύφλωσεν) unbelievers' minds and indicates the satanic purpose (εἰς τὸ μὴ αὐγάσαι) as preventing these people from seeing the light of the gospel (2 Cor 3:4). Nevertheless, God miraculously intervenes when the gospel is preached (2 Cor 4:5), trumping satanic efforts simply by exercising the same power that was exercised by divine fiat (2 Cor 4:6). God says "Let it be so" and unbelievers move from blindness to sight, able to see the light of the gospel.

78. See also Luke 8:17.

79. Tannehill, *Luke*, 94.

Jesus as the fulfillment of the Mosaic Law is easily seen through the attention he devotes to mercy and love directed toward the helpless of Jewish society. The nation of Israel had drifted far away from the prohibitions against defrauding, abusing, or misleading such persons. For example, one of the curses proclaimed from Mount Ebal was "Cursed is he who misleads a blind person on the road" (Deut 27:18). However, the Temple Scroll outlining the dimensions and procedures for a temple that was never built specifies that blind people did not have permission to enter Jerusalem for the duration of their lives "because blindness was seen as a form of impurity which could defile the sacred city."[80]

Jesus uses a rather unique verb in the first rhetorical question. In the NT, the word ὁδηγέω (n. ὁδηγός) only occurs in Matthew, Luke, John, Acts, and Revelation, each only once. The occurrences in Matthew and Luke pertain to the same subject matter, parallel material whose relationship will be discussed later (Matt 15:14; Luke 6:39). In John's writings, the verb is attributed to God. In the Gospel written by him, the word is used by Jesus to describe the role of the Holy Spirit that he will send (John 16:13). In Revelation, it refers to a future role of Jesus as the shepherd who leads redeemed saints coming out of the Tribulation (Rev 7:17). In the Septuagint (LXX), the word is most common in Psalms.[81] Jaroslav Rindoš says Luke prefers this word "when speaking of leadership," citing Luke 6:39, Acts 1:16 (where it occurs as a noun in reference to Judas), and Acts 8:31.[82] In Luke-Acts, however, this connection is not very apparent.[83] Darrell L. Bock says this is an everyday word used for a person guiding someone or something to another person or place.[84] It has this plain sense in Luke 6:39. In the first question, Jesus is concerned with one's capacity to lead another (δύναται ὁδηγεῖν), not about any destination. In the second

80. Avalos, "Blindness," 193. See also Crawford, *The Temple Scroll and Related Texts*, 80; Olyan, *Disability in the Hebrew Bible*, 104ff.; Charlesworth, "Introduction," 8–9.

81. The action is commonly attributed to God as the agent. It occurs in declarative statements, i.e., "He leads me . . ." and in petitionary statements, i.e., "Lord, lead me. . . ." On occasion it is something the psalmist ascribes to one of God's attributes, such as his truth.

82. Rindoš, *He of Whom It Is Written*, 96. Commenting about Judas, the word only refers to him as an escort who took the authorities to arrest Jesus (Sleeman, *Geography and the Ascension Narrative in Acts*, 87).

83. Major et. al. say it "is not necessarily implied in the saying as it stands in Lk." (*Mission and Message*, 349).

84. Bock, *Acts*, 342–43.

question, Jesus emphasizes the fate that would await both blind persons should one attempt to lead the other—both would undoubtedly fall into a pit (ἀμφότεροι εἰς βόθυνον ἐμπεσοῦνται).[85] A pit to which Jesus refers was common in the first-century world, especially in agrarian areas. It is also representative of God's judgment at times in the Septuagint.[86] The use of ὁδηγέω in Acts 8:31 is distinct. Philip, who is sent to a single Ethiopian traveling away from Jerusalem, hears him reading Isa 53:7–8. Philip asks the man if he understands the verses that he is reading, and the eunuch responds, "How could I if no one guides me?" (πῶς γὰρ ἂν δυναίμην ἐὰν μή τις ὁδηγήσει με). Philip becomes the Ethiopian's guide to Jesus. At first, the Ethiopian was seeing but not understanding. In the end, this Gentile understood and personally identified himself with Jesus through baptism (Acts 8:36–39). The use of the present indicative in Luke 6:39 is not surprising given the question is proverbial.[87]

Why does Jesus choose to use rhetorical questions? He must have a reason, right? Douglas Estes mentions how rhetorical questions add variety to a narrative:

> The most prominent [narrative function] is the ability of questions to structure narrative. Consider a story that is a sequence of events listed one right after another. A story structured in this way would be rather boring. In contrast when one reads a narrative and comes across a question—even if the question is not put to the reader but a character in the story—it elicits a pause and a momentary shift in thinking in the reader (John 9:35). Questions are very good tools for establishing boundaries or opening new avenues for pursuit in the reading process (John 11:9a).[88]

85. Concerning the textual variant πεσοῦνται present in some manuscripts (ℵ A C Ξ Ψ 33 𝔐), the prefixed preposition ἐν was probably regarded as unnecessary given the εἰς-phrase.

86. See Pao and Schnabel, "Luke," 298.

87. For a brief discussion of the gnomic present with Luke 6:39 as an example, see Young, *Intermediate New Testament Greek*, 110–11.

88. Estes, *The Questions of Jesus in John*, 10. It is important to note Estes's warning about equating Jesus's teaching with rabbinic teaching style as found in the Talmud:

> "[T]he Johannine Jesus was based on a product of the early 1st century; yet the Talmud, while it may possibly originate in as early as 1st or 2nd century thought, is received by us as a late 5th or early 6th century text. This late date—in contrast to the origin of the questions of Jesus—forces us to weigh heavily against relying on a rabbinic style." (ibid., 18)

This applies to the original teaching event as much as it does to the secondary audience, i.e., those to whom the biblical author writes. J. Ian H. McDonald, commenting on the series of rhetorical questions in Matt 5:43–48, says Jesus uses them to maintain a connection with the audience and to gain their assent before moving to a "final injunction."[89] In Matt 5:43, the audience is told to love their enemies and to pray for those who persecute them. At the end of the unit, they are commanded to do something even greater—to be perfect just as their heavenly Father is perfect (Matt 5:48). One reason Stein suggests is, "By drawing out the correct answer from his listeners rather than simply declaring it, Jesus impressed his point more convincingly upon their minds."[90] Arland J. Hultgren indicates Jesus often introduced parables with rhetorical questions in order to grab the hearer's attention.[91]

Jesus's use of rhetorical questions here differs from how he used simple questions, for example, at Caesarea Philippi (Matt 16:13, 15). There Jesus also posed two questions, one asking who people in general say he is (Matt 16:13) and the other asking specifically who the disciples say he is (Matt 16:15). In both cases, Jesus expected an answer. They were pure (or, true) interrogatives. In the case of Luke 6:39, no answer is necessary, although he may have accepted feedback. The answers to the questions are actually imbedded within. The first, using μή, expects a negative answer, while the second, using οὐκ, expects an affirmative one.[92]

He continues, "Jesus did not possess a 'rabbinic' style of asking questions because there is no such style; there are actually many different argumentative and discourse styles within rabbinic literature" (ibid.). Aspects of Jesus's teaching and discourse certainly bear common traits with some. On a similar note, Dawsey offers a warning about understanding Jesus's questions in light of Hellenistic rhetoric: "One must, in fact, be very hesitant when attempting to establish the influence of the Hellenistic diatribe on the characterization of Jesus in Luke, because the rhetorical question is a form of popular argumentation in general" (*The Lukan Voice*, 38). The goal is not to view Jesus's teaching solely in light of one or the other. Studying Jesus's teaching in the context where it appears and cross-analyzing it between common first-century teaching and discourse styles can help in an exegete's understanding of the biblical text—its structure, interpretation, and application.

89. McDonald, "Questioning and Discernment in Gospel Discourse," 342.

90. Stein, *The Method and Message of Jesus's Teachings*, 23.

91. Hultgren, *The Parables of Jesus*, 139, 162.

92. See Lenski, *St. Luke's Gospel*, vol. 1, 376; Black, *Using New Testament Greek in Ministry*, 98; Blass, *Grammar of New Testament Greek*, 254; Bock, *Luke: Volume 1 (1:1–9:50)*, 610; Robertson, *A Grammar of the Greek New Testament*, 1157 and 1175. Buttman suggests the translations "surely not?" and "perhaps . . . ?" (*A Grammar of the*

They are hybrid-interrogatives, questions that have a declarative tone.[93] A. T. Robertson mentions that while the anticipated answer is known, the "precise emotion in each case (protest, indignation, scorn, excitement, sympathy, etc.) depends on the context."[94]

The content Luke includes in the SOP is directed toward a predominantly Gentile audience. Under the direction of the Holy Spirit, Luke chooses to include aspects of the Sermon (Matthew 5–7//Luke 6:20–49) relevant to these Gentile communities in which this Gospel would become a disciple-making tool. For this reason, Luke's account does not include a direct Old Testament (OT) quotation, obviously different than Matthew who includes eight.[95] Jesus's SOP teaching also appears less combative than the record found in Matthew. Matthew places Jesus in opposition to the Pharisees and scribes. Not only does Jesus repeatedly provide the correct interpretation for the Mosaic Law,[96] whose interpretation had been tarnished over the years and placed as a burden on the Jewish people, but Jesus also clearly commands the people to not be like religious hypocrites (Matt 6:5, 8). At points he uses them as antitypes for how his disciples must live (e.g., prayer, 6:5; fasting, 6:16).[97] Jesus even warns his audience that they have no hope to enter the kingdom of God unless they possess a genuine righteousness that surpasses the perceived righteousness of the scribes and the Pharisees (Matt 5:20). In the SOP, there are no references to the scribes and Pharisees. However, this absence does not mean Jesus's intent in 6:39b and what follows does not

---

New Testament Greek, 254). Even though the speaker's expected answer is imbedded, for the rhetorical question to truly function properly it is necessary for the audience to share a common knowledge with the speaker. Park writes:

> "[I]t is necessary that the audience understands and shares the stereotyped knowledge presupposed by the text of the matter in question, otherwise the communication would fail and the hearer would mistake rhetorical questions for real questions" (*Mark's Memory Resources and the Controversy Stories [Mark 2:1—3:6]*, 129).

93. G. Guthrie, dealing specifically with rhetorical questions found in Hebrews 1–2, says they are "semantically equivalent to a proposition" (*The Structure of Hebrews*, 62).

94. Robertson, *A Grammar of the Greek New Testament*, 1175.

95. See Matt 5:21, 27, 31, 33, 35, 38, 43; 7:23.

96. The construction is ἠκούσατε ὅτι. . . . ἐγὼ δὲ λέγω.

97. Jesus only uses the Gentiles as an antitype once in the SOM (dealing with prayer, Matt 6:7).

have any connection to them.[98] When Jesus uses the imagery of two blind persons in 6:39b, he most likely has in mind the Pharisees and religious elite of his day. The two rhetorical questions are not present in Matthew's account of the sermon. Of the material in Luke 6:39–49 found in Matthew's SOM, Jesus clearly has "false prophets" in mind (Matt 7:15).

Matthew does include Jesus's teaching about the blind leading the blind elsewhere. It follows the rejection narrative in Matthew 12–13, which from this point forward shows marked increase in mutual hostility between Jesus and the scribes and Pharisees. In Matt 15:1–14, Jesus is approached and challenged by some of the Pharisees and scribes concerning his disciples' refusal to wash their hands before eating bread. He contrasts what their tradition says (Matt 15:5–6) with what God says (Matt 15:4). After refuting their interpretation of Exod 20:12//Dt. 5:16, Matthew indicates that Jesus called the crowd to himself so that he could use the recent conflict to teach them (Matt 15:10). The two declarative propositions are parabolic discourse; Peter indicates this with his question in Matt 15:15.[99] The disciples come to Jesus and tell him that he offended the Pharisees with his teaching about what actually defiles a person. Jesus responds with a prediction about the fate of the Pharisees and a warning for the disciples to leave them alone (Matt 15:13–14). Jesus says, "They are blind guides of the blind (τυφλοὶ εἰσιν ὁδηγοὶ τυφλῶν); and if a blind man guides another blind man, both of them will certainly fall into a pit (τυφλὸς δὲ τυφλὸν ἐὰν ὁδηγῇ, ἀμφότεροι εἰς βόθυνον πεσοῦνται)." On another occasion, sometimes referred to as "Busy Tuesday," Jesus heatedly called the scribes and Pharisees "blind guides" (ὁδηγοί τυφλοί, Matt 23:16, 24), as well as "blind men" (τυφλοί, Matt 23:19).

One problem (among the many) with attributing this illustration to a common source (whether it be Q, M, or L) is doing so assumes Jesus could have only used an illustration once throughout his approximate three-year ministry. Given the presence of similar imagery outside the NT, it is difficult to imagine that Jesus did not use the same imagery on

---

98. Fonck says this is possible but "neither the text nor the circumstances suggest this idea" (Fonck, *The Parables of the Gospel*, 270). True, but Jesus only occasionally mentions the customs and practices of Gentiles. Moreover, in the SOM Jesus discusses them by name and in a negative light. It is better to understand the absence of pharisaic references to Luke's preparation of a Gospel designed for use in predominantly Gentile communities.

99. The language ἀκούετε καὶ συνίετε is also reminiscent of Jesus's explanation for why he speaks in parables in Matt 13:13 (ἀκούοντες οὐκ ἀκούουσιν οὐδὲ συνίουσιν).

multiple occasions, especially with different audiences.[100] Nevertheless, Jesus could, and probably does, have the Pharisees and scribes in mind when he uses this imagery.[101] For him, they are the epitome and the worst kind of blind guides. They are the "false prophets" and chief "hypocrites" of their day (Matt 6:1, 5; 7:15) who pervert the Mosaic Law, nullifying it (ἀκυρόω, Matt 15:6) instead of fulfilling it (πληρόω, Matt 5:17).

In Luke 6:39–49, Jesus ultimately takes his audience's attention away from the illustrations and imagery. There is a flow to this unit of the Sermon on the Plain; the rhetorical questions in v. 39 grab the attention of the audience and hold them for the duration of the argument.[102] Major et al. say vv. 39–40 are general statements that Jesus explains the particulars of in 6:46–49.[103] In the climax of the SOP, Jesus places the attention on himself (vv. 46–47). His desire is for the audience to recognize that if they have any hope of carrying out his commands as children of God, they must do so by identifying who he is and, in response, placing their life under his lordship. Jesus has already chosen his twelve disciples (Luke 6:12–16). That he chooses them before this teaching indicates a shift in his ministry. From this point on he will continue teaching at large, but he is also concentrating on the spiritual and leadership development of these men. They, minus one, will be the foundational leaders in a new spiritual organism known as the church (ἐκκλησία; Matt 16:18 [first reference]; Eph 5:25).[104] Based on this and the immediate referent to αὐτοῖς as the disciples in Luke 6:20, it becomes clear that Jesus intends for his apostles to be spiritual guides capable of leading spiritually-blind souls to him, just as Philip does in Acts 8. Jesus is not directly warning about false teachers.[105] He is warning his disciples that people are completely incapable of leading others unless the one leading first has his blindness

---

100. While some present for the parable in Matthew 15 may have been present for the teaching recorded in Luke 6:20–49, the majority of persons present were most likely not present for the Sermon on the Plain.

101. Garland says they are blind on three levels: "blind to who Jesus is, what God is doing through him, and what their own faults are" (*Luke*, 283).

102. Reich, *Figuring Jesus*, 89.

103. Major et. al., *Mission and Message*, 349.

104. Of course, Paul is specifically commissioned to carry the gospel to the Gentiles (Acts 9:15). It is Paul who indicates in Eph 2:19–20 that the apostles and prophets were given for the purpose of laying the foundation of the church. He does not use the word ἐκκλησία but instead the imagery of a household.

105. See Luck (*Luke*, 58) who says this is a warning against false teachers.

turned into sight.[106] If there is a warning about false teachers, it is no one should be led by one who is spiritually blind; the consequences are dangerous and perhaps fatal.[107]

The Second Proverbial Unit (Luke 6:40)

2.1: οὐκ ἔστιν μαθητὴς ὑπὲρ τὸν διδάσκαλον·
2.2: κατηρτισμένος δὲ πᾶς ἔσται ὡς ὁ διδάσκαλος αὐτοῦ.

The relationship of a teacher and disciple is very similar to the idea of one person leading another.[108] It is to this relationship Jesus now turns. "An apprentice is not above his or her teacher; but each one, after having been fully trained, will be like his or her teacher" (Luke 6:40). This second unit consists of two maxims, marked as 2.1 and 2.2 above. Maxims dealing with likeness are present throughout the literature of different languages. George L. Apperson includes the following English maxims: "like cow like calf," "like crow like egg," "like father like son," "like fault like punishment," "like host like guest," "like mistress like maid," "like mother like daughter," etc.[109] The most commonly referenced maxim from the first century similar to Luke 6:40 is Petronius' *qualis dominus talis et servus*

---

106. See Guy, *Gospel of Luke*, 64; Dillersberger, *The Gospel of Saint Luke*, 211.

107. It is impossible to make a complete interpretation and analysis of Luke 6:39 apart from the three additional proverbial units, especially the third which deals also with the impairment of sight. For example, the disciples are commanded to not judge (6:37), yet they are also instructed to facilitate the removal of a speck in their brother's eye. Before they can have any involvement in this, they have to undergo a process of introspection. A more exhaustive consideration is thus postponed to the Semantic Frame, Pt. 1.

108. Rossé writes, "La metafora del cieco che guida un cieco ha facilmente creato l'associazione con l'immagine del discepolo-maestro, associazione conosciuta nel mondo giudaico (cf. *Rm* 2, 19s)" (*Il Vangelo di Luca*, 236). See also Dupont, *Les Béatitudes*, vol. 1, 53–58. Both ὁδηγός (ὁδηγέω) and μαθητής (μαθητεύω) fall under the same semantic domain.

109. Apperson, *Dictionary of Proverbs*, 338–40.

(*Sat.* 58).[110] Perhaps the only likeness proverb in the OT is in Hos 4:9 (καὶ ἔσται καθὼς ὁ λαὸς οὕτως ὁ ἱερεύς, LXX) pertaining to God's judgment.[111]

The structure and content of this unit bears some similarities with the previous one in 6:39b:

1. In each maxim, there are two participants—the former with two blind men and the present with a disciple and teacher.

2. Both maxims consist of two parts—the former with two rhetorical questions and the present with two declarative statements.

3. The second half of each maxim concentrates on the effect that the one participant has on the other. In the case of the two blind men, both will fall into a pit (εἰς βόθυνον ἐμπεσοῦνται); in the present maxim, the disciple will become like his or her teacher (ἔσται ὡς ὁ διδάσκαλος αὐτοῦ).

4. Finally, both second halves are designed to be more inclusive than the first. For example, in the first maxim, one blind man attempts to lead another blind man, yet both will end up falling into a pit. In the second, both obviously cannot become like the teacher (since one is the teacher). Instead, the proverb extends beyond a single disciple to include each disciple (πᾶς).

The first half of the maxim consists of a negated stative verb (οὐκ ἔστιν), an anarthrous subject (μαθητής), and a predicate prepositional phrase (ὑπὲρ τὸν διδάσκαλον),[112] occurring in that order. Proverbs and parabolic discourse alike often take the stative verb εἰμί since both attempt to show similarities between two persons or objects. In parables, one of the distinguishing features is the use of ὁμοία ἐστίν.[113] With proverbs, the goal is to state a principle that communicates something that is generally true (even common) but not universal. They are basically warnings

---

110. Trans. "As the master is, even so is the slave." Rubio writes, "The absence of a copulative verb, especially in proverbial expressions and in apodictic statements, is a common trend in Latin of all periods" ("Semitic Influence in the History of Latin Syntax," 218). He points out that verbal ellipsis occurs every time in the Vulgate with proverbs. The Vulgate reading of Luke 6:40 confirms his statement: *non est discipulus super magistrum* ("a disciple is not above his master").

111. Mays, *Hosea*, 70–71; Manser, *The Facts on File Dictionary of Proverbs*, 170; Seals, *Proverbs*, 24; Chomsky, *Lectures on Government and Binding*, 318.

112. Prepositional phrases can only be used as a predicate with a linking verb, written or implied. See Black, *It's Still Greek to Me*, 83.

113. Turner, *Matthew*, 296.

designed to lead someone to wise living. In cases like this, the verb serves as a linking verb.[114] The maxim has the same word order in Matt 10:24. Οὐκ ἔστιν comes at the beginning of two other proverbs (Matt 13:57// Mark 6:4; Matt 15:26//Mark 7:27),[115] as well as in Matt 18:14, when Jesus explains his illustration of a shepherd leaving all of his sheep to rescue one that is astray. The use in Mark 12:31 shows that the construction can appear at the end of a sentence. The use in material describing God as the God of the living and not the dead shows how the subject can be fronted if the author so chooses (Matt 22:32//Luke 20:38//Mark 12:27).[116] This construction is not prevalent in Proverbs (LXX) yet it does occur with great frequency in Ecclesiastes (LXX) and often maintains the same word order (i.e., the verb fronted before the subject and predicate).[117] Even John's similar material with δοῦλος-κύριος has οὐκ ἔστιν preceding the subject and predicate. In demotic proverbs, the verb is always fronted. However, Nikolaos Lazaridis says the word order in Greek proverbs is more fluid. The word order, he writes, "mostly depends on the style of the text and what is to be emphasized in each sentence. In proverb literature, sentences are short and therefore the weight of focus is balanced and may fall on any of the words employed."[118] Context is ultimately the deciding factor for determining emphasis, especially in short sayings like proverbs. In general, it appears that proverbial word order when using the stative verb is Verb + Subject + Predicate.[119] Deviations from this order are often markers of emphasis.[120] If Luke 6:40 were a quotation from the LXX, it would be easier to determine if any emphasis were intended by the position of οὐκ ἔστιν.[121] However, there is no OT parallel and no deviation among the Gospel authors. So, it is best to determine that there is not any intended emphasis (although impossible to rule out).

114. See Porter et al., *Fundamentals of New Testament Greek*, 72.

115. The position is maintained in indirect discourse.

116. In Luke 20:38, the subject θεός is placed before οὐκ ἔστιν.

117. For example: οὐκ ἔστιν πᾶν πρόσφατον ὑπὸ τὸν ἥλιον (Eccl 1:9). See also, Eccl 1:11; 2:11, 16, 24; etc.

118. Lazaridis, *Wisdom in Loose Form*, 60.

119. Of the three examples Lazaridis provides, the one using εἰμί maintains the V-S-P order: "οὐκ ἔστιν σοφίας κτῆμα τιμιώτερον" (ibid.).

120. For example, in Mark 6:3, the position of οὗτός is definitely emphatic.

121. For example, in Rom 3:10–18, Paul might intend some amount of emphasis with the fronted οὐκ ἔστιν if he is not doing so solely for the purpose of repetition as a rhetorical device. Cf. Eccl (LXX) 7:20 and Rom 3:10; Ps 52:3 (LXX) and Rom 3:10; etc.

The word μαθητής, the subject of the proverb, is the opposite of the word διδάσκαλος, found in the predicate prepositional phrase.[122] Without the latter, there would be no μαθητής.[123] The range of meaning for μαθητής is evident from the following glosses: disciple, learner, pupil, student, and follower.[124] In Classical Greek, the word is used in:

1. A general sense with reference to someone who is learning from another (e.g., an apprentice).

2. A technical sense with reference to someone who studies under a particular teacher or teaching.

3. A restricted sense referring specifically to a Sophist pupil.[125]

It is a gender-neutral word, able to refer to both a man and a woman.[126] When it occurs in the plural, as it usually does, only the context can determine if the group mentioned includes individuals from both genders. In the case of the present proverb, it is gender neutral, neither referring specifically to a man nor a woman, just a student or disciple in general. The noun appears nowhere in the LXX[127] and is confined to the Gospels and Acts in the NT (at least 250 occurrences).[128] The verb μανθάνω occurs over thirty times in the LXX, mostly in Deuteronomy and Isaiah. The noun μαθητής is used in each of the Gospels (seventy-two times in Matthew; forty-six in Mark; thirty-seven in Luke; and seventy-eight in John) and Acts (twenty-eight times). It can be used to refer to different groups defined by differing degrees of association.[129] In the present proverb, it has

122. Danker and Krug, *The Concise Greek-English Lexicon of the New Testament*, 95.

123. Rengstorf, "μαθητής," 416; Rausch, *Who is Jesus?*, 71; Meye, "Disciple," 947.

124. Trenchard, *Complete Vocabulary Guide to the Greek New Testament*, 67; Rausch, *Who is Jesus?*, 70–71.

125. Wilkins, "Disciples," 176.

126. Weren, "The Ideal Community," 183.

127. Fitzmyer mentions three uses of μαθητής in Jeremiah (13:21; 20:11; 46:9) and that there is no definitive support for their originality (*To Advance the Gospel*, 328 n.27). Likewise, Rengstorf says the variants lack support ("μαθητής," 426).

128. Some identify the number of occurrences at 264. See Müller, s.v. "μαθητής," 486; Tepedino, *Las Discípulas de Jesús*, 30. Rengstorf uses the number 250 because of questions in Mt. 20:17; Luke 9:1; Acts 1:15; etc. ("μαθητής," 441). Seventy-eight of the occurrences are found in the Gospel of John and, as Andreas J. Köstenberger notes, are usually accompanied with αὐτοῦ (*A Theology of John's Gospel and Letters*, 483). It only occurs in the Gospel of Luke thirty-seven times, often with αὐτοῦ as well.

129. Boring, *Mark*, 170.

the most general sense—student or learner. In each of the Gospels, there is a connection between following Jesus and being one of his disciples, and at points these two are connected with hearing (ἀκούω),[130] which is one of the central elements in the climax of the SOP (Luke 6:46–47). What is more, Jesus becomes the center of an individual's relationship to God, not just salvifically but also instructionally. In the NT, a μαθητής-διδάσκαλος-θεός (i.e., God the Father) relationship is formed.[131]

In the LXX, the root μαθ is used almost entirely to refer simply to learning something, having no connection to the type of teacher-student relationship known in Greek literature. Perhaps the closest lexical parallel to Luke 6:40 is 1 Chr 25:8 with the division of musical responsibilities in the temple. The passage teaches that Asaph and 287 additional Israelites (all children of Asaph, Jeduthum, and Heman) were included in the casting of lots for musical duties, small and great alike, groups consisting of teachers ("the advanced") and those still considered pupils ("ones still learning").[132] K. H. Rengstorf correctly distinguishes between the "schools" of prophets found in the OT (e.g., 2 Kgs 6:1) and the μαθητής-διδάσκαλος relationship encountered in Greek literature, including the Gospels.[133] His answer to why this concept is absent in Jewish history is:

> The religion of Israel is a religion of revelation. . . . In the sphere of revelation there is no place for the establishment of a master-disciple relation, nor is there the possibility of setting up a human word alongside the Word of God which is proclaimed, nor of trying to ensure the force of the divine address by basing it on the authority of a great personality.[134]

For the duration of Israel's history up to the birth and ministry of Jesus, when God wanted to correct the nation for its covenant disobedience

130. Brodie, *The Gospel according to John*, 159.

131. The clearest example of this is found in John 17:8. For a discussion of the structure of this passage, see Hudgins, "An Application of Discourse Analysis Methodology," 24–57. This essay applies discourse analysis methodology to the seventeenth chapter of John's Gospel. The familiar prayer of Jesus in that chapter has traditionally been analyzed in terms of the three referents (Jesus, his contemporary disciples, and future disciples). This analysis gives greater attention to the "mainline verbs," shifting the focus to Jesus's requests and final commitment. By giving greater structural significance to these verbs, a fresh understanding of the structural division and natural outline of Jesus's prayer are identified.

132. Wilkins, *Following the Master*, 55.

133. Rengstorf, "μαθητής," 428.

134. Ibid., 430–31.

and perversion of his revelation, he raised up prophets to call them back to covenant obedience. Is there another reason for why this concept is absent from the Old Testament? Perhaps. In the OT, the most important relationship, the one in which God's revelation was passed down from generation to generation, is the familial relationship. Parents were specifically commissioned to have the disciple-teacher relationship with their children (Deut 6:7–8, 20–25). Moreover, the relationship between Samuel and Eli is somewhat reminiscent of a relationship between a disciple and his teacher (see 1 Sam 2:11ff.).[135]

Disciples are those who associate themselves, often strongly, with a teacher in order to acquire from them his or her knowledge and experiences.[136] It is important to view this relationship as cognitive but not exclusively cognitive. For Jewish teachers, the μαθητής-διδάσκαλος relationship was a transmission of knowledge based on speaking-listening and always with the Torah at the center.[137] Only a partial glimpse of this relationship is given in the NT when Jesus spends three days at the temple sitting in the midst of the teachers (ἐν μέσῳ τῶν διδασκάλων), both listening to them (ἀκούοντα αὐτῶν) and asking them questions (ἐπερωτῶντα αὐτούς; Luke 2:46). Rengstorf even shows that content originating from the teacher was an important part of the relationship with Epicurus and his students. Part of his students' curriculum included memorizing verbatim the sayings of Epicurus (κύριαι δόξαι; Diog. L., X, 12 [6], 7 [3], 29 [18]).[138] Jacob Neusner says a person in rabbinic tradition becomes a μαθητήν τῶν σοφῶν "by hearing and repeating and memorizing the words of the sage set forth as Torah."[139] However, mere cognition was never the exclusive goal of learning and education in the Old or New Testaments. Charles F. Melchert says Jesus's relationship was completely different with his disciples: "There seems to have been no insistence on mastery of texts,

---

135. Keener, *A Commentary on the Gospel of Matthew*, 148 n.218.

136. Tepedino, *Las Discípulas de Jesús*, 30. The typical glosses (e.g., words like "disciple" and "student") do not capture exactly what Jesus is referring to. In fact, the word "disciple" has little meaning outside of Christian circles. Fisher Humphreys says, "[T]he word *students* does not give us an appropriate understanding of Christian disciples. . . . I want to suggest, therefore, that it is more helpful to speak of Christ's disciples as apprentices of rabbi Jesus rather than as students of rabbi Jesus" (Humphreys, *Friends*, 35).

137. Rengstorf, "μαθητής," 437.

138. Ibid., 422.

139. Neusner, *Theological Dictionary of Rabbinic Judaism*, 179.

on memorization, or on faithful transmission of Jesus' sayings."[140] This is a very important observation, and there are two answers for why. First, Jesus recognized the important ministry of the Holy Spirit. In the Farewell Discourse, Jesus tells the disciples, who were probably concerned that they would not remember everything, that the Holy Spirit would be sent from the Father to do two things: (1) teach them (ὑμᾶς διδάξει), and (2) remind them of all of the things Jesus taught them (ὑπομνήσει ὑμᾶς πάντα ἃ εἶπον ὑμῖν; John 14:26). Likewise, it is the Holy Spirit who is at work in the apostles and prophets in laying the foundation of the church (1 Cor 12–14; Eph 2:20), which includes the writing of inspired texts (πᾶσα γραφὴ θεόπνευστος, 2 Tim 3:16). Second, Jesus was most concerned with his disciples doing the things that he taught. The climax of the SOP is clear about this. Jesus demands that his disciples come to him, hear his words, and do them (Luke 6:47).

Education being more than cognitive is not anything new to the Jewish mind. James Limburg, commenting on Psalm 25, shows that education is theological-relational and cognitive-practical.[141] The theological element is evident as the Hebrew learner looks to God for instruction about his attributes and character (Ps 25:1, 4). The most important relationship a person has is his or her relationship to God. According to the psalmist, learning about God's attributes and Law requires a salvific relationship with him (Ps 25:1, 5) resulting in an obedient walk with him (Ps 25:12, 14). The cognitive aspect pertains to God's attributes, specifically what has been revealed to the Jewish people ("truth," Ps 25:4–5). But it also has an impact on how that person lives (i.e., praxis). God's "way" is the way a person is supposed to live (Ps 25:4–5, 8–9; cf. Ps 1:1–6).

Dio Chrysostom, in his fifty-fifth discourse, sheds additional light on the μαθητής-διδάσκαλος relationship and shows an important characteristic found in Greco-Roman literature and throughout the New Testament.[142] While μαθητής is confined to the Gospels and Acts, the idea of imitation is prevalent throughout the NT letters. Even though the authors of these works did not utilize the word μαθητής, for what reason remains unknown, they did carry on the important related concept of

140. Melchert, *Wise Teaching*, 223.

141. Limburg, *Psalms*, 81.

142. For parallels between Dio Chrysostom and the NT, see Mussies, *Dio Chrysostom and the New Testament*. Unfortunately, he does not provide the example that follows, a parallel between Dio and Luke 6:40 concerning the μαθητής-διδάσκαλος relationship.

imitation throughout their works. Likeness in the μαθητής-διδάσκαλος relationship involves knowing what the teacher knows as well as knowing his character and works. Dio's words connect the idea of sage to pupil, ἔχεις μοι εἰπεῖν ὅτου μαθητὴς γέγονε τῶν σοφῶν (55.1), and his own words show how this sort of relationship to a teacher is similar to the relationship of an apprentice. He specifically mentions the following relationships (55.1):

1. A sculptor, Pheidias, to an apprentice, Hegias.

2. A pair of brothers who learned painting from their father, Aglaophon.

3. Pherecydes, supposed to be the teacher of Pythagoras, and Pythagorus, supposed to be the teacher of Empedocles.

The purpose, according to Dio, in any μαθητής-διδάσκαλος relationship is this: μιμούμενος τὸν διδάσκαλον καὶ προσέχων ἀναλαμβάνει τὴν τέχνην (55:5). The two participle phrases, μιμούμενος and προσέχων ἀναλαμβάνει, stress the imitation of and allegiance or obedience to the teacher and his teachings. Kirk believes Luke 6:40 is imagery for "the educational relationship between sage and disciple," one marked by "the ancient ideal of education by mimesis: imitation of the master with the goal of likewise becoming a sage."[143] This is the ultimate goal of rabbinic Judaism as well.[144]

The proverb Jesus gives is more inclusive than a disciple's mere acquisition of what the teacher knows. Even in Greco-Roman culture, this sort of becoming like the teacher involves more than only knowing what the teacher knows. It involves imitation, a capacity to do what the teacher does. But, this is not an imitation that resembles entirely what Jesus has in mind. Jesus is instituting a new ethic in the SOP, one some would call perfectionistic. It is not enough for disciples to merely know what the teacher knows. In fact, if the tone of voice is maintained from Luke 6:39, Jesus is using this proverb negatively. The worst aspect about having a blind teacher is not that one's knowledge will be perverted or amiss of the truth; the worst aspect is rather that one's character is perverted as it becomes like that of the teacher. More consideration is given to imitation later in the analysis. This lexical analysis of μαθητής warrants including the concept in the semantic frame even though it is not mentioned specifically in Luke 6:39–49. Richard N. Longenecker, talking

143. Kirk, *Sayings Source*, 169.

144. Goldenberg, "Religious Formation in Ancient Judaism," 41.

about the absence of μαθητής in the majority of the NT, indicates semantically equivalent elements to likeness education as found in Luke 6:40. He mentions exhortations with verbs such as περιπατέω and μιμέομαι (to which is added the noun μιμητής) as well as the accompanying ideas of τύπος and ὑποτύπωσις.[145]

The illustration of a disciple's relationship to his or her teacher (or, a slave to his or her master) is "one of the frequent sayings of Christ."[146] Like the previous proverbial unit, part of this material is found elsewhere in the Gospels.[147] Again, it is difficult to imagine Jesus did not use the same imagery on multiple occasions, especially with different audiences.[148] Ray Summers explains that this imagery is used two different ways in the Gospels:

1. "If the teacher performs humble service for others (John 13:16), the disciple is not above such service."[149]

2. "If the teacher is reviled and persecuted, the disciple can anticipate the same thing; he cannot expect to be immune from persecution (Luke 6:40; John 15:20–21)."[150]

In the Gospel of Matthew, the similar description about a disciple and his teacher occurs during the commissioning of the twelve disciples (Matt 10:1–42). In the verses immediately preceding and following Matt 10:24–25, Jesus discusses persecution with them, anticipating rejection and persecution in place of repentance and a return to covenant obedience to God.[151] The word Jesus uses (ἀρκετόν) suggests that the disciples

145. Longenecker, introduction to *Patterns of Discipleship in the New Testament*, 5.

146. Thomas and Gundry, *A Harmony of the Gospels*, 69.

147. See Matt 10:24–25; John 13:16; 15:20. Thomas and Gundry also connect this proverb to Jesus's teaching in Luke 22:27 (ibid.).

148. Lenski correctly notes that these are uses of the same material at different points in Jesus's ministry: "A glance at Matt 10:24, 25 is sufficient to show that Luke most certainly did not take this saying of Jesus from that connection, for it is divided and combined with another figure in Matthew" (*St. Luke's Gospel*, 376). Similarly, Bock says the different occurrences record similar imagery and not the "development of a single saying" (*Luke: Volume 1 [1:1–9:50]*, 613).

149. Summers, *Jesus, the Universal Savior*, 79.

150. Ibid.

151. See Matt 10:23 (ὅταν δὲ διώκωσιν ὑμᾶς) and Matt 10:25b (πόσῳ μᾶλλον τοὺς οἰκιακοὺς αὐτοῦ). Thomas and Gundry write, "Jesus apparently did not expect widespread repentance to result from this mission. In the bulk of the discourse (e.g., Matt 10:14–39) He anticipated an unfavorable reception of the twelve. This anticipation was

should be satisfied, even happy, to become like their teacher—even if that involves suffering his same fate. A disciple becoming like Jesus in Matt 10:25 involves more than just taking on the teacher's character or having received all the teaching content that a teacher has at his disposal. For Jesus, this likeness transformation involves accepting the way others would or potentially could treat you, a manner with no distinction from how the teacher has been or could be treated. John's two references to the proverb, both occurring during the Farewell Discourse, do not include the μαθητής-διδάσκαλος relationship. He only includes the δοῦλος-κύριος relationship (John 13:16; 15:20). Every instance in the Gospels shows Jesus using the proverb to point to himself. For example, the proverb in John 13:16 follows Jesus's ultimate example regarding greatness when he washed each of the disciples' feet.[152]

Both Matthew and Luke include the prepositional phrase ὑπὲρ τὸν διδάσκαλον. Here the preposition serves as a comparative meaning "greater than," a metaphorical idea related to being positioned over someone or something.[153] In John the adjective μείζων is used (John 13:16 [2x]; 15:20). The prepositional phrase and the adjectival phrase are semantically identical.[154] When Jesus says a disciple is not above his or her teacher, the contrary is true: A teacher is greater than his or her disciple (ὑπὲρ τὸν μαθητήν). The prepositional phrase clearly refers to

based on earlier treatment of Himself" (*A Harmony of the Gospels*, 97).

152. Either Jesus does this in response to the disciples' quarrel about which of them was considered the greatest of his disciples (Luke 22:24), or they entirely disregard the most amazing example of servant-leadership ever. By the way, this was not the first time the disciples inquired about which of them was the greatest. Shortly after Jesus's transfiguration while still en route to Jerusalem by way of Capernaum, the disciples argued about who was the greatest and even approached Jesus with the question "Who is the greatest in the kingdom?" (Matt 18:1–5//Mark 9:33–37//Luke 9:46–48). At Jericho, another dispute arose when James, John, and their mother asked Jesus for seats of honor in his kingdom (Matt 20:20–28//Mark 10:35–45). In the first debacle, Jesus's illustration of the child apparently did not kill their selfish aspirations to hear Jesus identify one of them as the greatest. Jesus's final attempt to help them see how his kingdom is upside-down is found in the Farewell Discourse. This last attempt takes Jesus, the disciples' Savior and Lord, to the floor with towel and basin in hand just like a slave. For Jesus, it is imperative that the disciples have their minds resolute to be slaves of the gospel, not like the rulers of the Gentiles (Matt 20:25).

153. See Robertson, *A Grammar of the Greek New Testament*, 632–33; Riesenfeld, "ὑπέρ," 515; Bauer, *A Greek-English Lexicon*, 846.

154. Some older grammarians did not identify the semantic similarity between ὑπέρ with the acc. and μείζων with the genitive. See, for example, Dana and Mantey, *A Manual Grammar of the Greek New Testament*, 112.

two elements of the μαθητής-διδάσκαλος relationship. First, a student does not possess a superior amount or quality of knowledge than the teacher.[155] Second, not being "above" one's teacher definitely involves the idea of one not having authority over one's teacher.[156] This idea is not explicit in the proverb found in Luke, but it is very apparent when one compares the μαθητής-διδάσκαλος and δοῦλος-κύριος relationship joined side-by-side in Matthew's account. The authority element is clearly part of the latter comparison. Concerning this authority, Kirk believes that the proverb's placement in the unit "urges submission to the master (6:40) in place of arrogant presumption of leadership (6:39, 41–42)."[157] This is not impossible, but it is not a mandatory of understanding of the text. Proverbs have a sort of innate flexibility. Speakers and authors who utilize them clearly have an intended meaning. Nevertheless, Luke 6:40 can easily be understood negatively as well as positively. The negative aspect fits with the context.[158] Teaching and training by evil teachers will culminate in the reproduction of evil students. Likewise, teaching and training by good teachers culminates with good students on par with their teachers in content and character. Each of these proverbial units moves toward a final instruction about the wisdom of coming to Jesus (Luke 6:46–49), the actual "urging" for submission to the master. There is a third element present by default from reading the second part of the proverb. The corresponding phrase to ὑπὲρ τὸν διδάσκαλον in the second part of the proverb is ὡς ὁ διδάσκαλος αὐτοῦ. When Jesus says a disciple is not above his or her teacher, he must also mean that he or she is not like the teacher in the sense that he or she will be after having been fully trained (κατηρτισμένος, Luke 6:40b).

The second part of the maxim is not entirely unique to the Gospel of Luke: κατηρτισμένος δὲ πᾶς ἔσται ὡς ὁ διδάσκαλος αὐτοῦ. Matthew has a parallel continuation of the proverb in Matt 10:25: ἀρκετὸν τῷ μαθητῇ ἵνα γένηται ὡς ὁ διδάσκαλος αὐτοῦ. The presence of δέ is slightly adversative.[159] Jesus says what a disciple is not and follows now with what a disciple generally will be after a certain amount of instruction under the direction of the teacher. Unique to Luke, however, is the participle κατηρτισμένος

155. Reiling and Swellengrebel, *Translator's Handbook on the Gospel of Luke*, 282. They also suggest that the phrase means "not more important than" (ibid.).

156. Witherington III, *Jesus the Sage*, 179.

157. Kirk, *Sayings Source*, 172.

158. See Arndt, *Luke*, 197.

159. Lenski, *St. Luke's Gospel*, 377.

from καταρτίζω, which can carry any of the ideas of mending, restoring, completing, or maturing.[160] This form only appears here in Luke 6:40.[161] Other forms of καταρτίζω are fairly uncommon in the remainder of the New Testament. There are only three additional occurrences in the Gospels, two in Matthew and one in Mark. The remainder are found in the Pauline corpus (Rom 9:22; 1 Cor 1:10; 2 Cor 13:11; Gal 6:1; 1 Thess 3:10; Heb 10:5; 11:3; 13:21), with the exception of one use by Peter (1 Pet 5:10).[162]

While the lexeme itself is rare in the NT, its future-perfect form is extremely rare.[163] There are no occurrences in the active voice.[164] The use of the passive in 6:40b is obvious. The student does not train himself but is trained.[165] The perfect participle has the capacity to indicate simultaneous action with a finite verb. Here, however, the future perfect hinges the result (ἔσται ὡς ὁ διδάσκαλος αὐτοῦ) on a contingent factor or action, in this case "being fully trained."[166] The action described by the future perfect participle must precede the result (or, state).[167] Aspect in Greek does not connote anything about the duration of time that this training would require. Beyond that, this is a proverb. General statements like this usually concentrated on a beginning, an action, and a result without any reference to time. Perhaps the most famous "training" proverb in the Bible is Prov 22:6: "Train up a child in the way he should go and he will not depart from it." Even the verb יַזְקִין ("after he grows old") does not

---

160. Abbott-Smith, *A Manual Greek Lexicon of the New Testament*, 238.

161. Evans, *Saint Luke*, 338.

162. For a brief overview of each of these uses, see Balz and Schneider (eds.), "καταρτίζω," 268. See also Tuggy's overview of the uses in the OT, primarily in Psalms (*Léxico Griego-Español*, 512–13).

163. Robinson and House, *Analytical Lexicon of New Testament Greek*, 398; Luschnig, *An Introduction to Ancient Greek*, 162; Foley, *Biblical Translation in Chinese and Greek*, 179 n.102.

164. Mounce, *The Morphology of Biblical Greek*, 116.

165. Daniel B. Wallace provides two reasons for why the middle is not an option here: (1) Direct middles are rare in the NT, and (2) the perfect "is always to be taken as passive in the NT" (*Greek Grammar, Beyond the Basics*, 418).

166. Mateos, *El Aspecto Verbal en el Nuevo Testamento*, 130–31.

167. Antonakos, *The Greek Handbook*, 82. A similar construction found in Heb 2:13, ἐγὼ ἔσομαι πεποιθὼς ἐπ' αὐτῷ. Many translations miss the periphrastic construction here. J. Harold Greenlee brings out the meaning with these words, "I shall be in a condition resulting from previously having come to trust in him" (*A Concise Exegetical Grammar of New Testament Greek*, 51).

involve any specific duration of time. It only indicates the transition from one state (i.e., youth) to another (i.e., old).[168] The same is true in Luke 6:40b with κατηρτισμένος, and it is rather typical of proverbs.

The adverb ὡς, which Michael J. Wilkins identifies as an "'imitation' term,"[169] indicates who a student will resemble after receiving his or her training. They will be like their teacher. This adverbial phrase corresponds to the previous prepositional phrase (ὑπὲρ τὸν διδάσκαλον). It specifies that, according to Christopher R. Matthews, "the disciple is not in training to succeed the master, even though an essential part of being a disciple involves replicating the master's activity."[170] Instead, the training results in the disciple being like the teacher, not more than or greater than but liken to his or her knowledge, authority, and character.[171] It is more than cognitive growth. R. C. H. Lenski says a disciple "absorbs more from his teacher than mere learning."[172] The interpreter must remember the nature of proverbs. When they give a result or outcome, be it in connection to a certain lifestyle practice or relationship, that result is generally true, not universally true.[173]

To whom did Jesus intend the proverbs in Luke 6:39b–40? William Loader refutes the idea that the entire SOP is applicable only to the disciples. The clause καὶ αὐτὸς ἐπάρας τοὺς ὀφθαλμοὺς αὐτοῦ εἰς τοὺς μαθητὰς αὐτοῦ, he says, does not imply "that what follows excludes application to the crowds."[174] However, he entertains the possibility that 6:22 and vv. 39–40 are intended exclusively for his disciples (both in Jesus's audience and Luke's). It is dangerous to view this section as applicable only to disciples, whether directed toward the twelve disciples Jesus has already chosen and named apostles or to the broader group known as μαθηταί. The use of παραβολή in Luke 6:39a refers to the end of the SOP (Luke 6:47–49); its use so early is intentional, allowing Luke to mark 6:39–49 as a discourse unit. The relationship between these proverbs and the conclusion's climax must be considered. Since Jesus's exhortation in 6:47

168. Arnold and Choi, *A Guide to Biblical Hebrew Syntax*, 51.

169. Wilkins, *Following the Master*, 307.

170. Matthews, "Disciple," 109.

171. Reiling and Swellengrebel mention the first two (*Translator's Handbook on the Gospel of Luke*, 283).

172. Lenski, *St. Luke's Gospel*, 378.

173. Lenski cautions, "The warning is idle that we must not stretch this too far since some pupils become more learned than their teachers" (ibid., 377).

174. Loader, "What Happened to 'Good News for the Poor'?," 252.

involves three actions that would be involved in a μαθητής-διδάσκαλος relationship (coming, hearing, doing), the proverbs in 6:39–40 probably have a broader audience.

The Third Proverbial Unit (Luke 6:41–42)

The third proverbial unit consists of two rhetorical questions (marked below as 3.1 and 3.2), a vocative address (3.3), followed by an injunction consisting of two commands (3.4 and 3.5).

3.1: τί δὲ βλέπεις τὸ κάρφος τὸ ἐν τῷ ὀφθαλμῷ τοῦ ἀδελφοῦ σου,
   τὴν δὲ δοκὸν τὴν ἐν τῷ ἰδίῳ ὀφθαλμῷ;
3.2: πῶς δύνασαι λέγειν τῷ ἀδελφῷ σου,
   Ἀδελφέ, ἄφες ἐκβάλω τὸ κάρφος τὸ ἐν τῷ ὀφθαλμῷ σου,
   αὐτὸς τὴν ἐν τῷ ὀφθαλμῷ σου δοκὸν οὐ βλέπων;
3.3: ὑποκριτά
3.4: ἔκβαλε πρῶτον τὴν δοκὸν ἐκ τοῦ ὀφθαλμοῦ σου,
  καὶ τότε
3.5: διαβλέψεις τὸ κάρφος τὸ ἐν τῷ ὀφθαλμῷ τοῦ ἀδελφοῦ σου
  ἐκβαλεῖν.

Like the previous two units, the imagery here is not unique to this Gospel or to Judeo-Christian tradition.[175] The content is an elaboration of 6:39[176] and an illustration of the prohibitions in 6:37. The two rhetorical questions share a strong semantic relationship with the first proverbial unit (6:39b). Kirk writes:

> Besides the fact that both 6:39 and 6:41–42 are rhetorical questions based on sight-gags, they are correlated through key words from the semantic field of 'sight'—τυφλός, ὀφθαλμός, βλέπεις, κατανοείς—with the total blindness of verse 39 gradually giving way to the 'seeing clearly' (διαβλέψεις) of the final admonition.[177]

175. Nolland calls it a "secular proverb," yet none of them exactly resembles what comes from Jesus (Nolland, *Luke 1–9:20*, 310). Samuel Tobias Lachs writes, "This passage contains a popular Palestinian folk saying about individuals who refuse to take criticism or to see faults in themselves but who are quick to notice them in others" (*The Gospels of Matthew, Mark and Luke*, 137). For a few examples of this imagery used in rabbinic, Greek-Latin, and Arabic works, see Nolland, *Luke 1–9:20*, 307; Fillion, *Vida de Nuestro Señor Jesucristo II*, 115.

176. Summers, *Jesus, the Universal Savior*, 79.

177. Kirk, *Sayings Source*, 170. Bock also identifies the repeated sight-imagery (Bock, *Luke: Volume 1 [1:1–9:50]*, 613).

What Jesus describes in the two rhetorical questions is vivid imagery (hyperbole)[178] depicting what it is he has just commanded for his disciples not to do, specifically judging (μὴ κρίνετε) and condemning (μὴ καταδικάζετε) in 6:37.[179] The use of hyperbole, according to Nida and his associates, shows a significant increase in markedness. By using it here Jesus continues the sermon toward its climax in vv. 46–49.[180]

The first rhetorical question begins with τί and the second with πῶς. They are different than the rhetorical questions found in 6:39 in that these are more open-ended and have less of an indicative tone. Luke 6:39 is best translated something like "A blind person cannot lead another blind person, right?" Here in Luke 6:41, Jesus asks, "Why do you look at the speck in your brother's eye, but fail to notice the beam of wood in your own eye?" The imagery, which Jesus uses so that its application would not be restricted in the least, is obvious, but there is a general act and attitude which Jesus is addressing. The τί interrogative with the indicative mood implies this as an attitude regularly practiced by those who are present. The only use of the vocative follows these rhetorical questions. In this case it is a negative or condemning address. If it is not evident from the context preceding 6:37[181] that the uses of μή with the present indicative are prohibitive imperatives,[182] the two rhetorical questions here and the vocative certainly clarify how they should be

178. Craddock calls this a "tragicomical image" (Craddock, *Luke*, 92), while Nolland says it is "graphic to the point of being grotesque" (Nolland, *Luke 1–9:20*, 310). Is Jesus going for shock or for laughs? Is he being serious, or is he acting like a comedian as Morris (*Luke*, 147), Bock (*Luke*, IVP, 128), Lenski (*St. Luke's Gospel*, 382), and others seem to suggest? Certainly laughs could have been heard from among the crowd, however, there is nothing in the rest of the SOP, or the SOM for that matter, hinting of anything but a serious tone on the part of Jesus. Hyperbole is not synonymous with humor.

179. Marshall, *Gospel of Luke*, 270; Pao and Schnabel, "Luke," 298.

180. Nida et al., *Style and Discourse*, 23.

181. The uses of οὐαί in 6:24–26 clearly indicate that this is not a neutral teaching session. Jesus is not simply giving instructions about his kingdom ethic. Matthew's record of the same sermon shows Jesus's call to repentance, a call to find a righteousness that exceeds that of the Pharisees and to seek first God's kingdom (and the rightful heir to David's throne) before anything else. This sermon is part of Jesus's message of repentance and the kingdom (Matt 4:17). Whether Jesus entered the synagogues or taught on the side of a mountain, his teaching ministry prior to the rejection in Matthew 12–13 resembles what is recorded in Matthew 5–7 and Luke 6:20–49.

182. Concerning the imperative of prohibition, see Black, *Learn to Read New Testament Greek*, 189; Black, *Using New Testament Greek in Ministry*, 100; Swetnam, *Introduction to the Study of New Testament Greek*, 403–04.

understood. The interrogative πῶς is best understood as "How is it possible?" With these rhetorical questions, there is an "implied exhortation to do the opposite," says Stephen H. Levinsohn.[183] Without Jesus's injunction in 6:42, the audience might think that it is right to abstain entirely from spiritual assistance in someone else's life. Jesus's second command, however, mandates such involvement, but not before he introduces a prerequisite—introspection.

The meaning of κάρφος and δοκός is the primary topic in most discussions regarding this section. Major et al. say the word κάρφος means "any small dry object, a splinter or chip of wood, small twig or the like."[184] Lenski says it does not refer to a mote or a speck.[185] Concerning δοκός, Bock shows that the word refers to "the main beam of a building," a word with imagery greater than even a two-by-four captures.[186] The main beam of a building would have been much longer and thicker than a modern-day two-by-four; it would have been a load-bearing beam, sometimes stretched over numerous columns to provide support for a roof. This is something Jesus is very familiar with given his familial profession as a builder (τέκτων, Mark 6:3). A κάρφος is noticeable but not extremely obvious like a δοκός would be. A δοκός, as J. Reiling and J. L. Swellengrebel say, "is impossible not to notice."[187] The parallel to 6:39 is obvious as well. In 6:39, both blind persons have a sight handicap. Still, one blind person feels capable of leading the other, despite his own impairment. Likewise, in 6:41–42, both brothers have a sight handicap, one exceedingly worse than the other. It is the one with the more severe impairment who attempts to fix the other.

Despite the great amount of attention given to the contrast between κάρφος and δοκός, Bock says the "contrast in the verbs at the end of the passage is key."[188] The problem with the brother having a δοκός is his own failure to see (οὐ κατανοεῖς and οὐ βλέπων). At first glance, if consulting various translations, the two verbs may appear as synonyms.[189] The

183. Levinsohn, *Some Notes*, 31.

184. Major et. al., *Mission and Message*, 350. Turner says it can refer to a piece of straw (*Matthew*, 206). Also, the word was apparently used in Classical Greek to refer to cinnamon bark (Totelin, *Hippocratic Recipes*, 150).

185. Lenski, *St. Luke's Gospel*, 379.

186. Bock, *Luke*, IVP, 128–29.

187. Reiling and Swellengrebel, *Translator's Handbook on the Gospel of Luke*, 283.

188. Bock, *Luke: Volume 1 (1:1–9:50)*, 614.

189. Reiling and Swellengrebel, *Translator's Handbook on the Gospel of Luke*, 283.

first, however, is distinct from the simple sight-verb βλέπω. Κατανοέω is formed with the prefixed preposition κατά and the verb νοέω. The present indicative of κατανοέω is actually the introduction of the idea of introspection, not the command in 6:42b (ἔκβαλε πρῶτον). Different than the use of βλέπω, this verb carries the idea of mental consideration or assessment. Craig L. Blomberg and Mariam J. Kamell say this word "often implies intense or studied attention, not merely a passing glance."[190] This is evident in the other uses of κατανοέω in Luke-Acts.[191]

The most striking changes in verbs are: (1) Jesus's shift from βλέπω to his use of διαβλέπω, and (2) Jesus's shift from the indicative mood to the imperative in the injunction. Βλέπω, like ὁράω, is a simple sight-verb. Verbs like κατανοέω and θαυμάζω are sight-/sensory-verbs as well. However, they represent more complicated ideas. Διαβλέπεις is most likely emphatic. The only other two occurrences in the NT are found in Matt 7:5, a parallel passage, and Mark 8:25. In the latter, both βλέπω and διαβλέπω are used in the two-stage healing of the blind man at Bethsaida. After Jesus spit on the man's eyes and laid his hands on him, the man saw but his sight was still impaired. What he saw was men walking around who looked like trees. In the second stage, after Jesus reapplies his hands, Peter recalls that the man began to see everything clearly (καὶ διέβλεψεν καὶ ἀπεκατέστη καὶ ἐνέβλεπεν τηλαυγῶς ἅπαντα, Mark 8:25). In Mark 8:25, the idea of seeing clearly is either not sufficient with the word διαβλέπω or the word τηλαυγῶς is added for emphasis. The latter is most probable. Peter probably adds this because of his account of the first stage in which he did not see clearly. Although the blind man did see, it was not clear. Prior to his encounter with Jesus, he did not see at all. In Luke 6:42, the removal of the wooden beam results in being able to see clearly. The prefixed preposition διά helps communicate the idea of seeing without obstruction.

From Luke 6:39 to the second rhetorical question in 6:42, there is an absence of the imperative mood (or, equivalents in the subjunctive). The sermon is filled with a high concentration of imperatives given its brevity. Jesus tells the audience to:

1. Rejoice in the day they are persecuted (χάρητε, 6:23).

---

190. Blomberg and Kamell, *James*, 90.

191. Consider, for example, κατανοήσατε τοὺς κόρακας (Luke 12:24) and κατανοήσατε τὰ κρίνα πῶς αὐξάνει (Luke 12:27). The remaining occurrences in Luke-Acts are Luke 20:23, Acts 7:31–32 (2x); 11:6; and 27:39.

2. Love their enemies (ἀγαπᾶτε, 6:27).

3. Do good to people who hate them (καλῶς ποιεῖτε, 6:27)

4. Bless people who curse them (εὐλογεῖτε, 6:28).

5. Pray for people who ill-treat them (προσεύχεσθε, 6:28)

6. Offer the next cheek for people who want to smite it as well (πάρεχε, 6:29).

7. Not prevent a coat-thief from taking their shirts either (μὴ κωλύσῃς, 6:29; *subjunctive).

8. Give to those who ask for something (δίδου, 6:30).

9. Not demand the return of something stolen from them (μὴ ἀπαίτει, 6:30).

10. Treat people the same way they desire to be treated (ποιῶσιν, 6:31; *subjunctive).

11. Love their enemies (ἀγαπᾶτε, 6:35).

12. Do good to others (ἀγαθοποιεῖτε, 6:35).

13. Lend to others without even the expectation of a return (δανίζετε, 6:35).

14. Be merciful to others (γίνεσθε οἰκτίρμονες, 6:36).

15. Not judge people (μὴ κρίνετε, 6:37).

16. Not condemn people (μὴ καταδικάζετε, 6:37).

17. Release others [from their debts] (ἀπολύετε, 6:37).

18. Give (δίδοτε, 6:38).

There are a total of eighteen commands from 6:20–38. Only four are negated, and only two are in the subjunctive. Like the rhetorical interlude found in 6:39–42, these eighteen commands are broken up four times. Luke 6:32–34 contains two rhetorical questions and two statements about how even sinners (ἁμαρτωλοί) do what Jesus describes in the rhetorical questions. There are ten commands before Luke 6:32–34. Three commands follow (ἀγαπᾶτε, ἀγαθοποιεῖτε, and δανίζετε). Jesus adds that those who do these things will be sons of the Most High, who he says is the epitome of kindness to an ungrateful and evil people (6:35). This group is followed by another command to be merciful (γίνεσθε οἰκτίρμονες), to which Jesus adds a καθώς clause; the standard is God's own character and his measure of mercy (6:36). Then, there is a cluster of four commands, each with its own secondary statement (e.g., "and it will be given"). A single explanatory idea concludes, referring to a standard of reciprocity.

Luke 6:42b contains the final use of the imperative in the SOP, a shift from the indicative to the imperative. The transition from the rhetorical questions to the imperative, a reversal from the order in 6:23–34, is significant, but why? Kirk points out the shift and provides the following answer: "Though 6:42b maintains the images of log and splinter, its shift to imperative voice marks it out as the concluding admonition."[192] It is definitely an admonition. However, is this the final admonition? This section is marked not so much by the shift in mood, which is prevalent in the SOP, but by the use of the vocative and the accusatory tone in which Jesus speaks to the audience. The tone of the entire SOP has sought the repentance of the people. It is only here, though, that Jesus introduces the vocative. He calls the people hypocrites (sg. ὑποκριτά). Jesus used this term in the SOM three times referring to hypocrites in Jewish culture, particularly in the synagogues. Luke includes the only reference to hypocrites that is not used by Jesus in the sermon for a Jewish context. The word has a history of referring to actors, but by the time Jesus uses this word it has taken on a meaning apart from that word association. Dale C. Allison Jr. identifies the main concept underpinning hypocrisy. "Hypocrisy," he says, "involves, among other things, disjunction between word and deed."[193] This shift to the imperative mood foreshadows the final admonition found in 6:46–49, specifically Jesus's invitation for everyone to come to him. In this invitation, right before Jesus gives the parable mentioned in 6:39a, he draws everyone's attention again to this separation of word and deed. Allison writes, "One learns not just with the ears but also with the feet. Education is much more than heeding the infallible wordsmith. It additionally involves the mimetic following of Jesus, who is virtue embodied."[194]

In the second proverbial unit, Jesus says each disciple, "after having been fully trained, will be like his or her teacher" (6:40b). That unit provides no additional information as to what sort of training or instruction disciples needed before they will be like their teacher. C. F. Evans suggests that part of what Jesus intends with the participle κατηρτισμένος

192. Kirk, *Sayings Source*, 171.
193. Allison Jr., *Studies in Matthew*, 152.
194. Ibid., 153.

is a disciple's transformation from being the brother described in the rhetorical questions to one who conducts "necessary self-criticism."[195] Just
as in 6:39, where Jesus's emphasis is on "the necessity to see clearly before
one can guide others,"[196] here his emphasis is on the necessity of doing
introspective spiritual analysis before attempting to correct others. This
is a point that seems lacking in both Jewish and Greco-Roman education of the day. Moreover, the leadership, failing to make this an intimate
aspect of their investment into a student's life, spawned generation after
generation of pseudo-leaders unprepared to receive the Messiah and his
kingdom. It is significant that Jesus starts first in his likeness program
with the practical and with a disciple's character than with the deepest
theology. This is an idea later encountered in Paul's teaching—milk before solid food (Heb 5:12–14).

The Fourth Proverbial Unit (Luke 6:43–45)

4.1a: οὐ γάρ ἐστιν δένδρον καλὸν ποιοῦν καρπὸν σαπρόν,

4.1b: οὐδὲ πάλιν [ἐστιν] δένδρον σαπρὸν ποιοῦν καρπὸν καλόν.

4.2: ἕκαστον γὰρ δένδρον ἐκ τοῦ ἰδίου καρποῦ γινώσκεται·

4.3a: οὐ γὰρ ἐξ ἀκανθῶν συλλέγουσιν σῦκα

4.3b: οὐδὲ ἐκ βάτου σταφυλὴν τρυγῶσιν.

4.3c: ὁ ἀγαθὸς ἄνθρωπος ἐκ τοῦ ἀγαθοῦ θησαυροῦ τῆς καρδίας
προφέρει τὸ ἀγαθόν,
καὶ

4.3d: ὁ πονηρὸς ἐκ τοῦ πονηροῦ προφέρει τὸ πονηρόν·

4.4: ἐκ γὰρ περισσεύματος καρδίας λαλεῖ τὸ στόμα αὐτοῦ.

This proverbial unit consists of four parts. There are two main comparisons within:

1.   Trees (good, bad) and the fruit they bear (good, bad).

2.   People (good, bad) and the works they produce (good, bad).

The temptation is to analyze these comparisons by the content alone,
paying attention only to the lexical and other types of similarities. Doing
this, however, overlooks the discourse markers provided in the text. Luke
employs the use of γάρ four times. Outside of the fourth proverbial unit,

195. Evans, *Saint Luke*, 338.
196. Guy, *The Gospel of Luke*, 64.

there are only six occurrences of γάρ in the SOP (6:23 [2x], 26, 32, 33, 38). This unit contains the highest concentration of γάρ in the SOP and the Gospel as a whole. Luke 9:23–27 has the second highest concentration. Before looking at the content, it is necessary to understand how this conjunction functions and what the speaker's intent must have been in utilizing it four times in these three verses.

Steven E. Runge provides the best explanation of how authors utilize γάρ in discourse. Like other connectives, it is impossible to separate the content following γάρ with what precedes it. Γάρ, according to Runge, has a strengthening purpose. Whereas καί can move a narrative or argument along, γάρ keeps the narrative or argument still and "introduces offline material that strengthens or supports what precedes."[197] His summary of γάρ says:

> Γάρ introduces explanatory material that strengthens or supports what precedes. This may consist of a single clause, or it may be a longer digression. Although the strengthening material is important to the discourse, it does not advance the argument or story. Instead, it supports what precedes by providing background or detail that is needed to understand what follows.[198]

Richard A. Edwards offers a concurring opinion, saying most occurrences are "a way of supplying information after a statement or command."[199] What sort of information? Edwards refers to similar functioning γάρ clauses as ideological uses. They "reveal the assumptions of the speaker—the background of his/her thinking—after the command, statement, or question has been spoken."[200] It is not unusual for a γάρ clause to contain proverbial language.

This proverbial unit, if Runge's and Edwards' explanations about the uses of γάρ are correct, adds supplemental information to demonstrate Jesus's thinking about previous material. The content of vv. 43–45 must be understood in light of what Jesus has already taught. Craddock and Arndt tie the first γάρ clause to the vocative and admonition in 6:42.[201] A

---

197. Runge, *Discourse Grammar*, 52.

198. Ibid., 54.

199. Edwards, "Narrative Implications," 636.

200. Ibid., 646.

201. Craddock, *Luke*, 93; Arndt, *Luke*, 198. Marshall, holding a slightly altered position, says the connection is "weak" and that the γάρ progresses the argument forward (*The Gospel of Luke*, 272).

hypocrite is an unfit description for someone who claims Jesus as his or her Lord. Craddock writes, "Luke now strikes it down as totally inappropriate as a description of Jesus's followers. What one is, what one does, and what one says are an inseparable union, as are a tree and its fruit."[202] It is impossible to separate who a person is from what sort of fruit that person bears. Speech, mentioned in v. 45 with the final γάρ clause, is only an illustration of this inseparable union, and it reaches back further than verse 42. The warning in 6:39 leads to a question Jesus now answers, namely "How can one identify a spiritually blind person?" The answer is by his or her actions, which καρπός refers to.[203] Bock, for example, says "you will produce what you are and not something different."[204] José Manuel Díaz says the γάρ clauses confirm what Jesus says in each of the three proverbial units:

> De ahí que el guía inepto, el maestro mal formado en doctrina o en virtud, ningún bien podrá hacer de suyo a sus discípulos; o, más generalmente, que el hombre malo es de suyo incapaz de hacer el bien a los demás y de ejercer provechosamente el celo de la caridad.[205]

A blind person and a teacher who is deficient in knowledge and character have no capacity to effectively produce the type of disciples Jesus describes in the Sermon on the Plain. Jesus identifies the heart of the problem in this unit. Up until this point, when Jesus enters human history, all of mankind has suffered from the Fall and remain unregenerate. The problem is the heart of mankind.[206] Nolland points out that vv. 41–42 and vv. 43–45 differ in that the latter concentrates on "the necessary correlation between work of true goodness and the inner disposition"[207] or, as Arthur A. Just Jr. puts it, a person's "character."[208] The thrust of this passage is to show the warped nature of human beings and the character that accompanies it, a point that fittingly leads into Jesus's invitation for people to come to him, hear his words, and put them into action (6:46–49).

---

202. Craddock, *Luke*, 93.

203. Klein, *Das Lukasevangelium*, 264.

204. Bock, *Luke: Volume 1 (1:1–9:50)*, 616.

205. Díaz, *El Santo Evangelio según San Lucas*, 175.

206. Powell, *Luke's Thrilling Gospel*, 157.

207. Nolland, *Luke 1–9:20*, 309.

208. Just Jr., *Luke 1:1–9:50*, 282.

Jesus maintains his use of imagery and comparison, this time, drawing the connection between tree/fruit and people/speech. The imagery of a tree and its fruit is not uncommon. For example, John the Baptist uses the imagery in his call for the crowds to repent (Luke 3:8–9). The imagery is common for "describing human behavior" and is found in Galatians referring to Spirit-produced works.[209] The people's response to John's illustration is, "Then what shall we do?" (Luke 3:10, 12, 14). Luke records no response in the Sermon on the Plain. Like the SOM, the SOP is entirely a record of Jesus's teaching, not an exchange of discourse such as found elsewhere. Only Matthew records the response of the crowds at the end of the sermon. They were being amazed (ἐξεπλήσσοντο, Matt 7:28). Jesus's use of this imagery undoubtedly has the same effect on the crowds as when John used it earlier. The conclusion to the SOP is designed to answer the same question the crowds, the tax collectors, and the soldiers asked John in Luke 3:8—"What shall we do now?"

Each of the γάρ clauses is explanatory. The second clause, as Reiling and Swellengrebel note, "introduces the principle which underlies the statements of v. 43."[210] Arndt says it is parenthetical.[211] The use of ἕκαστος is resonant of πᾶς in 6:40b. Like πᾶς, no article is present, which Buttman says is "quite ordinary to analogy."[212] While the content (tree/fruit) is the same, it also serves as a transition from trees to people with the verb γίνομαι. How can a blind guide be avoided? How can a person know a teacher whose character matches one they would benefit from if they were trained into his or her likeness? The third γάρ introduces an illustration of people who do not gather fruit foolishly (6:44). In the same way that people do not foolishly attempt to gather figs or grapes from sources that obviously do not produce them, people should not look for guidance from those who lack sight or teachers who lack what it is that they truly need. All one needs to inspect is that person's actions.

Jesus shifts the illustration from trees and fruit to people in Luke 6:45. In v. 43, he used a negated ἔστιν (i.e., what does not exist). In v. 45, he speaks about what is. Thrice the word ἀγαθός is used. It is used to describe a man, his heart, and what comes forth from him. Likewise,

---

209. Rindoš, *He of Whom It Is Written*, 119–20.

210. Reiling and Swellengrebel, *Translator's Handbook on the Gospel of Luke*, 285.

211. Arndt, *Luke*, 198.

212. Buttman, *A Grammar of the New Testament Greek*, 120. He says the article would be expected only if the speaker/author intended to limit the quantity. In a general statement, like a proverb or analogy, the broadest application is intended.

the word πονηρός is used three times to describe the man, his heart, and what he produces. A man who is genuinely good is so because his heart is good. In general, these people are characterized by that which is good. The contrary is true for the one who is genuinely evil. This connection between a person's heart and speech is a known rabbinic saying (*Midr Pss* 9:2)[213] and "an ideal in Greek ethical thought."[214] Morris says, "It is what he has in his inner nature that determines what fruit his life will yield."[215] The fourth and final γάρ makes a final application of the two comparisons, identifying one way that a person's action can be identified and gauged, namely speech (λαλεῖ). Here it is equivalent to "for example" in English. Speech is not the only way by which someone's actions can be measured to the standard of Christ. It is an important way though and one which guides and teachers use often in the direction and instruction of those who they lead (v. 39–40).

The Meaning of Luke 6:46–49

The Transition to the Parable (Luke 6:46)

The end of the SOP consists of a final rhetorical question and the parable referred to in 6:39. Together they emphasize obedience to Jesus and what he commands.[216] Both Matthew's SOM and Luke's SOP include the parable found in Luke 6:46–49. The transition to the parable, however, is different. Matthew includes a longer section about people calling Jesus 'Lord' and the statement is declarative. In Luke, Jesus transitions to the parable with a rhetorical question, the only one lacking imagery in the entire Sermon on the Plain. The lack of imagery supports Levinsohn's point that this is a "rhetorical question of rebuke."[217]

Jesus asks, "Why do you call me, 'Lord, Lord,' and do not do the things that I tell you to?" This is the fifth question in the concluding section to the Sermon on the Plain. The first two rhetorical questions (6:39b) are the only questions that do not directly address the audience in the second person (βλέπεις, δύνασαι, καλεῖτε). The third and fourth

213. Major et. al., *The Mission and Message of Jesus*, 352.

214. Lieu, *The Gospel of Luke*, 53.

215. Morris, *The Gospel according to Matthew*, 148.

216. Garland, *Luke*, 285.

217. Levinsohn, *Some Notes*, 32.

questions are in the second-person singular, and the final is plural. It has two parts. The first deals with calling Jesus by a particular title (κύριος). The second, joined with a καί, deals with not doing what Jesus says. Levinsohn writes, "A person who calls Jesus 'Lord, Lord' and does not do what he says is a hypocrite (42c), and is like a bad tree attempting to bear good fruit."[218] In vv. 41–42, the problem is a person's endeavor to fix someone else without giving due attention to one's own character and actions. In v. 46, the ultimate hypocrisy is met. The crowds and the disciples were willing to follow Jesus, many perhaps calling him "Lord," but they failed at this point in his ministry to do the things he was teaching from synagogue to synagogue and city to city.[219]

The double-use of κύριος in the vocative is the subject of much discussion. Some believe that this is a later insertion by church tradition, a title synonymous with high Christology alongside Μεσσίας.[220] However, this is a term ascribed to persons with authority, especially teachers and rabbis in Jewish culture.[221] Luke does not include the crowd's response to the sermon that shows that the crowds identified this type of authority with Jesus (see Matt 7:29). He does, however, use the word ἐξουσία much more than Matthew. He shows that the synagogues were filled with people who recognized how his teaching differed in authority (Luke 4:32). He shows how people recognized the authority and power Jesus exercised over unclean spirits (Luke 4:36). Among the twelve other uses of the word in Luke, he shows how Jesus has the greatest authority of all, namely the authority to forgive sins (Luke 5:24).[222] People call him Lord

218. Ibid., 32. Bock adds, "The mention of speech in Luke 6:45 may have led to the thought of not uttering lightly one's commitment to Jesus" (Bock, *Luke: Volume 1 [1:1–9:50]*, 618).

219. This is most likely not the first time that some in the audience have heard Jesus's teaching. Jesus allows the crowds to follow, some so much that they become known as disciples. He eventually gives them a "difficult teaching" (σκληρός ἐστιν ὁ λόγος, John 6:60). By the time the events recorded in John 6:53–66 occur, Jesus has been rejected by the people (Matthew 12–13) and his ministry has shifted from being in Galilee to the regions surrounding it. The crowds continue to follow and gather to hear him speak. In the synagogue in Capernaum, Jesus gives the disciples a lesson (John 6:53–58) that causes many of them to withdraw from him and follow him no longer (John 6:60, 66).

220. Lenski, *St. Luke's Gospel*, 383.

221. Bock, *Luke: Volume 1 (1:1–9:50)*, 618.

222. Bock says that Luke's difference with Matthew's SOM, specifically that it leaves out the eschatological element connected to the "Lord, Lord" ascription, is because of his "tendency to play down the end-time judgment" (ibid., 619). There is an easier

not because of its Christological significance but because of its connection with authority.

The Meaning of the Parable (Luke 6:47–49)

Since 6:39, Jesus's teaching has been moving to this moment, a final admonition. It comes in the form of a parable, which Luke mentions at the introduction at the sermon conclusion. One finite verb (ὑποδείξω) is joined with a likeness clause (τίνι ἐστὶν ὅμοιος), which is typical of parable introductions.[223] The interrogative τίνι is modified by a chain of three present active participles (ἐρχόμενος, ἀκούων, ποιῶν),[224] which really constitutes a case of anacoluthon. By doing this, the participles are fronted, allowing the audience to feel the emphasis Jesus places on doing these three things: (1) coming to him, (2) hearing his words, and (3) doing them. The participle chain would function fine without the use of πᾶς, but, like v. 40, Luke includes it.[225] The last participle in the chain shows Jesus's attention to praxeology.[226] Moreover, the present tense for

---

explanation, though. Luke's sermon is systematically organized for brevity. The sermon is so important to the life and ministry of Jesus Christ that it could not be omitted entirely, especially if the Gospel of Luke would be an adequate training manual for Gentile believers. And the Gospel of Matthew with its account of the SOM was never intended to be replaced. It remained a most-valuable resource to early Christian communities, especially since it was this Gospel that Paul used on his missionary journeys. Luke simply could not include all of it, nor should he, if he hoped to include other parts of the life and ministry of Jesus Christ such as the early years of John the Baptist (1:5–80), the birth of Jesus (2:1–39), the anointing of Jesus's feet (7:36–50), and much of the latter Judean ministry and ministry around Perea (Luke 10–13). In addition to this, it is not necessary to assume that Luke changes Matthew's words. The rhetorical question is original, in fact, a question Jesus really asked. It may have occurred between Matt 7:20–21 or between Matt 7:23–24. The former is most likely. Statements like those by Anna Wierzbicka (*What Did Jesus Mean?*, 215) who says, "Luke's is the more original," show a danger in historical Jesus studies to the evangelical understanding of the inspiration of Scripture. The Scriptures' veracity is jeopardized if they present things as historical fact that never actually occurred.

223. Zerwick, *Biblical Greek*, 22.

224. Ἐρχόμενος is from the deponent ἔρχομαι. It is not active in form but is in voice.

225. Robertson says Luke has a fondness for πᾶς (*A Grammar of the Greek New Testament*, 122).

226. For a discussion on how praxis is addressed in Luke, see Chandler, "Love Your Enemies as Yourself," 37.

all three, according to David E. Garland, refers to "the ongoing process of discipleship."[227]

Construction analogies are not uncommon in the Greco-Roman or Jewish cultures. Rabbi Nathan (second century AD), for example, contrasts two builders—one who builds by placing smaller stones on top of larger stones, and another who does the reverse (*Aboth de Rabbi Nathan* 24:1–3).[228] This parable contrasts two persons. Different than Matthew's account, Luke does not include the qualifications of wise or foolish (Matt 7:24, 26), nor does he include Jesus's declaration "Not everyone who says to me, 'Lord, Lord,' will enter the kingdom of heaven" (Matt 7:21). Informing audiences of unfitness for his kingdom was common subject matter for him during his ministry, and Luke opts to include it in his section covering Jesus's ministry in and around Perea.[229] Jesus intends to show what the type of person who comes, hears, and does is like (ὑποδείξω ὑμῖν τίνι ἐστὶν ὅμοιος). He also, as is seen in the parable, intends to show what someone is like who comes (carried over from v. 37),[230] hears, and does not act, even though it is not stated (ὁ ἀκούσας καὶ μὴ ποιήσας, 6:49) in the transition to the parable. The most important elements of the parable are: (1) how and where the two different persons build a house, and (2) what happens to that structure when a flood occurs. Kenneth E. Bailey points out that the step parallelism used here emphasizes the climax, the result that transpires when the flood waters come.[231]

The first person (i.e., the type) does two things (v. 48). He digs deep and secures a foundation (ἔσκαψεν and ἐβάθυνεν). The verb ἔσκαψεν refers to the act of digging, and the latter verb ἐβάθυνεν stresses that great care was taken to make sure the house's foundation was secure below subsoil in bedrock, which acts as a footer (cf. Matt 7:25, ἐπὶ τὴν πέτραν). The second person (i.e., the antitype), does only one thing. He builds his house directly on the ground (ἐπὶ τὴν γῆν, v. 49), thus lacking

227. Garland, *Luke*, 286 (It appears that Garland is quoting someone but no citation is provided). Contrast this to the aorists used in v. 49 (ἀκούσας and μὴ ποιήσας). For a brief discussion on aspect, see Black, *Linguistics for Students of New Testament Greek*), 84–85.

228. Saldarini, *The Fathers according to Rabbi Nathan*, 205.

229. For a discussion, see Palachuvattil, "*The One Who Does the Will of the Father*," 115–16.

230. Or, it may be significant that Jesus leaves the first participle out when describing the second individual, as if the folly was never genuinely coming to him in the first place.

231. Bailey, *Jesus through Middle Eastern Eyes*, 321–22.

a foundation (χωρὶς θεμελίου). The reason for building the house on a foundation is seen in what did not happen to it when the flood water came (v. 48) and in what happened to the house built directly on the surface of the ground (v. 49). William W. Klein writes:

> Jesus' audience would instantly grasp the value of building on the limestone bedrock of the hill country rather than in a sandy wadi in the wilderness—a streambed likely to gush with a fast-moving deluge after a sudden rain.[232]

Like a blind person who allows another blind person to guide him into peril, like a student who does not first consider the character of a teacher before becoming like him, like people who go to pick fruit without first considering the source, the second builder does not consider the importance of looking below the surface of the ground and securing his own structure. Garland writes, "The builder who is deceived by the appearance of solid ground takes no precautions."[233] The result is catastrophic (τὸ ῥῆγμα μέγα, v. 49).

The Semantic Frame of Likeness Education, Part I

While Luke 6:40 is not the central text in the conclusion to the SOP, it communicates an important educative concept—students, whether trained in generally positive or negative ways, will take on the character and knowledge of their teachers. The following ideas are prevalent throughout Luke 6:39–49 pertaining to likeness education in a μαθητής-διδάσκαλος relationship:

1. *The selection of disciples.* Jesus does not describe in Luke 6:39–49 how two individuals enter into a μαθητής-διδάσκαλος relationship. However, the context leading up to the SOP and the conclusion shed much light on the subject. Jesus spends a whole evening in prayer to God prior to making his selection of the twelve apostles known (Luke 6:12–16). Each of these men are identified and personally invited by Jesus to leave their affairs to follow him (cf. Luke 5:27; John 15:16). None of the twelve apostles asked Jesus for his permission to follow him, to be his disciple, or to be an apostle. The initiation came from Jesus.

232. Klein, *Become What You Are*, 228.
233. Garland, *Luke*, 286.

2. *The uses of μαθητής and διδάσκαλος.* The word μαθητής does not appear outside of the Gospels and Acts.

3. *Imitation.* Since the relationship of a disciple to a teacher involves imitation, texts in Luke-Acts and the remainder of the NT will be evaluated for both positive and negative types of imitation, including the content of hortatory discourse either encouraging or discouraging imitation. The texts can be identified by the use of imitation words:

   a. μιμέομαι (or one of its cognates [μιμητής, συμμιμητής]);

   b. the use of walking-following words such as ἐξακολουθέω and περιπατέω;

   c. example-language such as τύπος (one of its cognates) or ὑπογραμμός;

   d. words like προσποιέομαι.

   What exactly should a disciple imitate? And how shared is the fate between Jesus and his disciples? For example, the δοῦλος-κύριος proverb is used by Jesus in the Farewell Discourse to show that persecution is not only possible for his disciples, but it is to be expected (John 5:20).

4. *Likeness language.* In Luke 6:40, Jesus uses a ὡς clause for the result of being fully trained. In Luke 6:36, he uses a καθώς clause to specify the standard to which disciples should exercise mercy. This sort of likeness language will be evaluated throughout Luke-Acts and the remainder of the New Testament. A quick glance at Robertson's grammar shows that Greek has many words and constructions for likeness: ὅμοιος ἀνθρώπῳ (Luke 6:48), καθώς (1 Thess 2:14), the intensive pronoun τὸν αὐτόν (Phil 1:30), etc.[234] Transformation and conformity fit under this section and must be evaluated.

---

234. Robertson, *A Grammar of the Greek New Testament*, 530.

Semantic Frame, Pt. I
(Luke 6:40)

---

1.   *The selection of disciples.* Likeness education involves a teacher and a disciple. How does Jesus select his disciples? How do the apostles select disciples?

2.   *The use of μαθητής and διδάσκαλος.* What do contexts in which they are used elsewhere contribute to the understanding of likeness education?

3.   *Imitation.* What does the New Testament say about imitation (positively and negatively)? How do hortatory discourses (either encouraging or discouraging imitation) contribute to the understanding of likeness education?

4.   *Likeness language.* In Luke 6:40, Jesus uses a ὡς clause for the result of being fully trained. In Luke 6:36, he uses a καθώς clause to specify the standard to which disciples should exercise mercy. This sort of likeness language will be evaluated throughout Luke-Acts and the remainder of the New Testament.

Table 1. Semantic Frame, Pt. I (Luke 6:39–49).

Summary

The conclusion to the SOP is an exceptional portion of the New Testament. While the Gospel of Matthew and his account of the SOM in particular contain content parallel to what is found in Luke 6:39–49, some parts are unique to Luke's record. None of these parts are more important than the inclusion of Luke 6:40b. Luke provides the proverb with the disciple-teacher imagery. The participle κατηρτισμένος is most interesting. The crowds followed Jesus because they were curious, and they had diseases and infirmities they desired to be healed of (Luke 6:18). Disciples followed Jesus with varying degrees of commitment. In fact, the majority of them eventually departed from Jesus because his teaching was, to use a modern idiom, hard to swallow (σκληρός, John 6:60). The majority were not looking for the type of training Jesus was offering. Most did not respond as the healed Gerasene, who, were it not for being a Gentile, might have had his prayer answered to join Jesus in the boat as one of his disciples (μετ' αὐτοῦ, Mark 5:18).

Foolishly, the Jewish audience had become a generation of blind people being led by blind people. The religious teachers of the day, under severe spiritual blindness, were doing their own sort of training and cultivating disciples unfit for the kingdom Jesus proclaimed. It is to their "students" that Jesus speaks. For example, they learned how to be pseudo-ophthalmologists by watching their teachers, the Pharisees, do it (Luke 6:41–42). The Gospel of Matthew concentrates heavily on the deficiencies of the Pharisees (and the Sadducees to a lesser extent). Luke is able to leave a majority of this out because of his audiences' ignorance of Jewish culture and their vast geographical separation from Israel and its temple. It was not irrelevant to Matthew; it was essential as the apostles had to continue showing the bankruptcy of a spiritually-blind religious system. Luke, on the other hand, includes what is most relevant to his predominantly Gentile audiences. Somewhere in his research, probably from an eyewitness (or maybe just the guidance of the Holy Spirit),[235] he came across these words of Jesus given in the sermon—"each, after having been fully trained, will be like his teacher."

Jesus gives no direct indication about what the training consists of. His concentration is on the main clause, "every single one will be like his or her teacher" (πᾶς ἔσται ὡς ὁ διδάσκαλος αὐτοῦ, 6:40b). From the passage, however, a few observations about the training are clear. First, it involves coming to Jesus (πᾶς ὁ ἐρχόμενος πρός με, 6:47) and hearing his words (καὶ ἀκούων μου τῶν λόγων, 6:47). The person and the teaching of Jesus are critical in likeness education (John 6:63, 68), even for disciples saved long after Jesus's death and resurrection. He is still the object of every disciple's faith. Second, likeness education necessitates a teacher who is not spiritually blind. As Jesus said, blindness renders someone unqualified to guide others (6:39b). Third, likeness education involves a spiritual capacity to do the things Jesus commands (καὶ ποιῶν αὐτούς, 6:47). In 6:45, Jesus speaks of a good person who does that which is good and a bad person who does that which is evil. The connection for each of them, according to v. 45b, is the correlation of their heart to their works. Jesus does not elaborate here on how someone acquires a heart that is filled with good. The beginning to this process is always the forgiveness of sins, which there is an account of before the SOP and after (Luke 5:18–26; 7:40–50).

---

235. Most scholars believe that Luke uses literary leeway in repositioning and altering the words of Jesus's saying, as if he only used this imagery once during his ministry. Not only is this dangerous for one's understanding of inspiration, it is completely unnecessary for properly understanding the biblical text.

3

Likeness Education in Luke-Acts

Introduction

The greatest development of the theme of likeness education occurs in the letters of the New Testament. Before turning there, it is necessary to consider the life of Jesus Christ, his works and teachings. After all, it is into Jesus's likeness that disciples are made (e.g., Rom 8:29), and, as Robert L. Thomas and Stanley N. Gundry point out, "the bulk of what we know about Jesus Christ is found in the four gospels, Matthew, Mark, Luke, and John."[1] The analysis that follows looks at Jesus's life concentrating on what the disciples saw and heard. Primary consideration is given to the Gospel of Luke (since Luke 6:40 is found within it) and Acts (Luke's second installment to Theophilus), which shows the consecration and growth of the church and the expansion of the gospel from Israel to the Gentile regions of the world. The analysis of the Gospel of Luke has three parts: (1) 1:1—4:13, (2) 4:14—9:50, and (3) 9:51—24:53. This is followed by a single analysis of Acts.

What exactly will the analysis look for? The semantic frame developed in chapter 1 is insufficient for analyzing the Gospel of Luke and Acts as a whole. Its insufficiency as a framing code is due in part to the proverbial nature of Luke 6:40. The SOP discourse is didactic and hortatory, but the concept of likeness education is left undeveloped. Instead of developing a framing code entirely off of non-canonical discussions about the μαθητής-διδάσκαλος relationship, it is best to use one already

---

1. Thomas and Gundry, *A Harmony of the Gospels*, 5.

present in the NT, one closely associated with Luke because of his relationship to the apostle Paul.

Paul tells Timothy, "Now you followed my teaching, conduct, purpose, faithfulness, patience, love, perseverance, persecutions, and sufferings" (2 Tim 3:10–11a). The word παρηκολούθησάς from παρακολουθέω is a cognate of one of the words (ἀκολουθέω) semantically related to μαθητής as identified in chapter 2 (see Luke 5:11, 27–28; 9:23; 18:22). In order to have a grid by which to analyze the Gospels and Acts, it is helpful to use these characteristics found in 2 Tim 3:10–11a as a supplementary code. Before moving into the Gospel and Acts, a brief lexical analysis for each of these words is provided. Then, the codes are applied to the Gospel of Luke and Acts. This is followed by a revised framing code and summary thus concluding the chapter.

A Supplementary Semantic Code Using 2 Timothy 3:10–11a

The Meaning of Διδασκαλία

The word διδασκαλία is formed on the root διδασκ ("teach"),[2] from which are formed words like διδάσκω ("I teach"), διδάσκαλος ("teacher"), διδαχή ("teaching," or "instruction"), and διδακτικός ("instructed").[3] Διδασκαλία contains the suffix -ια, which is a noun suffix "denoting quality or condition" for an abstract idea.[4] The word only occurs twenty-one times in the NT, two of which are in the Gospels (Matt 15:9//Mark 7:7) with the remainder being found in the Pauline corpus. With the exception of four occurrences, it is found in Paul's letters to Timothy and Titus where, according to H. F. Weiss, it refers to "apostolic or Christian teaching as a whole."[5]

Διδασκαλία simply refers to teaching in the most general sense, specifically content by way of verbal or written instruction. It can refer to teaching that is true (i.e., coming from God or in accordance to that which comes from him) or false (i.e., coming from satanically-energized sources or not in accordance to that which comes from God), namely

2. Stevens, *New Testament Greek Primer*, 244.

3. Trenchard, *Complete Vocabulary Guide to the Greek New Testament*, 30.

4. Black, *Linguistics for Students of New Testament Greek*, 66.

5. Weiss, "διδασκαλία," 317. See also Tuggy, *Léxico Griego-Español*, 231.

from false teachers. Daniel M. Doriani says it "typically refers to false teaching (Matt 15:9; Mark 7:7; Eph 4:14; Col 2:22; but not Rom 15:4); until we get to the Pastoral Epistles."[6] That it refers mostly to content and not the act of teaching[7] is apparent, first, by the lack of a process-morpheme suffix and, second, by uses of the noun with a teaching- or action-verb. For example, in the Gospels, διδασκαλία occurs with the verb διδάσκω (e.g., διδάσκοντες διδασκαλίας, Matt 15:9; Mark 7:7). In Eph 4:14, it occurs with περιφέρω (περιφερόμενοι παντὶ ἀνέμῳ τῆς διδασκαλίας).[8] In 1 Tim 1:10, the teaching is modified by ὑγιαίνω, stressing the positive quality of teaching consistent with that which has been handed down by Jesus and the apostles. Later in 1 Timothy, Paul refers to the "teachings of demons" (διδασκαλίαις δαιμονίων, 4:1). It is not the act of teaching by demons that causes people to fall away from the faith; rather, it is the content of this instruction that does so.

F. David Farnell makes a keen observation about the distinction between διδασκαλία and προφητεία ("prophecy") worth noting here. He writes:

> In the New Testament the presence or absence of revelation distinguishes prophecy from teaching. Prophecy always depended on a revelation from God, but by contrast no human speech act which is called a διδαχή or διδασκαλία ("teaching") done by a διδάσκαλος ("teacher") or described by the verb διδάσκω ("to teach") is ever said to be based on ἀποκάλυψις ("revelation").[9]

Paul's use of διδασκαλία in 2 Tim 3:10 most likely refers to the theological instruction Timothy received, embraced, and became a defender of. By the time Paul writes Timothy and Titus, the laying of the foundation of the church has nearly been completed (Eph 2:20). The prophetic gift has

6. Doriani, "A Redemptive-Historical Model," 110 n.73. See also Schnelle, *Theology of the New Testament*, 592–93.

7. The clearest example of διδασκαλία referring more to the act of teaching than the content is found in 1 Tim 4:13 (ἕως ἔρχομαι πρόσεχε τῇ ἀναγνώσε, τῇ παρακλήσει, τῇ διδασκαλίᾳ).

8. Clinton E. Arnold writes:
   "The threat that concerns Paul is teaching (διδασκαλία) that is at variance with the faith, which is at the foundation of all the Christian communities (4:4–6, 13b). Paul regards it as of utmost importance to have a clear and correct knowledge of who Jesus is ('the Son of God'; 4:13c) and the core convictions shared by all the churches" (*Ephesians*, 267).

9. Farnell, "When Will the Gift of Prophecy Cease?," 182–83.

almost ceased to exist in the local assemblies as more and more of the NT Scriptures had been written.[10] In these letters written near the end of Paul's life, he connects the idea of teaching with the written Scriptures (e.g., 2 Tim 3:16), which consisted of OT texts, the Gospels of Matthew and Luke, and letters that had been written up to that point.[11]

In the case of Jesus's teaching, there is no direct lexical link between his teaching and prophecy. However, it is clear that much of his instruction is revelatory (e.g., Matt 13:11//Mark 4:11//Luke 8:10). When using this supplementary semantic frame to analyze the Gospel of Luke and Acts, the simplest understanding of διδασκαλία is understood. What did Jesus teach during his approximate three-year ministry?

The Meaning of Ἀγωγή

The word ἀγωγή is a *hapax legomenon* in the NT from the root αγ ("to lead"). It occurs four times in the Apocrypha (2 Macc 4:16; 6:8; 11:24; 3 Macc 4:10), and it is found twice in the LXX (Esth 2:10; 10:3). Although almost entirely absent from the LXX and NT, it is "common in classical literature."[12] Johannes P. Louw and Eugene A. Nida classify it as a

10. Valeriy A. Alikin writes:

> "By the end of the first century, the oral utterances in the context of the gathering of Christians came to be designated more and more in terms of teaching and preaching and less as 'prophecy.' In the Pastoral Epistles there are three references to preaching, eleven to teaching given by the communities' leaders, but no reference is made to 'prophetic' activity." (*The Earliest History of the Christian Gathering*, 193)

11. Concerning what is included by the term γραφή, see Smith, "A Grammatical Exposition of 2 Timothy 3:16–17," 97. Black, in a forthcoming entry in the *EBR* ("Greek Grammar, NT"), also points out the following:

> "The Bible teaches its own inspiration. The key passage is 2 Tim 3:16: 'All Scripture is God-breathed . . . .' That is, everything written down (πᾶσα γραφή) in the text of Scripture is inspired by God (θεόπνευστος). But this includes not only the words. Words are not the minimal units of meaning of language, nor are they the most important. A proper understanding of biblical inspiration, based on the Greek, would include the words but also the tense, voice, mood, aspect, person, number, gender, case, word order, phrase order, clause order, discourse structure, etc. All of these features were put into the text by the Holy Spirit, and it behooves interpreters of the New Testament to do their best to unpack what is there."

12. Liefeld, *1 and 2 Timothy, Titus*, 278.

behavior-word: "to conduct oneself, with apparent focus upon overt daily behavior."[13] Harold K. Moulton provides the following glosses: "guidance, mode of instruction, discipline, course of life."[14] Abbott-Smith adds it can have a metaphorical meaning, different than "leading" or "guiding" associated with the verb ἄγω. For example, when used with the genitive τοῦ βίου as found in the work of Diodorus Siculus, it has the meaning "conduct, way of life,"[15] interchangeable with ὁδός.[16]

Ἀγωγή can refer to the manner in which the διδασκαλία is given (i.e., teaching methods). However, the word is best understood as living-διδασκαλία, a living example and outward expression of all that is taught. Karl Ludwig Schmidt prefers the translation "manner of life," saying it refers to "the way in which the man who is guided conducts himself in life, to his breeding, behavior, mode or manner of life."[17] Newport J. D. White thinks "manner of life" is not the best translation; he says it may have a "reference to guiding principles of conduct rather than to the external expression of them, which is meant here," referring to 2 Tim 3:10.[18] The word is semantically related to the μαθητής-διδάσκαλος relationship as Raymond F. Collins points out:

> The term *agōgē*, 'way of life' (see 1 Clem. 47:6; 48:1), sometimes used in reference to a person's training or reputation, suggests that a characteristic lifestyle has been adopted because someone has imitated a teacher or master.[19]

It is imperative that these two concepts, διδασκαλία and ἀγωγή, match, similar to what Jesus says in the conclusion of the SOP (Luke 6:43–45).

---

13. See "Behavior, Conduct" (41.1–41.24), Louw and Nida, *Greek-English Lexicon*, 504.

14. Moulton (ed.), *The Analytical Greek Lexicon Revised*, 6.

15. Abbott-Smith, *A Manual Greek Lexicon of the New Testament*, 8. See also Gingrich, *Shorter Lexicon of the Greek New Testament*, 4; Danker, *A Greek-English Lexicon of the New Testament*, 17.

16. Charles J. Ellicott shows the connection between ὁδός in 1 Cor 4:17 and ἀγωγή in 2 Tim 3:10 (*A Critical and Grammatical Commentary*, 158).

17. Schmidt, "ἀγωγή, παράγω, προάγω, προσάγω, προσαγωγή," 128–29.

18. White, "The First and Second Epistles to Timothy," 173.

19. Collins, *1 & 2 Timothy and Titus*, 255.

The Meaning of Πρόθεσις

The word πρόθεσις is present in the NT slightly more than ἀγωγή, occurring twelve times. Five of these occurrences are in the Gospels and Acts (Matt 12:4; Mark 2:26; Luke 6:4; Acts 11:23; 27:13). The remaining occurances are found in the Pauline letters (Rom 8:28; 9:11; Eph 1:11; 3:11; 2 Tim 1:9; 3:10; Heb 9:2). The majority of scholarly discussions concerning this word revolve around its uses in Romans 8–9. The following glosses are provided by Abbott-Smith, "a setting forth" and "a purpose,"[20] the latter meaning he ascribes to all Pauline uses (except for Heb 9:2). Danker adds "putting forth," "presentation," and, feeling the impact of the prefixed preposition, "that which is planned in advance, plan, purpose, resolve, will."[21] In rhetorical contexts, the πρόθεσις functions like a modern-day thesis—pre-established parameters from which an author works.[22] This word signifies the inward motivations, or resolve, that govern one's life.[23]

When Paul uses this word with παρακολουθέω in 2 Tim 3:10, he must mean that Timothy embraced this same "purpose" and that the purpose Paul possessed traveling thousands of miles in hardship and suffering was transferred to Timothy. There are no specific talking-points or list available to identify this single purpose that motivated Paul to pour out his entire life for the gospel. Spiros Zodhiates mentions, "When used of the purpose of God, it exclusively refers to salvation (2 Tim 1:9).[24] For Jesus, this purpose was two-fold: (1) to seek and to save those who are lost (Luke 19:10), and (2) to do the will of the Father (John 4:34). For Paul, this overarching purpose is the same (2 Tim 2:10). In order to identify the characteristics of this purpose, it is necessary to look underneath the surface of the biblical texts.

---

20. Abbott-Smith, *A Manual Greek Lexicon of the New Testament*, 380. See also Tuggy, *Léxico Griego-Español*, 814.

21. Danker, *A Greek-English Lexicon*, 869. Donald M. Lewis writes, "[T]he believer is to be described not only by what one believes and teaches, or how one lives, but also by way of one's purpose (*prothesis*, literally: objective, proposition or intention)" (*With Heart, Mind, and Strength*, 82).

22. Witherington III, *Letters and Homilies*, 356 n.233.

23. Also, "way of thinking" (Danker, *A Greek-English Lexicon*, 869); "'chief aim' in life" (D. Guthrie, *The Pastoral Epistles*, 172).

24. Zodhiates, *The Complete Word Study Dictionary*, 1219.

The Meaning of Πίστις

Πίστις (from the root πιθ) occurs over 200 times in the NT, the highest concentration being in the Pauline corpus. The base meaning of the word is "trust" or "belief." Desta Heliso mentions three ways that Paul uses the word:

> He refers to πίστις in relation to Jesus (Gal 3:23–25), notably connects it with the post-Easter community and its beliefs (Gal 1:23), and couples it as a virtue with others of the same kind, particularly ἀγάπη (1 Cor 13:13; 2 Cor 8:7; Gal 5:6, 22; 1 Thess 1:3; 3:6; 5:8). Paul also contrasts διὰ εἴδους [περιπατεῖν] (as the lower degree) with διὰ πίστεως περιπατεῖν (the higher degree) (2 Cor 5:7) almost in the same way as he contrasts πνεύματι περιπατεῖν with ἐπιθυμίαν σαρκὸς (Gal 5:16).[25]

Added to these is the Pauline definition of πίστις in Heb 11:1: ἔστιν δὲ πίστις ἐλπιζομένων ὑπόστασις, πραγμάτων ἔλεγχος οὐ βλεπομένων ("Now faith is the assurance of things being hoped for and the proof of things not yet being seen"). Option 1 is, therefore, a sort of belief-system,[26] comparable to τῆς καλῆς διδασκαλίας in 1 Tim 4:6.[27] Option 2 refers to a simple act of trust or, sometimes, a manner of living that involves trust even though one lacks sight (2 Cor 5:7; Heb 11:1). John C. Poierier mentions a third option:

> Scholars continue to argue over whether πίστις means 'faith' or 'faithfulness' in a number of contexts through the Pauline corpus, but they seldom note that the term's philological profile also extends *through* the notion of faithfulness into the related notion of stewardship.[28]

25. Heliso, *Pistis and the Righteous One*, 165 n.1; see also Wright, "Faith, Virtue, Justification," 472–97; Towner, *The Letters to Timothy and Titus*, 99–101 n.31. Heliso mentions a third use, a spiritual gift of πίστις (Rom 12:6; 1 Cor 13:2). However, the gift mentioned in Rom 12:6 is prophecy, not faith. Furthermore, Paul is writing rhetorically in 1 Cor 13:1–3 and not speaking of any spiritual gift in the same sense of prophecy, teaching, etc. The following is an interesting observation from Heliso: "Out of 55 occurrences of the substantive in Paul's Seven Letter Corpus, more than a third are in the ἐκ πίστεως form. Curiously, the use of this form is exclusively confined to Romans and Galatians" (*Pistis and the Righteous One*, 166).

26. See, for example, Hawthorne, *Philippians*, 57.

27. Mappes, "What Is the Meaning of 'Faith' in Luke 18:8?," 293.

28. Poirier, "The Meaning of Πίστις in Philippians 1:27," 335, emphasis original. See also Poirier, "The Measure of Stewardship," 145–52.

The idea of stewardship is not absent from 2 Timothy. On the contrary, a πιθ-word is even used in this sense in 1 Tim 1:12 (πιστόν με ἡγήσατο, "he considered me faithful") and 2 Tim 2:2 (πιστοῖς ἀνθρώποις, "faithful men"). In the case of Paul's use of πίστις in 2 Tim 3:10, the first option is impossible and ruled out given διδασκαλία is the only word in the list that refers to specific instruction. The remaining eight words are descriptors of Paul's person, not his instruction. But, in 2 Tim 3:10, does Paul refer to his lifestyle of trusting in God, whether it be for God's protection or provision, or to his faithfulness to the mission God had given him?[29] Douglas Moo writes, "[P]istis in Paul almost always means 'faith'; very strong contextual features must be present if any other meaning is to be adopted."[30] As to what these contextual features are, Moo does not say. Since the remaining characteristics following διδασκαλία concentrate on personal characteristics of Paul and are not content-oriented, 'faithfulness' appears to be the most appropriate understanding in 2 Tim 3:10.[31]

The Meaning of Μακροθυμία

Μακροθυμία, a combination of μακρός and θυμός, occurs in the NT fourteen times, all but three of which are found in Paul's letters. The verb μακροθυμέω occurs nine times, most notably in the parable of the king and his slaves (Matt 18:21–35) and Jas 5:7–8 (3x). The word refers to patience, but, as L. Thompson Wolcott says, it specifically refers to patience "with a provocative people."[32] Wolcott attributes to Paul its "wide currency among the Christians as a guideline for conduct,"[33] a conduct that can be followed as seen in 2 Tim 3:10.[34] Longsuffering is one of those

29. Paul is very interested in Jesus's faithfulness (πίστος). For example, in Hebrews 3, Paul contrasts the faithfulness of Moses to the superior faithfulness of Jesus Christ. See also Matt 23:23 where πίστις is used for "faithfulness." For a thorough discussion on the concept of faithfulness in the Scriptures, see Cunningham, *Christian Ethics*, 270ff.

30. Moo, *The Epistle to the Romans*, 225.

31. Another major support is that each description of Paul's character is a noun. Grammatically, an adjective (as πιστός is) could not have been included as the predicate of παρηκολούθησάς. In order to use πιστός Paul would have had to break the flow of just listing nouns. But why use more words than necessary? Paul is able to communicate the idea of faithfulness with no semantic strain by using πιστίς.

32. Wolcott, "Satyāgratha and Makrothumia," 40.

33. Ibid.

34. James W. Thompson says this kind of patience was not a virtue in Greco-Roman

prevalent attributes of God, even before Paul writes. John S. Feinberg mentions two OT examples of God's longsuffering: Exodus 34 and Numbers 14.[35] Concerning Exod 34:6–7, he writes:

> Verse 7 speaks of God's mercy and willingness to forgive sin. Though the reference in verse 6 is just to this divine attribute (among others), in the context of what happened, it was appropriate for God to underscore his longsuffering character. If he were not patient, he would not be merciful and forgiving to his people Israel, who had broken the first commandment at the very time it was being given. That there even is a second giving of the Decalogue, rather than destruction of the people, shows how longsuffering God is.[36]

The idea of forgiveness is closely tied to the attribute of longsuffering. The parable in Matthew 18 is prompted by Peter's question about forgiveness (v. 21). In the parable, Jesus says the king did two things (v. 27): (1) released his unfaithful slave (ἀππέλυσεν), and (2) forgave him (ἀφῆκεν). These two actions were prompted by the king's compassion (σπλαγχνισθείς), which he felt for the slave who humbled himself (v. 26).

The Meaning of Ἀγάπη

Ἀγάπη, one of the Greek words for love,[37] and its cognates (ἀγαπάω, ἀγαπητός) occur 320 times in the New Testament.[38] The word is "rare in classical writings."[39] One-third of the occurrences are found in the

---

thought (*Moral Formation according to Paul*, 105). However, E. M. Atkins and Carlos F. Noreña mention it in their discussions on the virtues of kings in Cicero's work, which predates Paul's writings by two centuries (Atkins, "Cicero," 461; Noreña, *Imperial Ideals in the Roman West*, 43). Howard Clark Kee says it is part of the Stoic tradition ("Sociological Insights," 348–49).

35. Feinberg, *No One Like Him*, 362–63.

36. Ibid., 363. It should be noted also that God could not have destroyed this people (Exod 32:10). This in no way minimizes Exodus 32–34 as an example of God's longsuffering toward his people. It just highlights also his faithfulness to his covenants and his word. Had he destroyed everyone except for Moses, a Levite, it would have been impossible for him to fulfill the promises passed down to Jacob's children (Gen 49:1–28).

37. Robinson and House, *Analytical Lexicon of New Testament Greek*, 4.

38. Schneider, "ἀγάπη," 9.

39. Willis, "Agape," 27.

Johannine corpus.[40] Ἀγάπη and ἀγαπάω span the NT and are only absent from Acts, something Schneider calls "striking."[41] In the Gospels, the words are usually found in Jesus's speech (e.g., the Farewell Discourse).

While the base meaning of the word (i.e., "love") has never been questioned, the word has been the subject of much debate. Some authors still maintain that ἀγάπη refers to self-sacrificing love expressed toward underserving persons, while ἔρως refers to "passionate love" and φιλέω to friendships.[42] The evidence against drawing sharp lexical distinctions apart from contextual analysis is staggering. Gary D. Badcock, for example, writes: "The fact is, however, that such a claim is both inconsistent with New Testament usage and theologically incoherent."[43] Citing uses in 1 John, he says, "The case for a unique concept of *agape* as self-giving is, then, far from proven in the New Testament."[44] Consider this from Joel B. Green:

> Ethelbert Stauffer wrote that, for John, *agape* (and its cognates) refers to Christian, self-giving love, thus neglecting the fact that we find in the Johannine corpus usages of the term that provides significant evidence to the contrary (e.g., John 3:19; 12:43; 1 John 2:15).[45]

John H. Hayes and Carl R. Holladay write: "[T]he New Testament word for love, *agape*, should not automatically be taken to mean some special form of self-giving concern (see Luke 11:43)."[46] D. A. Carson gives the following examples:

> The Bible has plenty to say about sexual love, for instance, and yet never uses the word ἔρως. In the Septuagint, when Amnon rapes his half-sister Tamar, the Greek text can say that he 'loved' her, using the verb ἀγαπάω (LXX 2 Sam 13:1, 4, 15). When John tells us that the Father loves the Son, once he does so with φιλέω,

40. Navarro, "Agápē en El Evangelio de Juan," 171–84.

41. Schneider, "ἀγάπη," 9.

42. Johnson, *The Writings of the New Testament*, 275; González, *Essential Theological Terms*, 2. For a tempered example that predates much of the research refuting sharp lexical distinctions between ἀγάπη, ἔρως, φιλέω, and other emotion-words, see Morris, *The Cross in the New Testament*, 340–42. For a sound response to Morris's exegesis, see Johnson Jr., "Divine Love in Recent Theology," 175–87.

43. Badcock, *The Way of Life*, 111.

44. Ibid., 111.

45. Green, "Context," 132.

46. Hayes and Holladay, *Biblical Exegesis*, 65.

and once with ἀγαπάω, with no discernible distinction in meaning (John 3:35; 5:20). When Demas forsakes Paul because he
loves this present evil world, the verb is ἀγαπάω.[47]

Clearly, these words are closely related. They appear interchangeable in
the biblical texts—nothing more than synonyms at times.

Most important to this analysis is how Paul uses the word and what
exactly Timothy was able to learn from Paul's character.[48] Paul recognized the importance of love. In 1 Cor 12–14, he places it over and supreme to prophecy. In Gal 5:22–23, it is placed first in the list describing
the fruit of the Spirit. Love is one of the characteristics of a transformed
heart.[49] In 1 Timothy, Paul identifies the "goal" (τέλος) of his and Timothy's instruction (1:5). The goal is love, which is modified by three genitive prepositional phrases:

1. The phrase ἐκ καθαρᾶς καρδίας ("from a pure heart") refers to the
   immediate result of regeneration in Christ through participation
   in the New Covenant (Ezek 36:25–27).

2. The phrase [ἐκ] συνειδήσεως ἀγαθῆς ("[from] a good conscience")
   refers to the believer's response to God's revelation and necessitates
   ongoing care.[50] Philip H. Towner says, "Paul regards an effectively
   functioning conscience to be intrinsic to the process that is to lead
   from teaching to the goal of love."[51] George W. Knight III calls this
   "an honest self-evaluation that one's conduct has been obedient
   rather than disobedient."[52]

3. The phrase [ἐκ] πίστεως ἀνυποκρίτου ("[from] a sincere faith")
   refers to a genuine trust in God for governance, provision, and
   protection in one's daily life (i.e., "a single-minded commitment
   to God").[53]

47. Carson, *Love in Hard Places*, 13.

48. See also 1 Tim 4:12; 6:11; and 2 Tim 2:22. Mario López Barrio examines four
Pauline texts dealing with ἀγάπη: Rom 13:8–10; Gal 5:13–15; 1 Cor 13:1–13; and Rom
8:31–39 (*El Amor en la Primera Carta de San Juan*, 98–108).

49. Jones, "Love," 66.

50. F. Alan Tomlinson writes, "The Pauline note of conscience (συνείδησις) appears, not in terms of weak and strong (cf. 1 Cor 8:7–12) but of 'good' (1 Tim 1:5,
19) and 'pure' (1 Tim 1:10; 6:3; 2 Tim 1:3; 4:3; Titus 1:9; 2:1)" ("The Purpose and
Stewardship Theme," 71).

51. Towner, *The Letters to Timothy and Titus*, 116.

52. Knight III, *The Pastoral Epistles*, 78.

53. Marshall, *The Pastoral Epistles*, 371.

Is the love to which Paul refers a love for God or toward people? While Peter Thomas O'Brien believes that the use of ἀγάπη in Phil 1:9 is unrestricted (referring to both love for God and love toward people), he points out that "the apostle normally used the term and its cognates of love toward one's neighbour."[54] He says the strongest reason for viewing ἀγάπη in this unrestricted sense is "'love' has no object."[55] In 2 Tim 3:10, ἀγάπη lacks an object as well. The two loves—vertical and horizontal[56]—are indeed inseparable. As one's love for God grows, so does the manifestation of it toward others. In 2 Tim 3:10, Paul speaks generally, as he does with all of the nouns following παρακολουθέω. As Towner writes, the word ἀγάπη "can serve as shorthand for the entire visible, outward life produced by genuine faith."[57] Most visible to Timothy is the love Paul had for others. This love, though, is only the overflow and extension of his love for God.

The Meaning of Ὑπομονή

Robinson and House provide the gloss "steadfast endurance" for ὑπομονή.[58] It occurs twice in the Gospel of Luke and eighteen times in the Pauline corpus. James, Peter, and John account for the remaining twelve occurrences: James (3x), 2 Peter (2x), and Revelation (7x). David M. Moffitt identifies the following words under the same semantic domain: προσέχω, κατέχω, ὑποστάσεως, παρρησία, and μακροθυμία.[59]

In Greco-Roman literature, especially stoical works, ὑπομονή was a "courageous virtue summoned from within the self . . . wholly from within."[60] In the LXX and NT this "steadfast perseverance" is undergirded by and never accomplished apart from a person's dependence upon God, both his character and promises.[61] Dan G. McCartney says it

54. O'Brien, *Introductory Thanksgivings in the Letters of Paul*, 30–31.

55. Ibid., 31.

56. *Vertical love* refers to one's love for God; *horizontal love* refers to love directed toward people.

57. Towner, *The Letters to Timothy and Titus*, 114.

58. Robinson and House, *Analytical Lexicon of New Testament Greek*, 357.

59. Moffitt, *Atonement and the Logic of Resurrection*, 241.

60. Dysinger, "Endurance," 486.

61. In the OT, believers looked back to the promises God made to his people in the covenants and certain eschatological promises revealed through the prophets. In the NT, believers especially look toward the eschatological return of Christ and the promises accompanying that return (Hauck, "ménō," 583).

"has a more active character than the English word 'patience,' which connotes passivity."[62] Passivity implies a sort of barren Christian living, one in which there is no spiritual fruit. However, the kind of perseverance Paul emphasizes is the same perseverance that Jesus speaks of in his first parable following Israel's collective rejection of him as their Messiah and heir to the Davidic throne (Luke 8:4–15). Regarding the seed that fell on "good soil" (καλῇ γῇ, Luke 8:15), Jesus explains that it represents people who:

1. Have heard (ἀκούσαντες) the message with a correct disposition toward God.

2. Continue to hold fast (κατέχουσιν) to the message.

3. Bear fruit by persevering (καρποφοροῦσιν ἐν ὑπομονῇ) no matter the resistance they meet.

John B. Weaver describes ὑπομονή in Luke 8 as "the disposition to persist in belief and obedience to the word of God."[63] For the Christian, steadfast perseverance is not forceful resistance. Ὑπομονή is one's unwavering resolve to holiness and active submission to the sovereignty of God, who alone brings about the consummation of sufferings and persecutions (see 1 Pet 5:6–7).

The Meaning of Διωγμός

Διωγμός means "persecution" motivated by or incurred because of religion.[64] Action or process is indicated by the suffix -μος.[65] It is the first of only two words in Paul's list that occurs in the plural. It is one of the words associated with the oppression of God's people, similar at times to θλῖψις.[66] Διωγμός is found in the LXX only twice (Prov 11:19; Lam

---

62. McCartney, *James*, 87. Charles C. Ryrie says it "does not denote a negative and passive resignation to persecution or problems, but rather a positive and optimistic fortitude in spite of indignities suffered" (*First and Second Thessalonians*, 25).

63. Weaver, "The Noble and Good Heart, 167.

64. Bauer, *A Greek-English Lexicon*, 200.

65. Black, *Linguistics for Students of New Testament Greek*, 64.

66. For θλῖψις in the LXX, see Exod 3:9; 4:31; Deut 4:29; etc. Karl P. Donfried and I. Howard Marshall indicate one difference between the two words: "Wheras *thlipsis* (affliction) needs to be specified according to its context, *diōgmos* always refers to persecution" (*The Theology of the Shorter Pauline Letters*, 87). Both share suffixed, derivational morphemes denoting process or action; in the case of θλῖψις, it is -σις (Black, *Linguistics for Students of New Testament Greek*, 64).

3:19),[67] which is substantially less than θλῖψις.[68] The cognate words διώκω and διωγμός are "terms often denoting persecution instigated by official authorities."[69] Luke refers to the persecution overseen by Saul as a "severe persecution" (διωγμὸς μέγας, Acts 8:1). Peter opts for the word πάσχω ("I suffer"). Even though he does not use διώκω or διωγμός, Lewis R. Donelson writes:

> [T]here is a range of terms that suggest verbal shaming: 'abuse' (*loidoreō, antiloidoreō*, 2:23), 'slander' (*katalaleō*, 2:12; 3:16; *blasphēmeō*, 4:4), 'disparage' (*epēreazō*, 3:16), and 'insult' (*oneidizō*, 4:14). It is impossible to reconstruct the precise context of this abuse or the social force of this verbal shaming from such a list of terms. Whatever the form of this public shaming, in a society built upon social status, such abuse could have been powerful.[70]

Similarly, Luke indicates that Paul hurled threats at Christians before his conversion (Acts 9:1).

To what persecutions does Paul refer? Fortunately, the NT provides a rather detailed account of the types of persecutions Paul underwent. Writing to the Thessalonians, Paul mentions how he and his associates had suffered and been mistreated in Philippi (προπαθόντες καὶ ὑβρισθέντες, 1 Thess 2:2). Timothy is one of the associates mentioned in 1 Thess 1:1. This is very interesting. Paul meets Timothy for the first time at the beginning of his second missionary journey (Acts 16:1–3). Timothy's introduction to the character of Paul, from nearly the day he first met him, involved persecution. The persecution they endured in Philippi involved being:

1. Seized by the Philippian authorities (Acts 16:19).

2. Dragged into the market place (Acts 16:19).

3. Misrepresented to the city officials (Acts 16:20–21).

4. Rejected and implicated by a crowd of people (Acts 16:22).

5. Beaten many times with rods (Acts 16:23).

6. Shackled and incarcerated (Acts 16:24).

67. It is also used once in 2 Macc. 12:23.

68. For a concise discussion on how this word is used in non-biblical texts, see Quinn and Wacker, *The First and Second Letters to Timothy*, 735.

69. Marshall et. al., *Exploring the New Testament*, 281.

70. Donelson, *I & II Peter and Jude*, 11.

Timothy is an eyewitness to all of these things bar the latter (Acts 16:4). Only Paul and Silas suffer all of these things, for they alone are mentioned by name (Acts 16:19, 25). This is not the only time Timothy witnessed the incarceration of his father in the faith for the sake of the gospel. For example, in Phil 1:7 and 14, Paul mentions another imprisonment (τοῖς δεσμοῖς μου). Timothy serves Paul in his imprisonment, is able to be dispatched by Paul, and is able to return to Paul for updates on the different regions where they had ministered.

The Meaning of Πάθημα

Πάθημα is the second and last noun Paul gives in the plural. It occurs sixteen times in the NT, all but four times by Paul.[71] It does not occur in the Septuagint. Wilhelm Michaelis and Barnabas Lindars note it always occurs in the plural in the NT except in Heb 2:9, where Michaelis says it "has the rare meaning 'passion,' 'impulse.'"[72] Trenchard provides the following glosses for πάθημα: "suffering," "misfortune," and "passion."[73] The original meaning in Greek is "suffering." It grew to include "passion," according to William V. Harris, no earlier than the fourth century BC (i.e., pre-Aristotle).[74]

The suffix -μα denotes result when used in the formation of nouns.[75] Διωγμός, with the -μος suffix indicating process or action, refers to the act of persecution; πάθημα, therefore, refers to the results of the persecution one suffers. J. Kremer writes, "In several instances τὰ παθήματα (like → θλίψις) clearly indicates the *sufferings* to which Christians and esp. the apostles are subject in this world and which result primarily from persecution" (emphasis original).[76] Sufferings apart from persecution, such as found in the example of Job's life, are not representative of the Christian's suffering. In fact, in the NT there appears only one example parallel to what is found in Job—Paul's "thorn in the flesh" (σκόλοψ τῇ σαρκί)—which he refers to as a "messenger of Satan" (ἄγγελος Σατανᾶ).[77]

71. Karrer, *Jesus Christus im Neuen Testament*, 86 n.39.

72. Michaelis, "πάσχω," 930; Lindars, "Paul and the Law in Romans 5–8," 186 n.12.

73. Trenchard, *Complete Vocabulary Guide to the Greek New Testament*, 86.

74. Harris, *Restraining Rage*, 342.

75. Black, *Linguistics for Students of New Testament Greek*, 65.

76. Kremer, "πάθημα," 1.

77. See Black, *Paul, Apostle of Weakness*, 98–101.

The uses of πάθημα in Romans show how the word can be used differently, even in contexts very near to one another. For example, the word clearly refers to "sinful passions" in Rom 7:5 given the qualifying phrase (τὰ παθήματα τῶν ἁμαρτιῶν; see also Gal 5:24).[78] In Rom 8:18, however, Paul refers to suffering, which is contrasted to glory.[79] Suffering, not passion, is usually what an author is referring to when using this word.[80] Part of what entails suffering is explained by Paul in 1 Cor 4:9–13, a description, says Black, "about the sad condition in which he and other preachers of the gospel find themselves."[81] Paul describes the apostles as "men condemned to death," "hungry and thirsty," "poorly clothed," "roughly treated," "homeless," and the "scum of the world."

One hardly thinks of suffering when thinking of education. Pamela Eisenbaum says suffering—"be it martyrdom or physical or verbal abuse—functions as a kind of training on the path to salvation, not simply as a response to historical contingency."[82] What is important in this quote is that she recognizes suffering as "a kind of training" (not the clause that follows it). A modified way to say it, in-line with an evangelical understanding of salvation, is that sufferings are part of a disciple's training subsequent to his or her salvation as that person is made into the image of God's Son (Rom 8:29). Not only is suffering part of the Christian's curriculum, Christ, as always, is the example *par excellence*. As Kar Yong Lim writes, "Modelling Christ's suffering is an expression of faith that leads to righteousness."[83] Even when Paul gives himself, or others, as an example, it is a mediated example pointing one to Jesus and his suffering unto death (Phil 2:8).

Summary of Supplementary Frame Based on 2 Timothy 3:10–11a

Paul provides nine areas in which his closest companion in the gospel work had followed him. These nine areas represent the clearest

---

78. Byrne, *Romans*, 215.

79. Suffering and glory often appear together in the NT. For example, see 1 Pet 1:11; 4:13; 5:1.

80. Matera, *Galatians*, 204; Byrne, *Romans*, 215; McDonald, *The Crucible of Christian Morality*, 126.

81. Black, *Paul, Apostle of Weakness*, 67.

82. Eisenbaum, "The Virtue of Suffering," 338.

83. Lim, '*The Sufferings of Christ Are Abundant in Us*', 49.

description of a holistic Christian education. Teaching is the only one that involves verbal and/or written instruction. However, the education that Timothy received from Paul included more than teaching. The eight nouns that follow διδασκαλία refer to aspects of Paul's life that could not be communicated by words alone. Even though the instruction Paul and the other apostles give is theological, it is impossible to miss their attention to praxis. As Jesus said, "After being fully trained, a disciple will be like his or her teacher" (Luke 6:40b). For Paul, being fully trained means following in his example in these nine areas: teaching, conduct, purpose, faithfulness, patience, love, perseverance, persecutions, and sufferings (2 Tim 3:10–11a).

Semantic Frame, Pt. I (Luke 6:40)	Supplementary Semantic Frame (2 Tim 3:10–11a)
The selection of disciples. Likeness education involves a teacher and a disciple. How does Jesus select his disciples? How do the apostles select disciples?	*Teaching.* *Conduct.*
The use of μαθητής and διδάσκαλος. What do contexts in which they are used elsewhere contribute to the understanding of likeness education?	*Purpose.* *Faith/Faithfulness.*
Imitation. What does the New Testament say about imitation (positively and negatively)? How do hortatory discourses (either encouraging or discouraging imitation) contribute to the understanding of likeness education?	*Patience.* *Love.* *Perseverance.*
Likeness language. In Luke 6:40, Jesus uses a ὡς clause for the result of being fully trained. In Luke 6:36, he uses a καθώς clause to specify the standard to which disciples should exercise mercy. This sort of likeness language will be evaluated throughout Luke-Acts and the remainder of the New Testament.	*Persecutions.* *Sufferings.*

Table 2. Supplementary Semantic Frame (2 Timothy 3:10–11a).

An Analysis of Luke 1:1–4:13

Imitation in Luke 1:1–4:13

While none of the imitation-words[84] are used in Luke 1:1–4:13, there are episodes in it that provide exemplary models. Part of any instruction using the Gospel of Luke would undoubtedly involve pointing out certain characteristics from the examples found in the birth and presentation narratives. For example, Burridge writes, "The pious figures of Elizabeth and Zacharias, and the humble acceptance of Mary, 'let it be with me according to your word', provide narrative examples to imitate in the opening chapters."[85] In the announcements of John the Baptist's and Jesus's conceptions and births, Luke actually provides a great example in Mary and a slightly tarnished one in Zacharias. Both Mary and Zacharias interject a question in the announcement narratives: "How will I know this is going to happen?" (Luke 1:18), and "How will this happen?" (Luke 1:34). Mary does not doubt what the angel says can happen; she only asks "how?" (πῶς) since she is a virgin. Zacharias, on the other hand, expresses his doubt with the prepositional phrase κατὰ τί, as if asking for a guarantee, and the verb γνώσομαι. Because of Zacharias's lack of faith, he is made mute until the day John is born (Luke 1:20). The remainder of Zacharias's testimony is exemplary (cf. Luke 1:67–79).

The example of the shepherds in Luke 2:8–20 is a model worth imitating as well. In the Gospel of Luke, Mary and Joseph are secondary characters at times in the birth narrative.[86] The shepherds are introduced in v. 8 as being in the region of Bethlehem and overseeing their sheepfolds in the night hours. Like Zacharias and Mary, an angel appears to them and the glory of God surrounds the pastors in the fields.[87] There are

---

84. In Chapter 1, these were identified as: (1) μιμέομαι (or one of its cognates [μιμητής, συμμιμητής]); (2) walking-following words such as ἐξακολουθέω and περιπατέω; (3) example words such as τύπος or ὑπογραμμός; or (4) words like προσποιέομαι.

85. Burridge, *Imitating Jesus*, 280.

86. Keith F. Nickle points out that the "narrative emphasis falls not on the birth itself but rather on the angelic announcement of that birth to the shepherds" (*Preaching the Gospel of Luke*, 24), thus placing Jesus's parents and their example on a level secondary to that of the shepherds. See also Litwak, "A Coat of Many Colors," 116.

87. The pronoun αὐτούς in Luke 2:9 has only one possible referent given the plural—the shepherds mentioned in 2:8. The appearance of the glory of God here is extremely significant. This is the first appearance of the glory of God since the days

three characteristics of the announcement the angel brings to the shepherds (2:10):

1. It is good news (εὐαγγελίζομαι).

2. It is a message that causes great joy (χαρὰν μεγάλην).

3. It is a message intended for everyone (παντὶ τῷ λαῷ).

Saying this, the angel makes them aware of the birth of a Savior, namely Christ the Lord.[88] How the shepherds respond to this message is an example of how disciples everywhere should respond to both Jesus's teachings and teachings concerning him.

First, they rush (ἦλθαν σπεύσαντες) to see the child that the angel announced (2:16). This is interesting because it parallels Jesus's teachings later about the importance of coming to him (cf. 6:47).[89] Even on the eve of Jesus's birth, he is worthy to come to. At this point in his life, he has no miraculous works to accompany him nor can he teach. It is the person of Jesus, first, that is worth coming to. Second, the shepherds make everything known to those around about the message that they received on the outskirts of Bethlehem (2:17). They first receive the message, but they become the teachers soon after, a pattern that will be emulated throughout Luke-Acts.[90] Two supplementary reactions are included here; everyone who heard the shepherds' report marvel (ἐθαύμασαν, 2:18), and Mary treasured all that she heard (πάντα συνετήρει, 2:19). The former is a reaction reminiscent of how the crowds respond to Jesus's teaching (cf. 4:22; 4:32).[91] The latter is unique, a word used once in Luke only to describe Mary's reaction at this moment. Third, they returned to their sheep in

---

of Ezekiel when it departed from the Temple (Ezekiel 8–11). That it appears first to shepherds, and not the religious elite in Jerusalem, points to the importance of the least important in the redemptive plan of God; that it appears on the eve of Jesus's birth outside Bethlehem, and not in the Holy of Holies where Zacharias received his announcement, shows the significance of the birth of the Savior of the world.

88. The birth had already taken place by the time the angel makes the announcement to the shepherds in the field (see ἐτέχθη in v. 11).

89. For a demonstration of how this narrative parallels Peter's imprisonment in Acts 12, see Ruis-Camps and Read-Heimerdinger (eds.), *The Message of Acts in Codex Bezae*, 372.

90. For λαλέω as a teaching-word, see Yen, *The Lucan Journey*, 83.

91. John B. F. Miller says amazement often follows a dream or vision as well in Luke 1:21; 2:18; 24:41; Acts 7:31 (*Convinced that God had Called Us*, 129 n.52).

a completely different manner than when they left. Luke says they were "glorifying and praising God for all that they had heard and seen" (2:20).

Likeness Language in Luke 1:1–4:13

Luke 1:1–4:13 contains no likeness language. Nevertheless, it presents an important aspect of likeness education that must be discussed here. The NT provides a few examples concerning how God should be imitated in his character and actions. For example, Jesus says, "Be merciful, just as your Father is merciful" (Luke 6:36). Matthew includes Jesus saying, "Be perfect, just as your heavenly Father is perfect" (Matt 5:48). In the OT, God told the people of Israel, "Be holy, for I am holy" (Lev 11:44; 19:2; 20:7). Paul, in the NT, adds, "Be imitators of God" (Eph 5:1). There is no question that people are to imitate God. However, the NT presents something entirely new. Nowhere in the Scriptures is a person held up as a supreme model, equivalent to these Old Covenant commands to be like God, as Jesus is in the New Testament. There are examples of model behavior and faith in the OT (see Hebrews 11), but there is no example where a person's entire life and character are set forth as an example to be followed. In the case of Jesus, his life is the supreme example. The believer is redeemed from sin so that he or she will be like him (Rom 8:29).

Before Jesus can be the supreme example found in the NT, he has to take on the likeness of human flesh. The following clauses in the NT all point to this fact:

1. ἐν ὁμοιώματι σαρκὸς ἁμαρτίας (Rom 8:3).

2. ἑαυτὸν ἐκένωσεν μορφὴν δούλου λαβών (Phil 2:7).

3. κατὰ πάντα τοῖς ἀδελφοῖς ὁμοιωθῆναι (Heb 2:17).

It would be helpful to consider each of these verses in greater detail, but space is limited. For now, it is important to consider briefly the genealogies and birth narratives.

Both Matthew and Luke provide genealogies for Jesus, each featuring important characteristics, similarities, and differences. The most probable explanation for the origins of the genealogies is Matthew's and Luke's Holy Spirit-guided and determined research of records available in the Temple prior to its destruction in AD 70.[92] From a macro-perspective,

92. Tony Evans calls the Temple "the records building of the day," saying in AD

Matthew introduces his Gospel with the genealogy, while Luke postpones the genealogy to the third chapter. Thomas and Gundry write, "The most obvious difference is that Matthew's list begins with Abraham and descends to Jesus, whereas Luke's list begins with Jesus and ascends to Adam, the son of God."[93] Matthew is most concerned with presenting Jesus as the heir to the Davidic throne and covenant (2 Samuel 7). Luke, who likewise traces Jesus's lineage back through David (Luke 3:31), concentrates much more on the humanity of Jesus, both in the genealogy and the birth narrative.[94] Thomas and Gundry write:

> Since Luke emphasizes the humanity of Jesus, His solidarity with the race, and the universality of salvation, it is fitting that Luke show His humanity by recording His human descent through His human parent Mary. His pedigree is then traced back to Adam.[95]

The authors of the NT letters refer to Jesus's humanity for different reasons. Each of them present Jesus's humanity as an essential aspect of the divine redemptive plan either for salvation or his ongoing ministry as priest before God on behalf of his brethren.

Why does Luke postposition the genealogy so far into the narrative? Garland believes the positioning of the genealogy between God's declaration that Jesus is his Son and the temptation minimizes the importance of Jesus's humanity in the narrative.[96] The presence of the genealogy beside

---

70 "all the records were lost" (*Our God is Awesome*, 315). See also Pentecost, *The Words and Works of Jesus Christ*, 39; Wilkins, *Matthew*, 57; Keener (who is open to the idea that certain families may have preserved their own genealogies), *Matthew*, 52. Concerning private records, R. J. Konczyk includes a letter from Julius Africanus to Aristides saying as much: "A few, however, of the studious, having private records of their own, either by remembering the names or by getting them in some other way from the archives, pride themselves in preserving the memory of their noble descent . . . on account of their connection with the family of the Savior" (*Melchizedek and the Temple*, 150).

93. Thomas and Gundry, *A Harmony of the Gospels*, 313.

94. Blomberg, *Jesus and the Gospels*, 242.

95. Thomas and Gundry, *A Harmony of the Gospels*, 317. That this is the genealogy of Mary, not Joseph, is clear by the parenthetical mention of Joseph in Luke 3:23, marked by a ὡς clause (ὡς ἐνομίζετο) and the absence of the definite article with his name (*A Harmony of the Gospels*, 317).

96. Garland, *Luke*, 171. He does agree that one of the purposes is to show "Jesus's connection to the human race" (172), just that this connection is less important in the narrative than others suppose.

the temptation, however, shows Jesus's humanity.[97] The statement by Luke that Jesus "became hungry" (ἐπείνασεν, 4:2) is not a divine action, but a human one. Luke stresses the importance of the Holy Spirit for Jesus's success in overcoming the temptations of Satan. He is "full of the Holy Spirit" (πλήρης πνεύματος ἁγίου, 4:1) going into the wilderness, and, following the temptation, Jesus returns to Galilee "in the power of the Spirit" (ἐν τῇ δυνάμει τοῦ πνεύματος, 4:14). Luke's account of the genealogy and the temptation shows what a believer can do, and withstand, via the presence of the Holy Spirit in one's life and a knowledge of the Scriptures.[98]

Teaching in Luke 1:1–4:13

Luke is the only author to include the account of Jesus "sitting in the midst of the teachers" at the age of twelve (2:46–47).[99] Lenski says the "teaching took place in one of the many Temple halls that were open to all and were used for this purpose,"[100] similar to where Jesus, and later Peter and John, taught (Luke 20:1; Acts 3:11). Lenski adds:

> Luke says not one word about his teaching. He listened and he asked respectful questions (this is the force of the participle). The next verse implies that he also answered questions. The teaching was not mere lecturing but was interspersed with questions both to and from the teacher. . . . He is a well-trained boy who knows his place and acts with respect toward these rabbis. But he is indeed intensely interested in all they have to say and eager to elicit more information, for these were more important men than the rabbis he could occasionally hear in Nazareth.[101]

97. Cook III, "Principles of Spiritual Warfare in Light of Jesus's Temptations," 14.

98. Jesus's use of the Scriptures to resist Satan's temptations is intriguing. He quotes three passages from Deuteronomy (8:3; 6:13; 6:16) and Psalm 91:11–12. The importance of the OT, even for Gentile believers, is reinforced here, especially a knowledge of the Pentateuch. David C. Hester disagrees and says this narrative "is not advanced as a paradigm for everyman's experience or temptation, since that description fails to do justice to the unique description of Jesus" ("Luke 4:1–13," 55).

99. Ronald T. Habermas says that by the age of twelve, Jesus both knew his Father's work and was doing it" (*Introduction to Christian Education and Formation*, 127).

100. Lenski, *St. Luke's Gospel* (2008), 164.

101. Ibid.

One answer for why Luke includes nothing about the content of the questions and answers, in part, has to do with where the focus is in the passage. Stein believes Luke includes the account "due to its christological significance" to show that Jesus had an astute awareness of his Father-Son relationship with God even at the age of twelve.[102] Luke's inclusion of this passage also shows that Jesus, at an early age, is interested in what the teachers of the Law have to say and, probably, keenly interested in whether or not the teachers' interpretations are accurate. By age 30, Jesus is aware of the Pharisees and their interpretations of the Law in two geographical and distinctly different locations, the Galilean country-side and the capital, Jerusalem.

Despite the fact that everyone present those three days was listening to an exchange between Jesus, a twelve year old 'Bar Mitzvah-ed' young man, and seasoned Jewish teachers in the Temple, they were all amazed. Luke indicates they were amazed at two things: (1) Jesus's understanding (τῇ συνέσει, 2:47), and (2) his answers (ταῖς ἀποκρίσεσιν, 2:47). This is similar, yet quite different, to what Luke records following Jesus's teaching in the synagogues of Nazareth, Capernaum, and elsewhere.

His message at Nazareth shifts from the audience speaking well of him and marveling at his words (ἐθαύμαζον, 4:22) to them being filled with rage (ἐπλήσθησαν θυμοῦ, 4:28).[103] In Luke 2:47, θαυμάζω is not used; there, Luke uses the verb ἐξίστημι. Luke does not record the crowds' response to the SOP, which Matthew does; Matthew includes, "The crowds were amazed at his teaching" (ἐξεπλήσσοντο οἱ ὄχλοι ἐπὶ τῇ διδαχῇ αὐτοῦ, Matt 7:28). This is the same verb that Luke uses to describe Mary and Joseph's amazement when they finally found him in the "place they least expected."[104] Matthew uses it later to describe a subsequent teaching opportunity at Nazareth (Matt 13:54). He also uses this verb to describe the disciples' astonishment to Jesus's teaching about the great difficulty that exists for a rich man trying to enter the kingdom of heaven (Matt 19:23–26). Matthew refers to the crowds' amazement at Jesus's teaching a final time on "Busy Tuesday," when Jesus silenced the Sadducees on the certainty of the resurrection (Matt 22:33). In each of the Synoptic Gospels, the authors indicate that those who heard Jesus teach were

---

102. Stein, *Jesus the Messiah*, 88. See also Serrano, *The Presentation in the Temple*, 152.

103. See also Luke 9:43.

104. Lenski, *St. Luke's Gospel* (2008), 163.

amazed at what they heard. The events following his age-thirty transition that speak of such amazement primarily indicate one factor that caused it—the authority with which Jesus taught (Matt 7:29; Luke 4:32; Mark 1:27). At the temple, when Jesus was twelve, no mention is made of his authority.

What happened when the crowds were amazed at Jesus's teaching? Stein says, "This reaction is external in nature and does not imply a change of heart."[105] The clause οὐχ ὡς οἱ γραμματεῖς αὐτῶν ("not like their scribes," Matt 7:29) distinguishes between the authority with which Jesus taught and the lack thereof in the teaching of the scribes.[106] Stein believes the authority referred to in Luke 4:32 refers more so to Jesus's "divine power to heal (4:39) and cast out demons (4:35–36, 41)."[107] This is certainly part of what is meant. Maria Do Thi Yen writes:

> Jesus' prophetic role is manifested in his words and deeds. . . . In regard to the deeds of Jesus, they represent a guarantee of what he has said. They confirm the effect of his words. Indeed, people often marvel at Jesus' teaching. But it is only when they witness his wonder(s) (7:16; cf. 9:7–8, 19) that they really exalt him as a prophet. It is worth noting that Luke very often mentions Jesus' teaching and healing together (4:21; 5:15, 17; 6:6–10, 18; 7:22; 8:1–2; 9:11).[108]

This is what the chief priests and scribes want to know in Luke 20:1–8: "By what (or whose) authority are you doing these things?" (ἐν ποίᾳ ἐξουσίᾳ ταῦτα ποιεῖς, 20:2). However, another example of this authority is found in Matthew 5–7, where Jesus repeatedly says, "You have heard it said. . . . But, I say to you. . . ." Similarly, the Pharisees are accustomed with linking quotations from different teachers one after another.[109] Jesus says what the Scriptures mean, how they should be applied in daily life, etc.

---

105. Stein, *Luke*, 162.

106. Iwe, *Jesus in the Synagogue of Capernaum*, 62–63.

107. Stein, *Luke*, 162. He adds in parentheses, "The term 'authority' is used over twenty times in Luke-Acts and is not associated with teaching in any other instance" (ibid., 162–63).

108. Yen, *The Lucan Journey*, 84.

109. McKenzie, *Dictionary of the Bible*, 780; Van Cangh, "Did Jesus Call Himself 'Son' and 'Son of Man'?," 4; Fredriksen, *Jesus of Nazareth*, 103; Barnett, *Jesus and the Rise of Early Christianity*, 102.

The account of Jesus at twelve years old interacting with the Jewish teachers in the Temple is quite unique. Only Luke provides a record of Jesus's activities prior to his departure from the building business and his divine encounter with the prophet John at the Jordan River.[110] Stein believes Luke includes the account "due to its christological significance" to show that Jesus had an astute awareness of his Father-Son relationship with God even at the age of twelve.[111] When Luke includes this narrative, he also provides the perfect example for every stage of life—Jesus the young child (τὸ παιδίον, 2:40), Jesus the young man (ἐτῶν δώδεκα [2:42] and ὁ παῖς [2:43]), and Jesus the adult (ἐτῶν τριάκοντα, 3:23). Concerning the former, Luke writes that the child "continued to grow and become strong, being filled with wisdom" (2:40). This wisdom, from Jesus's infancy onward, may refer to a heavenly source, a parental source, or both.[112] The text does not say specifically, just that Jesus receives the wisdom from outside of himself (stressing the humanity of Jesus). Robert H. Culpepper says it refers to "normal mental growth."[113] If a parental source is intended, there are striking similarities to 2 Tim 3:15 with Timothy and his relationship to his mother and grandmother. To Timothy, Paul writes: ". . . and that from infancy (βρέφους) you have known the sacred writings, which were able to make you wise (σοφίσαι) to salvation through faith in Christ Jesus."[114] The second stage is characterized by continued growth (Luke 2:52): (1) cognitively, i.e., in one's knowledge of the Scriptures; (2) physically (ἡλικία, "stature"); and (3) socially (χάριτι παρὰ θεῷ καὶ ἀνθρώποις, "favor with God and people").

---

110. There are apocryphal texts covering the early years of Jesus's life, but they are quite imaginative and very different from the Jesus of the canonical Gospels. For a discussion on the Infancy Gospel of Thomas (IGTh), see Klauck, *The Apocryphal Gospels*, 73–78; Horn and Martens, *"Let the Little Children Come to Me,"* 130–32. There is absolutely no reason to doubt the historicity of Luke's account and/or to interpret it as metaphorically significant alone, a sort of step above the apocryphal accounts.

111. Stein, *Jesus the Messiah*, 88. See also Serrano, *The Presentation in the Temple*, 152.

112. Klaus Issler, citing Sinclair B. Ferguson, opts for the former interpretation ("Jesus's Example," 219–20).

113. Culpepper, "The Humanity of Jesus," 16.

114. Paul has already mentioned the sincere faith of Timothy's grandmother and mother (2 Tim 1:5).

Conduct in Luke 1:1–4:13

There are only two episodes in Luke 1:1–4:13 that show the conduct of Jesus. They are 2:41–52 (Jesus in Jerusalem at twelve years old) and 4:1–13 (Jesus in the wilderness at thirty years old). As has already been shown, Lenski points out Jesus's conduct as a young man in the midst of some of Israel's most respected teachers of his day. He says Jesus is "a well-trained boy who knows his place and acts with respect toward these rabbis."[115] Jesus is sitting in the midst of the teachers, listening to all that they say, and asking questions when an opportunity is given. When he is asked a question, he responds as a twelve year old young man should. Nothing about the content of these exchanges is mentioned in the text. A curious mind can only speculate about what was discussed. What is clear is that nothing regarding Jesus's character is out of sync with what someone would expect from a twelve year old Jewish man. In addition to this, the narrative shows that Jesus, even from an early age, was intelligent, investigative, and seeking answers on things pertaining to God.[116] Kenneth E. Bailey writes, "[I]t is easy to assume that Jesus went on to spend eighteen years in sustained discussion with the brightest and best thinkers in Nazareth and the surrounding villages."[117]

Most striking in the passage is Jesus's relationship to his parents.[118] Did Jesus disobey his parents by staying in Jerusalem three extra days, causing them stress and worry because they did not know where he was, as well as probably costing Joseph financially since he was not able to return to work once back in Nazareth? Did Jesus violate the fifth commandment, "Honor your father and your mother" (Exod 20:12)? He certainly did not (2 Cor 5:21).[119] Luke 2:51 actually shows two things: (1) the primacy of the kingdom of God in Jesus's life, and (2) the humility and humanity of Jesus side-by-side. Concerning the former, the narrative shows a theme that recurs throughout the Gospel of Luke, namely that the kingdom and one's relationship to Jesus come before anything else, including family. Greg Jao says Jesus "models the primacy that must be

115. Lenski, *St. Luke's Gospel* (2008), 164.

116. Lenski writes, "But he is indeed intensely interested in all they have to say and eager to elicit more information" (ibid.).

117. Bailey, *Jacob and the Prodigal*, 25.

118. For cultural-sociological discussion of households in first-century Jewish life, see Moxnes, *Putting Jesus in His Place*, 32–38.

119. Doyle, *Jesus*, 32–33.

given to the kingdom of God," and "Luke emphasizes how the boy Jesus gave priority to God's work before he describes Christ's obedience to his parents."[120]

Concerning the humility of Jesus seen in his submission to his parents, Bruce A. Ware writes:

> It really is nothing short of astonishing that this same Jesus, who clearly understood his identity as the Son of the heavenly Father, would choose to put himself under the authority of his human parents. His submission to them indicated his commitment to follow the law of the Lord.[121]

Despite wanting to be in his Father's house, Jesus leaves with Joseph and Mary and, as Luke records, "was continuing in subjection to them" (ἦν ὑποτασσόμενος, Luke 2:51).[122] The sort of submission Jesus manifests even at twelve years of age is a relational submission that he is going to insist upon for his own disciples years later. Ware points out that Jesus's conduct here shows that submission "can be rendered by one who is in no way inferior or subordinate in essence to the one to whom he submits."[123]

Purpose in Luke 1:1–4:13

Jesus does not explicitly declare his purpose in Luke 1:1–4:13. There are, nevertheless, indications about the nature of his purpose nestled in the announcements of his and John's births and the prophecies found in the birth narratives. Three main characteristics of Jesus's purpose are found in this section of Luke:

1. The critical relationship of Jesus to God's covenants.

2. The unique relationship of Jesus Christ as Son to God the Father.

3. The salvific relationship of Jesus to Israel and the world.

First, Jesus's ministry is critical in God's fulfillment of his covenants with Abraham and David. In Luke 1:27, 32–33, Jesus is identified as the legitimate heir to the Davidic throne. Even though the birth of Jesus Christ comes through Mary alone, Luke indicates that Joseph is also from

120. Jao, "Honor and Obey," 52.
121. Ware, *The Man Christ Jesus*, 56.
122. Ryken et. al. (eds.), "Human Authority," 63.
123. Ware, *The Man Christ Jesus*, 57.

the house of David (1:27). In Gabriel's announcement to Mary, she is told God will give her Son "the throne of his father David" (1:32). "He will reign over the house of Jacob forever (εἰς τοὺς αἰῶνας), and his kingdom will have no end (οὐκ ἔσται τέλος)" (1:33). This is the one God refers to in 2 Sam 7:12–16, the descendent whose kingdom and reign will be forever.[124] Solomon and the descendants of David prior to Jesus could not be the one the covenant referred to. Whoever this covenant refers to must have a capacity to live forever, something Jesus demonstrates he has through the resurrection (Acts 2:24–31). Zacharias's prophecy in Luke 1:67–79 reinforces the centrality of Jesus in the Davidic covenant. The prophecy refers to Jesus when Zacharias says God raised up a horn of salvation "in the house of David his servant" (ἐν οἴκῳ Δαυὶδ παιδὸς αὐτοῦ, 1:69). Attention to the Abrahamic covenant is also found in this prophecy and Mary's Magnificat (1:54–55, 72–73).

Second, the purpose of Jesus is inseparable from his unique relationship to his Father as Son. Mary is told that her child will be called "the Son of the Most High" (1:32) and "Son of God" (1:35). Luke connects Jesus's sonship directly to the virginal conception (1:35). When Jesus remained in Jerusalem at twelve years of age while his parents returned home, he softly chides them for not knowing something they should have: "Did you not know that I had to be about my Father's business?" (2:49). The use of δεῖ indicates this is an absolute necessity. For some reason, unexplained in the text, Jesus must be at that place at that time. Even at the age of twelve, Jesus knows who his Father is and that he has a divinely orchestrated purpose, greater than the work of a builder that he does in and around Nazareth. Robert F. O'Toole writes, "Doing the Father's will is at the heart of Jesus's existence."[125] The importance of Jesus's sonship is most evident in Luke 3:21—4:13. Luke does not include as much information regarding the transition from John to Jesus and his baptism as Matthew and John do (Matt 2:13–17; John 1:19–37).[126] Luke 3:21–22 provides a transition to Jesus's ministry, and it also contrasts the obedience of two sons of God—Adam and Jesus (cf. 3:22, 38). How Jesus responds to Satan and overcomes his temptations shows his superiority as God's Son. Theodore J. Jansma writes: "Some have supposed that

124. The Hebrew word עוֹלָם occurs three times; it is translated in the LXX εἰς τὸν αἰῶνα (2x) and ἕως αἰῶνος.

125. O'Toole, *Luke's Presentation of Jesus*, 11.

126. Luke includes more information about the preaching of John the Baptist and his interaction with people in the crowd (Luke 3:1–20) than the other Gospel authors.

Satan's thrust was to raise a doubt in Jesus's mind as to that witness, as if Satan were trying to impress upon Jesus the incongruity of his present circumstances with the declared fact of his divine sonship."[127] Both Matthew and Luke show that each of Satan's temptations aim at disproving Jesus's sonship: "If you are the Son of God . . ." (Matt 4:3, 6; Luke 4:3, 9).

Third, Jesus's purpose is defined by his relationship as the Savior of the world. The first hint of Jesus's purpose as Savior is found in his name. The name Ἰησοῦς was not uncommon in the first century.[128] Surprisingly, Luke does not make the connection between his name and the Hebrew equivalent, Joshua (יֵשׁוּעַ). Matthew apparently does, including the angel's words "for he will save (σώσει) his people from their sins" (Matt 1:21b). Lidija Novaković observes: "Strictly speaking, the name Jesus means 'Yahweh is salvation.' However, Matthew ascribes the salvific activity not to God but to the bearer of the name, Jesus."[129] Mary's reference to "Savior" (τῷ θεῷ τῷ σωτῆρί μου) in Luke 1:47 refers to God the Father, not the child she bears. John's ministry is described as one that makes known salvation and the forgiveness of sins in Jesus (Luke 1:77). Gabriel's announcement to the shepherds highlights this purpose of Jesus. He tells them, "There has been born for you a Savior (σωτήρ), who is Christ the Lord" (Luke 2:11). Simeon, likewise, equates seeing the baby Jesus in the temple as seeing salvation (εἶδον οἱ ὀφθαλμοί μου τὸ σωτήριόν σου, Luke 2:30).[130] The last reference to Jesus as Savior in Luke 1:1–4:13 is found in the preaching of John the Baptist. The quotation from Isa 40:3–5 concludes with "And all flesh will see the salvation of God (τὸ σωτήριον τοῦ θεοῦ)" (Luke 3:6). What is striking about John the Baptist's declarations in Luke is there is no hint of the forgiveness of sins. Instead, Jesus, the salvation of God, is presented as an eschatological deliverer. There is "wrath

127. Jansma, "The Temptation of Jesus," 170.

128. Hare, *Matthew*, 11. In fact, a textual variant in Matt 27:16 says that the insurrectionist Barabbas (the one the Jews pled for Herod to release) and Jesus the Nazarene shared the same first name.

129. Novaković, *Messiah* 64. Novaković also notes replacement of Ἰσραήλ, found in Ps 129:8 (LXX), with ὁ λαὸς αὐτοῦ in Matt 1:21b. Her evidence showing the connection to Matt 21:43 is solid, and she demonstrates that the angel's announcement to Joseph points to the universality of God's redemptive plan, a plan that includes both Jewish and Gentile people (ibid., 64–65). See also Hurtado, *Lord Jesus Christ*, 392.

130. Simeon's response to Jesus also shows the universality of God's redemptive plan. He is called "the light of revelation to the Gentiles" and "the glory of your people, Israel" (Luke 2:32). Anna's response connects Jesus to an idea similar to salvation—redemption (λύτρωσις).

to come" (Luke 3:7) and "fire" and "burning" (Luke 3:9, 16, 17) found in his message of repentance, things generally associated with Jesus's second advent. Clearly, John, the greatest prophet, did not have a clear picture of the redemptive plan (cf. Luke 7:18–23).

Faith/Faithfulness in Luke 1:1—4:13

A majority of scholars recognize the temptation of Jesus as a test of his faithfulness to God's redemptive plan. O'Toole writes, "[T]hrough his temptation in the desert Jesus shows himself loyal to God and faithful to his will."[131] David L. Allen says this is a way Luke "emphasizes Jesus's faithfulness to God."[132] The temptation narrative is introduced with the name Jesus, not mentioned since the beginning of the genealogy (3:23). Warren Carter says of Ἰησοῦς in Matt 4:1: "The name Jesus recalls his God-given mission from 1:21–23. This mission is now at stake."[133] Don B. Garlington believes that the temptations are an attempt by Satan to make Jesus fallaciously fall in the same way that Israel as God's son had done time and time again.[134]

The contrast between Jesus and Adam shows the faithfulness of Jesus Christ and the lack of faithfulness exhibited by Adam. The similarities are striking. Both are called "son of God" (3:22, 38). Both have a purpose given to them by God before their temptation. God's purpose for Adam is found in Gen 1:26–30; 2:15, and it involves procreation in, care for, and oversight over God's garden and all of creation. Only one prohibition was given to Adam, and it was exactly at this that Satan took aim (Gen 2:16–17; 3:1–4). Jesus's purpose is not explicitly defined in this section of Luke, but different texts point to his salvific purpose (see "*Purpose in Luke 1:1–4:13*"). If Jesus fails to resist the temptations of Satan, the mission fails as soon as it starts.

Patience in Luke 1:1–4:13

Jesus's patience is shown both in his subjection to his parents (Luke 2:51–52) and his temptation by Satan (Luke 4:1–13). The first account of Jesus

131. O'Toole, *Luke's Presentation of Jesus*, 11.
132. Allen, *Hebrews*, 326.
133. Carter, *Matthew and the Margins*, 107.
134. Garlington, "Jesus, the Unique Son of God," 292.

in the temple demonstrates Jesus's eagerness, even at age twelve, to begin the work that the Father has for him. He sees nothing wrong with staying behind and allowing his parents to unknowingly return to Nazareth without him. In fact, from his perspective, it is an absolute necessity (δεῖ, 2:49), as if he could not be anywhere but in the Temple. Despite his desire and eagerness to begin doing the things the Father planned for him, Jesus places himself under ongoing submission[135] to his parents and his culture for the next eighteen years (3:23).

One of the reasons Jesus came is to put an end to the devil and the sting of death. In Gen 3:15, the pre-incarnate Jesus[136] tells Satan that one from the seed of woman will one day crush his head. He has been waiting thousands of years to put an end to the one who introduced sin into the world. The time when he is led out to the wilderness is not his opportune time to do so. Satan must first have his opportune time, which results in the crucifixion of Jesus on the cross. Despite being hungry and despite the fiercest satanic assault, Jesus opts to surrender to his Father's plan, first enduring the cross (Phil 2:8) before finally putting an end to the sting of death through the resurrection (1 Cor 15:51–57). Even after his resurrection, Jesus exercises great patience as he allows those whom he loves to undergo fiery trials (1 Pet 1:6) even though Satan prowls around like a roaring lion (1 Pet 5:8). As Peter writes, "The Lord is not slow concerning his promise" (2 Pet 3:9). He is "patient" (μακροθυμεῖ), "not wishing for

135. Note Luke's use of the imperfect ἦν with the participle ὑποτασσόμενος. The use of the imperfect here is similar to imperfect ἐγίνωσκεν in Matt 1:25. Both stress an action maintained over a period of time. In the case of Joseph, he did not have relations with Mary until after Jesus's birth, undoubtedly so that no charge could be made that Jesus was his son.

136. This statement may cause some surprise. However, that this is the pre-incarnate Jesus has the evidence of the Old and New Testaments. A sampling of the evidence is provided below:

1. There is a member of the godhead who speaks face-to-face with people in the OT and NT (e.g., Exod 24:9–11; 33:11).
2. There is a member of the godhead who is seen with the glory in the OT and NT (Isa 6:1–5; John 12:41).
3. There is a member of the godhead who cannot be seen and has never been seen (e.g., Exod 33:18–23; Judg 6:22–23; Matt 5:8; Luke 10:22; John 1:18; 6:46; 1 Tim 6:16).

John's language in 1:18 (οὐδείς and πώποτε) excludes every person at every period of time in human history (not just those in the first century). It is on the basis of this evidence that one determines Jesus (pre-incarnate) is the speaker in Gen 3:15.

anyone to perish" (2 Pet 3:9). This patience, however, does have its limit, as seen in Rev 20:7–10.

An Analysis of Luke 4:14—9:50

The Selection of Disciples in Luke 4:14—9:50

Luke includes the second call of the disciples in 5:1–11. A second call is understood in Luke for a few reasons. First, there is no mention of Peter and Andrew fishing in Matthew's or Mark's accounts. Second, Luke alone records that Jesus entered a boat and taught for a period of time. Finally, third, Luke alone records the miraculous catch of fish and Peter's prophet-like reaction.[137]

The first call is found in Matt 4:18–22. The reason behind Peter, Andrew, James, and John returning to the fishing business following the call in Matt 4:18–22 is unclear. They had met Jesus before. Andrew heard John's announcement of Jesus as "the Lamb of God" (John 1:36). He found his brother, Peter, and brought him to Jesus. Andrew is identified as one of John's disciples (John 1:35, 37, 40). Even though he is a disciple of John, he is able to continue his work (Matt 4:18). The gap between Matt 4:18–22 and Luke 5:1–11 may be similar to this relationship between John's and his disciples. Even though Andrew and Peter become disciples of Jesus, it is not until Luke 5:11 that they leave "everything" (πάντα) to follow him.

Luke's account exemplifies Jesus's teaching in Luke 6:46–49, namely hearing and doing what Jesus says. Not only did they listen to Jesus's message beside the Sea of Galilee, the content of which is not recorded, but the disciples also followed Jesus's command to re-launch their boat and tackle despite their already dry night of fishing.[138] Simon (Peter) is the central character in the call episode. He is solicited by Jesus to push off a little ways from the shore. Two options are possible. First, Peter could have pushed the boat out and remained in the water, holding it in place somewhere around five-feet deep. Second, he could have put out a sufficient distance and dropped a light anchor. Despite estimates about the

---

137. Barton et. al., *Luke*, 111.

138. Marshall, *The Gospel of Luke*, 199. For a thorough discussion of fishing on the Sea of Galilee in the first century, see Nun, "Cast Your Net upon the Waters," 46–56; Nun, "Ports of Galilee," 18–31, 64.

typical size of fishing vessels during the first century,[139] nothing in the text suggests Peter's boat necessitated a crew larger than 2 or 3 to operate (including the nets). That more are in the boat other than just Peter is clear by the command to "drop your nets" (χαλάσατε, 5:4), which is in the plural.[140]

Whether Peter is in the water holding the boat or inside the vessel listening to Jesus's words, he is nearer to Jesus than the crowd on the shore. It is not Jesus's teaching primarily that evokes Peter's response: "He fell down at Jesus's feet, saying, 'Depart from me, Lord, because I am a sinful man'" (Luke 5:8). Peter's response follows the great catch of fish that began to break the nets and sink the two ships (Luke 5:6–7). The conclusion to the narrative is clear—"they left everything and followed him" (Luke 5:11). The calling of Matthew includes Jesus's invitation to "follow him" (Luke 5:27), and it says Matthew "left everything" (καταλιπὼν πάντα, Luke 5:28), just like Luke 5:11.

In addition to these five disciples, Jesus adds seven more in his selection of apostles in Luke 6:12–16: Thomas, James the son of Alphaeus, Simon the Zealot, Judas the son of James, and Judas Iscariot, the traitor.[141] Jesus withdraws to the mountain and spends the whole night in prayer before selecting these men as apostles, an indication that this is a major shift in the ministry of Jesus.[142] Mark gives two purposes, each marked by a ἵνα clause, for why Jesus appointed these twelve men: (1) "so that they could be with him" (ἵνα ὦσιν μετ' αὐτοῦ), and (2) "so that he could send them out to preach and to have authority over demons" (ἵνα ἀποστέλλῃ αὐτοὺς κηρύσσειν καὶ ἔχειν ἐξουσίαν ἐκβάλλειν τὰ δαιμόνια, Mark 3:14). Concerning Mark's first ἵνα clause (Mark 3:14), Colin G. Kruse writes:

> The first part (to be with him) involved travelling up and down the country with him, sharing food and accommodation with

139. Shelley Wachsmann says the ideal size ranged from 23–30 feet long (*The Sea of Galilee Boat*, 364). Barton, Veerman, and Taylor say they were between sixteen and twenty feet (*Luke*, 112).

140. Johnson, *The Gospel of Luke*, 88.

141. On the number of apostles, see Luke 22:28–30; Acts 1:15–26. Morris Ashcraft writes, "The number twelve was so important that a replacement was sought when Judas killed himself" ("Apostle/Apostleship," 47), and no replacements were sought following the death of an apostle after that (Harrison, "Apostle," 86). On the addition of Paul, Ashcraft says, "Some speculate that Paul instead of Matthias was the choice of the Holy Spirit" ("Apostle/Apostleship," 48).

142. Johnson, *The Gospel of Luke*, 102.

him, experiencing the same acceptance and rejection which he encountered, and observing and sometimes participating in the ministry which he was carrying out.[143]

The word μαθητής actually corresponds most to the first ἵνα clause, while ἀπόστολος corresponds to the second.[144]

In Luke, Jesus is met with amazement and hostility. The attendees of the synagogue in Nazareth wanted to kill him (Luke 4:29). The Sabbath controversies found in Luke 6:1–11 only highlight this hostility even more. Recognizing this, Morris says, Jesus selected a group "who would carry on his work after him."[145] Green says the selection of these twelve, including four fisherman and one tax collector, is a "judgment on Israel's leadership for their lack of insight into God's redemptive plan and compassionate care for those in need."[146] He does not select any of the religious elite of his day, none who is likewise called "Rabbi" or "Teacher."

Sverre Bøe says this marks the beginning of a unique relationship, one he even considers entirely different from the μαθητής-διδάσκαλος relationship known in Jewish circles. Bøe writes:

> Compared to the traditional Jewish roles of teacher and student, Jesus breaks the mold; a student of Torah would follow the teaching of his rabbi until he someday became a rabbi in his own right. But neither Luke nor any of the other evangelists suggest that any of Jesus's disciples would ever grow equal to Jesus or take over his role. We also see the difference between the Jewish rabbis binding their students to the Torah, and Jesus, who binds his students to himself.[147]

Being with Jesus is essential to the training he wishes them to undergo. If teaching content were the only curriculum he desired to entrust them with (and the other characteristics mentioned in 2 Tim 3:10–11a were irrelevant), a second call may have been unnecessary. Jesus could have adequately taught the disciples around Galilee before moving on to Jerusalem. However, it is necessary for them to forsake everything, including their jobs, and travel with him. They needed to see his interactions with the Pharisees, with the sick and needy, and with the broken-hearted; they

143. Kruse, "Apostle," 31.

144. Harrison, "Apostle," 86.

145. Morris, *Luke*, 137.

146. Green, *The Gospel of Luke*, 259.

147. Bøe, *Cross-Bearing in Luke*, 97.

needed to see his devotion to prayer; they needed to see everything the Gospels record, especially his suffering, death, and resurrection.

Imitation in Luke 4:14—9:50

The concept of imitation is important to Luke. Richard A. Burridge says Luke is the "evangelist who makes the role of *mimesis*, imitation, most explicit."[148] He adds: "'Go and do likewise' may be Jesus' instruction to the lawyer to follow the example of the Good Samaritan (10.29–37), but in fact the whole of Luke-Acts is full of examples to follow or to avoid for moral conduct."[149] Of these examples, Burridge mentions the Rich Man and Lazarus, the Widow and the Unjust Judge, and the Pharisee and the Tax Collector. Each of them is given as "one to imitate and one not to follow."[150]

Aside from the comparisons in the SOP, the only examples like Burridge mentions in Luke 4:14—9:50 are Jesus's story of the moneylender with two debtors (Luke 7:40–50)[151] and the persons with a lamp (Luke 8:16–18). In the story of the debtors, the woman who anoints Jesus's feet with her tears and perfume illustrates the significance of how someone genuinely responds when his or her sins are forgiven. Jesus uses it to contrast the lack of deeds performed by the Pharisee, named Simon, to the abundance of love demonstrated by the woman, who is only called "a sinner" (Luke 7:37, 39).

Jesus uses a "moneylender" (or, "creditor;" δανειστής) in the illustration, one that is unique to the Gospel of Luke. James S. Jeffers says a person in this occupation was "a prominent figure in Roman and Hellenistic locales."[152] One debtor owes 500 denarii. The other owes only fifty. One denarius was equivalent to a "fair wage for one's work by a laborer" in the first century, according to R. T. France.[153] Jesus's use of the debt, however, is not the main focus of the illustration. He concentrates on the debtors,

---

148. Burridge, *Imitating Jesus*, 280.

149. Ibid.

150. Ibid.

151. Economic parables are quite common in the Gospels. Of the 30+ parables, Tomas Sedlacek, identifies nineteen that relate to economics in some way (*Economics of Good and Evil*, 132).

152. Jeffers, *The Greco-Roman World*, 65.

153. France, *The Gospel of Matthew*, 749.

particularly which of the two loves more once he is forgiven (Luke 7:42). It is important to know that moneylenders were not particularly popular in the days of Jesus. In fact, they were on par with the tax collectors— despised, shunned, and equated with a ἁμαρτωλός. Walter Wink writes, "Indebtedness was one of the most serious social problems in the first century Palestine."[154] During the first century, there were "large estates owned by absentee landlords, managed by stewards, and worked by servants, sharecroppers, and day laborers."[155] So culturally detested was this issue that "the first act of the Jewish revolutionaries in 66 CE was to burn the temple treasury, where the record of debts was kept," says Wink.[156] Then, there are the debtors, who are far more common in society than creditors.

J. P. Louw says that each of the characters is a potential example for the audience.[157] For example, Jesus's message is not received well by the Pharisees, even one as open to Jesus as Simon. Luke's audience hears the comparison and knows which example Jesus commends. Those who are forgiven of their sins should have this same outpouring of love as the sinful woman for the one who has the capacity to forgive all sins.

Not only are these examples provided by Jesus given for imitation, he actually commissions the Twelve to proclaim the kingdom and heal the sick in neighboring villages (Luke 9:1–6), thus replicating his ministry through them for the first time. From the very beginning Jesus has this intention. A. B. Bruce writes:

> [The Twelve] were to be something more than travelling companions or menial servants of the Lord Jesus Christ. They were to be, in the meantime, students of Christian doctrine, and occasional fellow-laborers in the work of the kingdom, and eventually Christ's chosen trained agents for propagating the faith.[158]

The absence of repentance in Luke 9:1–6 is not representative of a message lacking a call to repentance, nor does Luke postpone the use of the word for the time following Jesus's resurrection. The phrase "kingdom of God" (ἡ βασιλεία τοῦ θεοῦ) encompasses all that Jesus (and John) taught since the beginning of his ministry (Matt 4:17; Mark 1:15). Although few

154. Wink, "Neither Passivity nor Violence," 107.

155. Ibid.

156. Ibid.

157. Louw, "Macro levels of Meaning in Lk 7:36–50," 134.

158. Bruce, *The Training of the Twelve*, 30.

scholars discuss the content of the disciples' message, it would not be unlikely for them to (1) reproduce the content of Jesus's messages like the SOP and (2) proclaim the works of Jesus that they had been eyewitnesses of up to that point. The latter is similar to what Luke describes in 4:37 and 7:22–23; the only difference is that these twelve men were equipped to manifest Jesus's power along with the message, whereas previously people could only report what they heard. More than this, they were to represent the very person of Jesus—his teaching and his character (i.e., his likeness).[159] In order to adequately receive what they needed in order to fulfill this mission, Jesus spends about one year with these twelve men.[160]

Jesus gives his disciples "power and authority" (δύναμιν καὶ ἐξουσίαν) over all the demons and a capacity to heal people from their infirmities (Luke 9:1). The power Jesus possesses, enabling him to cast out demons and heal people, comes directly from the Holy Spirit. What then enables the apostles? What is the power that is given to them, especially since they are not baptized with the Holy Spirit until Acts 2? The most likely answer is that the twelve apostles received the Holy Spirit[161] in a manner similar to the prophets and judges found in the OT. When Luke 10:1–22 and Acts 1:8 are considered, it is clear that this endowment of the Holy Spirit is temporary in Luke 9 and 10. In Acts 1:8, Jesus says the disciples will receive power (λήμψεσθε δύναμιν) and be his witnesses (ἔσεσθέ μου μάρτυρες),[162] both referring to an event in the future.

159. Elwell and Comfort, "Apostle, Apostleship," 96.

160. Thomas and Gundry, *A Harmony of the Gospels*, 348. Sections 51 and 54 refer to the call of the disciples. They place this around the winter of AD 28. The commissioning of the Twelve occurs in the winter of AD 29 (see Section 99 at the end of the ministry in and around Galilee).

161. Black, *Luke*, 182; Hooker, "John's Baptism," 34; Warrington, *The Message of the Holy Spirit*, 62ff.; Yen, *The Lucan Journey*, 165.

162. In his Gospel, Luke states the apostles' purpose in terms of what they will do. Note the use of action verbs. In Acts, however, he uses a form of the stative verb εἰμί. This may be a stretch, but it is possible that Luke intends to stress who the apostles have finally become, having been fully trained in their 3+ years with Jesus. The giving of the Holy Spirit in Acts 2 is entirely different than anything prior; the presence of the Holy Spirit in the Gospels and the OT represents the ministry of the Holy Spirit under the Old Covenant. Beginning in Acts 2, the Spirit is given in accordance to the New Covenant; one of its characteristics is an ongoing, permanent presence of the Holy Spirit in the life of a believer-participant.

It is interesting that Jesus uses a form of situational leadership[163] here, supervising the apostles while also maximizing the work that is being done for the kingdom. Gareth Weldon Icenogle writes:

> Jesus' determination to share leadership authority and power, first with the Twelve (Luke 9:1–2), then with the seventy-two (Luke 10:1–11), then with the one hundred twenty (Acts 1:15–2:4), and finally with all who are afar off (three thousand on the first day of Pentecost, Acts 2:14–21, 38–41) is foundational to the meaning, purpose, goal and process of his leadership among the Twelve. Of all the Gospels, Luke is most clear about this revolutionary practice and concept of a leader sharing power with wider and wider groups of persons. Shared and empowered leadership development is unique to the good news of Jesus' discipleship model.[164]

Luke 8:1–3 indicates that Jesus is traveling around, from one city and village to the next, spreading the message of the kingdom of God.[165] The Twelve are "with him" (σὺν αὐτῷ, 8:1), just as they have been since Luke 5.[166] Ringe refers to 6:17—8:56 as "their time of preparation for the task."[167] Mark C. Black writes, "Jesus has been with the disciples long enough now for them to begin to imitate him in preaching and healing."[168] Just as situational leadership affirms, the wisest thing to do when preparing future leaders and releasing them with very important tasks is to stage the levels of supervision over time. Talbert points out that "Jesus does not assign a task until he has first equipped those who are to perform it."[169] This is true here in Luke 9 as well as in Acts, where the disciples had to remain in Jerusalem to first receive the Holy Spirit.

---

163. See Hersey et. al., *Management of Organizational Behavior*; Blanchard and Hodges, *Lead Like Jesus*, 138–52; Northouse, *Leadership*, esp. 99ff.; Cousins, "Overseeing Staff," 141–44.

164. Icenogle, *Biblical Foundations for Small Group Ministry*, 168.

165. Guy D. Nave Jr. says Luke's use of "kingdom of God," "demons," and "healing" is "to connect the ministry of the Twelve in 9:1–6 with the ministry of Jesus in Chapter 8" (*The Role and Function of Repentance in Luke-Acts*, 193).

166. Luke also includes the presence of many women (ἕτεραι πολλαί, 8:3), three of whom are named. These women assisted Jesus financially in his work.

167. Ringe, *Luke*, 128.

168. Black, *Luke*, 181.

169. Talbert, *Reading Luke*, 101.

Ken Blanchard and Phil Hodges identify four learning stages: (1) Novice, (2) Apprentice, (3) Journeyman, and (4) Master.[170] During the first stage, trainees are given basic information, which they describe as "What, How, Where, When, and Why" information. Actually, information like this continues throughout the different learning stages.[171] Jesus's teaching never ceases in the disciples' lives. From Luke 5:1 to 8:56, the disciples fall under this first learning stage. Stein writes, "The Twelve's mission served as an apprenticeship for their ultimate mission (24:45–49)."[172] Beginning in 9:1, the Twelve move, for the first time, into the apprentice stage, which is characterized by instruction, practice, and evaluation.[173] Jesus continues his own involvement in the preaching mission, for the first time since Luke 5:1, without his twelve disciples alongside him (Matt 11:1).

Luke provides more detail regarding these characteristics in Luke 10 than here. Matthew, on the other hand, is rather comprehensive about Jesus's instructions given to the Twelve before their commission (Matt 10:1–42).[174] In Luke 9:3–5, Jesus tells the disciples three things. First, he instructs the Twelve on what they will need for their journey—nothing (μηδέν, 9:3). Second, he tells them how they should conduct themselves with hospitality when they arrive in a city (9:4). And, third, he instructs them on how they should depart a city that does not receive them (9:5). Each of these commands is characteristic of Jesus's own ministry. While the Gospels say nothing explicit about Jesus's luggage and possessions on his journeys, he must have travelled with some things; nevertheless, he no doubt travelled light.[175] Morris says the reason for traveling light is the disciples are not to concentrate on "elaborate preparations," and they must rely on God's provision for everything that they need.[176]

170. Blanchard and Hodges, *Lead Like Jesus,* 138.

171. Blanchard and Hodges write, "No one is totally a novice, apprentice, journeyman, or master/teacher in the things he or she does. At any one time in our work life or in one of our role relationships, we could be at all four learning stages" (ibid.).

172. Stein, *Luke,* 266.

173. Blanchard and Hodges, *Lead Like Jesus,* 138.

174. John does not include anything about the Galilean apprentice mission. Kruse believes Jesus refers to the commissioning of the Twelve in John 4:38 (Kruse, *John,* 140).

175. It may have even been Jesus who gave the previously demon-possessed man the clothes that the herdsmen and townspeople find him wearing in Mark 5:15.

176. Morris, *Luke,* 179. On the use of πήρα, Michaelis refutes the idea that Jesus refers to some sort of "beggar's bag." All that Jesus prohibits the Twelve from taking along with them are things related to traveling, common in the first century (Michaelis,

Jesus is accustomed to traveling in a way that trusts God for every provision. No example is greater than Luke 9:58. To a man on the road who desires to follow Jesus, he says: "The foxes have holes and the birds of the air have nests, but the Son of Man does not have a place to even lay his head down." There are times in Jesus's travels where he has nowhere to sleep. As well, there are times when he does.

1.   In John 1:38, two disciples (one of them being Andrew) ask Jesus, "Where are you staying?" (ποῦ μένεις). John provides no information about where that place is; he only says the disciples "saw where he was staying" and they spent the day there with him. Andrew is able to lead his brother, Simon, there later because he has visited with Jesus at the same place.

2.   In Luke 4:38, Jesus is at Peter's home and heals Peter's mother-in-law.

3.   In Luke 10:38, he is welcomed into the home of a woman named Martha.

4.   In Luke 19:5, Jesus tells Zaccheus that he absolutely must stay at his house (ἐν τῷ οἴκῳ σου δεῖ με μεῖναι).

Jesus is entirely familiar with depending on the hospitality of others. In fact, Luke mentions that the ministry of Jesus is funded in part by women who had been healed by Jesus (8:1–3).[177] When he tells his disciples to stay in the first house that welcomes them in, he is teaching them to be content and respectful; it is a warning against seeking out "better" sleeping accommodations, which would insult the host and the God who provided them. The Scriptures are silent on much of Jesus's accommodations during his ministry. Given he told his disciples to do this, one can expect this is how Jesus acted toward hosts in cities and villages he visited.

Likeness Language in Luke 4:14—9:50

One of the most important events in the life of Jesus is the Transfiguration, which each of the Synoptic Gospels contains (Matt 17:1–13//Luke 9:28–36//Mark 9:2–13). Lewis Sperry Chafer says the importance of

---

"πήρα," 119–21). For its uses referring to a bag itinerant preachers would carry, see Bauer, *A Greek-English Lexicon*, 662.

177. The use of αὐτοῖς as the direct object indicates that they were not just taking care of Jesus, but even his twelve disciples.

this event is evident "by the fact that it appears at length in each of the Synoptics."[178] Under consideration here is what actually happens to Jesus during the Transfiguration. What happens to him—his face, his clothing, and the presence of the glory of God?

Before considering Luke 9:29–31, it is helpful to think about verse 32. Luke records that the disciples were asleep, and when they woke up they saw his glory. Whatever takes place in the transfiguration of Jesus so that he takes on this glory, the disciples are unaware of it. Luke uses a pluperfect periphrastic construction (ἦσαν βεβαρημένοι) to indicate that what takes place in Luke 9:29–31 occurs during this period of sleep.[179] It is remarkable that for two of the most significant events in the life of Christ, his closest three disciples cannot/do not stay awake (cf. Matt 26:36–46; Luke 22:45–46).[180]

Two changes occur in Luke 9:29. First, the appearance of Jesus's face changes. The finite verb is ἐγένετο. Its subject is τὸ εἶδος τοῦ προσώπου.[181] Its object is ἕτερον. Ἐγένετο, from γίνομαι, is a verb of being. Francis J. Moloney says the verb is "versatile and thus has many possible meanings."[182] Different than the verb εἰμί (a stative verb), γίνομαι is able to communicate transition. Beuford H. Bryant and Mark S. Krause write, "[T]he verb γίνομαι (*ginomai*, 'to become') signifies that something changed its features or began a new situation by becoming what it was not beforehand."[183] Thus, it can be used in discourse to further a narrative or provide a temporal framework.[184] Or, as it does here, it can be used to show how something changes from one state to another. Reiling and Swellengrebel, as well as Yen, say the sentence as a whole only says the appearance changed, "without indicating the nature of the change."[185] Matthew and Mark use a different verb. Whereas Luke uses a

178. Chafer, *Systematic Theology*, 86.

179. Yen, *The Lucan Journey*, 121.

180. Holleran says Luke contains more parallels between the Transfiguration and Gethsemene than do Matthew and Mark: "Not only are the disciples depicted as asleep, but in both scenes Luke describes the action as taking place on a mount at night, he has the disciples 'follow' Jesus there, and he shows Jesus, in contrast to his weak disciples, praying and strengthened by heavenly messengers" (*The Synoptic Gethsemene*, 47).

181. Matthew has only τὸ πρόσωπον.

182. Moloney, *Gospel of John*, 42.

183. Bryant and Krause, *John*, 47.

184. Runge, *Discourse Grammar*, 299.

185. Reiling and Swellengrebel, *Translator's Handbook on the Gospel of Luke*, 380.

simple verb to mark the transition from one state to another, they use the verb μεταμορφόω.[186] The second change involves Jesus's clothing. Luke records, "And, his clothing *became* super bright white." The two changes share a single verb—ἐγένετο.

Yen believes the two changes are semi-symbolic. She says, "The face and clothing refer to Jesus's entire existence. The face is to represent his person/being, the clothing his status."[187] There are other options, however. There are references in the OT, and elsewhere in the NT, that speak of someone's face being changed in connection to the glory of God. Moses, who is present at the Transfiguration, had his face changed on Sinai (Exod 34:29–35).[188] Moses's face was changed because he was speaking with God. Similarly, Jesus's face is changed when he is praying to the Father. Moses, however, did not have his clothing changed. By the change in Jesus's clothing, his transfiguration is presented as superior to the transfiguration of Moses. There may also be a connection to Isa 6:1. John says Isaiah saw Jesus's glory (εἶδεν τὴν δόξαν αὐτοῦ, John 12:41). The same thing is said of the three disciples at the Transfiguration: "they saw his glory" (εἶδον τὴν δόξαν αὐτοῦ, Luke 9:32). In the Isaiah vision, there is no mention of the glory except in the angel's pronouncement that the entire earth is filled with the glory of God (Isa 6:3). There is another connection, though. The language Isaiah uses of the train of the Lord's robe "filling the temple" (מְלֵאִים אֶת־הַהֵיכָל [πλήρης ὁ οἶκος τῆς δόξης αὐτοῦ, LXX]) is reminiscent of the glory of God filling the temple in the Old Testament. This is why the LXX explicitly states as much. In Isaiah, the train of the Lord's robe and the glory of God are synonymous.

What is important here is God's capacity to entirely transform the appearance of Jesus Christ. When the disciples go to sleep, Jesus is as they have always known him. When they awake, he is different. In the Pauline corpus, Paul talks a great deal about God's transforming power and purposes. For example, in Phil 3:21, he speaks of Jesus Christ as being the one "who will transform the body of our humble state into conformity with the body of his glory." Jesus is the agent of the believer's transformation in Phil 3:21. If God has this capacity to transform a believer from a humble

---

See Yen, *The Lucan Journey*, 113.

186. This word is significant given it occurs twice in reference to a change believers undergo (Rom 12:2; 2 Cor 3:18).

187. Yen, *The Lucan Journey*, 114.

188. Paul, likewise, speaks of the face of Christ and the glory of God together in 2 Cor 4:6.

state to a glorious state, he also has the capacity to transform a believer in this life from one likeness into the likeness of Jesus Christ (Luke 6:40; Rom 12:2). The Transfiguration has huge Christological significance. It is also critical for one's understanding of the theme of likeness education in the New Testament.

The Use of Μαθητής and Διδάσκαλος in Luke 4:14—9:50

One of the elements of the μαθητής-διδάσκαλος relationship identified in the exegesis of Luke 6:39–49 is the importance of both hearing and doing the things Jesus says (Luke 6:47). Jesus's teaching in Luke 8 provides more information about this aspect of hearing and doing in discipleship. Jesus gives the parable of the sower and the seed in Luke 8:1–8; he interprets it for the disciples in 8:11–15. Hearing not only plays an important role in Jesus's own interpretation of the parable, but he also concludes the parable with a call for those listening to be sure they are listening to what he says. The saying "He who has ears to hear, let him hear" (ὁ ἔχων ὦτα ἀκούειν ἀκουέτω) occurs only in Luke 8:8 and 14:35.[189] It is very similar to the injunction found in the letters to the seven churches in Revelation: "He who has an ear, hear what the Spirit is saying to the churches" (Rev 2:7, 11, 17, 29; 3:6, 13, 22).[190] Structurally, it is more similar to the injunction found in Matt 19:12: "Let him who is able to accept this, accept it" (ὁ δυνάμενος χωρεῖν χωρείτω).[191] These injunctions are used rhetorically to point out a significant teaching or event.[192] Runge shows how they function in discourse: "The commands to hear and understand are not needed for semantic reasons. It is comparable to someone in English saying, 'Listen up!' or 'Pay attention!'"[193] He adds, "The metacomment ensures that the gravity of what follows is not missed."[194]

189. See also Matt 11:15, 13:9, and 13:43.

190. The primary differences between the two forms are the use of the plural ὦτα in Luke (where John has the singular) and the present active imperative ἀκουέτω (where John has the aorist).

191. Turner, *Matthew*, 463 n.13.

192. See Rowland and Morray-Jones, *The Mystery of God*, 115.

193. Runge, *Discourse Grammar*, 115.

194. Ibid. Willem S. Vorster discusses its use in Matt 13:9 saying it is used to foreshadow the theme of hearing and understanding that develops in 13:10–23, particularly in Jesus's answer for why he has begun to speak in parables to the people ("The Structure of Matthew 13," 145–46).

In Jesus's interpretation of the parable of the sower and seed, "hearing" is present throughout. One sower goes out to sow seed. The seed falls in four different locations marked by four different prepositional phrases:

1. παρὰ τὴν ὁδόν ("beside the road," 8:5).

2. ἐπὶ τὴν πέτραν ("upon rocky soil," 8:6).

3. ἐν μέσῳ τῶν ἀκανθῶν ("between the thorns," 8:7).

4. εἰς τὴν γῆν τὴν ἀγαθήν ("into the good soil," 8:8).

In each case, the word of God (i.e., "the seed," 8:11) is heard:

1. "beside the road" (8:5) → οἱ ἀκούσαντες (8:12).

2. "upon rocky soil" (8:6) → οἳ ὅταν ἀκούσωσιν (8:13).

3. "between the thorns" (8:7) → οἱ ἀκούσαντες (8:14).

4. "into the good soil" (8:8) → οἵτινες ἀκούσαντες (8:15).

Hearing the word of God is essential in the discipleship relationship. Like Paul says in Rom 10:14, "How will they believe in him whom they have not heard?" What is marked in Jesus's explanation is not the hearing but what follows that hearing:

1. "beside the road" (8:5) → "the devil removes the word" (8:12).

2. "upon rocky soil" (8:6) → "receive the word with joy," yet no root (8:13).

3. "between the thorns" (8:7) → "are choked" and "bear no fruit" (8:14).

4. "into the good soil" (8:8) → "cling to it" and "bear fruit" (8:15).

The final illustration of the seed that fell into good soil is the only one that modifies the verb ἀκούω. Consider the following diagram:

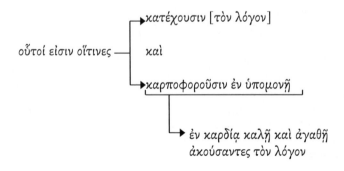

The discipleship that Jesus commends and urges his listeners to have is one that does two things: (1) clings to the word of God (κατέχουσιν), and (2) bears fruit (καρποφοροῦσιν).

Each of these two results to hearing the word of God contains a single prerequisite, the only thing not present in the three other illustrations. Ultimately, it is not the worries, riches, or pleasures of life that cause the people described in the third illustration to not be saved. Ultimately, it is not temptation in a person's life that causes him or her to not believe (see the second illustration). The first and fourth illustrations are parallel in that both mention the importance of the heart. In the first, Satan is responsible for removing the word of God from the heart, which is an idea similar to Paul's teaching that the god of this world has blinded the minds of the unbelieving (2 Cor 4:4). What is necessary for the word of God to take root is "a good and genuine heart" (καρδία καλῇ καὶ ἀγαθῇ). This is also reminiscent of Jesus's teaching about the good man and the good treasure of his heart (τοῦ ἀγαθοῦ θησαυροῦ τῆς καρδίας, Luke 6:45). Hearing Jesus's words and hearing the word of God are synonymous in Luke 6:47 and 8:4–8. Before one can genuinely embrace the word of God and bear fruit, a person's heart has to be transformed so that it takes on the attributes of "honest" and "good."

The interpretation of the parable leads into a second event with further teaching about hearing and doing. Jesus tells his audience that no one lights a lamp just to cover it up or hide it; a person lights a lamp and puts it on a lampstand so that (ἵνα) people coming into the house will see its light (8:16). Robertson mentions an unusual difference between Matthew and Luke's account. Matthew says the purpose (ὅπως) is people might see their good works (τὰ καλὰ ἔργα). Robertson writes, "The purpose of light is to let one see something else, not the light."[195] So, why does Luke's account say so that they might see the light? Most importantly, Lucan redaction is not the answer. Jesus, like the Luke 6:40 proverb, uses this comparison on multiple occasions (see also Luke 11:33–34). On this occasion, he chooses to use light instead of good works. Light in this comparison is representative of the word of God (cf. 8:11).[196] This comparison is expanding Jesus's statement in Luke 8:10, the Isaiah 6 quotation, and why Jesus is now revealing and concealing teachings about

---

195. Robertson, *Gospel according to Luke*, 128.
196. Patella, *Gospel according to Luke*, 56.

the kingdom of God. Even though he teaches in parables, he makes the teaching known to those considered to be his closest disciples.[197]

Connected to this is Jesus's warning for his audience to be careful on how they listen (βλέπετε οὖν πῶς ἀκούετε, 8:18). The γάρ is explanatory in Luke 8:18. There is a manner by which disciples can listen to the word of God where they receive more knowledge; there is also a manner by which a person can have all spiritual knowledge taken away from them. The idea of the devil taking the word of God out of people's hearts in 8:12 is connected here through the use of αἴρω in 8:18. The purpose of the parables is to reveal and conceal. What Jesus says through these two illustrations is some do not have a capacity to understand what he is saying due to a divine judgment for their rejection of him (Isa 6:9–10). They are not prevented from hearing the teaching. No one is; nor are they prevented from perceiving that they have true spiritual insight from the word of God. In the second illustration, the ones who hear do so with joy only to have it disappear through temptation (8:13). In the third illustration, those who hear apparently continue for a long while, perhaps even their whole life, thinking they have genuinely received the word of God—but they bear no fruit to maturity (8:14). God exercises the decision to grant one a capacity to genuinely understand the word of God (ὑμῖν δέδοται γνῶναι, 8:10). Satan is the one who takes away in 8:18. Even though the devil (ὁ διάβολος) is mentioned only in the first illustration, he is alluded to with references to temptation (πειρασμός) in 8:13 and the references to the worries, riches, and pleasures of life in 8:14.

At this very moment, Jesus's mother and brothers try to reach Jesus but cannot because of the crowd around him. Jesus uses this opportunity to teach about relationships he has that are greater than earthly relationships and far more important. Someone in the crowd informs Jesus that his mother and brothers are "standing outside" the house he and the

197. The disciples are the ones who ask the questions about the parables. It is to them that Jesus directs his answers (8:9–10). Matthew records that the disciples waited until they were away from the crowds and settled in a house to ask Jesus about a parable, i.e., the parable of the tares of the field (Matt 13:36). The explanation of the parable in 8:11–15 probably occurs in the house as well since the report Jesus receives about his mother and brothers is that they are "standing outside" (εστήκασιν ἔξω), presumably the house. Even they, the ones to whom it had been given to know, lack understanding pertaining to the secrets of the kingdom (τὰ μυστήρια τῆς βασιλείας). Jesus's teaching remains public, but he conceals the teaching in parabolic form, explaining it further to those whom he chooses—particularly the Twelve who are responsible for proclaiming it later.

disciples were visiting (Luke 8:20; see Matt 13:36). Jesus leaves everything at the age of thirty (Luke 3:23) to do the work of his Father. This had serious ramifications, even within his own family. When he tells future crowds, "If anyone comes to me and does not hate his own father and mother and children and brothers and sisters, and even his very own life, he cannot be my disciples" (Luke 14:26), he does not place upon anyone a burden he has not himself considered. Considering one's relationship to the kingdom of God far surpasses any earthly relationship. One's love for family should pale in comparison to one's love for the kingdom. Ringe writes:

> For the ancient Jews . . . an individual existed only as part of an extended family unit, whose authority structure, obligations, and customs governed every aspect of life. Any action by an individual was a reflection on the whole family, and any breach of family honor would usually meet with severe discipline.[198]

When Jesus's family comes to him, they do so out of shame, anger, and maybe a desire to save his life (i.e., if he keeps this blasphemy up, he might die).[199] Peter recounts them saying "He is out of his mind" (Mark 3:22) and that they tried to do a citizen's arrest. Instead of surrendering and giving up the work of the kingdom, Jesus pronounces ties that he has superseding all earthly relationships. He says his mother and brothers are actually those who "hear the word of God and do it" (οἱ τὸν λόγον τοῦ θεοῦ ἀκούοντες καὶ ποιοῦντες, 8:21). Just like Luke 6:47, the discipleship required by Jesus is one that not only hears, but one that does. And using the parable of the sower and the seed, it is one that bears fruit with perseverance, no matter what sort of trial or temptation arises.

Teaching in Luke 4:14—9:50

There are five major teaching sections in Luke 4:14—9:50:

1. The Inaugural Sermon at Nazareth (4:14–30).

2. The Sermon on the Plain (6:20–49).

3. The Teaching concerning John (7:24–35).

198. Ringe, *Luke*, 75.

199. Mary probably accompanies Jesus's brothers as any mother would, i.e., to supervise, protect, etc. Nowhere in the Scriptures is there a testimony of her like that of Jesus's brothers: "For his brothers were not even believing in him" (John 7:5).

4. The Rejection-Day Parables (8:4–21).

5. The Teaching at Caesarea Philippi (9:18–27).

Woven between these sections are works and events accompanied by lesser teaching units. For example, in Luke 8:22–25, Jesus commands the storm to calm. Jesus uses this opportunity to chide the disciples for their lack of faith. Their question about "who" (τίς) Jesus is foreshadows Jesus's question to the disciples later in Luke 9:18. Another example is found in Luke 9:46–48. Jesus responds to an argument between the disciples about who among them was the greatest of the Twelve. Jesus tells his disciples that the least is the greatest in his kingdom (9:48). Of the five major teaching sections in Luke 4:14—9:50, three have already received sufficient discussion. The following analysis will concentrate on the teaching concerning John the Baptist (7:24–35) and the teaching at Caesarea Philippi (9:18–27).

Not all of John's disciples left him to follow Jesus as the two disciples did in John 1:37, Andrew being one of them (John 1:40). Some apparently heard John's message and received his baptism only to depart from the Jordan region and be found by Paul later in Ephesus (Acts 19:1–7). The Pharisees and the scribes even compare John's disciples to Jesus's disciples, indicating some disciples still follow John (Luke 5:33). Why would Jesus permit some of John's disciples to continue as disciples of John? Why would he not challenge them for not leaving John to follow him? On this the Scriptures are silent; however, there are at least two options. First, Jesus may have permitted them to remain with John so that they could care for him during his imprisonment. Second, the work of John and his disciples, mainly the message that they carry, does not stop with the baptism of Jesus. They have a message that is closer than any other to the message of Jesus—"Repent, for the kingdom of heaven is at hand."

In Luke 7:19, John selects two of his disciples while he is in prison to go and inquire about Jesus and his mission.[200] John the Baptist asks two questions (Luke 7:19–20):

1. Is Jesus the one they have been waiting for?

2. Should John and his disciples look for someone else?

---

200. According to Josephus, John was being held at Machaerus some fifteen miles southeast of where the Jordan River connects to the Dead Sea. See Trost, *Who Should Be King in Israel?*, 92–93; Rousseau and Arav, "Machaerus (Hebrew, *Makhwar*)," 187–89; Dvorjetski, *Leisure, Pleasure and Healing*, 172ff.

Jesus answers their questions by performing miracles in their presence. Presumably, John the Baptist had not witnessed any of Jesus's miracles firsthand before being thrown into prison; he had seen the Holy Spirit descending on Jesus at his baptism, and he heard the Father's pronouncement that Jesus is his Son (Luke 3:21–22; John 1:32–34). John's questions reveal a moment of weakness in the life of Israel's greatest prophet. Part of this moment of doubt is attributed to John's perceived incompatibility with his message and the ministry of Jesus. For John, the Messiah's coming has the following characteristics: (1) salvation (Luke 3:6); (2) wrath (Luke 3:7, 9, 17); and (3) the fulfillment of the covenants (Luke 3:8). None of these, from John's perspective, is being fulfilled. He views salvation eschatologically, just like God's wrath; salvation is viewed more as national deliverance from Israel's oppressors, similar to Qumranic expectations.[201] Jesus's response for John is meant to assure him that he is indeed the one they have been waiting for. He quotes Isa 35:5–6 and 61:1, the latter being his text in the sermon at Nazareth (Luke 4:18–19).[202]

Luke 7:24–35 contains a large amount of Jesus's teaching concerning the kingdom of God. Jesus speaks about John's identity and purpose in the redemptive plan of God (7:24–27). He uses the greatness of John to segway into who is the greatest in his kingdom (7:28). Luke includes how Jesus's comparison of John to his genuine disciples is received and rejected (7:29–30). Then, Jesus issues a sharp condemnation on the entire generation, comparing them to children playing songs in a market place. "Luke 7:31–35," writes Tannehill, "is addressed to people who reject both John and Jesus, for opposite reasons (vv. 33–34)."[203] Jesus's concluding remark is entirely related to the reception of the kingdom and the future ministry of Jesus's disciples in proclaiming it. First, consider the comparison:

1. John comes isolated from society → He is rejected → He has a demon.

2. Jesus comes engaged in society → He is rejected → He is a glutton, a drunk, and, worst of all, a friend of tax collectors and sinners.[204]

---

201. See Tso, *Ethics in the Qumran Community*, 148ff.; Lichtenberger, "Messianic Expectations," 9–20.

202. Jesus's report does not include a phrase from Isaiah that may have been particularly important to John and where he was. When the disciples report back to John, there is no mention of freedom for prisoners, as found in Isaiah 61:1.

203. Tannehill, *Luke*, 133.

204. Although Luke does not include it, the Pharisees and scribes ascribed Jesus's

John is characterized by abstaining from certain foods and all alcohol. Jesus does not abstain, and he socializes with the rejected ones of society. Jesus responds saying, "Nevertheless, wisdom is vindicated by all her children" (Luke 7:35). Rindoš points out the connection to the wisdom of God in Luke 11:49. There, the wisdom of God "can send her messengers like prophets."[205] Explaining the difference between Luke 7:35 and 11:49, he writes:

> In Luke 7,35 the divine emissaries, John and Jesus, together with all those who adhere to God's purpose are simply counted among the children of wisdom in contrast to the official religious leaders. In Luke 11,49 the emphasis is on the destiny of emissaries of wisdom who continue to experience the rejection and persecution of prophets from of old.[206]

Despite the rejection Jesus and his disciples experience, God's plan is unwavering. God's vindication of himself through his apostles and prophets is guaranteed.

Luke does not include any geographical references in transitioning from the feeding of the 5,000 to the teaching in Caesarea Philippi (see Matt 16:13). The disciples had previously asked themselves, "Who then is this one, that he even commands the winds and water and they obey him?" (Luke 8:25). Arriving in Caesarea Philippi, Jesus now turns the question on them. In the time since the disciples previously asked the question, they have seen Jesus heal another demoniac (8:26–39), a recently deceased twelve year old girl (8:41, 49–56), and a woman with a long running illness (8:43–48). For the first time in over a year, the Twelve have gone out without Jesus. Though he is not with them, they are accompanied by his power and authority, and they are ready to imitate the ministry they have seen spoken and performed through their teacher (9:1–11). They have also witnessed Jesus feeding over 5,000 people from "no more than five loaves of bread and two fish" (9:12).

Jesus asks two questions. First, "Who do people say that I am?" (9:18). The second question asks the disciples to tell Jesus who they think Jesus is (9:20). The people were puzzled, some supposing Jesus was Elijah

---

capacity to do miracles to his connection with Beezebul, "the ruler of the demons" (ἄρχοντι τῶν δαιμονίων, Matt 12:24).

205. Rindoš, *He of Whom It Is Written*, 187.

206. Ibid.

(see Mal 4:5) or a resurrected (ἀνέστη) prophet (9:19).[207] When Peter answers collectively for the group, he tells Jesus they believe he is "the Christ of God" (τὸν Χριστὸν τοῦ θεοῦ, 9:20). The answer in Matthew is rather emphatic. The personal pronoun σύ is used and placed at the beginning of the sentence, followed by four definite articles: Σὺ εἶ ὁ Χριστὸς ὁ υἱὸς τοῦ θεοῦ τοῦ ζῶντος (Matt 16:16).[208]

This event in the life of Christ is extremely significant, as it contains four firsts:

1. This is the first time God says Jesus is the Christ (Matt 1:16–17). He has previously been identified as the "Lamb of God" by the prophet John (John 1:29) and the Son of God (i.e., Luke 1:32, 35; 3:32). But this is the first time he is called the Christ (ὁ Χριστός).

2. This is the first time Jesus explicitly speaks of his church. Previously, he has spoken about wheat and tares existing side by side in his kingdom until the latter are gathered up and burned (Matt 13:24–30, 36–43). By the way, this is one of the parables that causes the disciples great concern and difficulty in understanding. Here, however, Jesus directly speaks about a new community and his role as its builder. He says, "I will build my church" (οἰκοδομήσω μου τὴν ἐκκλησίαν, Matt 16:18; note the future tense).

3. This is the first time Jesus speaks specifically about his suffering, death, and resurrection (Matt 16:21).

4. This is the first time Jesus teaches on the glory of God (Matt 16:27).

Conduct in Luke 4:14—9:50

The most striking aspect of Jesus's conduct, perhaps in his entire life, is his association with social outcasts who were despised and avoided, especially by the Pharisees and scribes. Matthew, Luke, and Mark contain the narrative of the "large banquet" (δοχὴν μεγάλην, Luke 5:29),[209] which

207. Matthew's account records two other possibilities the crowds were considering, namely John the Baptist and Jeremiah.

208. The use of the restrictive attributive position (i.e., τοῦ θεοῦ τοῦ ζῶντος) is emphatic (Black, *Learn to Read New Testament Greek*, 44). Χριστός normally occurs with the definite article in the NT; exceptions include when it is joined with Ἰησοῦς and when it is a translation (John 1:41; 4:25).

209. Arthur A. Just Jr. says this language is common in Luke, "reflecting the table fellowship language of Luke" and refers to Luke 14:13, 16, and 22:12 (*The Ongoing Feast*, 134).

Jesus attended in his honor (αὐτῷ)[210] at Matthew's home (Matt 9:9–13; Luke 5:27–39). Luke says "there was a large crowd" (ἦν ὄχλος πολύς) made up "of tax collectors and others" (τελωνῶν καὶ ἄλλων, Luke 5:29). The "others" are identified as sinners (ἁμαρτωλοί) in each of the Synoptics as well. Bruce B. Barton, Dave Veerman, and Linda K. Taylor point out how this is a crowd "that Jesus could not reach in the synagogues, for they had been excommunicated because their profession was seen as traitorous against their countrymen."[211] That is the case for the tax collectors. Ἁμαρτωλοί refers to persons characterized by an immoral lifestyle. They are people "of proved dishonesty or followers of suspected and degrading occupations."[212] The sick and needy of society, like the lepers, are the "down and outs" of society; Blomberg says the tax collectors are viewed as the "up and outs."[213]

Jesus's association with these people is driven by his mission as Savior. His conduct is completely different than the Pharisees who scold him for his association with the ceremonially unclean and those, who according to their standards, were morally bankrupt. Daniel J. Scholz writes, "The Jewish social norms of Jesus's day left the call of Levi nothing short of scandalous. . . . In Jewish culture, who you reclined at table with was directly tied to your identity and to the identity of your kinship group."[214] For this reason, the Jews are upset, although mistaken. For them, according to Johnson, "[T]o eat and drink with 'sinners and tax collectors' meant that one shared their indifference or defiance of the codes of holiness."[215] But Jesus does not share their indifference or default on his standard of holiness (Matt 5:48; Luke 6:36). He is drawn to them as their Savior. And they are drawn to him. Jesus is exceptionally popular, especially with this group of people. It is the tax collectors and

210. Eugene LaVerdiere believes the banquet is not to "honor Jesus" so much as it is "to enable Jesus to invite tax collectors and others . . . so they could become his followers along with Levi" (*Dining in the Kingdom of God*, 42). Of course, this is possible; however, one might expect one of the co-laborer pronouns if this were the case, such as σύν. More likely, Jesus defers to Matthew, his host, who wants to honor him, knowing that by doing so he will have an amazing opportunity to share the gospel and Matthew's testimony with his other guests. Jesus did allow people to honor him in certain ways, such as the woman who wiped his feet with perfume and tears.

211. Barton et al., *Luke*, 130.

212. Lachs, *The Gospels*, 168.

213. Blomberg, *Jesus and the Gospels*, 164.

214. Scholz, *Jesus*, 10.

215. Johnson, *Prophetic Jesus, Prophetic Church*, 142.

sinners, all of them (πᾶς), who draw near to Jesus in Luke 15:1. Despite the type of people Jesus associated with, his conduct never deviated in holiness. Accusations were obviously made, as they are in Luke 7:34, but they never carried any weight.

Luke 8:22–56 contains three demonstrations of Jesus's power. Marshall writes:

> Jesus is revealed to his disciples as the possessor of divine power over the elements, demons and physical evil, including death itself. Thus to the witness of Jesus by word is added that by power, and the whole sequence prepares the way for the confession of Jesus as Messiah in 9:18–27. The emphasis, however, is not simply on the power of Jesus; the mighty works reveal his compassion and willingness to save in situations of human need.[216]

The four demonstrations of Jesus's power over nature, demons, and infirmities are aimed at demonstrating to his disciples and Israel as a whole that Jesus is the Son of God (referring to his deity) and the legitimate heir to David's throne (Luke 1:32–35). He is, answering John the Baptist's questions, the one all Israel and all the world has been expecting (Luke 7:20).

Part of the complete training that Jesus mentions in Luke 6:40 is a proper understanding of his identity. The calling of the disciples is accompanied both by a change in a disciple's understanding about the identity of Jesus and a demonstration of the distinctiveness of his identity (cf. Luke 5:1–11; John 1:43–51).[217] Interestingly, Peter and the disciples did not have a comprehensive understanding about Jesus's identity before he commanded them to follow him (Matt 5:18–22; Luke 5:27–28). Nor did

216. Marshall, *The Gospel of Luke*, 332.

217. Andrew had already been drawn to the preaching of John the Baptist (John 1:40). The first person that he leads to Jesus is his brother, Simon. At this point, Jesus had issued no invitations for disciples to leave everything and follow him. In the "second call" of the early disciples, Peter shows a change in his understanding of Jesus's identity (Luke 5:1–11). Peter is asked to push out from the water a small distance, probably anchoring the boat with his own feet as Jesus teaches from inside the vessel. After Jesus teaches, he tells Peter to take the boat to deeper waters to fish. Between his hesitation to do so and his reaction at the fullness of his nets, Peter moves from calling Jesus "Master" (ἐπιστάτα, v. 5) to "Lord" (κύριε, v. 8). Alfred Plummer says, "The change from ἐπιστάτα is remarkable, and quite in harmony with the change of circumstances" (*A Critical and Exegetical Commentary on the Gospel of S. Luke*, 145). For Plummer, the title "Master" corresponds to the command; "Lord" corresponds to the sinfulness of Peter and the sinlessness that Peter recognized in Jesus. His understanding of the identity of Jesus was already changing and developing.

they have such a knowledge before being selected and named his apostles (Luke 6:12–16). Coming to Jesus, one of the elements of likeness education found in the conclusion to the SOP, undoubtedly involves gaining a proper understanding of who he is. These four miracles in Luke 8:22–56 are used to show the disciples who Jesus is.

Likeness education is not about making someone take on the attributes of God, just his character. It is his character found in these three episodes that most concerns the investigation at hand. As Marshall points out, these three episodes "reveal his compassion and willingness to save in situations of human need."[218] Peter recalls that this event takes place after the rejection and Jesus's long day of teaching in parables, as recorded in Matt 12–13 (Mark 4:35). A long day of teaching, especially one with an intensity matched only by the so-called "Busy Tuesday," caused Jesus to be extremely tired. Morris says he "would have been weary after a full day's teaching."[219] Weariness is an element of Jesus's life and ministry that comes up often. He is busy doing the work the Father has given him to do, never wasting a moment.

Purpose in Luke 4:14—9:50

Prior to Luke 4:14, descriptions of Jesus's purpose are found primarily in the announcements concerning his birth. Coming out of the wilderness, having just been tempted intensely by the devil, Jesus begins his ministry. When Jesus returns from the wilderness, he goes straight to Galilee and begins teaching in the synagogues.[220] The first synagogue he teaches at is in Nazareth. The passage that Jesus teaches from is Isa 61:1, indicating:

1. The presence of the Holy Spirit upon him and its anointing.

2. The purpose of Jesus's work, which involves preaching good news to the poor and doing miraculous works.

---

218. Marshall, *The Gospel of Luke*, 332.

219. Morris, *Luke*, 169.

220. Later, Jesus returns to where John the Baptist is. The beginning of his call of the disciples begins by returning to the Jordan. When he returns, John reminds everyone of who Jesus is—"the Lamb of God who is taking away the sins of the world" (John 1:29). John also reminds every one of the descent of the Holy Spirit upon Jesus, which he witnessed forty days prior (John 1:32), and he testifies that this is "the Son of God" (John 1:34).

Four groups of people are mentioned in Luke 4:18–19: (1) the poor (πτωχός), (2) the captives (αἰχμάλωτος), (3) the blind (τυφλός), and (4) the oppressed (τεθραυσμένοι).

In order to understand the type of people Jesus's ministry engages, consider the first group—the poor.[221] This is a group Luke gives special attention to. This word appears in Luke twice as many times (10x) as it does in Matthew and Mark (5x each).[222] Ekkehard W. and Wolfgang Stegemann say πτωχός refers to those "who live on the verge or even below minimum existence,"[223] someone who is "utterly destitute."[224] It can have a non-literal meaning, such as someone being spiritually poor. In this sense, the poor in the OT are characterized by their "weakness and dependence on God,"[225] like those who Jesus refers to in the SOM—"the poor in spirit" (οἱ πτωχοὶ τῷ πνεύματι, Matt 5:3). This is one of those places where Jesus and the Scriptures are intentionally ambiguous so that both groups (i.e., those who are literally poor and those who are spiritually poor) are referred to without any issue. Both interpretations represent people having serious need of assistance.

Having read from the Isaiah scroll, Jesus tells the people something they have never heard before. He says, "Today this Scripture has been fulfilled" (Luke 4:21).[226] Yen writes:

> When Jesus applies the prophecy of Luke 4:18–19 to himself, he clearly declares his own prophetic role. He again affirms this when he says to the crowd: "I must preach the good news of the kingdom of God to other cities also; for I was sent for this purpose" (4:43).[227]

Jesus is resolute about this purpose of preaching the good news of the kingdom to the poor, captives, blind, and oppressed. As Jesus says in Luke 19:10, his purpose for coming is to seek and to save those who are lost,

---

221. For a discussion on τυφλός, see Chapter 2.

222. Bosch, *Transforming Mission*, 99.

223. Stegemann and Stegemann, *The Jesus Movement*, 89.

224. Blomberg, *Neither Poverty nor Riches*, 128.

225. Ireland, *Stewardship and the Kingdom of God*, 169.

226. Dennis M. Sweetland says that "prophecies found in Isaiah play an extremely important role in Luke-Acts" ("Luke the Christian," 53). Luke, he shows, also uses prophecies found in Malachi, Micah, Joel, Amos, 2 Samuel, Psalms, and Deuteronomy.

227. Yen, *The Lucan Journey*, 85.

the sick who need a physician and not those who consider themselves healthy (Luke 5:31).

The second most striking part of Jesus's declaration in the synagogue is his identification of his own ministry with great prophets like Elijah and Elisha[228] and the way God used them to reach out to those outside the fold of Israel (Luke 4:25–27). Luke does not record Jesus's instructions to the twelve disciples before sending them out that prohibited them from going to the Gentiles or the Samaritans (even though Jesus did; cf. Matt 10:5 and John 4:4). Jesus's purpose has been defined from his birth (and before), and this purpose clearly involves being the Savior of the Gentiles in fulfillment of the OT Scriptures (e.g., Isa 9:1–2, גְּלִיל הַגּוֹיִם [Γαλιλαία τῶν ἐθνῶν, LXX]; Matt 4:12–17; John 10:16, ἄλλα πρόβατα ἔχω).[229] During his earthly ministry, Jesus concentrates on giving the good news to Israel, not to Gentiles. Nevertheless, the latter are not excluded from his work. If the disciples had never seen Jesus interact with or give the good news to Gentiles, it would have damaged their motivation and willingness to take the gospel to the ends of the earth. Peter is hesitant in Acts 10 to accept God's command to reach beyond the nation of Israel with the gospel, despite having the same vision three times (Acts 10:16). He even tells God, "By no means whatsoever [will I do what you say]! I have never eaten anything unholy or unclean!" (Acts 10:14). It is not only the vision that softens Peter's heart to reaching out to the Gentiles; it is also the example that he has from the time he spent with Jesus.

---

228. Koet, "Isaiah in Luke-Acts," 59.

229. See Bird, *Jesus and the Origins of the Gentile Mission*; Köstenberger and O'Brien, *Salvation to the Ends of the Earth*, 83–86. Little justly says Jesus is not aloof to the inclusion of the Gentiles in the redemptive plan. He writes:

> "In reality, his teachings prepare the way for it (Mt. 8:10–12; 24:14; 25:31–46; 26:13; Mark 13:9–10; Luke 13:28–30), his parables allude to it (Mt. 21:33–44; 22:1–14; Mark 12:1–11; Luke 10:30–37; 14:16–24; 20:9–18), his consistent openness to Gentiles assumes it (Mt. 8:5–7; 15:21–28; Mark 7:24–30; Luke 7:1–10; John 4:1–54), and his post-resurrection accounts confirm it (Mt. 28:19–20; Mark 16:15; Luke 24:46–47; Ac. 1:8). In fashion, Jesus set the stage for Gentile mission subsequent to his earthly ministry." (*Mission in the Way of Paul*, 80)

Faith in Luke 4:14–9:50

Matthew, Luke, and Mark include the healing of a demon-possessed boy (Matt 17:14–20; Luke 9:37–43a; Mark 9:14–29). Luke leaves out Jesus's answer to the disciples' question, "Why could we not drive it out?" (Matt 17:19). Matthew, however, includes it: "Because of the littleness of your faith" (Matt 17:20). Ian G. Wallis says the disciples are already trying to imitate Jesus:

> One of the distinguishing features about this miracle is that it records an attempt by the disciples to put into practice the commission they had received earlier to assist Jesus in making the kingdom known through proclamation and demonstration.[230]

Mark includes, "All things are possible to him who believes" (Mark 9:23). Why did the disciples, who had previously exercised the power and authority to cast out demons, fail to cast out the demon that was in control of this young boy?

Jesus gives his disciples "power and authority" (δύναμιν καὶ ἐξουσίαν) over all the demons and a capacity to heal people from their infirmities in Luke 9:1. This power comes directly from the Holy Spirit. Even though the Twelve are not baptized with the Holy Spirit until Acts 2, they receive the Holy Spirit[231] in a manner similar to the prophets and judges found in the Old Testament. This is a temporary endowment of the Holy Spirit, whereas in Acts 2:1–4 (cf. Acts 1:8) it is a permanent giving of the Spirit as a result of the commencement of the New Covenant. The Twelve receive power and authority in Luke 9. While there is no similar statement in Luke 10:1–16, seventy-two additional persons apparently receive this same power and authority, since they report to Jesus that the demons are subject to them (Luke 10:17). After the journeys of the Twelve in Luke 9:1–2 and the seventy-two in 10:1 were complete, the power and authority recedes or is taken away. Jesus tells the disciples in Acts 1:8 they will receive power (λήμψεσθε δύναμιν) and will be his witnesses (ἔσεσθέ μου μάρτυρες), both referring to an event in the future.

If they needed to receive this power again in Acts, why would it be difficult to suppose Jesus issued his power and authority only for the duration of their journeys in Luke? If this is the case, they may have assumed

---

230. Wallis, *The Faith of Jesus Christ*, 28.

231. Black, *Luke*, 182; Hooker, "John's Baptism: A Prophetic Sign," 34; Warrington, *The Message of the Holy Spirit*, 62ff.; Yen, *The Lucan Journey*, 165.

that they could cast out the demon on the basis of this authority alone (which they no longer possessed). Peter, for example, recalls that Jesus told them, "This kind is not able to come out by anything except prayer" (Mark 9:29). Matthew records the answer to their question on why they could not do it: "Because of the tininess of your faith" (Matt 17:20). These two statements coupled together indicate that the disciples failed to even offer up prayers on behalf on the young boy. They depended instead on what they knew they were previously able to do, and thus did not trust in God to cast the demon out. The disciples, even at this point in Jesus's ministry, having spent over a year with him, still lacked the faith that Jesus possessed. This is an area that he has to work on with them. They are not "fully trained" at this point. They are not like him, who never once failed to cast out a demon from a person that was brought to him. They are not like him—yet.

An Analysis of Luke 9:51—24:53

Imitation in Luke 9:51—24:53

There are two key areas in this period of Jesus's ministry concerning imitation in need of analysis here. The first deals with the way Jesus presented the Pharisees and the scribes as an anti-example for his disciples and the crowds. The second concerns Jesus's own personal example in Luke 22:14–23//John 13:1ff.

Jesus's use of an anti-example is important in likeness education. When Paul gives examples of how disciples are to imitate his conduct, he generally provides examples of the conduct that they should not follow as well (e.g., Phil 2:19–30; 3:17–19). The Pharisees and scribes are usually cast in a negative light throughout the Gospels. Nicodemus, in John 3:1–21, is really the only exception, since he reappears in John 7:50–52 and 19:39–42, defending Jesus and later coming to care for his body. Gamaliel is presented in a fairly positive light. Although nothing is said of his acceptance of the Jesus movement, he comes to its defense with sound wisdom in Acts 5:34. Jesus is clear that the scribes and Pharisees lack a righteousness sufficient to gain entry into his kingdom (Matt 5:20). They are the ones opposing the work of Jesus Christ, working behind the scenes to trick and trap him (e.g., Matt 19:3).

Jesus's condemnation of the Pharisees reaches its height on "Busy Tuesday" (Matt 23:1–39; Luke 20:45–47; Mark 12:38–40). Matthew indicates that Jesus's teaching concerning the scribes and Pharisees is given to the crowds and disciples (Matt 23:1) while teaching at the temple (Matt 24:1). They are his chief example on how not to live. They are not Jesus's primary audience; the crowds and disciples are. The scribes and the Pharisees are his primary example, or, as Keener calls it, "a negative paradigm."[232] Jesus only uses the Gentiles as an example on occasion (e.g., Matt 20:25; Luke 22:25; Mark 10:42). For what does Jesus criticize the scribes and Pharisees? What exactly is their anti-example?

Matthew 23:1–39 is one of the longest teaching discourses in the New Testament. It deals entirely with the scribes and the Pharisees. Leon Morris writes, "There is nothing comparable to this sustained denunciation of the scribes and Pharisees in any of the other Gospels."[233] During this denunciation, he refers to them as "hypocrites," "blind fools," "blind guides," and the "offspring of vipers." In general, they represent exactly what Jesus does not want his disciples to look like or become. First, consider what Jesus says about the teaching of the Pharisees. In the SOM, Jesus issues a striking condemnation of the pharisaic interpretation of Torah. Throughout the sermon, Jesus repeatedly cites the teachings of the Pharisees and their interpretations (e.g., Matt 5:21, 27, 38, 43). Sometimes, their interpretations are not included. For example, in Matt 5:27–28, Matthew only records the Torah citation (Exod 20:14; Deut 5:18). He follows this with Jesus's correct interpretation: "But I say to you. . . ." (Matt 5:28). Matthew is not correcting what God has said in Exodus and Deuteronomy. There is a gap in what Matthew includes. Basically, Matthew leaves out the Pharisees' interpretation of those passages and concentrates on Jesus's interpretation (cf. Matt 5:43). In Matt 23:4, Jesus refers to their teaching as heavy burdens (φορτία βαρέα). The Pharisees gave no consideration to "mercy or love as the supreme criterion of what God wants."[234] When Jesus tells them to do and keep "all that they tell you," he cannot mean everything. Jesus has clearly led his disciples to not do everything that the Pharisees told people to do (cf. Matt 15:1–3; Luke 6:1–11; 7:36–50). Jesus must intend for them to do and keep everything the Pharisees and scribes tell them that is correctly interpreted from

232. Keener, *A Commentary on the Gospel of Matthew*, 536.

233. Morris, *The Gospel according to Matthew*, 569.

234. Byrne, *Lifting the Burden*, 171.

Torah. Moreover, he certainly intends for them to have a different relationship between teaching and works, specifically one where the latter corresponds to and reflects the former.

Thomas G. Long says, "According to Jesus, the basic problem with the scribes and the Pharisees is not with what they teach; it is with what they do or fail to do."[235] Concerning their conduct, in Matt 23:3, Jesus says the Pharisees' teachings did not carry into how they live. Jesus tells the disciples and those in the crowd, "Do not act according to (κατά) their works" (Matt 23:3). The use of κατά signals the standards by which the Pharisees were living (i.e., their own, not God's);[236] and, even then, they did not live up to them.

Jesus reveals the underlying purpose for everything that the scribes and Pharisees do in Matt 23:5—recognition. He says, "They do all their works to be recognized by people." Jesus lists six things in Matt 23:5–7 that they do:

1. They make their phylacteries elaborate.

2. They lengthen their tassels.

3. They love the seats of honor in people's homes.

4. They love the chief seats in the synagogues.

5. They love respectful greetings when they are out in the market.

6. They love the title Rabbi when they are in the synagogues.

The use of phylacteries and tassels, for example, was intended to remind a man of his covenant responsibilities to God (based on Deut 6:8; 11:18). These are the three leather pouches (for the hand, arm, and forehead) that Jewish men put tiny notes of Scripture inside. Instead of using them in humility, they developed a standard that one's flashiness spoke to his righteousness and holiness.[237] In place of preparing people for the kingdom and concentrating on upholding Israel's covenant obedience (see Lev 26; Deut 28), Jesus says the scribes and Pharisees prevented people from entering God's kingdom (Matt 23:13). Instead of being reproducers of faithful servants of God, they had their own perverted Great Commission—"You travel around on sea and land to make a single proselyte," not disciples (Matt 23:15).

235. Long, *Matthew*, 259.
236. Bruner, *Matthew, A Commentary*, 433.
237. Pickup, "Matthew's and Mark's Pharisees," 107.

In the middle of Jesus's teaching, he makes a distinct application for the crowds and disciples. He tells them not to be like the Pharisees. His disciples should not be called by titles, and they should not call anyone else, among themselves, by titles. It is to his disciples that Jesus says, "But, you, don't ever let people call you 'Rabbi'" (Matt 23:8a). Immediately after prohibiting it, he tells them why: "Because one is your teacher, and you all are just brothers and sisters" (Matt 23:8b). The next prohibition tells the disciples to not call anyone on the face of the earth "Father" (Matt 23:9a). Why? He answers, "Because one is your Father—the Father who is in heaven" (Matt 23:9b). The final prohibition returns again to what the disciples should not allow themselves to be called by anyone. Jesus says, "And don't let anyone ever call you 'Leader'" (Matt 23:10a). Again, why? The answer Jesus gives is, "Because one is your leader, and that's the Christ" (Matt 23:10b). Jesus tells his disciples that they should seek greatness according to the new standard they have been given by him, namely servant-leadership.

Servant-leadership is exactly what Jesus demonstrates on the eve of his crucifixion. The Farewell Discourse (John 13–17) is a rather lengthy section of Scripture devoted only to a few hours of teaching. It is the greatest amount of space devoted to the shortest period of time in all the Gospels. John records the historic act of the one and only Son of God assuming the role of a household servant, but he does not record the circumstances following the foot-washing scene. Luke, on the other hand, does.

After supper, John says Jesus "laid aside his outer robe, and taking a towel, he girded himself" (John 13:4). Andrew Lincoln says Jesus did not just do the work of a servant, but he took on the dress of a servant.[238] Then, Jesus filled a bowl with water and washed the disciples' feet (John 13:5). Lincoln describes with vividness:

> Most footwashing in the ancient world was a menial task. It involved washing off not just dust and mud but also the remains of human excrement (which was tipped out of houses into the streets) and animal waste (which was left on country roads and town streets). The task of doing this is an act of hospitality to honour guests was therefore normally assigned to slaves

---

238. Lincoln, *The Gospel according to St. John*, 367. See also Carson, *The Gospel according to John*, 462–63.

or servants of low status, particularly females, so much so that footwashing was virtually synonymous with slavery.[239]

Jesus's purpose in doing this act of service was not to honor the disciples; he did it in response to their quarrel about greatness. In vv. 13–14, Jesus says, "You call me Teacher and Lord, and you are correct because I am. If then I washed your feet, you should likewise wash one another's." In v. 15, he says that he gave them an example "so that (ἵνα) you should do also, exactly as (καθώς) I did unto you." The ἵνα clause indicates the purpose. The use of καθώς, a characteristic of John's Gospel, indicates the exactness there should be between the conduct of Jesus and the conduct of his disciples. Partaking of the bread and wine is not the only thing the disciples were to do this night forward in remembrance of Christ. They were commanded to live the rest of their days as slaves one to another.

Luke adds that a "dispute" arose among the disciples. What about? On the eve of Jesus's betrayal and crucifixion, the disciples are inclined once again to fight among themselves about who is the greatest in the kingdom. They had this heated discussion among themselves before (Matt 18:1–5; Luke 9:46–48; Mark 9:33–37). Previously, Jesus had used a visual aid, a living example, to illustrate the way his kingdom works. He stood a child beside him, and he told his disciples that the greatest is one who receives a child in his name (Luke 9:46–48). He also told them that unless they became like that child, they would not enter into his kingdom. Adding to this, he said the one who humbles his or herself to the level and stature of a child is the one who is the greatest. The disciples did not receive Jesus's teaching. They did not hear it and do it. On the eve of Jesus's betrayal, knowing his time is limited and knowing the absolute importance of this kingdom lesson, he resorts to a final example, the greatest example ever. It is imperative that the disciples never have this argument again. In fact, the mission depends on their unity.[240]

Conduct in Luke 9:51—24:53

Jesus's living example of servant-leadership has already been discussed. While there are many aspects of Jesus's conduct that can be considered here, none pose greater difficulty to likeness education than the apparent

239. Lincoln, *The Gospel according to St. John*, 367.

240. Hudgins, "An Application of Discourse Analysis Methodology," 35–36.

anger Jesus demonstrates when he scolds the Pharisees (Matt 23:1–39; discussed earlier) and drives the traders from the Temple as recorded in Matt 21:12–17, Luke 19:45–48, Mark 11:15–19, and John 2:13–22.[241] Jesus enters Jerusalem on Sunday and goes straight to the Temple (Luke 19:28–29, 37, 41, 45). William S. Kurz views Luke 19:45–48 as transitory, foreshadowing the showdown with the religious elite on Tuesday.[242] This is not the first time that Jesus has entered the Temple and caused a scene. John records Jesus's first Passover visit to Jerusalem since the beginning of his ministry.[243]

What Jesus found during this first Passover is strikingly similar to what he found on the week of his crucifixion. First, there were people in the Temple selling animals for sacrifice. What is striking here is not that animals were being sold and provided for sacrifice in Jerusalem. It might seem striking that they were doing so "in the Temple" (ἐν τῷ ἱερῷ, John 2:14), that is in the court of the Gentiles.[244] Michael F. Patella says the merchants "are not out of place in conducting their affairs in this area;" the area was "constructed for this very purpose."[245] There were people inside the Temple changing money, presumably from Roman currency to Jewish currency, for the payment of the Temple tax.[246] As Larry Woodruff points out, the temple, which was designed for the holiness of God, was turned into a common marketplace.[247] Even though the glory of God had not dwelt there since the days of Ezekiel (see Ezek 8–11), Jesus's anger was aroused. It was not just how the Temple looked, though. His anger is lit because of the abuses that were undergirding all the practices in the Temple. They had turned it into a robber's hide-out (σπήλαιον λῃστῶν, Matt 21:13). When people thought about the Temple, they would not

241. See also Luke 11:37–45, where one lawyer demonstrates that Jesus was willing to insult the religious elite of his day when their actions were reprehensible.

242. Kurz, *Reading Luke-Acts*, 54. Discussions about the relationship of this passage in the structure of Luke, i.e., whether or not it concludes the travel narrative to Jerusalem or begins the Jerusalem ministry, are important but irrelevant here. For one analysis, see Denaux, *Studies in the Gospel of Luke*, 24–26.

243. The evidence supporting this as a distinct event is summarized by Bock: "John's use of Psalm 69 and the way his placement works in the account suggest a distinct event, especially as it is linked to John 2:23–25" (*Luke*, IVP, 316).

244. Black, *Luke*, 317.

245. Patella, *Gospel according to Luke*, 128.

246. Black writes, "[T]he temple tax had to be paid with a 'half-shekel,' a coin only minted in Tyre at the time, thus necessitating the money exchanging" (*Luke*, 318).

247. Woodruff, *The Proclamation of Jesus*, 290.

have thought about it as a place of prayer so much as they would have remembered the hustle and the bustle, not to mention the corruption if they ever got jipped when exchanging currency. Sadly, there is not much difference from the Temple the glory left in Ezek 8–11 and the Temple Jesus visited for just over thirty years.

Jesus's outburst seems harsh. He pours out all the money changers' coins and flips their tables over (John 2:15). John records that Jesus made a scourging instrument and used it to chase everyone (πάντας) involved out of the Temple. His reaction is uniform toward both the money changers and sellers. Why was he so angry? Kathleen A. Cahalan says "the very idea that God's love or favor could be bought through animal sacrifice infuriates him."[248] This is not the reason. Animal sacrifice is commanded by God under the Mosaic covenant, as is the Passover, which was made a perpetual practice even before the ratification of the Mosaic covenant. Moreover, Jesus and his disciples participated, as they should, in the sacrifices according to the Law. If this infuriated him so much, he would never have allowed his disciples to do so. Until the ratification of the New Covenant (only a few days away from Palm Sunday), his disciples (and all the Jewish people everywhere) were obligated by covenant to offer these sacrifices, albeit with a correct disposition and right standing with their God. The Temple was never supposed to have vending or greed and gross profit by the priests. It is this perversion that angers Jesus.[249]

Bruce Chilton mentions the actions of other Jewish teachers in the first century found in Josephus, as well as regulations taught by different Pharisees current in Jesus's day. His conclusion is, "Jesus' action seems almost tame; after all, what he did was expel some vendors, an act less directly threatening to priestly and secular authorities than what some earlier Pharisees had done."[250] Making a scourging instrument, calling the culprits "robbers,"[251] and flipping over tables is far from nice. These two events describe the angriest Jesus ever was during his earthly ministry. Andrew D. Lester says Matthew, Luke, and Peter [via Mark] had

---

248. Cahalan, *Introducing the Practice of Ministry*, 83.

249. Patella, *Gospel according to Luke*, 128.

250. Chilton, "The Trial of Jesus Reconsidered," 488ff. One of the more interesting pharisaic prohibitions is no purses were to be permitted inside the Temple walls (ibid., 492).

251. Either those selling animals were charging more money than they should, or the money changers were charging an abusive exchange rate, or both.

their concept of emotions, especially Jesus's emotions, challenged by what they saw, and they opted to leave out the more colorful language John employs.[252] Punning on the acronym "WWJD," David T. Lamb asks, "WWJW?," that is "Who would Jesus whip?"[253] He says the Synoptics do not play down his anger; instead, they all "apparently thought it was important for the anger of Jesus to be emphasized, since all four of them include the incident."[254]

Outside of this event, there are two key texts to briefly consider concerning anger in the Gospels: (1) Mark 3:5, and (2) Matt 5:22, each appearing earlier in the ministry of Jesus. In the SOM, Jesus teaches his disciples and the crowds about unjustified anger: "But I say to you, 'Everyone who is angry with his or her brother without cause will be guilty before the court.'" Black and I, in a forthcoming chapter on the originality of the textual variant εἰκῇ, have argued that anger is a legitimate emotion for the followers of Jesus.[255] Jesus does not prohibit all forms of anger; he prohibits anger that is unjustified or "without cause (or, reason)." Peter gives another glimpse of Jesus's anger in the messages Mark transcribed. In Mark 3:5, Jesus looks around at the people "with anger" (μετ' ὀργῆς). This is the only Gospel text that explicitly says Jesus got angry.[256]

Likeness education involves becoming like Jesus entirely and being conformed to his person as described in the Gospels. This means the

252. Lester, *The Angry Christian*, 163.

253. Lamb, *God Behaving Badly*, 42.

254. Ibid., 43.

255. So why would such a tiny word be omitted from certain manuscripts, which are confined really to a single geographical region? The Gospel authors did not struggle with Jesus's person or his teaching on anger. Instead, the struggle came years later as part of the church wrestled with it and eventually incorrectly succumbed to the view that the two were incompatible. The answer provided in the essay mentioned below is Jesus's teaching on righteous anger was seen as too indulgent to anger in the eyes of some ancient scribes, and, its modern-day absence from the majority of Bible translations is due to an unjustified preference given to 01 and B. See Black and Hudgins, "Jesus on Anger (Matt 5,22a)," 91–104.

256. Saussy, *The Gift of Anger*, 95. Boring and Craddock say the absence in Matthew and Luke of Jesus's anger is attributed to them viewing this as problematic (*People's New Testament Commentary*, 116). They argue this from the post-twentieth-century perception that Matthew and Luke write after Mark. Following the Patristic evidence for Matthean priority and that Luke followed Matthew, it is understandable why Mark includes it—Peter recognizes the importance of this emotion in Jesus's ministry, recognizes that Matthew and Luke have not explicitly stated it and thus inserts it into his messages delivered at Rome.

disciples were being trained in how to be righteously angry while tempered by the meekness and gentleness Isaiah speaks of describing Jesus (see Isa 42:3; repeated by Matthew in 12:20). He is described as being so gentle that he could walk past a bruised reed and it would not break off; he could walk past a dimly burning wick, a candle that was just about to extinguish, and it would not be put out. The whole range of Jesus's emotions and character are included in likeness education, not just the one's convenient to twenty-first century social norms and modern-day culture.

Love in Luke 9:51—24:53

The Gospel of Luke is not silent on demonstrations of love. On the contrary, every single healing and miracle in the Gospel is a demonstration of Jesus's love. It is his love that causes him to meet the needs of the people he encounters.[257] No Gospel reveals the love of Jesus more than the one penned by John.[258] The Gospel authors even stress Jesus's love for the worst and detestable of society, including Gentiles (e.g., Luke 7:1–10; 8:26–39; 17:11–21). However, Luke does not expressly communicate Jesus's love, as John does. Matthew and Luke do point out a related emotion—Jesus's compassion. For example, when Jesus returns from a moment of solitude following John's murder, he travels across the Sea of Galilee again. When he goes ashore, Matthew writes, "He saw a large crowd and he had compassion on them (ἐσπλαγχνίσθη ἐπ' αὐτοῖς)" (Matt 14:14). Also, when Jesus enters Nain, Jesus sees a widow whose only son had died. Luke writes, "When the Lord saw her, he had compassion on her (ἐσπλαγχνίσθη ἐπ' αὐτῇ)" (Luke 7:13).

This expression is common in the Gospels. Alfredo Sampaio Costa helps to show where the expression is used in the Gospels:

> Esta expresión es aplicada sólo a Dios y principalmente a Jesús: cuando Jesucristo mira la multitud cansada y sin pastor (Mt 9, 27.36), se encuentra con el leproso, el ciego, el paralítico (Mt 14, 14; Mt 9, 27; Mc 1, 41), con la viuda de Naím, enterrando su hijo (Lc 7, 13).[259]

257. For example, Tiegreen says the feeding of the 4,000 (Mark 8:2) "wasn't just for the purpose of astounding the people with a miracle. It met a need" (*Feeling Like God*, 125. For an examination of four demonstrations of Jesus's compassion in Luke, see Sam, *The Love Commandment*," 70–82.

258. See, for example, John 11:3; 13:34–35; cf. 1 John 4:19.

259. Costa, "Compasión," 357.

The use of the verb σπλαγχνίζομαι is confined to the Gospels, usually with Jesus as its subject.[260] The verb, says Keri Wyatt Kent, means "to be deeply moved with compassion."[261] Another proposed translation is "his heart went out to the people."[262] Richard A. Hughes says translations like these do not even capture what Jesus felt, writing, the phrase means "hit in the guts."[263] Walter Brueggemann et al. add, "The feeling described is more than a superficial kind of sympathy—Jesus is deeply moved."[264] It is Jesus's love for all peoples that causes his heart to break for others. In Luke, this verb always appears with εἶδον.[265] This is a deep, deep emotion Jesus feels for people in dire situations and grave need. His compassion is very important for his earliest followers. Paul is heavily influenced by the compassion of Jesus. For example, he tells the Philippians not just that he longs for them (ἐπιποθῶ), but that he longs for them with "the compassions of Christ Jesus" (ἐν σπλάγχνοις Χριστοῦ Ἰησοῦ, Phil 1:8).[266]

Another event demonstrating Jesus's love for people is the account of his interaction with the rich young ruler (Matt 19:16–30; Luke 18:18–34; Mark 10:17–31). While Luke says nothing directly about Jesus's emotions in the conversation, Mark adds, "Jesus looked at him and loved him" (Mark 10:21). This is the first and only time Peter recalls Jesus loving someone in his messages delivered in Rome.[267] Voorwinde says

260. Cachia, *The Image of the Good Shepherd*, 87. He believes this is an evidence of Jesus's divinity, saying it "characterizes the divine nature of his acts" (ibid.). Indeed, God is characterized as the God of mercy. The standard Jesus issues in the SOP is God's mercy (Luke 6:36). Disciples are to be merciful to the measure that God himself exercises mercy. Again, Jesus does with perfection that which he commands his disciples to do. See also Eph 2:4.

261. Kent, *Deeper into the Word*, 44.

262. Ryken et. al. (eds.), "Mercy," 547–48.

263. Hughes, *Lament*, 52.

264. Brueggemann et al., *Texts for Preaching*, 150.

265. Reiling and Swellengrebel, *Translator's Handbook on the Gospel of Luke*, 380. See Yen, *The Lucan Journey*, 300.

266. Wenham, *Paul*, 351–52. From where did this influence come? There are four possibilities: (1) Paul learned of Jesus's compassion from eyewitness testimony, such as when he was in Jerusalem; (2) Paul learned of Jesus's compassion from his use of Matthew's Gospel; (3) Paul learned of Jesus's compassion directly from the Lord, either prophetically or through his three-year period in Arabia (Gal 1:17); or (4) a mixture of two or more of the above.

267. John Bowman says this "may well be a Petrine reminiscence" (*Gospel of Mark*, 213). James R. Beck incorrectly says this is the only example where "the Gospel records explicitly state that Jesus loved a specific individual" (*Jesus and Personality Theory*,

Jesus gives him more than "a fleeting glance," adding, "the Greek word (*emblepō*) suggests that he looked intently."[268] Why does Peter share how Jesus felt toward the rich young ruler? According to Voorwinde, "There was something about the young man that was deeply appealing to Jesus."[269] John R. Donahue and Daniel J. Harrington say it is due to "the sincerity and integrity" of the young ruler.[270] More likely, Peter just adds this, perhaps as a contrast to the sadness with which the ruler departs from Jesus (Mark 10:22). Imagine Jesus loving someone and that person walking away from him, turning down the invitation to follow him. Voorwinde adds, "Because he loves this young man Jesus is not afraid to challenge him. The words of v. 21 are not meant to put him off, but they do lay bare the true state of his soul."[271] It is Jesus's love that leads to his declaration, "Still there is one thing you lack . . ." (Luke 18:22). Jesus's love is what leads to confrontation, similar to "speaking the truth with love" (ἐν ἀγάπῃ) in Eph 4:15.

Perseverance, Persecutions, and Sufferings in Luke 9:51—24:53

Perseverance is a significant topic toward the end of Jesus's ministry, especially the last week of his life which makes up about thirty percent of the Gospels. In Luke 21, Jesus speaks of the trials and persecutions his disciples will face in the future. In v. 12, he tells them that before the natural disasters of the last days occur, people will lay their hands on the disciples (ἐπιβαλοῦσιν ἐφ᾽ ὑμᾶς τὰς χεῖρας αὐτῶν) and persecute (διώξουσιν) them. Some suggest the subject of the verbs is unnamed in each case because Jesus is talking about persecution in general.[272] However, the

---

149). The problem is in the distinction which he and many other scholars perceive between ἀγαπάω and φιλέω. He views the statement in Mark differently than John's statements in 13:23; 19:26; 21:7, and 20, as if in Mark the statement is spoken by Jesus. It could just as easily be said that nowhere in the Gospels does it explicitly state that Jesus loved someone since it says nowhere, "And, Jesus said, 'I love you.'" The disciples do explicitly state Jesus's love for an individual, both in Mark 10:21 and the verses cited from John. That's exactly how the disciples perceived Jesus's interaction, Peter with the rich young ruler and John with himself.

268. Voorwinde, *Jesus's Emotions in the Gospels*, 109.

269. Ibid.

270. Donahue and Harrington, *Gospel of Mark*, 303.

271. Voorwinde, *Jesus's Emotions in the Gospels*, 110.

272. Reiling and Swellengrebel, *Translator's Handbook on the Gospel of Luke*, 665.

order of "synagogues" before "prisons" suggests an order found in the arrest and trials of Jesus and future disciples, namely beginning with the Jews and culminating with the Gentiles. Jesus's words as the "common lot of Christians" find their beginning in Acts (cf. 4:3; 5:18; 12:1, 14; 21:27).[273] He says this persecution will present opportunities for his disciples to give testimony to their faith and the life of Jesus Christ (Luke 21:13). They will do so through his power, requiring no preparation except a mental and spiritual resolve to be used by him (Luke 21:14–15). He gives them three different fates: (1) familial betrayal, (2) death, and (3) hatred (i.e., they will be the recipients of hatred).

Jesus presents these as literal future events, as sure to transpire as the "great earthquakes," "plagues and famines," and "terrors and great signs" mentioned in Luke 21:11. What does Jesus mean when he says, "By your endurance you will gain your souls" (Luke 21:19)? Mark uses endurance substantivally, i.e., "the one who endures" (ὁ ὑπομείνας). He also adds the prepositional phrase εἰς τέλος, which Luke does not have. Jesus does not say that the one who endures can hope to avoid persecution that results in death, thus saving their lives. He is referring to an eschatological salvation of their souls. Yen writes, "[A] guarantee of life is promised for those who keep steadfast."[274] This is the only way to understand Jesus's words, where he places martyrdom and persecution beside the promise that "not even one of the hairs on your head will perish" (Luke 21:18).

There is nothing equivalent to the crucifixion of Jesus Christ anywhere or at any time in the history of the world. The fourth Servant Song of Isaiah contains the following description of the crucifixion: "His appearance was marred more than any man's" (Isa 52:14). The crucifixion has no comparison in the history of the world. It is to this end that Jesus has been moving since the beginning of his ministry. In Luke 12:49–53, Jesus indicates how great his approaching death was distressing him. There are a number of different translations for συνέχομαι, the word Luke uses.[275] Luke's use is early in the Gospel narrative, showing that, very soon after he resolves to go to Jerusalem (Luke 9:51), Jesus is already feeling the weight of the approaching cross. Matthew and Mark refer to his distress in Gethsemane (Matt 26:37, ἤρξατο λυπεῖσθαι καὶ ἀδημονεῖν;

---

273. O'Toole, *The Christological Climax of Paul's Defense*, 36.

274. Yen, *The Lucan Journey*, 246.

275. For a discussion on different translations (including those by authors of different commentaries), see Voorwinde, *Jesus's Emotions in the Gospels*, 133.

Mark 14:33, ἤρξατο ἐκθαμβεῖσθαι καὶ ἀδημονεῖν).[276] Jesus's third prediction of his suffering, death, and resurrection is found in Luke 18:31–34.[277]

How Jesus suffers is tantamount for likeness education. The ultimate litmus test for the teachings of Jesus, particularly about loving one's enemies, is whether or not he will do as he has instructed his disciples to do. Luke records that Peter is present for the sufferings of Jesus Christ (Luke 22:54, 61; see also 1 Pet 3:22–23; 5:1, μάρτυς τῶν τοῦ Χριστοῦ παθημάτων), as are John (John 19:26) and others. Luke records the first round of sufferings Jesus experienced in 22:54–65. Of them, the first is the denial of Peter (Luke 22:54–61; cf. Luke 21:16). Jesus is betrayed, mocked, beaten, blindfolded, and blasphemed against. Before Herod, Luke adds in 23:8–12 that Jesus receives harsh accusations; he is treated with contempt, mocked, dehumanized, and demoralized.

On the way to the cross and while he is on the cross, Jesus cares for others and gives the disciples their example to follow:

1.   Jesus responds to the mourning women on the way to the cross (perhaps negatively) and teaches on the way to the cross.

2.   He prays for the forgiveness of everyone present who is participating in his crucifixion (Luke 23:34).

3.   He forgives a criminal who is being crucified near him and promises the man will be with him in paradise (Luke 23:43).

4.   He makes provisions for his mother, asking a disciple to care for her in his stead (John 19:25–27).

5.   He prays to and entrusts his soul to his Father.

As Green writes: "Love is expressed in doing good—that is, not by passivity in the face of opposition but in proactivity: doing good, blessing, praying, and offering the second cheek and the shirt along with the coat."[278] Jesus models all of this in the last six hours of his life.

---

276. The use of this verb with the infinitive is similar to a periphrastic imperfect (ἦν + participle).

277. See Luke 17:25; 22:15; 24:26; Acts 1:3; 3:18; 17:3.

278. Green, *The Gospel of Luke*, 272.

An Analysis of Acts

The following outline is presented as an aid for the analysis of Acts. It is the one proposed by Thomas D. Lea and David Alan Black,[279] provided here with only slight modification:

I. Witness in Jewish Culture (1:1—12:25)

    a. Birth of the Church (1:1—2:41)

    b. Initial Spread of the Gospel in Jerusalem (2:42—6:7)

    c. Three Leaders: Stephen, Philip, and Paul (6:8—9:31)

    d. Initial Spread of the Gospel among Gentiles (9:32—12:25)

II. Witness in Gentile Culture (13:1—21:17)

    a. First Missionary Journey (13:1—15:35)

    b. Second Missionary Journey (15:36—18:22)

    c. Third Missionary Journey (18:23—21:17)

III. The Arrest and Trial of Paul, and His Transfer to Rome (21:18—28:32)

    a. Events in Jerusalem (21:18—23:35)

    b. Events in Caesarea (24:1—26:32)

    c. Journey to and Ministry in Rome (27:1—28:32)

Selection of Disciples in Acts

Acts directly mentions two younger men who are enjoined to the mission of the gospel. The first, John Mark, is found in Acts 12, first mentioned in v. 12. Having been delivered from prison, Peter goes straight "to the house of Mary, the mother of John who was also called Mark." This takes place following the radical change in Peter's understanding of the Great Commission. Acts 9:32—12:25 covers the initial spread of the gospel among the Gentiles. Luke records that before Barnabas and Paul embark on the first missionary journey, they enlist John Mark, who they take

---

279. Lea and Black, *The New Testament*, 326–28. For a more detailed outline, see Appendix I: Outline of Acts.

with them from Jerusalem back to Antioch (Acts 12:25—13:1). As to why they chose him is the subject of great debate.[280]

In Acts 13:5, John Mark is described as a ὑπηρέτης ("helper"). Paul is also referred to as a ὑπηρέτης (Acts 26:16). Luke's designation of Mark as a helper or assistant is not something uncommon in first-century Judaism. Even the heads of synagogues had assistants similar to Mark's role (see Luke 4:20).[281] It is not uncommon in Hellenistic literature either. C. Clifton Black shows where the word is used in historical texts with reference to a soldier's assistant:

> [I]n the works of the later Attic historians, Thucydides (*Peloponnesian War* 3.17) and Pseudo-Xenophon (*Cynegeticus* 2.4.4; 6.2.13), ὑπηρέτης is used in military contexts to designate an armed foot soldier's attendant (who carried the warrior's baggage, rations, and shield) or any adjutant, staff officer, or aide-de camp.[282]

Mark's role is distinct from the designation of Paul by Christ as a ὑπηρέτης. Luke does not use the word μαθητής to describe Mark, even though follow-ship is included in the word's meaning.[283] He will use this word later to refer to the second young man. Luke may have avoided this word with Mark because of the short amount of time in which Paul invested in his life. The separation of Barnabas and Paul as missionary partners is related in some way to Mark (Acts 15:39). Unless including Mark's presence in the narrative for this reason, i.e., connecting it to the sharp disagreement

---

280. For a discussion on different possibilities, see Black, "John Mark in the Acts of the Apostles," 103–4; Black, *Mark*, 28–30. The two are basically verbatim. Both are provided here in case one is easier to locate than the other.

281. Bailey, *Paul through Mediterranean Eyes*, 142. The very presence of this word in synagogal use should serve as a serious caution to exegetes and preachers tempted to use the under-rower, nautical imagery in explaining what this word means. In the minds of someone who heard it, they simply heard "helper" or "assistant," without any exegetical fool's gold included. Statements like, "The Greek word for minister is *huperetes*. It means 'an under-rower of a ship'" really are not helpful (Wood, *A Passion for His Passion*, 178). For a discussion on how this word differs from οἰκονόμος, see Thiselton, *The Hermeneutics of Doctrine*, 496–97.

282. Black, "John Mark in the Acts of the Apostles," 106. This essay contains an excellent discussion on the use of ὑπηρέτης in Luke-Acts. Or, see Black, *Mark*, 30–32; Moon, *Mark as Contributive Amanuensis of 1 Peter?*, 57–60.

283. See, for example, Xenophon, *The Education of Cyrus*, 280.

(παροξυσμός)[284] between Paul and Barnabas, there appears no reason to include him in the narrative.

By including him, Luke also:

1. Shows it was Paul's desire to train future leaders in the work of the gospel.

2. Contrasts Mark and Timothy, the former as a poor example of a second-generation disciple and the latter as a good example.

How Mark is related to the sharp disagreement has been the subject of great debate, especially why Paul did not want Mark to accompany him any longer. The most logical explanation is Mark was considered unfaithful, not sharing the same purpose, faith, perseverance, persecutions, and sufferings as Paul. Paul viewed what Mark did as desertion (Acts 15:38). Even though the mission to the Gentiles had been proclaimed by Peter, Mark had not seen it firsthand. The salvation of the proconsul must have troubled him, especially how Paul did not require customs according to the Law. So he departed and returned to Jerusalem, his home, probably taking a ship from Salamis to Sidon and on to Caesarea (Acts 13:13). Mark had not travelled more than 300 miles with Paul before turning away.[285]

The next disciple selected, after Paul and Barnabas part ways, is Timothy.[286] Luke introduces Timothy in Acts 16:1. He serves as the replacement of Mark, and Silas the replacement of Barnabas.[287] The description of Timothy as μαθητής in place of ὑπηρέτης probably points to Paul's lifelong relationship to Timothy as διδάσκαλος, until his departure to be with Christ in the early AD 60s.[288] Timothy would spend more

284. Earl S. Johnson Jr. says this is a "strong, almost violent" word that involves heightened emotions, even anger (*Hebrews*, 52). See also Acts 17:16; Nave, *The Role and Function of Repentance in Luke-Acts,* 215 n.320.

285. This number includes the distance from Jerusalem to Antioch. For the mission, they had only travelled about forty-one miles, the distance from Antioch to Salamis on the island of Cyprus.

286. For an overview of Timothy in the NT, see Lancaster, "Timothy," 1313.

287. Johnson, *The Gospel of Luke*, 288.

288. The word μαθητής occurs sixteen times in this section of Acts (13:1—21:17). There are three episodes dealing with disciples. The first episode takes place during Paul's travels from Iconium, Derbe, and, finally, back to Antioch (Acts 14:1–28). The second episode concerns Luke's introduction of Timothy to the narrative (Acts 16:1). The third episode concerns the relationship of μαθητής to persons only familiar with the baptism of John (Acts 18:23—19:10).

than ten years as Paul's μαθητής.[289] It is one of only five designations of an individual (whose name is given) as μαθητής in Acts (cf. Acts 9:10, 26, 36; 21:16). Another difference between the narrative referring to the inclusion of Mark in the gospel work and this narrative is Luke's record that Paul desired (θέλω) that Timothy go with him (σὺν αὐτῷ)[290] (Acts 16:3). Timothy is immediately plunged into the difficulty of traveling and laboring with Paul for the gospel.

His first trip to Lystra allows him to bear witness to the sufferings and persecutions that Paul mentions last in 2 Tim 3:10–11a. Thomas C. Oden writes: "When Paul and Barnabas visited Lystra, the populace first treated them as gods; later they tried to stone Paul, leaving him for dead (Acts 14:6–20)," adding "if the young Timothy did not actually see this event, he surely must have heard of it."[291] Even before this, however, Timothy sees a great deal about Paul's purpose and perseverance. The gospel first arrived in Europe via Philippi between AD 49 and 52 during Paul's second missionary journey. Luke records in Acts 16:7 that Paul (along with Timothy who had just joined the team) intended on entering Asia to preach the gospel. It is very interesting that the change that leads the missionary team into Macedonia is the direct result of a Trinitarian roadblock.[292] Paul is resolute about taking the gospel into Asia (Acts 16:6), so resolved that he travels 500+ miles before arriving at Troas (Acts 16:11). Timothy witnessed nothing less than a determined laborer of the gospel, who would not falter on his purpose. Only a divine intervention could alter the plans of Paul.

Along the way, Timothy became the recipient of personal apostolic instruction, receiving the teaching of Paul both in private and in public. John Pollock describes him this way:

> Timothy was a complicated character. He had a weak stomach and looked very young. Nervous, a little afraid of hardship, though enduring it without flinching, he was tempted occasionally to be ashamed of Paul and the gospel. But he was no

289. Köstenberger, et al., *The Cradle, the Cross, and the Crown*, 643.

290. In the Gospels, μετ' αὐτοῦ (or similar expressions) is used of the disciples. Σύν may reflect the co-laborer relationship that Paul intended to develop from the beginning with Timothy.

291. Oden, *First and Second Timothy and Titus*, 4.

292. Acts 16:6 reads that they were "forbidden by the Holy Spirit." Acts 16:7 says that the "Spirit of Jesus did not permit them" to go into Bithynia. And in Acts 16:10 the team had concluded that "God" had called them to preach the gospel in Macedonia.

weakling. Warm-blooded—Paul had to warn him to flee youth-
ful lusts—and equally virile spiritually, Timothy became an able
preacher who soon could be trusted with important missions
of his own.[293]

He is Paul's brother through their common faith in Christ (Col 1:1); he
becomes Paul's most trusted son in the faith (1 Tim 1:2; 2 Tim 1:2), his
representative (e.g., 1 Thessalonians 3), his co-laborer in the work of the
gospel (e.g., Phil 1:1), and an example in his own person to the churches
at large (Phil 2:19–24).

Imitation in Acts

Like the Gospel of Luke, Acts is replete with examples for his audience to
imitate. For example, Burridge writes:

> Within Acts, examples of Christian conduct abound for readers
> to emulate, such as Barnabas, Dorcas and Lydia (Acts 4.36–37;
> 9.27, 36; 16.14–15). Stephen imitates his Lord's last words and
> attitude in committing his spirit and praying for forgiveness for
> those who bring about his death.[294]

This is different than saying Luke's second work is a paradigm for the life
of the church today. It is not intended to be a paradigm, no more than
one of the narratives in the OT was to be a paradigm for the nation of
Israel. Still, there are exemplary teachings and works presented therein
that would behoove the modern-day church to pursue in likeness. What
are some of these? The following is an annotated list:

1. An astute attention to the OT in the study and teaching of God's
    word (e.g., Acts 2:17–36; 6:4).

2. A marked focus and attention to the apostles' teaching, which is
    now recorded in the NT (e.g., Acts 2:42).[295]

293. Pollock, *The Apostle*, 117–18.

294. Burridge, *Imitating Jesus*, 280

295. Clark M. Williamson and Ronald James Allen give the following three ways
Luke shows the importance of teaching in Acts: (1) Teaching is marked as "one of
the characteristic elements of the life of the ideal Jerusalem community (Acts 2:42);"
(2) Teaching is mentioned numerous times "as part of the ministry of early church"
(Acts 4:2; 5:21, 42; 11:26; 13:1; 15:35; 17:19; 18:11; 20:20; 28:31); and (3) Teaching is
emphasized by one of the book's most influential characters—Paul—as seen in Acts
20:17–35 (*The Teaching Minister*, 42). David Peterson writes, "Luke uses a strong

3. A resolved devotion to prayers, both corporately and individually (e.g., Acts 1:14; 6:4).

4. A compassionate interrelationship among believers marked by a steady remembrance of the Lord's Supper and the sharing of possessions to meet needs (e.g., Acts 2:42; 4:32).

5. A fixed commitment and dedication to further the gospel to the ends of the earth, even at the risk of personal loss, suffering, and persecution.

6. A consistent reevaluation of the church's focus and the nature of the gospel (e.g., Acts 15:4–21).

7. A concerted and loving involvement in the development of leadership around the world (e.g., Acts 20:17–38).

In addition to these, Luke provides anti-examples in the Acts narrative. One has already been mentioned, that of John Mark. Another includes the negative example of Ananias and his wife Sapphira in Acts 5. The account of this husband and wife is preceded by a positive example—Barnabas (and the community as a whole).[296] Luke says his name is Joseph and that he was a Levite (Acts 4:36). If there was an opportunity for someone to meet the needs of a brother and/or sister in Christ, disciples would sell some of their possessions and use the proceeds in order to be a blessing. Here is the early Christian community following in the teaching and example of Jesus Christ, who taught his disciples and the crowds to generously and mercifully give to everyone (e.g., Luke 6:30, 38; Acts 20:35). Barnabas does exactly this (Acts 4:37).

Ananias and his wife Sapphira do something that warrants divine discipline. A few details are clear from the text:

1. While they sold a piece of land, they withhold part of the proceeds (Acts 5:2).

2. What they do is "lie to the Holy Spirit" (ψεύσασθαί σε τὸ πνεῦμα τὸ ἅγιον; Acts 5:3; "to God" [τῷ θεῷ], 5:4), which is directly attributed

---

verb in 2:42, 46 (προσκαπτεροῦντες, 'devoting themselves to') to stress that the earliest disciples were pre-occupied with and persevered in the activities he lists. Their first pre-occupation was with the apostolic teaching" ("The Worship of the New Community," 390). Clark adds, "Luke shows the apostles as perceiving their main activity as ministering the Word of God (6:2, 4)" ("The Role of the Apostles," 179).

296. Talbert, *Reading Acts*, 50.

to Satanic influence (ἐπλήρωσεν ὁ Σατανᾶς τὴν καρδίαν σου, Acts 5:3).

3. Sapphira also lies to Peter (Acts 5:5).

The first verb used to describe what the two did is νοσφίζω. Witherington says this verb "always has a negative connotation, and means something like 'embezzled,' referring to a secret theft of a part of a larger amount, sometimes of something placed in trust."[297] They were struck dead "not because they refused to give all their possessions to the church," says Charles C. Ryrie, "but because they pretended to give all away," thus lying to God.[298] Why is this negative example given to the church? Douglas A. Hume says Luke includes it because it shows the continued triumph of God over Satan who has infiltrated and attempted to disrupt God's redemptive plan again.[299] Alan Thompson suggests it shows God's displeasure and wrath against threats to the unity of the fellowship, something the church had experienced without fail until now.[300] There are other answers proposed as solutions. These two go hand in hand. One addresses the spiritual element at work, which Luke draws attention to, without ignoring the human element. It is a heinous sin, one John F. MacArthur Jr. says is "to the book of Acts what Achan's sin is to the book of Joshua."[301] "Both," he writes, "were deceitful, miserly, selfish acts that interrupted the victorious progress of God's people and brought sin into the camp at the height of great triumph."[302]

The account of Ananias and Sapphira is redolent of Jesus's teaching on possessions. Tannehill says, "Jesus in Luke speaks repeatedly about the dangers of possessions and commands his disciples to sell their goods and give to charity (Luke 12:33)."[303] He draws a very interesting parallel to the life and teaching of Paul regarding his view on possessions, which is very germane to the discussion here. In his farewell discourse to the Ephesian elders (Acts 20:35), Paul paraphrases Matthew's Gospel (δωρεὰν ἐλάβετε, δωρεὰν δότε, Matt 10:8), saying:

297. Witherington III, *The Acts of the Apostles*, 215 n.74.
298. Ryrie, "Perspectives on Social Ethics, Part IV," 314–28.
299. Hume, *The Early Christian Community*, 142.
300. Thompson, *One Lord, One People*, 72.
301. MacArthur Jr., *Ashamed of the Gospel*, 57.
302. Ibid.
303. Tannehill, *The Narrative Unity of Luke-Acts*, 260.

> In everything I have done, I showed you that it is absolutely nec-
> essary for you to help the weak, working in this same manner
> [v. 34]; and, remember the words of the Lord Jesus, which he
> himself said, "It is more blessed to give than to receive."

Tannehill says there is "a twist in the application,"[304] adding:

> Paul does not follow Jesus' teaching by selling his possessions
> and distributing the proceeds. Instead, he gives by working with
> his hands. This is a new application of Jesus' teaching to fit the
> situation of church leaders such as the elders being addressed.
> Church leaders who do not work to support themselves will
> have to be supported by the church. Because Paul did not want
> to take other people's money and clothing (20:33), he worked
> with his own hands so that he could give rather than receive
> from others, in accordance with Jesus' teaching.[305]

The connection to the teachings of Jesus is important. Paul is following
the example of Jesus, and he is now presenting to the Ephesian elders his
own example as one to follow. This is the only instance in Acts where Paul
does so. Nevertheless, this is a common theme, i.e., imitation, in Paul's
letters (e.g., 1 Thess 1:6; 2:14; 1 Cor 4:16; 11:1; Eph 5:1; Heb 6:12; 13:7).
Christopher R. Little says, "Paul, in his Miletus discourse to the Ephesian elders (Ac. 20:17–35), viewed his entire experience among them as
a model to follow."[306] The SOM and the SOP stress this more than anywhere else, which may reflect why Paul paraphrases it like a beatitude.[307]

More than simply presenting positive and negative examples, Luke
demonstrates how Jesus's disciples carry on his mission in his likeness.
Susan Wendel shows, for example, how the apostles' teaching now imitates the teaching of Jesus. She writes:

> An excerpt from the sermon of Peter in Acts 3:12–26 provides
> a cogent example of the way that Luke also portrays the preach-
> ing of the followers of Jesus as a continuation of the message of
> Jesus.[308]

304. Ibid.

305. Ibid. See also Black, "The Thessalonian Road to Self-Support," and Black, "El
Camino para Auto-Apoyo según Tesalonicenses."

306. Little, *Mission in the Way of Paul*, 80.

307. On the similarities, see O'Toole, "What Role Does Jesus's Saying in Acts 20:35
Play?," 334–35.

308. Wendel, *Scriptural Interpretation*, 112.

One similarity is dependence on the Old Testament. In the same way that Jesus used the OT to verify and explain his ministry, Peter now uses it in Acts 2 to declare the resurrection of God's Son (e.g., Deut 18:15–16a, 19; Lev 23:29).[309] Wendel also shows the similarity in how Peter used the Scriptures to communicate "a revolutionary understanding of the Jewish scriptures that aims to correct previous misunderstanding," just as Jesus did.[310]

If it is important for Luke to show the continuity between Jesus and Peter and the rest of the disciples, it is tantamount that he shows continuity between Jesus and Paul. Tannehill writes, "[I]f the mission of Paul is to be comparable to the missions of Jesus and Peter, the narrator must not only demonstrate his power as a preacher but also as a worker of signs and wonders."[311] Like Peter, Paul's first miracle is the healing of a lame man (Acts 14:8–10). In addition to this, Paul casts out a demon (Acts 16:16–18), performs extraordinary miracles (Acts 19:11–12; cf. 5:1–10), raises Eutychus to life (Acts 20:9–12), and more.

The parallels between Peter and Paul have a nice rhetorical effect in the book of Acts.[312] However, could there be more to why these parallels exist? Both Peter and Paul spent approximately three years with the Lord. While there is a cloud surrounding the nature of Paul's time with the Lord (Gal 1:17–18), could not they both have received the same training from the Lord, learned the same things about his purpose, his character, his love, etc.? Acts certainly shows continuity between Jesus, Peter, and Paul (and others) concerning their teaching and works.[313] Most studies on the parallels have concentrated on these two, but what about the other aspects of likeness education? While Acts does shed some light on the

---

309. Ibid., 113. Peter may not have arrived at these verses on his own. It is very likely that these were part of the τὰ περὶ ἑαυτοῦ ("all the things concerning himself") in Luke 24:27b (cf. Luke 24:44–47).

310. Ibid., 114.

311. Tannehill, *The Narrative Unity of Luke-Acts*, 162.

312. For a list of parallels, see Table 6.3 in Witherington III, *The Indelible Image*, 673. The name of this rhetorical device is σύγκρισις and, according to Andrew Clark, was common in forms of biographies and other genres of literature ("The Role of the Apostles," 185). See this Clark essay, pages 185–89, for a detailed discussion on the parallels between Peter and Paul in Acts (dealing only with miracles and speeches) and the following for a historical discussion, Moessner, "'The Christ Must Suffer,'" 117–53.

313. See the chart and discussion on the parallels between the Gospel of Luke, Acts 1–12, and Acts 13–28 in Rothschild, *Luke-Acts and the Rhetoric of History*, 115–19.

apostles' purpose, faith, love, etc., their letters really communicate each so well and fill in what is lacking in Acts.

Conduct in Acts

Anthony C. Thiselton opens up his biographical sketch of the apostle Paul with these words:

> Very many people, perhaps even millions, view Jesus of Nazareth with admiration and respect, but see Paul as the founder of a different system of doctrine and the inventor of established churches. They regard Jesus as a religious idealist, who taught a simple religion of love and tolerance; they regard Paul very differently, as one who imposed his ideas onto others, and who, unlike Jesus, undervalued women and the marginalized of society.[314]

The reasons for beginning the section on conduct in Acts with this quote are three-fold. First, the real problem above, for many people, is an incorrect and incomplete view of who Jesus is. At the heart of this problem is a spiritual issue, but that is beyond the scope of this investigation. Second, anyone who understands Paul as Thiselton describes has an incorrect and incomplete view of who he is. Few men have lived with a purpose, faith, conduct, love, patience, and perseverance with which Paul lived. While Paul does not entirely represent any of these areas like a mirror reflecting Jesus, his life is a testimony to the life Jesus lived and died for. None of the eleven original disciples had a life transformed like that of Paul's, saved from the crowd Jesus hurls his woes against and saved from a life whose greatest pleasure was putting into chains and death those who followed the foolishness of the cross.

The conduct encountered in the book of Acts is an extension of the conduct that the disciples witnessed in the life of Jesus Christ. The very first thing Luke records the disciples doing after the ascension of Jesus Christ is obedience to what Jesus commanded them to do (Acts 1:4). The very next thing he records is their continual devotion to prayer (ἦσαν προσκαρτεροῦντες ὁμοθυμαδὸν τῇ προσευχῇ, Acts 1:14). The apostles had recognized in Jesus an unwavering commitment to prayer during his earthly life. Matthew and Mark both record Jesus sending the crowds away so that he could give himself time to pray, away from the disciples

314. Thiselton, *The Living Paul*, 1.

(Matt 14:23; Mark 1:35; 6:41, 46; 8:6–7; 14:22–23). John includes the longest record of one of Jesus's prayers and its content.[315] No one mentions Jesus's commitment to prayer more than Luke (e.g., Luke 5:16; 6:12; 9:28). Morris writes, Luke "lets us see Jesus at prayer often. . . . Some of the instances are found in the other Gospels, but seven times it is Luke alone who recorded that he prayed. . . . The example of the Master is very clear in this Gospel."[316] Marshall says as much. Given the sheer quantity and attention to content, he says Luke must have been "consciously aware of the significance of prayer in Jesus's ministry and teaching."[317] Luke alone declares Jesus's prayer life as a discipline, not just an event: "Jesus himself was often withdrawing (ἦν ὑποχωρῶν) to the wilderness and praying (προσευχόμενος)" (Luke 5:16).[318] Jesus's example is extended into Acts as Luke shares the continuing example of God's Son as intercessor for his people.[319]

The disciples in Acts are found praying continually (Acts 1:14, 24; 4:31; 9:40; 10:2, 31; 12:5; 13:3; 14:23; 20:36; 28:8). They are found praying "with the appointment of someone to a particular service, with the giving/reception of the Holy Spirit, [and] with the eschatological hope of redemption," per Geir O. Holmas.[320] The order found in Acts 6:4 is

315. See Hudgins, "An Application of Discourse Analysis Methodology," 24–57. John 17 is not the first prayer of Jesus found in the Johannine discourse. It is actually the third. The two other prayers are found in John 11:41–42 and 12:27–30. Preceding both of these, John includes in his account of when Jesus fed the multitudes that Jesus prayed prior to distributing the bread and fish (John 6:11). However, in John 6, the act of Jesus having prayed is mentioned in passing as part of the narrative. The accounts in John 11 and 12 contain the actual words of Jesus as he prayed—direct discourse—just as is found in John 17. The similarities between the prayers, specifically the introduction and the concluding purpose statement, are extremely important. See Appendix 2: Jesus's Prayers in John.

316. Morris, *New Testament Theology*, 213.

317. Marshall, "Jesus—Example and Teacher of Prayer," 115.

318. It is possible that the periphrastic imperfect is durative, but not likely. If it is, Luke is saying that when Jesus prayed, he prayed at length.

319. Brad Blue writes:

In as much as ancient Judaism maintained that heavenly intercessors continued to do in heaven what they had done successfully on earth, it is not surprising that Acts 7:55–56 suggests that the intercession of Jesus is a continuing reality. That is "Jesus continues to intercede for his disciples in heaven in order to testify to their faithfulness in times of trial, and to ensure their perseverance in discipleship at such moments." ("The Influence of Jewish Worship," 496)

320. Holmas, *Prayer and Vindication in Luke-Acts*, 113.

significant. The apostles viewed their primary ministry as consisting of two things—first prayer, then the ministry of the Word. In Acts 2:42, the order is reversed, but this is Luke's statement. In Acts 6:4, he is reporting what the apostles said of their own ministry, and prayer came first. Having prayer as one's first priority, especially in leadership, does not mean a person needs to lead some sort of monkish lifestyle. The early Christian community is settled in prayer only to be thrust into mission by way of persecution. Even when the mission takes them outside Jerusalem, hundreds and thousands of miles away from home, to prisons and dungeons, their devotion to pray does not fail. Jesus had trained them well in this area of life, both in his numerous teachings on the subject and by his living example.

The Semantic Frame of Likeness Education, Part II

The semantic frame developed in Chapter 2 was found insufficient to adequately analyze Luke's Gospel as a whole and Acts. Therefore, this chapter began with a supplemental analysis of 2 Tim 3:10–11a. Instead of developing a code from outside of the biblical texts, Paul's second letter to Timothy offers a more than sufficient text on likeness education. In 2 Tim 3:10–11a, Paul identifies nine areas in which Timothy was trained under his mentorship. These are: (1) teaching, (2) conduct, (3) purpose, (4) faithfulness, (5) patience, (6) love, (7) perseverance, (8) persecutions, and (9) sufferings.

1. *Teaching* refers to the theological instruction in the broadest sense. It includes instruction given in one-to-one settings, small groups, and larger venues.

2. *Conduct* is the desired effect of teaching. When teaching is successful, it becomes incorporated into the way a person leads his or her life.

3. *Purpose* refers to the inward motivations, or resolve, that governs a person's life.

4. *Faithfulness* is one's responsible commitment to the mission and resources that God gives a person.

5. *Patience* (i.e., longsuffering) refers to a person's extended, active patience toward individuals or groups that are hostile to him or her.

6. *Love* is a part of the fruit of the Holy Spirit, the result of a transformed heart toward fellow-believers as well as enemies of the cross of Christ.

7. *Perseverance* refers to one's unwavering resolve to holiness and active submission to the sovereignty of God in pursuing one's purpose in Christ.

8. *Persecutions* refer to the acts of ill-will or hostility toward others, often for religious reasons.

9. *Sufferings* refer to the effects of persecutions.

In addition to beginning the chapter with this supplementary analysis, the resulting code was applied to Luke-Acts. Instead of surveying the text for every instance in which the code appears, the most important (sometimes the most evident, sometimes not) examples were investigated in further detail. The result is a definite continuity between Jesus and the apostles. For example, the analysis in Acts demonstrates that the apostles followed in Jesus's teaching, conduct, and persecutions. They value prayer like Jesus valued prayer. They place a high value on the needs of others and service.

Summary

The analyses in this chapter demonstrate that likeness education extends far beyond the realm of cognition. Jesus is never satisfied with a mere transfer of knowledge. He is concerned with the accurate interpretation and explanation of God's word, as seen in the SOM and the Sermon on the Plain. However, he places a huge emphasis on praxis, i.e., putting such knowledge into practice. Some of the greatest instructions the disciples received in their likeness training came from moments in which Jesus said little or nothing. His living example, such as his example on the importance of prayer by slipping away just to do so, spoke as loud or louder than an exposition on the nature of prayer. Being "fully trained" as Jesus describes in Luke 6:40 involves exposition and visual instruction. Jesus proves the truthfulness of his proverb through the likeness cultivated in his own disciples. Fishermen, tax-collectors, and persecutor alike all became like their one Teacher—the Lord Jesus Christ.

4

Likeness Education
in the New Testament

Introduction

Jesus said, "After being fully trained, each apprentice will be like his or her teacher" (Luke 6:40b). According to Paul, Timothy had followed him in nine different areas, such as teaching, conduct, love, and even persecutions and sufferings. The following analysis is a survey of these characteristics of likeness education in the writings of the NT, particularly the writings of Paul. What sort of conduct does the NT present as exemplary conduct for a participant of the New Covenant? What is the type of love that Timothy would have learned from Paul? How were believers to view persecutions and sufferings? All of these are important questions for determining what likeness education is in the NT and what sort of continuity exists between the life and person of Jesus to future disciples. In addition to this, the following analysis considers what the NT says about who believers will be like after they are fully trained.

Conduct in 1–2 Thessalonians

None of Paul's letters presents a more detailed picture of his personal conduct like his letters to the Thessalonian believers. The densest discussion concerning his conduct, and that of his missionary co-laborers, is found in 1 Thess 2:1–12. Throughout this section, Paul reminds the

Thessalonians of their character and conduct, which the Thessalonian believers witnessed firsthand.[1]

The first mention of his character is found at the closing of Paul's thanksgiving section transitioning to the letter proper. The καθώς clause in 1 Thess 1:5 reads "just as you know what kind of men we proved to be among you for your sake" (καθὼς οἴδατε οἷοι ἐγενήθημεν ἐν ὑμῖν δι' ὑμᾶς).[2] The καθώς clause parallels the idea of knowing in v. 4 (εἰδότες) and provides a perfect transition into the next section of Paul's letter (καὶ ὑμεῖς μιμηταὶ in 1:6), which concentrates heavily on the missionaries' personal example. Frank J. Matera writes, "[B]ecause they already know (*kathōs oidate*) what kind of a person Paul is, they have become imitators (*mimētai*) of him and the Lord (1:6)."[3] The only other two uses of καθὼς οἴδατε in the NT, both in 1 Thessalonians (2:2, 5), contain only those two words.

What is it that the Thessalonians knew, according to Paul? He says they knew "what kind" (οἷοι) of persons he and his co-laborers "were shown to be" (or, "proved to be," ἐγενήθημεν).[4] Paul includes two prepositional phrases: (1) ἐν ὑμῖν, and (2) δι' ὑμᾶς. Generally the preposition ἐν has the meaning "in," however this understanding makes no sense in 1 Thess 1:5. The most plausible understanding is "among," referring to missionaries' presence in Thessalonica (cf. ἐν ὑμῖν in Rom 1:12; Jas 5:13–20

1. Furnish, *1 Thessalonians, 2 Thessalonians*, 45; Morris, *The First and Second Epistles to the Thessalonians*, 47.

2. What is the main idea to which this clause belongs? How does it relate to the thanksgiving in 1 Thess 1:2–5? Robert E. Picirilli believes it serves as the conclusion to Paul's thanksgiving. He writes, "The 'as' apparently makes this parallel to the 'knowing' in v. 4: Paul knows the election of the Thessalonians (because of the powerful demonstration of the Spirit's work there), even as they know the kind of people he and his co-workers were" ("1 Thessalonians," 18). G. K. Beale says it parallels the idea of the Holy Spirit's power and deep conviction: "to indicate that what follows confirms for the readers that they themselves knew well the truth that the apostolic preaching was delivered with the Spirit's power and deep conviction" (*1-2 Thessalonians*, 54). Earl J. Richard sees a looser connection to the thanksgiving section and hints that it introduces what follows, particularly the Thessalonians' imitation of Paul and his co-laborers:
> "Such a phrase functions as a paraenetic commonplace since it reminds the readers of what they already know; the Thessalonians have witnessed the missionaries' pastoral activity and are simply reminded of this in terms of power ('what sort of persons we were') and focus ('for your sake')" (*First and Second Thessalonians*, 48).

3. Matera, *New Testament Ethics*, 126.

4. Judge, *The First Christians in the Roman World*, 687.

[3x]).[5] About the δι' ὑμᾶς in the καθώς clause, Beale says it "indicates that Paul's preaching was for the readers' advantage and not for selfish motives."[6] Paul's conduct among the Thessalonian believers is more than exemplary. Just as how the Thessalonians proved to be God's beloved and elect (1 Thess 1:4), how Paul and his co-laborers conducted themselves in their presence proved the value of their example, which he repeatedly appeals to throughout the letter, and the validity of the teaching they received.

It is no doubt that the Thessalonians received the word of God as they did, in some part, because of the testimony that Paul and his missionary friends had in their presence. Leon Morris writes:

> Several times he recalls to their minds the manner of life of the preachers. This must have made a profound impression on the mixed population of the city, and it was evidence of the power the apostle has just been talking about. While many preachers in modern times will be hesitant about directing attention to their own lives, it yet remains true that no preacher can expect a hearing for his gospel unless it is bearing fruit in his own life.[7]

Beginning in 1 Thess 2:1, Paul refers eight times to what the Thessalonians know about his conduct, four being found between 1 Thess 2:1–12 (2:1, 2, 5, 11).[8] Jeffrey A. D. Weima also points out how Paul also uses the verb μνημονεύω in 2:9 and ὑμεῖς μάρτυρες (with ellipsis) in a manner similar to how he uses οἶδα these eight times.[9] The following list comprises what the Thessalonians knew about Paul and his co-laborers. The Thessalonians knew firsthand that Paul and his co-laborers:

1. "Did not prove to be a waste" (οὐ κενὴ γέγονεν, 1 Thess 2:1) in their work of sharing the gospel to them.

2. Suffered and were mistreated in Philippi. Despite all of this, they were resolved to speak the gospel in Thessalonica with even more opposition there (1 Thess 2:2).

---

5. See, for example, Byrne, *Romans*, 55.

6. Beale, *1–2 Thessalonians*, 54. E. A. Judge says it is "for their sake" (*The First Christians in the Roman World*, 687).

7. Morris, *The First and Second Epistles to the Thessalonians*, 47.

8. Weima, "The Function of 1 Thessalonians 2:1–12," 121.

9. Ibid., 121. He does not believe that Paul uses these recollections to encourage them toward imitation; rather, he believes this is a response to polemical issues in Thessalonica.

3. Never used flattery speech; they never had monetary motivations (1 Thess 2:5); they never sought glory from people; and they never asserted their authority (1 Thess 2:6).

4. Worked, and worked hard at that, night and day even (1 Thess 2:9).

5. Proved to conduct themselves devoutly, uprightly, and blamelessly (1 Thess 2:10).

6. Treated them like a father treats his own children (1 Thess 2:11).

For the sake of space, only a couple of these will be considered in greater detail below.

First, Paul did not exert authority. Instead of using his authority, Paul and his co-laborers proved to be "gentle" (ἤπιοι),[10] which he presents as the complete opposite of ἀπόστολοι. He gives a metaphor to describe this character trait. In 1 Thess 2:7, he says the missionaries were like a τροφός, that is a "nursing mother."[11] This is one of three feminine illustrations Paul's uses in order to describe his own person and conduct (cf. 1 Cor 3:2; Gal 4:19). Paul's conduct can be demonstrated effectively by examining and comparing the ideas of authority with gentleness. Paul's commission from Jesus Christ was to preach the gospel, both to suffer and to extend the gospel to the Gentiles (e.g., Phil 3:10). However, for Paul it was imperative that he do so not as the apostle to the Gentiles

10. Burke, "Pauline Paternity in 1 Thessalonians," 75 n.47. For a discussion on the textual variant νήπιοι, see Williams, *1 and 2 Thessalonians*, 2–7 (E-book accessed on March 9, 2013, from Google Books). Williams believes the ν is omitted accidentally. However, the ν could have been accidentally included just as easily. It is not just "an easy way out of a textual problem," as Collins thinks (*The Power of Images in Paul*, 18). The strongest supports for viewing ἤπιοι as original are Paul's use of "child" imagery elsewhere in his letters (usually not positive) and the unusualness of Paul's mixture of metaphors in the same sentence; in other words, it seems unlikely Paul would use one metaphor in the mainline part of a sentence and then switch to a different metaphor in a subordinate clause. Using different metaphors within a larger discourse unit like a paragraph is understandable, such as Paul's switch from ὡς τροφός in 2:7 to ὡς πατήρ in 1 Thess 2:11. A switch from νήπιοι to ὡς τροφός changes the idea instead of expands it or builds upon it. In addition to all of this, ἤπιος is used by Paul in 2 Tim 2:24 as a character trait a slave of the Lord absolutely must have (δεῖ) in ministry. To be fair, though, see also the article to which Williams refers: Fowl, "A Metaphor in Distress," 469–73. Fowl, like Williams, opts for νήπιοι.

11. This is a role that could be performed by a house servant; however the use of τὰ ἑαυτῆς τέκνα supports the view that he is not thinking about a servant or slave who performed nursing duties, but the actual mother of the children (see Witherington III, *1 and 2 Thessalonians*, 80–81; Green, *The Letters to the Thessalonians*, 127–28).

but by serving just as he was and in ways society might view as weak or inferior. He recognized that exertions of authority, for the sake of demonstrating one's superiority, were completely contrary to the nature of the gospel. Charles A. Wanamaker on 1 Thess 2:7 writes:

> [A]lthough he was entitled to wield authority and command recognition (vv. 6, 7a), Paul chose a different pattern of conduct. He acted with gentleness toward the Thessalonians, as ἤπιοι implies. As Paul told the Corinthians, he preferred to abstain from using his rights even to the point of personal deprivation, lest he do anything to hinder the communication of the gospel (1 Cor. 9:12).[12]

Paul's mentions his authority only in dire circumstances, especially when a believing community challenges his apostleship or fails to heed his calls to change some area of their moral conduct. The verb Paul uses in the ὡς clause with τροφός is θάλπω, used only here and in Eph 5:29 in the New Testament. The verb is also found in the LXX with reference to a mother bird nesting over her eggs (Deut 22:6). Beale captures the idea of its use in Deuteronomy precisely. The mother "conforms her life to meet the needs of the new lives of her young, just like human mothers do. . . . Ultimately, she sacrifices her needs to meet the needs of her offspring."[13] As Richard suggests, a "hint of affection" is needed in any accurate translation of this word (such as "lovingly cares for" or "tenderly cares for").[14] This sort of tenderness is evident in the life of Christ as well (cf. Matt 12:20; Isa 42:3) and is echoed in the verse that follows, where Paul says the Thessalonians had become beloved to his cohort (ἀγαπητοὶ ἡμῖν ἐγενήθητε, 1 Thess 2:8).

In 1 Thess 2:10, Paul uses three adverbs to describe the conduct the Thessalonians were witnesses of: (1) ὁσίως, (2) δικαίως, and (3) ἀμέμπτως. The first word (and its cognate, ὅσιος)[15] is semantically related to ἅγιος in Paul's writing. Both carry the ideas of purity, especially moral purity, in relationship to God.[16] The adjective ὅσιος is used substantivally in two speeches found in Acts, one of Peter and one of Paul, in reference to Jesus

12. Wanamaker, *The Epistles to the Thessalonians*, 101.

13. Beale, *1–2 Thessalonians*, 73.

14. Richard, *First and Second Thessalonians*, 83.

15. The adjective is used more than the adverb in the NT (e.g., 1 Tim 2:8; Titus 1:8; Heb 7:26). Louis Berkhof writes, "It describes a person or things as free from defilement or wickedness, or more actively (of persons) as religiously fulfilling every moral obligation" (*Systematic Theology*, 528).

16. Ridderbos, *Paul*, 264.

Christ (τὸν ὅσιόν; Acts 2:27; 13:35). Marshall, explaining the distinction between ἅγιος and ὁσίως (ὅσιος), writes, "The word *hosios* is more expressive of an attitude of piety. . . . [I]t does not have the same sense of being called by God and belonging to him that we find in *hagios*."[17] Morris, however, sees a closer connection between the two words. Concerning ὁσίως, he says it "points to the character involved in being set apart for God."[18]

The second adverb Paul uses is δικαίως from the root δικ, which is one of those very important Pauline roots. While the adverb only appears here, 1 Cor 15:34, and Titus 2:12 in the Pauline letters, its cognates formed off of δικ are found throughout the Pauline corpus. The adverb here is used ethically, i.e., referring to one's conduct as opposed to one's relationship before God because of Christ, although, these are not two exclusive ideas. Daniel C. Arichea Jr. explains it as "describing the proper lifestyle of people who have been 'justified' by God."[19] Wanamaker, with reference to ὁσίως and δικαίως in 1 Thess 2:10, says they

> were commonly used together to indicate the keeping of divine and human law respectively. . . . This is why Paul specifies that both the Thessalonians and God are witnesses to his and his coworkers conduct. God is witness to the pious or holy way in which they had acted in their responsibility toward God. The Thessalonians are witnesses to the uprightness of their behavior toward the people with whom they had dealings. Ἀμέμπτως strengthens the formulation and applies equally well to behavior in relation to God and behavior in relation to the Thessalonians: neither God nor the Thessalonians could reproach their conduct.[20]

Why does Paul need to add the third adverb if he has covered dealings with people and God with the first two respectively? Most likely, it is due to his attraction to groupings of three, found throughout his letters. Still, the word ἀμέμπτως adds more than just a synonymous thought. This word deals specifically with the opposition, which Paul described as "great" (ἐν πολλῷ ἀγῶνι) in 1 Thess 2:2. Even though Paul and his group were charged with various accusations, they were "without blame."

17. Marshall, "Holiness in the Book of Acts," 115–16.

18. Morris, *The First and Second Epistles to the Thessalonians*, 59.

19. Arichea Jr., "Reading Romans in Southeast Asia," 209.

20. Wanamaker, *The Epistles to the Thessalonians*, 105.

Another area worth considering briefly, since it appears throughout the Thessalonian correspondence, is Paul's work ethic. In 1 Thess 2:9, Paul reminds the Thessalonians how he, Silvanus, and Timothy worked night and day (νὺκτος καὶ ἡμέρας). This phrase occurs five times in the NT, all of which occur in the Pauline letters. Three of the occurrences are found in the Thessalonian correspondence (1 Thess 2:9; 3:10; 2 Thess 3:8); two are found in the letters to Timothy (1 Tim 5:5; 2 Tim 1:3).

Νυκτὸς καὶ Ἡμέρας in the Pauline Letters

Verse	Text
1 Thess 2:9	νυκτὸς καὶ ἡμέρας ἐργαζόμενοι
1 Thess 3:10	νυκτὸς καὶ ἡμέρας ὑπερεκπερισσοῦ δεόμενοι
2 Thess 3:8	νυκτὸς καὶ ἡμέρας ἐργαζόμενοι
1 Tim 5:5	προσευχαῖς νυκτὸς καὶ ἡμέρας
2 Tim 1:3	ἐν ταῖς δεήσεσίν μου νυκτὸς καὶ ἡμέρας

Table 3. Νυκτὸς καὶ Ἡμέρας in the Pauline Letters.

Three of the five occurrences deal with prayer (1 Thess 3:10; 1 Tim 5:5; 2 Tim 1:3). The remaining two deal with work, both being used with the participle ἐργαζόμενοι (1 Thess 2:9; 2 Thess 3:8). In fact, both of these occurrences include the same descriptors (κόπος and μόχθος) of their work. There are two possibilities in how this expression can be understood—literally or rhetorically. Did Paul mean that he and his co-laborers actually worked and, even more, worked "night and day?" Or, did he use this expression similar to the English expression "day and night?"[21]

In Acts, Luke identifies Paul as having a profession (and it was not the ministry!).[22] In Acts 18:2–3, Luke records that Paul stayed with a married couple who made tents for a living. Luke says they were of "the same profession" (τὸ ὁμότεχνον).[23] What Luke records after that is also interesting. First, he says that Paul worked with Aquila and Priscilla

---

21. In English, the expression can be understood as referring to the amount of work being performed, i.e., "constantly," or to the amount of labor being performed (something like, "I worked like a dog").

22. See Black, "The Thessalonian Road to Self-Support."

23. Brian Rapske says Paul could have acquired this trade as part of Rabbinic training or through paternal relationship (*The Book of Acts in its First Century Settings*, 111).

(ἠργάζετο, Acts 18:3).[24] Given the way Luke presents the information, it appears Paul concentrated on work a great deal of the time once he arrived in Corinth. The only teaching that he records is Paul's involvement in teaching on every Sabbath (κατὰ πᾶν σάββατον, Acts 18:4) in the synagogue (singular). Only after Silas and Timothy arrive from Macedonia does Paul give himself entirely to the Word (συνείχετο τῷ λόγῳ, Acts 18:5). There are a few possibilities:

1. Paul could have used this as an opportunity to save up some money for their travels.

2. Paul could have postponed being devoted completely to the ministry of the Word because of Jesus's plan (and the church's plan) on sending missionaries out in groups.[25] Once they arrive, he transitions from reasoning (διελέγετο) to solemnly bearing witness (διαμαρτυρόμενος) to the Jews, presumably every day and everywhere, until they blasphemed and resisted him.

3. Paul could have postponed his full-throttle witness to the Jews, waiting for Silas and Timothy to arrive, because he was afraid. In Acts 18:9–10, God has to tell Paul, "Do not be afraid; speak and do not stop speaking." Why would God tell Paul to not fear if he was not afraid?[26]

Actually, each of these plays a part in what takes place in Acts 18, not just one. In 1 Cor 4:12, Paul says he works with his very own hands. Luke alone, however, reveals his profession. Returning to the phrase νὺκτος καὶ ἡμέρας, Jeffers says:

> Paul began his work before sunrise and continued it during much of the day. Apprentice contracts usually specified sunrise to sundown as the expected workday. He would likely have followed the Mediterranean custom of taking several hours in the middle of the day for rest and a meal.[27]

24. See Lai, *Tentmaking*, 12ff.

25. The similarity to Jesus's plan in Luke 10:1–16 is strengthened even more since Paul's reaction to the Jew's rejection of his message is wiping the dust off of his feet (cf. Luke 10:10–12; Acts 18:6).

26. This is not the only place where Paul demonstrates his fear. See also Gal 2:2. When he reported to the leaders of the church in Jerusalem about his labors in the gospel, especially toward the Gentiles, he makes the presentation in private. Why? He was afraid of the possibility that his efforts might have been in vain.

27. Jeffers, *The Greco-Roman World of the New Testament Era*, 28.

This lifestyle was part of Paul's philosophy of ministry from the very first missionary journey (1 Cor 9:6).[28] Ronald F. Hock says, "[W]e may picture Paul plying his trade wherever he was preaching the gospel."[29] There is nothing in the NT that indicates Timothy had a trade; however, social norms in general indicate that it would have been extremely uncommon for him to not have one. Although entirely speculation, it is not difficult to imagine him working with Paul. Paul uses his own work ethic as an example for the believers in Thessalonica. In 2 Thess 3:7–10, Paul tells them that they should remember his example, which he describes as disciplined.[30] When he and his co-laborers stayed in Thessalonica, they paid for their own food. He gives three purposes behind his work ethic:

1. They did not want to be a burden to the Thessalonian believers (2 Thess 3:8).

2. They intentionally wanted to give their own lives as an example on how the Thessalonians should live and work by being upstanding citizens (2 Thess 3:9).

3. They wanted the example they provided to be followed. It was not enough for them to just give the example; they wanted to see it bear fruit in the Thessalonians' lives, probably correcting some aspects of their lifestyle that they found troublesome (or unbecoming) of a believer in Christ (2 Thess 3:9).

Conduct, Imitation, and Παιδαγωγός in Galatians

The Conduct of the Galatian Believers

There are three different areas of conduct in Paul's letter to the Galatians. They are:

1. The Galatian believers' reprehensible conduct in relationship to the gospel.

2. Paul's own conduct, particularly toward the Galatians as a whole and Peter in particular.

3. The works of the flesh and the fruit of the Spirit.

28. Ronald F. Hock believes Paul's words in 1 Cor 9:19, i.e., his enslavement of himself, refers to Paul's devotion to self-support in ministry whenever possible ("Paul's Tentmaking," 6).

29. Hock, *The Social Context of Paul's Ministry*, 26.

30. Paul states this using a negative construction (οὐκ ἠτακτήσαμεν, 2 Thess 3:7).

In each there is continuity from the teaching and person of Jesus Christ. Moreover, each expresses different intricacies of likeness education, particularly what Timothy would have received from the investment Paul made in his life.

Most notable in Paul's letter to the Galatians is the absence of any thanksgiving before moving into the letter proper.[31] The only other Pauline letter lacking a thanksgiving is Hebrews, but for different reasons.[32] Instead of giving any thanks, Paul launches directly into the main content of the letter. R. Alan Cole writes:

> After the opening greeting, Paul normally in his letters moves onwards to some prayer for the local church. He very often first finds some point on which he can commend them. Then he gradually introduces the real purpose of the letter, which is not always so pleasant to the recipients. . . . But on this occasion there is no easy and gradual transition to the subject: Paul is too deeply moved for that.[33]

This is very unusual for Paul. He did not even do such a thing to the Corinthian believers. Even to them, with all of their church disorders,[34] Paul writes, "I always give thanks to my God concerning you" (1 Cor 1:4).

Not only does he refrain from commending the Galatian believers on anything positive, Paul uses a strong verb to describe how their conduct absolutely baffles him (θαυμάζω, 1:6). This is the only occurrence of this verb in a context like this found in the Pauline corpus. Something concerning the conduct of the Galatian believers absolutely troubled him, and the use of this verb indicates that Paul pounced on the Galatians immediately for it.[35] Martinus C. De Boer writes, "The use of the verb *thaumazō* to express astonishment with an undertone of irritation or annoyance in letters is conventional; the verb functions to introduce

---

31. McDonald and Porter, *Early Christianity and its Sacred Literature*, 415.

32. Hebrews is entirely unique since it lacks the letter opening (which identifies the author[s], recipients, location, etc.) and thanksgiving.

33. Cole, *Galatians*, 74.

34. These include leadership issues, divisions, sexual misconduct, lawsuits, divorce, dress codes, as well as abuses of the Lord's Supper and spiritual gifts. See Richardson, "Corinthians, First Letter to the," 281–83.

35. Beaudean Jr., *Paul's Theology of Preaching*, 67.

a rebuke."[36] What conduct could be so dumbfounding and dangerous to Paul that he jumps right into a rebuke in one of his letters?

The content ὅτι in Gal 1:6 following the verb indicates what caused Paul such concern. The Galatian brothers and sisters were not guilty as it were for tolerating sexual sins like the Corinthians, or lawsuits, or abuses to the Lord's Supper. They were guilty of something much more heinous and much more dangerous. The verb Paul uses is μετατίθεσθε, a verb that carries the idea of deserting someone or becoming a traitor.[37] Kenneth L. Boles shows how the word was used to describe a person's act of changing from one philosophical school to another.[38] The present tense here is almost certainly durative, referring to the treacherous act that Paul catches the Galatians in the process of doing.[39]

Paul specifies what the Galatians are turning from (or better yet, from whom):

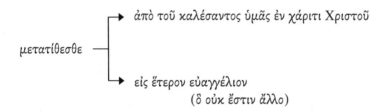

$$\mu\varepsilon\tau\alpha\tau\acute{\iota}\theta\varepsilon\sigma\theta\varepsilon \longrightarrow \begin{cases} \mathring{\alpha}\pi\grave{o} \; \tauo\tilde{\upsilon} \; \kappa\alpha\lambda\acute{\varepsilon}\sigma\alpha\nu\tauo\varsigma \; \mathring{\upsilon}\mu\tilde{\alpha}\varsigma \; \mathring{\varepsilon}\nu \; \chi\acute{\alpha}\rho\iota\tau\iota \; X\rho\iota\sigma\tauo\tilde{\upsilon} \\ \\ \varepsilon\mathring{\iota}\varsigma \; \mathring{\varepsilon}\tau\varepsilon\rho o\nu \; \varepsilon\mathring{\upsilon}\alpha\gamma\gamma\acute{\varepsilon}\lambda\iota o\nu \\ (\mathring{o} \; o\mathring{\upsilon}\kappa \; \mathring{\varepsilon}\sigma\tau\iota\nu \; \mathring{\alpha}\lambda\lambda o) \end{cases}$$

First, Paul says who the Galatians were turning away from—"the one who called you." There are three possibilities. Paul could be referring to himself, i.e., he is the one who called the Galatians. While possible, it is very unlikely. When Paul refers to being deserted by persons elsewhere in the NT, he explicitly says so (cf. 2 Tim 4:10); moreover, the verb καλέω he almost always reserves for a divine act (e.g., Gal 1:15; Rom 8:30).[40] He could be referring to Jesus, but it is unlikely given he does not use a possessive pronoun with χάριτι. The most probable answer is the Galatians were in the process of turning away from God the Father, the one Paul

36. Boer, *Galatians*, 39.

37. Borchert, *Worship in the New Testament*, 125.

38. Boles, *Galatians and Ephesians*, 32.

39. Jervis, *Galatians*; Longenecker, *Galatians*, 14; Beaudean Jr., *Paul's Theology of Preaching*, 67.

40. For an exception, see 1 Cor 7:24.

identifies in his salutations as calling Paul as an apostle and raising Jesus from the dead (1:1).[41] John William Beaudean Jr. writes:

> This is a serious indictment, especially in view of the fact that later Paul will describe their condition prior to their conversion as a form of slavery in which they "did not know God" (4:8–9). Paul implies that they are throwing away their entire relationship to the true, living God (cf. 1 Thess 1:9–10).[42]

Is it possible that Paul is comparing the actions of these believers to the Israelites at Sinai? Frank Thielman believes so. He writes, "Paul is astounded that they would imitate the error of ancient Israel and turn aside from God's redemption."[43] There is nothing more embarrassing in the history of Israel than their quick desertion from the one who brought them out from bondage in Egypt, allowed them to see his glory, and made provisions to dwell with them forever (Exod 19:1—32:10).

What did Israel exchange everything for? –A molten calf. By God's grace and because of his faithfulness to his own word, they were not destroyed nor was the covenant he made with them revoked. Paul's audience here is not guilty of deserting God for a golden calf. They are in the process of deserting God for a false gospel (εἰς ἕτερον εὐαγγέλιον, Gal 1:6). The primary difference between the gospel that Paul preached in Galatia and the gospel that is luring the believers away is the absence of *sola fide*. The absence of this most critical aspect of the gospel renders it a non-gospel, which is what Paul means by the clause ὃ οὐκ ἔστιν ἄλλο.[44]

"Open table-fellowship with Gentiles and no requirement for circumcision were, for Paul, non-negotiable positions," says Robert M. Royalty Jr.[45] Believers in Galatia were turning away from the gospel that taught justification apart from works (Eph 2:8–9). The change in their understanding of the gospel impacted how they lived in the new community that Jesus promised in Matt 16:18 (see also Eph 2:19–20). The allure of this man-oriented gospel (Gal 1:11) was not only tempting to the baby believers in regions where Paul preached, but it was apparently so powerful it could lead astray even the strongest of believers. For example, Paul specifically mentions Peter, who he identifies as one of the

---

41. Boles, *Galatians and Ephesians*, 33.

42. Beaudean Jr., *Paul's Theology of Preaching*, 67.

43. Thielman, *Paul and the Law*, 136.

44. Grassmick, "Galatians," 370.

45. Royalty Jr., *The Origin of Heresy*, 74.

pillars (στῦλοι, Gal 2:11) and who had received a vision from God (Acts 10:9–16) concerning the Gentiles,[46] as being caught up on the wrong side of the controversy (Gal 2:11–14).

Imitation in Galatians

There are two key examples of imitation in Paul's letter to the Galatians.[47] The first, a negative example, concerns Peter's example in Antioch (Gal 2:11–13). The second, a positive example, is Paul's exhortation for the Galatian believers to be like him (Gal 4:12). Luke does not record anything about the conflict mentioned in Galatians between Paul and Peter (Acts 15:36–41); he presents the disagreement as one concerning whether or not John Mark would accompany Barnabas and Paul.[48] Paul adds more information here, a bigger picture, surrounding the controversy. The fol-

46. God needed to show Peter the exact same vision three times (τοῦτο δὲ ἐγένετο ἐπὶ τρίς, Acts 10:16) before he would finally surrender to God's will and recognize his required participation in facilitating the gospel's spread to the Gentiles.

47. The previous analysis of μαθητής and διδάσκαλος in chapter 2 has already shown that μαθητής occurs nowhere outside of the Gospels and Acts. The noun διδάσκαλος, on the other hand, does occur elsewhere in the NT, albeit rarely (9x), only one of which is found outside the Pauline corpus. As the analysis of Luke 6:39–49 has already shown, there are other elements to the μαθητής-διδάσκαλος relationship that can be identified in the NT beyond simply identifying occurrences of the lexemes. For example, in the Gospels, Jesus calls his disciples to be "with him" (μετ' αὐτοῦ; e.g., Mark 3:14; 14:33; 16:10). In Gal 1:2, Paul uses an interesting phrase—οἱ σὺν ἐμοὶ πάντες ἀδελφοὶ ("all the brothers and sisters who are with me"). Is there sufficient reason to understand this as a reference to Paul's own disciple-making efforts?—Probably not. So much cannot be read into a simple prepositional phrase. But, some observations can be made.

The phrase σὺν ἐμοί is found in four of Paul's letters (nowhere in the non-Pauline corpus). Paul is always accompanied by others in ministry; some of these, though not all, were in a μαθητής-διδάσκαλος relationship with him, such as Timothy, Titus, and Luke. Twice Paul uses the phrase in reference to someone he considers a spiritual son in the faith (Phil 2:22; Gal 2:3 [Titus1:4]). Titus, who Paul mentions in Gal 2:1, accompanies him and Barnabas on their trip to Jerusalem for the first council on the nature of the gospel.

48. Helmut Köster believes that Paul "lost out in this conflict" since Paul and Barnabas, mentioned in Gal 2:13, sever their missionary partnership (Introduction to the New Testament, Volume 2, 113). There is another option. Peter unaligned himself with the party sent by James, reestablished fellowship with the Gentile believers, and Barnabas followed suit. Luke, therefore, records the disagreement between Paul and Barnabas specifically concerning the accompaniment of his cousin, John Mark, because this was the main dividing line between the two. The other issue was resolved in Antioch before Paul's departure for the second missionary journey.

lowing characteristics describe Peter's actions, from Paul's perspective, in Antioch:

1. Peter had been in the habit of fellowshipping with Jewish and Gentile believers alike (Gal 2:12). The use of the imperfect συνήσθιεν, a customary imperfect,[49] refers to this as a characteristic description of Peter's daily life and ministry.[50]

2. After certain disciples arrived from Jerusalem, Peter started withdrawing and distancing himself.[51] He may have been distancing himself from the Gentiles in general, keeping away from them in conversation and all sorts of interaction. Paul may, however, only be referring to dining with the Gentiles, particularly eating the foods that they were accustomed to eating.[52]

3. The reason causing Peter's own desertion was fear of what those from the party of the circumcision might say about him (Gal 2:12, φοβούμενος), possibly fearing what they might do to him (i.e., persecution).[53]

Paul makes it very clear that this is a conscious decision by Peter out of his own volition to withdraw from the Gentiles. Paul does not say that Peter is guilty of what the Gentiles are doing (μετατίθεσθε, 1:6). Peter's conduct changes out of fear, not because he is convinced by the gospel brought by the περιτομαί.[54] Nevertheless, Peter's actions carried devastating theological undertones. For example, instead of stressing the explicit teachings of Jesus for one's conduct (as they did with Paul; see Gal 2:10), this sort of gospel emphasizes conduct according the Law, which does not justify; if it does not justify, how can it be emphasized as the source

---

49. For a brief discussion on the different uses of the imperfect, see McLean, *New Testament Greek*, 109.

50. Schreiner, *Galatians*, 139; Schnelle, *Theology of the New Testament*, 134.

51. On the inceptive uses of the imperfect here, see Niang, *Faith and Freedom in Galatia and Senegal*, 100 n.29.

52. Schnelle writes, "The context (2:12, συνήσθιεν [he used to eat with]) indicates that compelling Gentiles to live in the Jewish way refers primarily to the keeping of the Jewish food laws" (*Theology of the New Testament*, 134).

53. Peter readily accepts and endures imprisonment elsewhere (e.g., Acts 4). Something causes him to be afraid though.

54. The use of the verb συνυποκρίνομαι in v. 13 may add more support since the word has overtones of acting, such as in a drama (i.e., playing a role). See Fung, *The Epistle to the Galatians*, 110.

of life and godliness (cf. Gal 3:1–14)? While Peter did not embrace a different gospel, his actions were representative of the different gospel the Galatians were so quickly turning to.

Peter's actions are evidence of the proverb in Luke 6:40. They show just how quickly a person's character/actions can become like those of someone else, in this case negatively. Paul says, "The rest of the Jews joined together [or, aligned themselves with; συνυπεκρίθησαν] him" (Gal 2:13). The presence of the party coming from where James was would certainly cause some disruption, especially if they arrived in opposition to Peter and Paul's work among the Gentiles, which did not stress Jewish dietary obedience. However, had Paul been joined by Peter in an opposing stance against them, any sort of problem would have been squashed. The unanimity of Peter and Paul would have been sufficient to quell the spread of a false gospel, especially since both were present in Jerusalem for the council. Peter bowed out of the fight before it even started. Paul recognized Peter's actions and was forced to confront him, especially since his actions were so quickly leading many astray, not to mention causing division.[55] As Paul says in v. 14, Peter's actions did not stand the test of the gospel.

In addition to this, Paul gives himself as an example for the Galatian believers. They can continue this turn to a false gospel, as the rest of the Jews turned and followed Peter and the pharisaic party in Antioch, or they can have a different example, namely Paul's. In Gal 2:14–21, Paul records his reaction to Peter. Chapter 3 contains an exhortation to the Galatian believers to consider the nature of the gospel and the relationship of the Law to history in general and Israel in particular. Finally, in Gal 4:10, Paul deals with the adoption that believers have in Christ, regardless of whether they are Jew or Gentile. Verses 11 and 20 in Galatians 4 form an *inclusio*, beginning and ending with Paul's reminder of his labor over and with the Galatians. According to 4:11, if the Galatian believers turn 180 degrees, thus abandoning the true gospel, all of Paul's work will have been for nothing, including his weakness (Gal 4:13–14).

Paul exhorts the believers to be like him (γίνεσθε ὡς ἐγώ) in Gal 4:12. This is semantically equivalent to Paul's exhortation to the Corinthians, "Be imitators of me" (μιμηταί μου γίνεσθε, 1 Cor 11:1). In fact, the passages appear more similar given the accompanying clauses:

---

55. Köster, *Introduction to the New Testament, Volume 2*, 113–14.

Gal 4:12: γίνεσθε ὡς ἐγώ → ὅτι κἀγὼ ὡς ὑμεῖς

1 Cor 11:1: μιμηταί μου γίνεσθε → καθὼς κἀγὼ Χριστοῦ

Galatians includes a causal ὅτι, explaining why Paul's audience should be like him. He has, according to Gal 4:12, also become like them. This is a rather difficult statement to explain. In what manner was Paul like (ὡς) the Galatians? There is, of course, an absence of the word μιμηταί in Galatians. Still, ὡς stresses the similarities existing between the two groups (i.e., Paul and the Galatians). In 1 Cor 11:1, the imitation Paul encourages is directly linked to the person and example of Jesus Christ. Moreover, in both, Paul uses the present imperative to underscore the ongoing state of being like his example.[56] Even though this is in the imperative, De Boer views this as an earnest request, not a command.[57] There are competing examples at work in Galatia. Undoubtedly, the fake gospel the Galatians are being lured away by has its own examples, just as Peter became one in Antioch. Paul is not just earnestly requesting them to follow his example; he is begging them (δέομαι ὑμῶν, 4:12; cf. 2 Cor 10:2). This is of utmost importance; that he begs them is evidence of the urgency at hand.

De Boer believes Paul is referring to liberty from the law. The logic is as follows:

1. "Become and remain as I am now, free from the law."

2. "Because I also have become as you are now, free from the law."[58]

The latter half of De Boer's interpretation is difficult to grasp. If they are free from the law, how would they become like him in his freedom from the law? Elizabeth A. Castelli helps clarify:

> Paul's action of forsaking the law had the result of Paul becoming like the Gentiles, but the action was not motivated by any

56. De Boer, *Galatians: A Commentary*, 278. Robert W. Wall says it "envisages a work in progress" (*Community of the Wise*, 78). Bruner says the present imperative can refer to the time needed for this transformation to take place. Concerning its use in Matt 24:44, he says, the "use of the present tense shows an appreciation that this adjustment does not come all at once. It takes time to learn hope" (Bruner, *Matthew*, 530). It really seems as if scholars draw a hard line between the imperatives of εἰμί and γίνομαι, the latter referring to the process of change into a state. However, Dan G. McCartney is right; the translation "be" best translates the "ongoing character" of the imperative (*James*, 119).

57. De Boer, *Galatians: A Commentary*, 278.

58. Ibid.

> intention to become like the Gentiles. The reverse is not the
> case; the Gentiles are called upon to free themselves from the
> law, and to do so by becoming like Paul.[59]

Ὡς clauses like this one, when referring to a person, seem to deal more with the person's character or actions than one's condition or natures. Thus, Paul is not referring to their becoming like him salvifically, in Christ, etc. He is indeed referring to his own conversion experience, specifically how he left the Mosaic Law and its requirements, becoming as it were a Gentile in lifestyle.[60]

De Boer's interpretation of ὅτι κἀγὼ ὑμῶν (Gal 4:12) is not the best. The idea that Paul is begging the Galatians to be like him, i.e., free from the law, hinges on a past-time form of γίνομαι (such as γέγονα) being supplied in the second half. However, the most common form of verbal ellipsis in Greek is with the verb εἰμί.[61] Ellipses must have been understood in their contexts, or the author would have been obligated to or felt inclined to supply the verb.[62] What is the action or characteristic that Paul immediately describes of the Galatians? He says they did nothing unjust to him (Gal 4:13). He even describes in detail how they treated him. In his weakness, when his "thorn in the flesh" became manifest before the Galatians and somewhat hindered his ability to serve at peak performance, they treated him as an "angel of God" and as "Christ Jesus" (Gal 4:14). Paul's latter phrase demonstrates that he learned something from the Galatian believers and is now imitating them. His letter is not designed to treat them unjustly or cause them any harm. He has their best interests in mind, just as they had his when he first preached the gospel to them.

This is extremely important in likeness education. Because all are "in Christ" together, μαθηταί and διδάσκαλοι inside this spiritual union in Christ have the capacity to imitate one another. There exists a mutual and reciprocal *mimesis* among believers. Epaphroditus, a fellow-Philippian,

---

59. Castelli, *Imitating Paul*, 115.

60. Lopez, *Apostle to the Conquered*, 141.

61. Abasciano, *Paul's Use of the Old Testament*, 184. Filippo Belli specifically mentions the need for a form of εἰμί with ὡς clauses (*Argumentation and Use of Scripture in Romans 9–11*, 209 n.65). It is true that ellipses often imply the thought of the previous phrase, as Joseph D. Fantin points out (*The Greek Imperative Mood in the New Testament*, 255). This does not mean that the exact same verb has to be carried over into the ellipsis, only the idea; the idea in Gal 4:12 is *mimesis*.

62. DeMoss, *Pocket Dictionary*, 51.

for example, is given as an example for the Philippians to imitate (Phil 2:25–30). However, Gal 4:12–14 is the only place in the NT where the mutual and reciprocal *mimesis* includes an apostle acknowledging that he imitates other believers (especially non-apostles). This is significant because normally there appears a hierarchy with *mimesis*. For example, in 1 Cor 11:1, there is Christ, who is imitated by Paul, who then gives himself as an example to others. Galatians 4:12 teaches how Paul recognized his ability to see Christ in others and imitate them as well. He does not do this for mere rhetorical effect, wishing to charm the Galatians into following his example. Imitation in the NT is designed to be horizontal; Christ alone is at the top, always as the chief example.

Leaders are supposed to be examples. The qualifications of pastors and deacons found in 1 Timothy and Titus demonstrate this. They are required to have exemplary lifestyles. Paul even tells believers to imitate them (Heb 13:7). But, just as Jesus was able to pull a child to his side and find something in that child's character or person for his disciple's to imitate, so Paul acknowledges here in Gal 4:12 the reciprocal nature of *mimesis*. Even he, an apostle of the Lord Jesus Christ, imitates fellow believers when their conduct merits it. Even babes in Christ, in whom the Spirit dwells, can have Christ living through them in ways worthy of *mimesis*. While Paul skips over the thanksgiving section in his letter and moves right into the matter concerning the gospel, his words in Gal 4:13–14 are more than tender and genuine. Of no other group does he say he was received in a manner like this group received him, especially at a time when his "thorn" was acting up.

The Meaning of Παιδαγωγός in Galatians 3:23–25

The word παιδαγωγός is extremely rare in the NT, occurring only three times (Gal 3:24–25 [2x]; 1 Cor 4:15).[63] According to Witherington, παιδαγωγός "means literally a boy or child leader and it refers to a member of the household entrusted with the care and guardianship of a minor."[64] N. R. E. Fisher defines it as a "domestic slave charged with attending and watching a free child."[65] The following glosses are provided by Trenchard:

63. Smith, "The Role of the Pedagogue in Galatians," 197. For one of the most detailed discussions on the use of παιδαγωγός in ancient sources, see Young, "*PAIDA-GOGOS*," 150–176.

64. Witherington III, *Grace in Galatia*, 263.

65. Fisher, *Slavery in Classical Greece*, 120.

"attendant," "custodian," and "guide."[66] They were most often utilized in the upper echelons of society.[67] These persons are always older and often rather advanced in age.[68]

From where did well-off families acquire these attendant-guides? Moreover, what were they tasked to do? Witherington answers:

> This person was almost always a slave, and very often in the first century A.D. was a foreigner. Generally speaking these persons were taken captive during a war, sold at a slave auction, and were bought by well-to-do heads of households looking for slaves who had some knowledge of Greek, and perhaps some smattering of philosophy so they could aid in the moral upbringing of the 'master's' children, in particular his male heirs.[69]

Mark Golden lists a παιδαγωγός as one of the three types of slaves that directly interacted with children in the ancient world; the other two are the τιτθή (wet-nurse) and τροφός/παιδοτρόφος.[70] Witherington says, "There were both bad and good pedagogues and the latter were not rare exceptions to a rule."[71] He lists the following duties performed by a παιδαγωγός:[72]

1. Responsibilities characteristic of a shepherd caring for sheep.

2. Escorting a child in public, providing supervision and protection.[73]

3. Providing a sound moral example to a child under supervision.

4. Guiding those under their supervision in their academic studies.

5. Performing servant/slave responsibilities.

---

66. Trenchard, *Complete Vocabulary Guide*, 85.

67. Some suggest Paul uses this imagery in Galatians and 1 Corinthians because he himself had a παιδαγωγός in his youth. See Hock, "Paul and Greco-Roman Education," 216; Lull, "'The Law Was Our Pedagogue,'" 489–95.

68. Matera, *Galatians*, 139. Artwork depicting a παιδαγωγός-παιδίον relationship sometimes shows an elderly man (see Young, "The Figure of the *Paidagōgos* in Art and Literature," 80–86).

69. Witherington, *Grace in Galatia*, 263–64.

70. Golden, "Slavery and Homosexuality at Athens," 164. Golden says a τροφός refers more generally to someone involved in the "rearing" of a child.

71. Witherington, *Grace in Galatia*, 263.

72. Ibid., 264–65.

73. Fisher, *Slavery in Classical Greece*, 55.

Included in these is the responsibility a παιδαγωγός had to discipline the child as necessary and as permission allowed.[74]

Scholarly investigations, especially from a social-science approach as found in Witherington's work, show the fallacy of equating παιδαγωγός with διδάσκαλος.[75] The translations "teacher," "tutor," and "schoolmaster" are misleading.[76] Even in Classical literature, there is a difference between παιδαγωγός and instructors in different fields, e.g., γραμματιστής and παιδοτρίβης; these latter two were more likely to be classified a διδάσκαλος than a παιδαγωγός. One key difference between these is a παιδαγωγός "gave no formal instruction but administered the directives of the father in a custodial manner."[77]

How long did such a relationship last? Clearly a child could not remain under the supervision, guardianship, and tutelage for the duration of his life. This is a temporary relationship, one that has an anticipated

74. Calvert-Koyzis, *Paul, Monotheism, and the People of God*, 103. Gene Getz writes, "[T]he tutor was a disciplinarian. Sometimes he was harsh and cruel. In ancient art, the paidagogos was often pictured as a man with a rod in his hand, ready to strike a disobedient boy" (*Loving One Another*, 12).

75. Witherington, *Grace in Galatia*, 264; Collins, *The Power of Images in Paul*, 98; De Boer, *Galatians: A Commentary*, 240; MacGorman, "The Law as Paidagogos," 99–111.

76. Smith, "The Role of the Pedagogue in Galatians," 198. Scholars, like Anthony T. Hanson, still affirm the educative role behind the word, which joins famous theologians like Martin Luther and others ("The Origin of Paul's Use," 73).

77. Longenecker, "The Pedagogical Nature of the Law," 55. One of Clement of Alexandria's educational works is actually titled "Παιδαγωγός." A. P. Sharma describes it this way:

> "In *Paidagogos* [Clement] is more concerned with the character formation of youth. The theme of morality has been discussed at a great length, as for him the inculcation of virtue is more important than knowledge. . . . In *Paidagogos* Christ is presented as the teacher of humanity; not as a professor cultivating intellect and mental skills, but as a model in whom men could find example." (*Development of Western Education Thoughts*, 43)

Clement's work shows that character-transfer was more important in thinking about education than the mere transfer of information. His own "Timothy," Origen, carried on the work in Alexandria, which Arthur F. Holmes says was characterized by μαθητής-διδάσκαλος relationships similar (though not identical to) what is found in the Gospels. Holmes points out, "As was often the case then, students met and sometimes lived in their teacher's home, so that he became a mentor and model of virtue" (*Building the Christian Academy*, 18). See also Wagner, *Christianity in the Second Century*, 171–86.

end from the day it is begun (although that exact date is unknown at the time). The τιτθή and τροφός (παιδοτρόφος) relationships began much earlier; the παιδαγωγός-παιδίον relationship could begin as early as a child learned to speak (see Xenophon, *de Rep. Lac.* 2.1) or later, such as at the age of seven (e.g., Plato, *Axiochus*, 366d–e).[78] Boles says this relationship usually ended by age sixteen.[79] While there is no consensus or fixed date for the completion of this relationship, Norman H. Young indicates it extended well beyond puberty.[80]

In Gal 3:23–25, Paul indicates that the Israelites had this sort of relationship with the Law—corporately and individually. Does he refer to the temporariness of Israel's relationship to the law by comparing it to a παιδαγωγός-παιδίον relationship?[81] Or, does Paul refer to the negative elements characterized by the παιδαγωγός-παιδίον relationship?[82] Paul clearly has temporal ideas in his mind in the context. For example, Paul says:

1. The Law was added "until the seed would come" (ἄχρις οὗ ἔλθῃ τὸ σπέρμα, Gal 3:19).

2. A child remained under the care of the παιδαγωγός "until the date fixed by his father" (ἄχρι τῆς προθεσμίας τοῦ πατρός, Gal 4:2).

3. He maintains his close relationship with the believers in Galatia "until Christ is formed" in them (μέχρις οὗ μορφωθῇ Χριστὸς ἐν ὑμῖν, Gal 4:19).

There is also evidence that Paul viewed the Law negatively.[83] Stephen Finlan writes:

78. James Riley Estep Jr. says the role of teacher as παιδαγωγός corresponds to the earlier years (i.e., preschool age) in Greek education. The earlier a child had a παιδαγωγός, the more the παιδαγωγός would teach. Once the child became of age to receive formal instruction in music, grammar, and gymnastics, the παιδαγωγός took over a more supervisorial-guardian role ("It's All Greek to Me! Education in Greek Culture," in *C.E.: The Heritage of Christian Education*, ed. James Riley Estep Jr. (Joplin, MO: College Press, 2003), 4.6.

79. Boles, *Galatians and Ephesians*, 91.

80. Young, "The Figure of the *Paidagōgos* in Art and Literature," 80.

81. For example, see Burton, *Epistle to the Galatians*, 200; Bruce, *The Epistle to the Galatians*, 183; Longenecker, "The Pedagogical Nature of the Law in Galatians 3:19–4:7," 56; Meyer, *The End of the Law*, 172.

82. For example, see Hübner, *Law in Paul's Thought*, 31–33; Betz, *Galatians*, 177–78.

83. Collins says the negative tone is apparent given the parallel ideas of being

The disciplinarian analogy is an excellent one: these disciplinarians were reputed to be strict and demanding, and they were temporary, for the period just preceding adulthood. Coming out from under the disciplinarian was a much-desired event. In the same way, coming out from under the domineering Torah and into the age of faith was a real coming of age.[84]

However, this negative view does not concern the quality and essence of the Law itself. Paul views it negatively in relationship to the New Covenant, especially as it relates to participants of the covenant who have been released from the care of a παιδαγωγός. For example, it is likened to enslavement in Gal 4:3–5 (ἤμεθα δεδουλωμένοι). Entering again, be it as an adult, into such a relationship would be a heinous suggestion and ludicrous idea. But this is all in reference to after someone has come to believe in Jesus Christ.

There are three possible interpretations for Gal 3:24. One option is the Law, even before the ratification of the New Covenant, was designed to be a guide that led persons to Christ (εἰς Χριστόν).[85] Another option is, since the ratification of the New Covenant, the Law took on a different purpose than it previously had—it "has become our guide into Christ" (ὁ νόμος παιδαγωγὸς ἡμῶν γέγονεν εἰς Χριστόν). In Gal 3:19–20, Paul clearly specifies that, before the ratification of the New Covenant, the purpose of the Law was mediatorial and temporal (e.g., ἄχρις).[86] James D. G. Dunn says this of the Law:

> In the sequence of Israel's history, the law was given as an act of God's magnanimity for Israel's benefit, probably as a means of dealing with Israel's sins, and certainly with constrictive consequences,[87] but basically to protect, instruct, and discipline.[88]

The ratification of the New Covenant occurs at the cross (Luke 22:20; 23:44–46). Since then, the Law does not disappear; instead, God uses

---

"under" (ὑπό) something (e.g., the law [Gal 3:23], sin [Gal 3:22], and a curse [Gal 4:3]). All of these, he says, have a "negative connotation" (*The Power of Images in Paul*, 98).

84. Finlan, *The Apostle Paul and the Pauline Tradition*, 88.

85. Erickson, *Christian Theology*, 196.

86. Dunn, *The Theology of Paul the Apostle*, 143; Cosgrove, *The Cross and the Spirit*, 71.

87. See Leviticus 26 and Deuteronomy 28. The consequences are more numerous than the blessings.

88. Dunn, *The Theology of Paul the Apostle*, 142.

it as a means to bring people to Christ through faith. Once a believer comes to Christ through faith, the Law has fulfilled its purpose and is no longer needed, just as a child no longer needs his παιδαγωγός (Gal 3:25). Of course, not everyone would agree with this understanding, especially concerning the εἰς prepositional phrase. This leads to the third option. Under this view, the Law only served as παιδαγωγός as long as the Mosaic Covenant was in effect. De Boer, for example, says, "Verse 25, with its claims that since 'this faith has come, we are no longer under a *paidagōgos*,' meaning 'under the law' (v. 23), only makes sense if the *eis* in v. 24 also has a temporal meaning."[89] His translation would be something like, "Therefore the Law had become our tutor until Christ."

Still, Paul uses similar language in Gal 4:19 to suggest that believers have not exited the παιδαγωγός-παιδίον relationship only to be found in no relationship at all. Paul neither abandons this metaphor entirely, as indicated by his use of τέκνα μου ("my children"), nor the enslavement imagery. Fẹmi Adeyẹmi, says:

> Unlike the *paidagogos* (the Mosaic Law) that Paul affirms he and the New Covenant church are no longer under (cf. 1 Cor 9:20, Gal 3:25), Paul presents himself and the New Covenant church as under this Law of Christ (cf. 1 Cor 9:21, Gal 6:2).[90]

Does Paul view himself as a new type of παιδαγωγός, in service to younger believers until a new fixed end—"until Christ is formed in you" (μέχρις οὗ μορφωθῇ Χριστὸς ἐν ὑμῖν)? Believers, upon entry into the New Covenant, are generally considered infants. Consider how he speaks to the Corinthians believers: "I gave you milk to drink, not solid food" (1 Cor 3:2; cf. Heb 5:12–13; 1 Thess 2:5–7). Of course, here Paul seems to compare his relationship to believers more so to the role of a μήτηρ or τιτθή. In 1 Cor 4:15, the third of three uses of παιδαγωγός in the NT, Paul explicitly identifies himself as a "guide" to the Corinthian believers.[91]

---

89. De Boer, *Galatians: A Commentary*, 240. See also, Adeyẹmi, *The New Covenant Torah*, 122; Matera, *New Testament Theology*, 161.

90. Adeyẹmi, *The New Covenant Torah*, 123.

91. Sakharov, *I Love, There I Am*, 200. Paul may also view each believer as having Christ as their new παιδαγωγός, which may warrant further investigation.

Love in 1 Corinthians 13

1 Corinthians 13 contains the Pauline equivalent to John's attention to love found within his Gospel and letters. The περὶ δέ construction found in 1 Cor 12:1 signals Paul's shift to a new topic.[92] Between 1 Corinthians 12 and 14, Paul discusses spiritual gifts, in particular issues of abuse in the Corinthian church that need attention and correction.[93] The root concern in 1 Corinthians 13 is the Corinthian believers lack one thing— love. Imbedded within this chapter are teachings that are important to understanding the cessation of spiritual gifts (1 Cor 13:8–10). Cessationism, however, is not the primary teaching from this chapter, nor can it be proven on the basis of this chapter alone. Garland writes, "Far from being a displaced hymn singing the praise of love as a virtue, chapter 13 is a call to a way of life that addresses real problems in the church."[94] Like most of the Corinthian correspondence, Paul is hard at work trying to correct major issues impeding the spiritual growth of these believers and the testimony that they have in and beyond Corinth.

Paul is always concerned with praxis when he teaches and writes his letters. 1 Corinthians 13 is sandwiched between two key chapters on the misuse and misappropriation of the gifts of the Spirit.[95] By analyzing what Paul says about love in 1 Corinthians 13, it is possible to gain a better understanding of the type of love Paul modeled to Timothy (2 Tim

92. Paul rarely uses this construction outside of Corinthians, in fact only twice (1 Thess 4:9; 5:1). They either mark Paul's responses to the Corinthians' questions outlined in a previous letter, or they correspond to reports Paul heard concerning their conduct in Corinth on a number of issues: (1) marital relations (7:1–24), (2) singleness (7:25–40), (3) food sacrificed to idols (8:1—11:1), (4) spiritual gifts (12:1—14:40), (5) the collection of money (16:1–4), and (6) Apollos (16:12). Most believe they are issues identified by the Corinthians in a letter sent to Paul. The first use contains a modifier, ὧν ἐγράψατε; even though subsequent uses of περὶ δέ lack the modifier, they believe it is implied. See Dunn, *1 Corinthians*, 19; Fee, *To What End Exegesis*, 91; Roetzel, *The Letters of Paul*, 92; Klauck, *Ancient Letters and the New Testament*, 451. However, it is possible that this is a rhetorical device used by Paul to shift from one topic to the next, e.g., see Mitchell, "Concerning *peri de* in 1 Corinthians," 229–56; Fitzmyer, *First Corinthians*, 277.

93. MacArthur Jr., *Charismatic Chaos*, 275; Thomas, *Understanding Spiritual Gifts*, 210–11.

94. Garland, *1 Corinthians*, 608.

95. The position proposed by Anthony C. Thiselton (via Moffatt) is interesting. He believes Paul "composed this chapter over several days or more as he reflected upon the situation in Corinth, and subsequently inserted it into the flow of his letter after he had formulated it" (*1 Corinthians*, 218).

3:10). The chapter begins with three conditional statements (marked by ἐάν), each containing an antecedent (A#) and consequent (C#):[96]

A₁: ἐὰν ταῖς γλώσσαις τῶν ἀνθρώπων λαλῶ καὶ τῶν ἀγγέλων
     ἀγάπην δὲ μὴ ἔχω
C₁: γέγονα χαλκὸς ἠχῶν ἢ κύμβαλον ἀλαλάζον

A₂: καὶ ἐὰν ἔχω προφητείαν
     καὶ [ἐὰν]εἰδῶ τὰ μυστήρια πάντα
     καὶ [ἐὰν] πᾶσαν τὴν γνῶσιν
     καὶ ἐὰν ἔχω πᾶσαν τὴν πίστιν ὥστε ὄρη μεθιστάναι
     ἀγάπην δὲ μὴ ἔχω
C₂: οὐθέν εἰμι

A₃: κἂν ψωμίσω πάντα τὰ ὑπάρχοντά μου
     καὶ ἐὰν παραδῶ τὸ σῶμά μου ἵνα καυχήσωμαι
     ἀγάπην δὲ μὴ ἔχω
C₃: οὐδὲν ὠφελοῦμαι

Common to each unit is the phrase ἀγάπην δὲ μὴ ἔχω ("but I do not have love"). Paul is not minimizing the importance of the spiritual gifts of prophecy and tongues in 13:1–2. If anyone understood the importance these spiritual gifts played in the early life of the church, Paul did. As an apostle, Paul understood his ministry as being one of a builder laying the foundation of the new community Jesus promised to build in Matt 16:18 (see Eph 2:19–20; 1 Cor 3:10).[97] Apostolic instruction was not the only way that God guided and instructed New Covenant participants who did not have the totality of the NT teachings as believers today do. Prophecy was critical for this period of time in the life of the church while the foundation was being laid. However, if believers did not exercise these gifts with love, they failed miserably.

96. Abilities and actions found in the conditional statements do not necessarily reflect reality. In other words, just because Paul mentions an angelic language does not necessarily imply that such a language exists. He is speaking rhetorically.

97. Please note the use of the future in Matt 16:18. The church is a unique community of believers that did not exist prior to the life, death, and resurrection of Jesus Christ. It is dangerous hermeneutically to see the church in the Old Testament. One of the biggest "secrets" (see τὰ μυστήρια in Matt 13:11) includes the church, which shocked the disciples. The idea of a kingdom community that included both tares and wheat until the consummation of the ages simply was not expected nor foreshadowed in the Old Testament.

Ministry in Corinth was extremely divisive (1 Cor 11:16–19). In-dividuals sought their own best interests and tried to find any avenue to exalt themselves. Some viewed themselves as better than others on the basis of who baptized them (1 Cor 1:12–14; 3:1–4). Some viewed themselves as better than others on the basis of which spiritual gift had been imparted to them. Such is the case in 1 Corinthians 12–14. Thomas summarizes the issue in 1 Corinthians 13 best: "Love is exclusively outgo-ing and other-directed."[98] The first thing Paul does in 1 Corinthians 13 is recalibrate the Corinthians' sights and attempt to focus their attention on what they lack, showing that it is in fact the most important element of the Christian life. Garland writes, "Paul's strategy is to place in center stage the gift that the Corinthians prized the most and that was causing the greatest disruption in their assembly and then to bring it down sev-eral notches by showing its emptiness without love."[99] George Klein says, "In the opening three verses Paul states the worthlessness of anything we may have or do without love. He is not speaking of the way into the kingdom of grace but of living and working in it."[100] What does Paul say about someone who does not have love?

Paul says a believer who lacks love is a nuisance and an annoying presence in an assembly that is trying to glorify and honor God. Alan F. Johnson, explaining χαλκὸς ἠχῶν and κύμβαλον in 1 Cor 13:1, says this: "[T]here is no 'gong' in the phrase. The older KJV is closer to the correct translation, 'sounding brass.' Paul may be thinking of the resonating jars lined up on a stage to project the voices of acts and music."[101] The next two consequents (C2 and C3) are easier to explain than the first; since they are parallel to one another, the last two can be informative of the meaning of the first. The best explanation is Paul believes even wonderful spiritual gifts are absolutely useless in the body of Christ if they are not done by and with love as the motivation. Richard E. Oster Jr. calls it a "cacophony,"[102] completely different than the sound of sweet melody it should have been. The image is clear. A believer stands up and begins to speak. To the ignorant, this believer appears to be used by God. How-

---

98. Thomas, *Understanding Spiritual Gifts*, 212.

99. Garland, *1 Corinthians*, 611.

100. Klein, "Christian Love according to 1 Cor 13," 433.

101. Johnson, *1 Corinthians*, 244. Collins says Paul uses this illustration due to the Corinthians' familiarity with the manufacturing of bronze. He agrees with Johnson that these are "acoustical devices" (Collins, *1 Corinthians*, 473).

102. Oster Jr., *1 Corinthians*, 302.

ever, from God's perspective (and in-tune believers), the words fail to accomplish the purpose they were designed to accomplish. They fail not because God fails to accomplish what he desires through the utterance (cf. Isa 55:11); they fail because of the bankrupt character of a believer whose heart lacks love. The two remaining consequents contain a form of οὐδείς. The first, οὐθέν εἰμι, is striking. To use this word with the stative verb εἰμί is harsh; equivalents are found in every language (e.g., "Yo soy nadie," "I am a nobody"). If such a person did exist (i.e., one who had the prized prophetic gift, knew all God knows, had all the faith that Jesus described), that person would be elevated in Corinth to superstar status. However, Paul says that what defines whether or not a person is someone or no one in the body of Christ is whether or not a person has love.[103]

Between vv. 4–8a, Paul gives sixteen descriptions of love (eight positive and eight negative):[104]

Paul's Sixteen Descriptions of Love in 1 Corinthians 13:4–8a

Positive Statements about Love	Negative Statements about Love
Love is patient.	Love is not jealous.
Love is kind.	Love does not brag.
Love rejoices with the truth.	Love is not arrogant.
Love bears all things.	Love does not act unbecomingly.
Love believes all things.	Love does not seek its own best
Love hopes all things.	interests.
Love endures all things.	Love is not provoked.
Love never fails.	Love does not take into account a
	wrong suffered.
	Love does not rejoice in
	unrighteousness.

Table 4. Paul's Sixteen Descriptions of Love in 1 Corinthians 13:4–8a.

While Paul does not explicitly say so, it is reasonable to think the contraries may be descriptive of the Corinthians. For example, love is not jealous; the Corinthians, however, were. Part of their carnality and immaturity in Christ, according to Paul, was their jealousy of one another

103. The third consequent is very similar. Paul says that a believer can even appear motivated by love. However, there is a difference between doing things—good things—and doing these things out of love. Paul says that if love does not accompany or drive these acts, then they do not benefit anyone, including the one doing the act.

104. Thomas, *Understanding Spiritual Gifts*, 72.

(ἐν ὑμῖν ζῆλος, 1 Cor 3:3).[105] He also feared finding this jealousy among them during a subsequent visit (2 Cor 12:20). Jealousy is among Paul's list of characteristic works of the flesh (τὰ ἔργα τῆς σαρκός) in Gal 5:19–20.[106] It is not inherently sinful. In 2 Corinthians, Paul speaks of his own jealousy for the Corinthians believers (11:2); the word, however, is aptly clarified θεοῦ ζήλῳ ("with God's jealousy").[107] Moreover, love does not brag; the Corinthians did. Their declarations (e.g., "I am of Paul" and "I am of Apollos)" are pompous being clearly seen with the emphatic personal pronoun ἐγώ (1 Cor 1:12 [4x]; 3:4 [2x]). Thomas says this:

> Any effort to gain the applause of others for outstanding performance comes under this heading. The Corinthians were woefully lacking in this respect, specifically in expending themselves to 'show off' their own outstanding abilities. Unfortunately they did this at the expense of consideration for the rights and well-being of others.[108]

In 1 Corinthians 3, Paul is attacking the Corinthians' perception that they are spiritual (πνευματικός) and identifies them instead as fleshly (σαρκικός). Here, in 1 Corinthians 12–14, Paul is dealing with spiritual gifts (τῶν πνευματικῶν, 12:1), and he plainly says spiritual men and women act from love not jealousy.[109] James W. Thompson writes:

> [Paul's] eighteen months of pastoral leadership (cf. Acts 18:12) among the new converts were insufficient for the shaping of the Corinthian church. . . . He fears that the same quarreling, jealousy, anger, and sexual immorality that characterized the Corinthians in their spiritual infancy will continue to be present (cf. 1 Cor. 3:1–5; 2 Cor 12:20–21).[110]

---

105. Garland, *1 Corinthians*, 536.

106. Ciampa and Rosner, *The First Letter to the Corinthians*, 141.

107. While not quite an exact semantic antonym for θεοῦ ζήλῳ in 2 Cor 11:2, James alone uses a negative adjective with ζῆλος (ζῆλον πικρόν, "bitter jealousy"). On the subjective genitive, see Bell, *Provoked to Jealousy*, 26.

108. Thomas, *Understanding Spiritual Gifts*, 72. See also Clarke, *Secular and Christian Leadership in Corinth*, 110.

109. Pickett, *The Cross in Corinth*, 40.

110. Thompson, *Pastoral Ministry according to Paul*, 119–20.

Apparently, Paul's words did not settle in, at least in the long-term. Clement, writing from Rome, wrote a very similar letter to the Corinthians exhorting them "to avoid strife, party spirit, and sedition."[111]

Allison provides an interesting discussion on how 1 Corinthians 13 parallels the life and teachings of Jesus Christ. He says, "Jesus wrote nothing to the Corinthians, but without him 1 Corinthians 13 would not have been written."[112] The descriptions of love in 1 Corinthians 13 are easily identified in the person of Jesus as found in the Gospels. Nevertheless, there is no mention of Jesus in 1 Corinthians 13. Richard B. Hays writes:

> While we may be sure that Paul's understanding of love is fundamentally formed by the love of God shown in the death of Jesus Christ (cf. Rom 5:8; Gal. 2:20b; 1 Cor 13:13), there is no explicit reference in this chapter to Jesus or to christology.[113]

Paul's solution to believers' waywardness in living mature Christian lives is directly linked to the life of Christ. Yung Suk Kim writes, "[A]sking the audience to imitate him (4:1), Paul sternly challenges them to return to a 'crucified living' just as Paul himself embodies in his life (4:1–21)."[114] This love now spans three generations: Jesus → Paul → Timothy (and those of the Corinthians who heed Paul's words and imitate him). He is calling them to be controlled by the love of Christ as he is (see 2 Cor 5:14).[115] Immediately after the call for imitation (μιμηταί μου γίνεσθε, 1 Cor 4:16),[116] Paul indicates that he is sending Timothy with the letter. Timothy's objective per Paul is to remind the Corinthians about Paul's "ways in Christ" (τὰς ὁδούς μου τὰς ἐν Χριστῷ, 1 Cor 4:17). Timothy is not only able to offer audible reminders about Paul's ways, which include this love discussed in 1 Corinthians 13, but he is able to offer his own personal example. Paul sends Timothy because Timothy is already following in his example. By sending Timothy, Paul knows that he will aid the Corinthians in being able to imitate him, giving them a

---

111. Hagner, *The Use of the Old and New Testaments*, 6. See also Walker, *In the Steps of Saint Paul*, 128.

112. Allison Jr., *The Historical Christ*, 28.

113. Hays, *First Corinthians*, 221.

114. Kim, *Christ's Body in Corinth*, 83.

115. Frye, *Jesus the Pastor*, 173 n.9.

116. The verb παρακαλέω in 1 Cor 4:16 marks very important sections in Paul's letter, usually "when he sets forth a main purpose of his letters" (Dahl, "Paul and the Church at Corinth," 88).

firsthand, living example. This is the best understanding of the purpose clause διὰ τοῦτο. The antecedent is obvious.[117] Furthermore, paternal language is used for both the Corinthians and Timothy (1 Cor 4:14–15, 17). The only difference between the two is the additional adjective πιστός to describe Timothy. Perhaps Paul adds it in a subliminal manner to nudge the Corinthians, either silently asking them if they would be faithful or graciously pointing out their lack of faithfulness.

Eschatological Likeness in Romans 8:28 (and Other Passages)

Paul gives the most comprehensive explanation of the gospel in Romans 1–8. Romans 1:18—3:20 shows the depravity of humankind. Beginning in Rom 3:21, Paul explains that it is on the basis of faith that God has always justified and saved individuals—both Jew and Gentile alike. In Romans 6–7, he discusses how the justified person lives following God's act of justification by faith. His discussion is far from pretty; Paul even uses his own personal struggle with sin in Rom 7:14–25 to show the continued struggle with sin even though he has been justified before God. Paul's hope is eschatological. If Rom 7:14–25 was all that believers could see, there would be no hope. Turning to God's eternal purpose in Rom 8:26ff., Paul outlines what God intends for all believers everywhere, namely to make them look like his Son Jesus Christ.

In Rom 8:29–30, Paul uses five verbs to outline God's redemptive plan, i.e., his "purpose" (πρόθεσιν, Rom 8:28). They are: (1) foreknew (προέγνω); (2) predestined (προώρισεν); (3) called (ἐκάλεσεν); (4) justified (ἐδικαίωσεν); and (5) glorified (ἐδόξασεν). That Paul intends to show a chain of events in the redemptive plan is clear through the repetition of all verbs except the first and the last.[118] The first two verbs refer to divine acts that take place prior to the creation of the world. Moreover, these two verbs should be viewed together since they are joined together with a καί and appear elsewhere grouped together (e.g., Acts 2:23). Greta Grace Kroeker says, joined together, they allow Paul to "set the matter

---

117. Not everyone connects διὰ τοῦτο to antecedent material. Nevertheless, it only makes sense here in relationship to what precedes. See Bailey, *Paul through Mediterranean Eyes*, 157. For an additional example in Romans, see Matera, *Romans*, 129.

118. Lee, *Paul's Gospel in Romans*, 413, 415.

forth more vividly."[119] Out of all the verbs in the chain, only the first two (προέγνω and προώρισεν) are expanded with additional information:

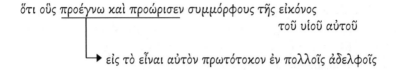

ὅτι οὓς προέγνω καὶ προώρισεν συμμόρφους τῆς εἰκόνος
                                          τοῦ υἱοῦ αὐτοῦ

→ εἰς τὸ εἶναι αὐτὸν πρωτότοκον ἐν πολλοῖς ἀδελφοῖς

The entire chain is part of a subordinate clause marked by a causal ὅτι.[120] The ὅτι corresponds to the verb οἴδαμεν in Rom 8:28. What follows the ὅτι answers the implied question, "How can we know?," specifically that God causes all things to work together for good. There is a case of ellipsis following the two verbs, common in Paul's letters (but perhaps because he needs the stative verb in the purpose clause that follows). What does God preplan and predetermine for believers before the foundation of the world? Paul's answer is, "[To be] conformed into the likeness of his Son."

Before investigating what it means to be conformed, it is necessary to figure out what it is that constitutes the "likeness of his Son" (τῆς εἰκόνος τοῦ υἱοῦ αὐτοῦ). By no means whatsoever can the concept of "the image of God" be dealt with exhaustively here. However, it is important to delve briefly into the subject in order to properly identify what Paul is talking about and what God has purposed from long ago. The first reference to the image of God is found in Gen 1:26–27. God says, "Let us make man in our image, according to our likeness;" and, the author of Genesis writes immediately after that, "God created man in his own image, in the image of God he created them." Whether the image mentioned in Genesis deals with relationship or substance is a big debate.[121] In the OT, the nation of Israel was prohibited from making an image attempting to depict God's likeness (Lev 26:1). The only exception is God's making of humankind in his own image.[122] James McKeown writes:

119. Kroeker, *Erasmus in the Footsteps of Paul*, 75–76.

120. Forlines, *Romans*, 232.

121. For a discussion, see Hall, *Imaging God*; Middleton, *The Liberating Image*. The arguments on both sides, however, are as plentiful as those surrounding the election-free will discussion. In both discussions, the answer is probably both sides are right to certain degrees.

122. Brodie, *Genesis as Dialogue*, 136; Towner, *Genesis*, 26.

Although it is difficult to ascertain the meaning of the 'image,' it is closely associated with the uniqueness and distinctiveness of humans in the created order; the image of God sets humans apart from all other creatures. The corollary of this is that God can have a closer relationship with humans than with the animals. To put it another way, if God was to appear on earth, it would be inconceivable for him to appear as an animal but perfectly appropriate for him to appear in human form.[123]

That Adam was distinct from all of creation is undeniable. The reference to God's likeness is only attributed to mankind. God speaks and fellowships only with Adam and his wife. These two are the only creatures given a blessing and the only two given a prohibitive command. Is there something about the likeness mentioned in the NT in particular that is distinct from the likeness that Adam (and Eve) knew before and after the Fall?

There must be something different about the "likeness" into which Adam was made and the "likeness of his Son" into which believers are made. For example, the NT directly connects the latter to God's glory (e.g., 2 Cor 3:18; Phil 3:21),[124] something not experienced by Adam in Gen 1:26–27.[125] Even in Rom 8:29–30, the final verb is ἐδόξασεν ("he glorified"). While 1 Cor 15:50–58 does not mention anything about the image of Christ, the transformation of the body is described in ways similar to Phil 3:21. The idea behind the transformation of the body in 1 Cor 15 is that the believer's resurrected body will be "imperishable" and "immortal," also qualities that Adam's likeness to the image of God never possessed. In addition to this, both Paul and James refer to humankind as still being in possession of the likeness of God, referring to Gen 1:26–27 (and perhaps Gen 9:6 for James).[126] The similarities between Phil 3:21 and other passages dealing with this eschatological transformation clearly make reference to the body (σῶμα), especially its weakness (e.g., τὸ σῶμα τῆς ταπεινώσεως, Phil 3:21). Likewise, Rom 8:26 speaks of believers' weakness (τῇ ἀσθενείᾳ ἡμῶν), and the reference to Jesus as "firstborn"

123. McKeown, *Genesis*, 27.

124. Cf. 1 Cor 11:7, where the image and glory of God are descriptive of a male (not in an eschatological sense); Thiselton, *The First Epistle to the Corinthians*, 834ff.; Matthews, *Genesis 1–11:26*, 171–72.

125. In Rom 1:23, the glory is connected to εἰκών and ὁμοίωμα, another likeness word. The inclination is that mankind has not exchanged the glory of God for simply a copy but rather, worse, a likeness of an image (i.e., a copy of a copy). See Poggemeyer, *The Dialectic of Knowing God*, 263–64.

126. Matthews, *Genesis 1–11:26*, 171.

(πρωτότοκον) is generally believed to refer to the resurrection (Rom 8:29; cf. Col 1:18; Rev 1:5).[127] Judith M. Gundry Volf, for example, believes that the conformity Paul describes is an eschatological reality consisting of a change, not into Jesus's humble state but into his glorified state.[128] The reference to Christ's likeness in Rom 8:29 may refer to something more than a physical description. In Phil 3:21, there is some physical similitude involved, at least concerning the substance that body is made up of (see also 1 Cor 15:50–58 describes). However, in Rom 8:29 the expression is so general that it seems to include much more. Stanley J. Grenz writes:

> Romans 8:29 lacks the explicit reference to the transformation of the mortal body found in the Philippians text. But rather than being a point in favor of a this-worldly interpretation of the Romans passage, the absence of resurrection language here suggests that in both verses Paul has a broad and inclusive eschatological goal in view, one that goes beyond any mere outward and superficial resemblance. He anticipates nothing short of the radical transformation of the entire person.[129]

Ben Witherington says it refers to "conformity to Christ's character."[130] When the NT authors tell believers to imitate God, which is to say be like him, they do not refer to his substance but to his character. For example, in Ephesians 5, believers are told to imitate God and walk in love, and Christ's demonstration of love is held up twice as the chief example (Eph 5:2, 25–26).

Elsewhere, when the NT refers to the person of Jesus Christ, it presents Jesus as the exact representation of the Father. For example in Hebrews, Paul says God's Son is "the exact representation of his nature" (χαρακτὴρ τῆς ὑποστάσεως, Heb 1:3). Concerning this expression, O'Brien says, this language "was used of a mark or impression placed on an object, especially on coins, and came to signify a 'representation' or 'reproduction.'"[131] Donald Guthrie cautions interpreters and says the engraving (i.e., stamp) imagery should be used with caution:

> The illustration cannot be pressed too far, for it must not be supposed that the Son is formally distinct from the Father as the

127. Cottrell, *Romans*, 286.

128. Volf, *Paul and Perseverance*, 11.

129. Grenz, *The Social God and the Relational Self*, 229.

130. Witherington III, *Paul's Narrative Thought World*, 330.

131. O'Brien, *The Letter to the Hebrews*, 55.

stamp is from the impression it creates. There is nevertheless an
exact correspondence between the two.[132]

It refers not to a physical description but to the exactness of Christ's embodiment (both before the incarnation, during the incarnation, and after
the incarnation) of the character and person of God. There may be a difference between χαρακτήρ in Heb 1:3 and εἰκών in Rom 8:29, but given
the use of both words in reference to images on coins, the illustration
should be applied carefully.[133] While the latter is used both of Jesus and
believers, the former is never used to describe believers. The additional
description of Jesus in Heb 1:3 is expressly unique to God's Son. Even
more, the use of the present participle ὤν signifies that this is who Jesus
always is, whereas believers are being made into the likeness and image of
God. Conformity to his image does mean identicalness. There will always
be certain differences.[134] For example, Stanley J. Grenz writes, "Rather
than sharing Christ's unique Sonship, believers are transformed into the
image of the Son. They share the imprint of the Son but do not become
the imprinting exemplar."[135] What is communicated in Heb 1:3 is parallel
to what is found in John's Gospel, from John's narration as well as teaching
coming from the mouth of Jesus himself (e.g., John 1:18; 10:30; 14:8–11).
No one has seen God (the Father) at any time, but seeing Jesus incarnate
was equivalent to seeing God the Father because of his exactness to the
Father. The capacity of a believer to reflect the character of God is limited
and only possible through the spiritual work of God in his or her life.

The word σύμμορφος ("having a like form with")[136] is unique to
Paul, occurring only here and in Philippians. Philippians 3:10 has the
present passive participle συμμορφούμενος and Phil 3:21, like Rom 8:29,
has the noun form. A similar word is used in 2 Cor 3:18—μεταμορφόω.
While Rom 8:29 does not say anything beyond God's goal in election,
the reference in Phil 3:10 clearly shows Paul's understanding that God
accomplishes this through the experiences of believers in this life, which
includes their active participation in humbling themselves like Christ
(Phil 2:5–8).[137] Philippians 3:21 shows that it is never fully accomplished

132. D. Guthrie, *Hebrews*, 66.

133. It should be noted that both of these words are used for images on a coin. This
just goes to show how the words could be used synonymously (Kuhli, "εἰκών," 389).

134. Andria, *Romans*, 159.

135. Grenz, *The Social God and the Relational Self*, 230.

136. Bullinger, *Foundations of Dispensational Truth*, 106 n.2.

137. Bockmuehl, *The Epistle to the Philippians*, 216–17.

until the eschatological transformation at the return of Jesus Christ (1 Cor 15:50–58; Phil 3:21). Grenz writes, "By declaring that believers are destined for conformity to the *eikon tou huiou autou*, Paul is reminding his readers of God's purpose to imprint them with the very qualities of Christ,"[138] who is the image of God. What qualities? Millard J. Erickson, looking at the life of Jesus, points out three areas: (1) fellowship, (2) obedience, and (3) love.[139] F. Leroy Forlines says this is "an inward conformity," in which the "believer's personality (the way he thinks, feels, and acts) is being conformed to the image of Christ."[140] For example, if Paul is concerned with believers having the same mind that is in Christ Jesus in Philippians 2, it is because this is an area in a believer's life that needs to be conformed to the Son. Likewise, Paul recognizes that even his own sufferings are part of God's plan to conform him to the image of the Son (e.g., Phil 3:10).[141]

In the age to come, when finally glorified, all of these areas will be like God's character, exactly the way Jesus embodied them during his earthly ministry as presented in the Gospels. In the New Covenant, by the working of the Holy Spirit, believers are being shaped into the image of God's Son. They can surrender to the power of the Holy Spirit and allow him to bring about the work he is doing. How?—By putting off the old self and continually pursuing the example of Christ, imitating him and others who bear the fruit of the Spirit and Christlikeness in their lives. It is this here-and-now transformation that Paul speaks of in Rom 12:1–2. While no reference is made to the "image of his Son" there, it is into this that Paul desires for believers to be transformed. As elsewhere in Paul (e.g., Eph 4:17ff.), believers are faced with two options: (1) conformity to the world (or, the way the Gentiles live), and (2) conformity to the likeness of God and his Son.

Conduct and Likeness in Ephesians

The idea of a new walk with God is prevalent in Paul's letter to the Ephesian church. Seven times in the letter Paul refers to how a person walks using a form of the verb περιπατέω:

138. Grenz, *The Social God and the Relational Self*, 230.

139. Erickson, *Introducing Christian Doctrine*, 176.

140. Forlines, *Romans*, 238; or, see Forlines, *The Quest for Truth*, 225.

141. Donfried and Marshall, *The Theology of the Shorter Pauline Letters*, 144.

The Seven Walks in Ephesians

Verse	Text
Eph 2:2	ἐν αἷς ποτε παριεπατήσατε κατὰ τὸν αἰῶνα τοῦ κόσμου τούτου
Eph 2:10	κτισθέντες . . . ἐπὶ ἔργοις ἀγαθοῖς ἵνα ἐν αὐτοῖς περιπατήσωμεν
Eph 4:1	ἀξίως περιπατῆσαι τῆς κλήσεως ἧς ἐκλήθητε
Eph 4:17	μηκέτι ὑμᾶς περιπατεῖν καθὼς καὶ τὰ ἔθνη περιπατεῖ
Eph 5:2	περιπατεῖτε ἐν ἀγάπῃ
Eph 5:8	ὡς τέκνα φωτὸς περιπατεῖτε
Eph 5:15	βλέπετε οὖν ἀκριβῶς πῶς περιπατεῖτε

Table 5. The Seven Walks in Ephesians.

This is Paul's choice word for referring to the overall conduct of a person's life (31x).[142] At times, he uses the verb ζάω as well as ἀναστρέφω, which is found in Eph 2:3 synonymous to περιπατέω.[143] He uses it not just to describe a Christian's life but also as a reference for anyone's overall conduct, regardless of being Jew or Gentile, saved or unsaved, etc. The word might not be a form of imagery;[144] it is probably just a standard way for referring to lifestyle in the first century[145] (cf. John's writings [15x]) or a common lexical Semitism (e.g., LXX Ps 1:1; LXX Prov 8:20; Mark 7:5).[146] Deviations from this, when imagery is definitely intended, are found in places like Phil 1:27 (πολιτεύομαι) and 3:20 (πολίτευμα).[147] Either way, Margaret Y. MacDonald is correct; "the more literal translation 'walk' better captures the active dimension of the concept."[148]

The first two descriptions of a walk in Ephesians come in Eph 2:1–10, actually forming an *inclusio* (Eph 2:2, 10). The first is a description of one's life before he or she is saved by God (Eph 2:1–3). The second is a description of the life that a person is saved to (Eph 2:10). In between,

142. Belleville, *2 Corinthians*, 251; Freed, *The Apostle Paul and His Letters*, 50; Picirilli, *Gospel of Mark*, 194.

143. Cassidy, *Paul in Chains*, 278; Muddiman, *The Epistle to the Ephesians*, 105.

144. Collins says "Paul employs the verb in a figurative sense. . . . He never uses the verb to speak about movement by foot from one place to another" (Collins, *The Power of Images in Paul*, 21).

145. Sumney, *Colossians*, 47 n.48.

146. Collins, *The Power of Images in Paul*, 21.

147. Melick Jr., *Philippians, Colossians, Philemon*, 89.

148. MacDonald, *Colossians and Ephesians*, 48.

Paul gives a unique description about how a believer is saved (Eph 2:4–9). He describes people prior to salvation as being dead in their trespasses and sins (ὄντας νεκροὺς τοῖς παραπτώμασιν καὶ ταῖς ἁμαρτίαις ὑμῶν, Eph 2:1). Paul favors using dichotomies in his teachings, as here with death and life. Looking at the end of the section, it becomes clear that Paul does not use an outright antonym for the spiritual death he describes in Eph 2:1–3. The reason is, for Paul and others, περιπατέω and its cognates are synonymous with life and living. The following ideas are parallel in Eph 2:1–3 and 2:10: (1) death → walking, and (2) trespasses and sins → good works.

The walk before someone is in Christ, according to Paul, is characterized by two things, which are marked by two κατά-prepositional phrases (Eph 2:2):

1. κατὰ τὸν αἰῶνα τοῦ κόσμου τούτου

2. κατὰ τὸν ἄρχοντα τῆς ἐξουσίας τοῦ ἀέρος

The preposition κατά, frequent in Paul's letter to the Ephesians (24x), refers here to a standard by which a person acts or, in this case with the verb περιπατέω, conducts his or her life.[149] Abbott-Smith offers "like" as a possible gloss, along with "according to" and "after."[150] Likeness certainly has a connection to what Paul describes here. Unbelievers are characterized by a lifestyle that is in accordance with the patterns established by this present world[151] and, even worse, the pattern of satanic rebellion against God (found in the second κατά phrase). Paul does refer to satanic/demonic influence, which is to say these supernatural forces bring about the trespasses and sins because people are under their control. For example, E. Best writes, Paul "describes the pre-Christian condition of his readers, not only as one of sin (v. 1), but also (v. 2) as one of control by supernatural evil forces; in sinning they were not their own masters but were under external control."[152] Demonic activity and influence are not absent themes from the Pauline corpus (e.g., 2 Cor 4:3–4), and they are found elsewhere in the letter to the Ephesians (e.g., Eph 6:11). However,

149. Hoehner, *Ephesians*, 26–27, 198. Sam Storms provides the following possible understandings: "in conformity with" and "based on" (*Chosen for Life*, 106).

150. Abbott-Smith, *A Manual Greek Lexicon of the New Testament*, 232.

151. On the meaning of αἰών, MacDonald convincingly argues that Paul is not referring to a personal being, like he does in the second κατά phrase. Here, Paul is using αἰών in the temporal sense (*Colossians and Ephesians*, 229).

152. Best, *Ephesians*, 198.

this is only apparent by the supplemental clause attached to the second of the two κατά-phrases—τοῦ νῦν ἐνεργοῦντος ἐν τοῖς υἱοῖς τῆς ἀπειθείας ("which is now working in the sons of disobedience").

There is a huge difference between the lifestyle that believers are characterized by and the life they have been saved from. In Eph 2:10, Paul calls believers God's "workmanship" (ποίημα).[153] The personal pronoun αὐτοῦ is placed in an emphatic position. The purpose for God's salvific work (Eph 2:4–9) is "for good works" (ἐπὶ ἔργοις ἀγαθοῖς), the exact opposite of the trespasses and sins mentioned in Eph 2:1. Whereas demonic influence is working in the sons of disobedience, Paul has already indicated twice in the letter that God the Father has been at work in his Son (Eph 1:19–20) and everything else (Eph 1:10–11, τοῦ τὰ πάντα ἐνεργοῦντος). This demonic influence is now working (τοῦ νῦν ἐνεργοῦντος), but God has been at work since before the foundation of the world (προητοίμασεν, Eph 2:10; cf. 1:4). God prepared these good works so that (ἵνα) those he saves will walk in them (Eph 2:10).

Underlying these verses is an idea of likeness. Unbelievers are like both the present age and the prince of the power of the air. Unbelievers act like the ones who are at work in them (ἐν τοῖς υἱοῖς τῆς ἀπειθείας). Likewise, believers who have been (1) made alive together with, (2) raised up with, and (3) seated with Jesus Christ (Eph 2:5–6a) act like the one who is at work in them (Rom 8:1–17). This is why four of the nine characteristics of likeness education in 2 Tim 3:10–11a are found in Paul's list outlining the fruit of the Spirit (faithfulness, patience, love, and perseverance). Likeness education involves not just an overhaul in one's

---

153. This cannot be translated, "We are his 'poem,'" as some do. Doing so is an exegetical word-study fallacy. For example, Witness Lee writes: "This Greek word means something which has been made, a handiwork, or something which has been written or composed as a poem. . . . We, the church, the masterpiece of God's work, are also a poem, expressing God's infinite wisdom and divine design" (*The Divine Dispensing of the Divine Trinity*, 244). The word may indicate care in design, but it is usually the supplementary context that unveils this understanding. In the LXX, this word is used at times simply to refer to divine acts/works in general (e.g., Ps 63:10; 142:5). See Arnold, *Ephesians*, 141. Christian educators need to exercise extreme caution with word-studies and better familiarize themselves with up-to-date methodologies. Instead of reading a modern-day idea back into the understanding of an inspired text, regardless of how powerful the illustration might prove to be, the goal in exegesis is to identify what the author (and the Holy Spirit) intended when he penned the word. Paul did not intend to say that the church is a "poem." He intended for all of v. 10 to be communicated, and what happens so often is exegesis of this passage is confined to this one word.

lifestyle but an overall change in one's lifestyle brought about by God's divine power (Eph 1: 19–20; 2:10).

This lifestyle is in conformity to one who is at work in a believer. Nevertheless, is this simply a work of God or does the believer play a role in this transformation? The answer is "Yes." Richard and Shera Melick write:

> Some people exert no effort to change. They expect the Holy Spirit to override their inclinations and actions so that they are carried along by a power higher than they know. Others believe the Holy Spirit only points the way. It is up to them to walk the road indicated by the Spirit. Both are wrong. The Holy Spirit seldom does what a person will not do, and He seldom supplies power to those who do not think they need him. Instead, there must be a conscious sense of trust in the Holy Spirit's power. At the same time, it is necessary to act in order to put the process into motion.[154]

God has made every provision for believers to be transformed. The whole theme of Ephesians 1–3 is what God has accomplished and done on behalf of those who are the recipients of his great mercy and love. God is the subject of nearly every single verb (e.g., he chose [Eph 1:4]; he predestined [Eph 1:5]; he bestowed [Eph 1:6]; he lavished [Eph 1:8]; he made known [Eph 1:9]). When people are the subject, often the content or description is negative or the passive is used (e.g., you were sealed [Eph 1:13]; you were dead [Eph 2:1]). Every provision has been made including the preparation of every good work even before the foundation of the world (Eph 2:10). The greatest thing God has done is make believers the beneficiaries of his great love (τὴν πολλὴν ἀγάπην, Eph 2:4) through Jesus Christ. In addition to this, Jesus Christ has given a single gift to those who are in him—the Holy Spirit (Eph 4:7). By God's grace, each believer receives the Holy Spirit, which is vital to likeness education (Eph 4:18).[155] Moreover, Jesus is building the church (the foundation was not finished at the time Ephesians was written; Eph 2:19–20). Inside of this body, according to Eph 4:11, God provides certain leaders (apostles, prophets, evangelists, pastors, and teachers[156]).

154. Melick Jr. and Melick, *Teaching that Transforms*, 97.

155. O'Brien, *The Letter to the Ephesians*, 265.

156. For a brief discussion on τοὺς δὲ ποιμένας καὶ διδασκάλους, see Wallace, *Greek Grammar, Beyond the Basics*, 284.

God's purpose is stated in Eph 4:12–13, though his overarching purpose is not stated immediately. The shift to purpose is indicated by a πρός + accusative construction[157] in Eph 4:12. These leaders themselves are gifts and given, says Paul, "for the equipping of the saints" (πρὸς τὸν καταρτισμὸν τῶν ἁγίων). This marks the macro-purpose of God's plan. Two additional prepositional phrases, both with εἰς, identify the micro-purposes. God's purpose for equipping these saints through the leaders mentioned in Eph 4:11 is two-fold: (1) εἰς ἔργον διακονίας ("for works of service"), and (2) εἰς οἰκοδομὴν τοῦ σώματος τοῦ Χριστοῦ ("for building up the body of Christ"). Walter L. Liefeld says the leaders in Eph 4:11 "are themselves gifts to the church and become the equippers of the church, so that ultimately all participate in ministry to one another."[158] This work is supposed to continue until (μέχρι) three things are accomplished in all believers. Each of these is marked with the preposition εἰς as well: (1) εἰς τὴν ἑνότητα τῆς πίστεως καὶ τῆς ἐπιγνώσεως τοῦ υἱοῦ τοῦ θεοῦ ("we all reach the unity of the faith and the knowledge of the Son of God"), (2) εἰς ἄνδρα τέλειον ("we all reach [the goal of being] a mature person"), (3) εἰς μέτρον ἡλικίας τοῦ πληρώματος τοῦ Χριστοῦ ("we all reach the level of maturity [exhibited] fully in Christ").[159]

According to Eph 1:23, the church is already the "fullness" of Christ. On a similar note, Paul tells the Colossian believers they had already been made complete/full (ἐστὲ ἐν αὐτῷ πεπληρωμένοι) due to their new positional relationship in Christ (as opposed to the "domain of darkness" in Col 1:13). Already, but not yet (and not even referring to eschatology!). O'Brien says believers are "to become what they already are."[160] In Ephesians 4, Paul mentions two key elements for how believers become what they already are. First, the relationship between those who teach in the church and Jesus Christ himself is inseparable. Three verbs in Eph 4:20–21 have Jesus as the immediate direct object: (1) ἐμάθετε τὸν

157. Brooks and Winberry, *Syntax of New Testament Greek*, 59; Wallace, *Greek Grammar, Beyond the Basics*, 380ff. Given this important use of πρός with the accusative, it is a shame introductory Greek grammars generally do not include it along with the spatial use.

158. Liefeld, *Ephesians*, 23.

159. Obviously this last translation deviates a great deal from most renderings. The "fullness of Christ" makes absolutely no sense to the majority of people who hear it. My translation is a small attempt to help Paul's words make sense to a modern day hearer. Cf. Col 1:19; 2:9.

160. O'Brien, *The Letter to the Ephesians*, 265. Cf. Eph 4:5 and the reference to the unity of the faith in 4:13.

Χριστόν, (2) αὐτὸν ἠκούσατε, and (3) ἐν αὐτῷ ἐδιδάχθητε. Each of these verbs is associated with the μαθητής-διδάσκαλος relationship. Each verb concentrates on the recipient of instruction, but implies a teacher (e.g., the passive ἐδιδάχθητε). The first two verbs and their direct objects refer to the content of the instruction—Jesus. Hoehner says, "The implication is that factual learning is insufficient, the goal is to know Christ personally. . . . Believers continually 'learn' Christ."[161] The final verb has the common Pauline[162] and Johannine[163] phrase ἐν αὐτῷ ("in him"). John Paul Heil believes this refers to believers being taught "within the realm of being 'in Christ.'"[164] Is the locative the only way this can be understood? Given how Paul uses ἐν αὐτῷ elsewhere, the instrumental use of the dative is not entirely certain. However, it is not impossible, especially since it accompanies the passive voice.[165] The implication would be Christ is not only the content of their instruction, but he is also the one who is teaching, albeit through the leaders he has given for the building up of his body (Eph 4:11). For this reason, Peter S. Williamson says, "Christ is the content and the medium of what is preached and taught."[166] The latter two verbs (ἠκούσατε and ἐδιδάχθητε) are used as two antecedents in a conditional statement whose consequent, the main verbal idea, is the "putting off" and "being renewed" material in vv. 22–23.

161. Hoehner, *Ephesians: An Exegetical Commentary*, 594.

162. The phrase "in him" occurs nine times in Ephesians; the similar phrase "in Christ" occurs fourteen times.

163. For a discussion on the use of ἐν in John's writings, see Moule, *The Origin of Christology*, 63–66.

164. Heim, *Ephesians*, 192.

165. Cf. 1 Cor 1:5 (ἐπλουτίσθητε ἐν αὐτῷ). Maria Pascuzzi writes:

> "The prepositional phrase *en Cristô* is important, ubiquitous and used with various significations in Paul. At times *en* + *Cristô* (or *en autô* as at 1Cor 1,5) has an instrumental sense, cf. e.g., Rom 3,24; 6,11; 1Cor 1,4; 2Cor 3,14; 5,19. In these instances the accent is on Christ's mediation and the phrase is similar in meaning to *dia* + the gen. *Christou* at e.g. 1Thess 5,9." (*Ethics, Ecclesiology and Church Discipline*, 157 n.51)

"In Christ" is a rather vague translation for a very important theological concept. Sometimes, it seems, the locative is adopted without much consideration, if any at all, being given to other possibilities. Either translators have done a very poor job in capturing Paul's ideas behind this very common phrase, or teachers, for centuries, have neglected explaining with adequate attention a very important concept in Pauline and Johannine theology.

166. Williamson, *Ephesians*, 128.

Because believers have learned about Christ, his person/character and work (especially the cross), they should work toward completely removing any semblance of their old life (Eph 4:17–19).[167] Instead of being characterized as empty-minded (ἐν ματαιότητι τοῦ νοὸς αὐτῶν, 4:17), these believers are exhorted to put off their old way of life and put on a new way of life, which allows them to be renewed mentally. In Eph 4:18, Paul mentions the old way of life as one in which a person's mind is darkened; in Eph 4:23, this new way of life consists of a person's mind being renewed. Paul's use of the present indicates the renewing is a continual process.[168] This is very similar to the idea that Paul presents in Rom 7:14–25 and 12:2. In as much as believers put away their old way of life and shun the lifestyle that once characterized their spiritual death, God is at work through the teaching (Eph 4:21) in renewing their minds more and more in conformity to Christ.

Paul says what the believers are to put on is κατὰ θεόν (Eph 4:24). The idea of likeness behind κατά-phrases has already been shown. Here, the new life is referred to as one that is like God, just as the old life was like the present age and the prince of the power of the air (Eph 2:1–3).[169] Like the good works mentioned in Eph 2:10 (which are prepared beforehand), this new creation is created (κτισθέντα) before it is put on (indicated by the aorist) and by someone other than the one putting it on (indicated by the passive).[170] Just as God prepared the good works and believers must walk in them, God has already determined the likeness which they should put on and they must, by their own volition, put off the old so that they can put on Christ (see Gal 3:27).

There are five additional walk-references in Ephesians. Ephesians 5 is considered here.[171] In Eph 5:1, Paul tells believers specifically to be

167. For a discussion on how Paul uses communal antitypes and prototypes here, see Shkul, *Reading Ephesians*, 216ff.

168. Hoekema, "The Reformed Persepctive," 81.

169. Stephen E. Fowl thinks differently here. He believes κατὰ θεόν refers to being "created according to [the desires and plan of] God in the righteousness and holiness that come from the truth," which follows how the phrase is understood in 2 Corinthians 7 (*Ephesians*, 152). While no one really discusses Eph 4:24 as likeness language, the NAS provides this translation: "and put on the new self, which *in the likeness of* God has been created. . . ."

170. Schnackenburg, *Epistle to the Ephesians*, 201.

171. In Eph 4:1–3, Paul gives more information about what the believer's new walk is like, specifically five areas believers can focus on if they aim to walk in a manner that honors God. Three are characteristics that should describe their person (humility,

"imitators of God" (μιμηταὶ τοῦ θεοῦ). Twice in Ephesians 5, Paul gives Jesus Christ as the example they should imitate. Both references (5:2, 25–26) refer to his sacrificial love on the cross. The οὖν directly links the command to what precedes.[172] In Eph 5:1, believers are told to "walk in love" (περιπατεῖτε ἐν ἀγάπῃ). Only here does Paul connect a believer's "walk" to the imitation of God, followed immediately by an example. In fact, they are inseparable.[173] Just as in Eph 2:1–3, being a child of disobedience is connected with one's walk, so also is it here. Allen Verhey and Joseph S. Harvard say the parental language here is indicative of *mimesis*: "Every parent knows (to their shame, sometimes) how children learn to speak and to act by imitating a parent. God's actions and dispositions are a model for God's beloved children to follow."[174] Paul's relationship to the churches and to his own closest disciples and co-laborers never superseded or usurped the relationship between God and his children. True likeness education consists of God as teacher and everyone else as μαθηταί. It is transference of God's character, exhibited fully in Christ, to his adoptive children.

Imitation in Hebrews

Hebrews is rich with teaching about the supremacy of Jesus Christ. Compared to other letters of the NT, it has proportionally less to say about likeness education. Nevertheless, what it contributes to the areas of imitation, suffering, and general Christian conduct is profound.

There are two verses in which Paul outright tells his audience to imitate someone. The first, in Heb 6:11–12, reads:

> And we earnestly desire that each of you show the same diligence
> resulting in complete assurance until the end, so that (ἵνα) you

---

gentleness, and patience); two are actions dealing with unity in the body. In Eph 4:17, Paul exhorts the Ephesians to not walk like the Gentiles. The only other negative walk-reference is found in Eph 5:15, where Paul tells them to not walk like unwise people.

172. MacDonald, *Colossians and Ephesians*, 310. The similarities between Eph 4:31–32 and Gal 5:19–23 are interesting to note. Verse 31 offers characteristics of the flesh supplementary to Gal 5:19–21. Likewise, verse 32 offers characteristics of the Spirit supplementary to Gal 5:22–23. The driving difference between the two is in Ephesians, Paul concentrates on how believers relate one to another.

173. Hoehner, *Ephesians: An Exegetical Commentary*, 646.

174. Verhey and Harvard, *Ephesians*, 206.

> will not prove to be lazy, but imitators[175] of those who through
> faith and steadfast endurance are inheriting the promises.

Paul has already referred to the audience as being νωθροί ("lazy," Heb 5:11). He has been working hard to show them the superiority of Jesus Christ to everything preceding the ratification of the New Covenant. Unfortunately, these believers were not responding to the exhortations about Christ. Tempted to return to the old way of life they lived as Jews, they did not give New Covenant teaching an open ear (Heb 5:11). O'Brien says Paul does not consider their present condition as fixed. "It can be avoided," he says, "if they heed both warning and encouragement, and renew the same earnest concern demonstrated in the past."[176] In having this diligence rekindled in their hearts, Paul says that they will prove to be "imitators" of a certain group of people.

Who then does Paul refer to in the ἵνα clause found in Heb 6:12? There are two options. First, Paul could be anticipating the sort of diligence and steadfast endurance exemplified in Hebrews 11, believers found throughout the Old Testament. The second option, proposed by a minority, believes Paul includes Christians in this exhortation.[177] Given the second use of imitation language in Heb 13:7, the most likely answer is the second option.

In Heb 13:7, Paul specifically tells believers to imitate the faith (μιμεῖσθε τὴν πίστιν) of those who led them (τῶν ἡγουμένων ὑμῶν) and spoke the word of God to them. Despite the two other references to leaders, which clearly refer to leaders who are still alive and ministering, Bruce (and others) believes the reference in Heb 13:7 is intentionally general and inclusive of "those who led them in earlier days but have now completed their service."[178] He says of them, "being dead they yet speak, and the record of their faith is still alive in the memory of those who knew them."[179] Neither the verb μνημονεύω nor ἔκβασις in Heb 13:7

175. David L. Allen says it is viable to translate the noun as an infinitive ("to imitate") "since semantically the noun conveys an active rather than a static sense" (*Hebrews*, 396).

176. O'Brien, *The Letter to the Hebrews*, 233.

177. D. Guthrie, *Hebrews*, 149.

178. Bruce, *The Epistle to the Hebrews*, 374.

179. Ibid. See also Schenck, *Understanding the Book of Hebrews*, 89; Rothschild, *Hebrews as Pseudepigraphon*, 199; Getz, *Elders and Leaders*, 173–74; Hughes, *A Commentary on the Epistle to the Hebrews*, 569; Salevao, *Legitimation in the Letter to the Hebrews*, 132; O'Brien, *The Letter to the Hebrews*, 15.

require the interpretation that Paul is referring to leaders who have already died (or been martyred).[180] Barnabas Lindars writes, "Some commentators think that the unusual word for 'outcome' (*ekbasis*) of their life is intended to suggest martyrdom, but it need not do so."[181] Paul may also be referring to leaders who were imprisoned at the time he wrote the letter.[182] It is only when this verse in Heb 13:7 is compared to Heb 6:12 that the interpretation favored by Bruce becomes the most plausible understanding. Hebrews 6:12 includes the clause "the ones who through faith and steadfast endurance are inheriting the promises." The ἔκβασις in Heb 13:7 has the most logical explanation as being the same inheritance mentioned in 6:12.[183] The promises of God are realized in two ways: (1) When a believer exits this world for the next, and (2) when God brings the consummation of his promises about according to his own perfect, fixed time. Since the latter is not yet realized, the former implies their steadfast endurance unto the end of their lives. When Paul refers to the word of God (τὸν λόγον τοῦ θεοῦ), he either refers to:

1. The message of the gospel. The aorist then refers to when these believers were saved.[184]

2. The preaching/teaching of leaders. The aorist then refers to the message they have stopped listening to (see Heb 5:11), which they previously heard.

Paul's audience is exhorted to imitate (μιμεῖσθε) their leaders,[185] specifically their faith (τὴν πίστιν). In fact, the two imperatives go hand in

180. If not leaders who have already died, then Paul is referring to living Christian witnesses—current leaders in the church—as he does in Heb 13:7 and Heb 13:24.

181. Lindars, *The Theology of the Letter to the Hebrews*, 8. See also Hagner, *Hebrews*, 280. Comparing the use of ἔκβασις in 1 Cor 10:13 is really not helpful. Both here and in 1 Cor 10:13, the attention in the context is placed on God's faithfulness (cf. Heb 13:5–6). However, the prepositional phrase emphasizes the conduct of these leaders, and Heb 13:7 appears to be loosely related (if at all) to what precedes. These are Paul's closing instructions to the believers, and he appears to have fired off an entirely new one in 13:7.

182. Just as Paul continued his ministry throughout his imprisonments, so these pastors would continue theirs. See Heb 13:1–3 for a possible connection.

183. This is not to say that the leaders' conduct does not have any meaningful earthly results from being virtuous in the way that they live.

184. Attridge, *The Epistle to the Hebrews*, 391.

185. The notion that Paul is referring also to himself is highly unlikely. Elsewhere, when he desires to use himself as an example, he explicitly says so using the first person.

hand: (1) remember, and (2) imitate. In between the two commands is a participial clause modifying μνημονεύετε. These believers are supposed to pay special attention to one thing about these leaders—their "conduct" (ἀναστροφῆς).[186] Concerning its use in James, Patrick J. Hartlin says, it "refers to one's whole way of life," mentioning Paul's use of it in Gal 1:13 "to embrace his way of life before his call."[187] In the NT, says Georg Bertram, this word refers to "moral conduct," and, in Hebrews particularly, it "embraces the whole walk including the conflict of suffering which is essential for the Christian community.[188] Likewise, Johnson points out that suffering is wrapped up into this idea of imitation in Hebrews, since the letter as a whole "emphasizes the essential connection between the life of faith and the experience of suffering."[189] The conduct to which Paul refers is the "'sum total' or 'achievement' of their day-to-day behavior, manifested in a whole life."[190]

Undoubtedly, this word refers to all of those characteristics Paul gives Timothy in 2 Tim 3:10–11a. In the midst of deep suffering and persecution, these leaders, just like those in Heb 13:17, fulfilled their ministry of watching over the souls of those entrusted to them—and they did so in a virtuous manner.[191] In Hebrews 11, Paul reaches back through the annals of Israel's history, citing from his own memory areas of exemplary faith. Here, in Heb 13:7, he allows the readers to use their own memory of the leaders they once knew. Paul is always mindful of the impact his own example has on believers to which he ministers. He always lives as though he is giving believers dear to him, especially Timothy, a τύπος for their own lives to follow after. Here in Hebrews, it is clear that Paul recognized again the importance of other people's examples. Instead of presenting himself as the example to a group of believers he probably had little contact with (given his intense missionary travels and close association with the church in Antioch), he does not attempt to give himself

---

186. In 1–2 Peter, the noun is used eight times and, as Quinn and Wacker point out, it often occurs with an adjective, e.g., καλός, ἀγαθός (*The First and Second Letters to Timothy*, 383). Obviously, there is no adjective in Heb 13:7; this only indicates the overall reputability of the leaders who once ministered to Paul's audience.

187. Hartin, *James*, 191.

188. Bertram, "στρέφω," 717.

189. Johnson, *The Writings of the New Testament*, 275.

190. Hughes, *A Commentary on the Epistle to the Hebrews*, 569.

191. Patterson, "The Meaning of Authority in the Local Church," 252.

as an example.[192] Instead, he reveres the godly leadership these believers knew firsthand, which he no doubt knew from his travels and stays in and around Jerusalem. Then, he tells them to imitate that faith.

Persecutions and Sufferings in 1 Peter

No letter is geared more toward persecutions and sufferings quite like 1 Peter. J. N. D. Kelly writes:

> Running through the whole letter, sometimes overtly expressed but never far below the surface and giving point to the writer's reiterated appeal to Christ's sufferings as a precedent and a ground for confidence, is the assumption that the recipients are being, or at any moment are liable to be, subjected to trials and persecutions.[193]

When biblical inspiration is taken into consideration, this letter is really what God has to say to those who are presently or will in the future experience severe testing, persecutions, and sufferings on account of the gospel, not just a mere human attempt to provide comfort and hope as best as humanly possible. This is divinely prescribed medicine for the ailing bodies and souls of regenerated believers. The noun for suffering (πάθημα) occurs four times in 1 Peter (1:11; 4:13; 5:1, 9), and:

1. In each case, the word occurs in the plural (παθήματα; παθήμασιν; παθημάτων [2x]).

2. In all but one case, the word occurs with a form of Χριστός connected to it (exc. 1 Pet 5:9).

3. In each case, a reference to the glory of God closely follows in the context.

---

192. Andrew D. Clarke mentions this when he discusses Romans:

> "Paul's letter to the Romans is not characterized by the presence of imitation language, and this has widely been considered a consequence of the reality that the apostle has not had the opportunity to visit Rome, and there his lifestyle is not personally known to them—although, we should note that Romans 16 presupposes that he is remembered by a number in the city." (*A Pauline Theology of Church Leadership*, 180)

Had Paul ministered among them day-in and day-out, as he had in Thessalonica and Corinth, he most likely would have presented himself as an example.

193. Kelly, *Peter and of Jude*, 5.

Writing to a predominantly Gentile audience throughout Asia Minor, these new believers may have never realized that adoption into God's family could involve anything like the persecutions and sufferings they were facing, or would face. Talbert has shown that suffering is not foreign to Greco-Roman ideas of God and humanity, particularly that suffering has a pedagogical function in a person's life. He writes:

> In the Greco-Roman world one was believed to be educated through suffering viewed as struggle that results in increased strength. Suffering in this view is not so much correction of one's misdirection, as in the mainstream of Jewish thought, but rather conditioning that builds one up for greater virtue.[194]

Maybe persecution and suffering seemed incompatible to the gospel they embraced. An individual's involvement in sufferings and persecutions are aspects of the redemptive plan that are generally not covered in one's first hearing of the gospel. Anticipating the persecutions and sufferings, Randy Hall says Peter writes "to assure them that they are blessed, that this is a true part of the Christian life, and that they should be steadfast in their suffering."[195] They may have not received or grasped yet the teaching Paul shared with the Philippians—it is as much a gift and part of God's plan for believers to suffer as it is to believe in Jesus Christ (Phil 1:29). Suffering, as George Eldon Ladd says, "occurs under the providential hand of God, brings added blessings with it, and gives assurance of sharing Christ's future glory."[196] In doing so, Peter gives the most beautiful explanation of suffering, showing its divine purposes far exceed the ways humankind previously imagined.

Peter needed to communicate a proper understanding of persecutions and sufferings for those who were suffering (and would suffer in the future). Different than the apostle Paul, who uses himself occasionally as a supplementary model for enduring persecutions and sufferings (e.g., 1 Thess 2:14; 2 Cor 1:5–6; Col 1:24), and James, who uses the imagery of a farmer and the example of the prophets (Jas 5:7–11), Peter continually uses Jesus Christ as his sole example. Even though Jesus had forewarned his immediate disciples of the likeness they would experience (i.e., similar persecution, similar suffering, and similar fate), such as found

---

194. Talbert, *Learning through Suffering*, 20.

195. Hall, "For to This You Have Been Called," 138.

196. Ladd, *A Theology of the New Testament*, 648.

in Matt 10:24–25 (a passage parallel to Luke 6:40),[197] Peter's letter gives much more information about persecutions and sufferings. He especially covers how God views persecutions and suffereings and how believers should respond to them. Peter's letter addresses three key questions about suffering:

1. How does Peter intend for his audience to view persecutions and sufferings?

2. How does Peter intend for his audience to respond to persecutions and sufferings?

3. How does God promise to respond to persecutions and sufferings?

Peter's letter begins with a foundation on the foreknowing and pre-determining work of God in the redemptive plan. This idea has already been discussed in the discussions on Rom 8:16–18, 28–29. There, Paul says believers know that God causes all things to work together for good for those who love God because of God's redemptive plan, which began even before the foundation of the world. Peter, in a similar fashion, wants believers to recognize God's involvement in the trials and sufferings that they are experiencing (or will experience). It is necessary, if persecutions and sufferings are going to be met with the proper response, for believers to understand who they are. In 1 Pet 1:1, Peter identifies his audience as ἐκλεκτοῖς παρεπιδήμοις ("chosen ones, sojourners . . . ").[198] The first word corresponds to what follows κατά in v. 2, while the latter corresponds to διασπορᾶς and the geographical locations that follow.[199] Because ἐκλεκτοῖς corresponds to what follows the κατά-phrase, most translations position it after the geographical references, thus losing something theologically significant for the letter and Peter's purpose, namely God's election of them.[200] There are three prepositional phrases describing God's choice of

197. Donald P. Senior says this letter "joins many other New Testament texts that alerted the Christians to the prospect of suffering, particularly in anticipation of the final age," of which he mentions Matt 10:24–45 and Luke 6:40 (*1 Peter*, 128).

198. It is best to view these two words in apposition, the first designating their relationship to God and the latter referring to their temporary relationship to their geography (Jobes, *1 Peter*, 75; Green, *1 Peter*, 14). Peter, Paul, and John each begin one letter identifying believers with the word ἐκλεκτός in the *salutatio* (1 Pet 1:1; Titus 1:1; 2 John 1:1).

199. This is not to say that παρεπιδήμοις only has a geographical function in the letter opening. Fagbemi argues that this term further strengthens the idea that these are the chosen people of God (*Who Are the Elect in 1 Peter?*, 57).

200. Harink, *1 and 2 Peter*, 28–29.

these believers: κατά, ἐν, and εἰς. The purposes of the prepositions are as follows:

1.   Κατά "indicates the basis of divine election," which includes more than just "knowing beforehand" who would be saved (cf. 1 Pet 1:20).[201]

2.   Ἐν "signifies the means by which eternal election was effected in time."[202] Note that ἁγιασμῷ contains a process morpheme. Peter's choice of this word allows him to refer to all that the Holy Spirit does in bringing believers to Christ.

3.   Εἰς "denotes the goal or outcome of election,"[203] which is obedience to Jesus and participation in the New Covenant ratified by his blood (cf. Exod 24:8).

In addition to this, Peter refers to salvation with the verb ἀναγεννήσας, an aorist active participle from ἀναγεννάω (found only here and 1 Pet 1:23). The verb is not in the passive voice, resulting in the idea that God makes or causes this new birth to happen.[204] It is on the basis of God's "abundant mercy" (τὸ πολὺ αὐτοῦ ἔλεος) that believers are born again. God's election of believers is a comfort. Later in the letter, Peter is going to show how Jesus, who is also chosen (1 Pet 2:5), likewise experienced rejection and the ultimate persecution and suffering via the cross (1 Pet 2:21–24). Utilizing an OT reference to Israel, Peter calls them a "chosen people" (γένος ἐκλεκτόν; Isa 43:20; Deut 7:6; 10:15). These believers have been called for this very purpose (εἰς τοῦτο γὰρ ἐκλήθητε, 1 Pet 2:21)—to do what is right, suffer, and patiently endure (1 Pet 2:20).

From God's perspective (and Peter's), the persecutions and sufferings that believers endure are temporary; in fact, the amount of time is considered tiny in comparison to the eternal state that awaits them. In 1 Pet 1:6 and 5:10, Peter refers to it as "a little while" (ὀλίγον)[205] compared to the everlastingness (τὴν αἰώνιον) of God's eternal glory in Christ in 5:10. Thomas R. Schreiner makes this distinction as well. He says "it does not mean it will only last for a brief interval during the earthly sojourn"

201. Demarest, *The Cross and Salvation*, 134.
202. Ibid.
203. Ibid.
204. See Schreiner, *1, 2 Peter, Jude*, 61.
205. The same word is used 1 Pet 3:20 in reference to eight persons in comparison to the entire world's population in the days of Noah.

but that it "refers to the entire interval before eternal glory commences."[206] Of course, Peter is writing to individuals who would take comfort in knowing the duration of the trials they are enduring are short compared to eternity.[207] God ultimately decides when someone's suffering is complete; he has fixed the duration for each one. For some, God's acts described in 1 Pet 5:10b will take place (at least in part) before their death and resurrection; for others, they take place after. Either way, the amount of time between suffering and God's perfecting, confirming, strengthening, and establishing work is brief compared to the eternal state of glory that awaits.

This perspective on suffering does not minimize the severity of the persecutions and sufferings that believers are called to endure. Peter refers to them as πειρασμός (1 Pet 1:6; 4:12). This noun occurs twice in James (1:2, 12), and the verb πειράζω is found in Jas 1:13. The adjective ἀπείραστός with the alpha-privative (ἄλφα στερητικόν)[208] occurs once as well in Jas 1:13.[209] The same word is used for tests (or, trials) and temptations. Because of what James says in 1:13, that "God does not πειράζει anyone," when God is the subject of the verb, the translation is "test," and when it is Satan (or, demonic) it is translated as "temptation."[210] At times, both God and Satan (or, demonic forces) are involved. Consider Job's entire ordeal and the fact that the Holy Spirit was responsible for

206. Schreiner, *1, 2 Peter, Jude,* 245.

207. Witherington III, *The Indelible Image,* 337–38; Nienhuis, *Not by Paul Alone,* 175; Donelson, *I & II Peter and Jude,* 151.

208. Hamilton, *The Negative Compounds in Greek,* 6–15; Swetnam, *Introduction to the Study of New Testament Greek,* 145–46.

209. For a discussion of these words and semantically related words, such as δοκιμάζω (which occurs in 1 Pet 1:7) in the *Testaments of the Twelve Patriarchs,* see deSilva, *The Jewish Teachers,* 235.

210. Moo, *The Letter of James,* 53–54; Crump, *Knocking on Heaven's Door,* 151–55. Crump has a very helpful diagram worth reviewing. Joel B. Green believes the word is intentionally vague in 1:6 so as to encompass both, in his words, forming a "paradox" (*1 Peter,* 30). He writes, "With the potential for both glory and tragedy, the very process that can develop and deepen human life (testing) is the one that can stunt and corrupt human life (temptation)" (ibid.). Perhaps this is what both Peter and James intend by the use of ποικίλος (1 Pet 1:6; Jas 1:2). Yet, Green's statement seems to confuse. Can God test and the result be as Green describes for temptation? Can Satan tempt and the result be as Green describes for test? The answer is yes to both questions. It is best to base one's translation, whether test or temptation, on from where the πειρασμός originates based on careful consideration of the context and author.

Jesus's delivery into the wilderness where Satan tempted him.[211] Grant R. Osborne says this word "has no single meaning but only meaning potential."[212] He adds, "It is a symbol waiting for a context, when its meaning will be decided by interaction in a sentence."[213] Just as there is question as to whether or not James speaks of tests or temptations in Jas 1:12 (clearly he refers to temptations in 1:13), there is some concern as to which Peter refers in 1 Pet 1:6. Did Peter want his audience to view their persecutions and suffering as originating from God or Satan (or, demonic influence)? Or, perhaps this is what both Peter and James intend by the use of ποικίλος (1 Pet 1:6; Jas 1:2), hoping to capture both ideas under one heading. The only way to determine this is to examine the context.

Even before looking at the rest of 1 Peter, there is a monumental event that takes place in Peter's life, a πειρασμός that he would never forget, not to mention one that would forever shape his theology of πειρασμός. While the word is not present in Luke 22:31–33, the idea certainly is. Matthew and Mark do not include the conversation Jesus reveals concerning Satan and Peter;[214] they only include Peter's response to Jesus's statement about everyone falling away that night (Matt 26:33–35; Mark 14:29–31).[215] Satan, Jesus says, pleaded with him for permission to sift Peter like wheat (Luke 22:31). While Jesus does not say he or the Father granted permission, the granting of permission is implied since what transpires later that night reflects exactly what Jesus describes would happen. Jesus's words, καὶ σύ ποτε ἐπιστρέψας ("and you, after you have turned back . . ."), refer to when Peter denied Christ. The need for him to strengthen his brothers, which follows, refers to the falling away of each of the eleven remaining disciples. This permission request is extremely familiar, and it is impossible to read and not recall when the sons of God were called before the throne of God in Job, where God and Satan discuss the temptation of Job (see Job 2). In fact, Job and 1 Peter use related verbs to describe Satan's movement around the earth (LXX Job

211. France, *The Gospel of Matthew*, 251.

212. Osborne, *The Hermeneutical Spiral*, 94.

213. Ibid.

214. Who did Satan request this permission from? Jesus? God the Father?

215. This author personally believes that Jesus reveals the conversation with Satan after the content recorded in Matt 26:35//Mark 14:31. Because Peter especially (though not only him) kept insisting that he would not deny Christ, Jesus told them about Satan's request for permission to sift Peter like wheat, the implied permission granted, and the comfort in knowing that Jesus prayed specifically for him.

1:7 [ἐμπεριπατήσας]; 1 Pet 5:8 [περιπατεῖ]). This leads to the only other evidence for suggesting that Peter refers to temptations. A look at 1 Pet 5:8, shows that Peter is well aware at the time he wrote his letter of the presence of Satan in attacks on God's elect. From Peter's perspective, it must be hard to imagine the persecutions and sufferings of believers as arising from anyone other than Satan. It is no wonder he describes Satan as a "roaring lion" (ὡς λέων ὠρυόμενος) who goes about the earth "seeking someone to rip apart" (τινα καταπειεῖν). While it is difficult to arrive at any definitive conclusion, Peter must be referring to both in 1 Pet 1:6. He does not want his audience to view what is transpiring in their lives as only being that of temptation. All of what he says pertaining to the promises of those who persevere and remain faithful applies, whether or not the trial is a test or a temptation.

What do the references to fire in 1 Pet 1:7 and 4:12 communicate about the trials these believers are facing? In 1 Pet 1:7, Peter says they are "being tested through fire" (διὰ πυρὸς δὲ δοκιμαζομένου). In 1 Pet 4:12, he refers to the "fiery ordeal among you" (τῇ ἐν ὑμῖν πυρώσει). The first reference has the imagery of a goldsmith who melts and purifies gold by fire.[216] The same imagery is found in Jas 1:3 and 1 Cor 3:10–15, the latter being applied to a different circumstance.[217] Paul's use in 1 Corinthians has eschatological overtones;[218] Peter's (and James's),[219] on the other hand, compares the here-and-now trials to performing the work of a goldsmith and fire. The imagery says nothing about quality of the suffering; it refers, on the other hand, to the purpose behind the trial.[220] Daniel Keating writes, "If gold, the most precious of earthly substances, requires purification, how much more does our faith—more precious than any earthly gold—benefit from the purifying fire of our trials."[221] Given the use here and the connections to Mal 3:1–4, the translation "fiery ordeal" probably is not the best translation; something like "purifying process" (note the -σις morpheme), pointing back to the purpose of fire in 1 Pet 1:7, would be better.

---

216. Ryken et. al. (eds.), "Gold," 341.

217. Howard, *Paul, the Community,* 121. See also Job 23:10; Ps 66:10; Prov 17:3; Zech 13:9.

218. Mihaila, *The Paul-Apollos Relationship,* 36; Garland, *1 Corinthians,* 117–19.

219. Hartin, *James, First Peter, Jude, Second Peter,* 12.

220. Richard, *Reading 1 Peter, Jude, and 2 Peter,* 17.

221. Keating, *First and Second Peter, Jude,* 33.

In addition to viewing these trials as temporary and as having a purifying purpose, Peter wants his audience to understand that even in the midst of persecutions and sufferings, they are "protected by the power of God through faith" (τοὺς ἐν δυνάμει θεοῦ φρουρουμένους διὰ πίστεως, 1 Pet 1:5a). Whatever Peter's view of divine protection in the midst of persecutions and sufferings, it must be in conformity to the teaching of Jesus. Douglas Harink recalls Jesus's words to the disciples before sending them out:

> [H]e makes clear to them not only that there is no guarantee of their safety, but that their message and deeds will in fact become the occasion of conflict (Matt 10:16–42). Resistance to the reign of God and the mission of God's people is often fierce and violent. Jesus does not assure us that no sparrow will fall, but that a sparrow, though it fall, does not fall "apart from" (*aneu*; 10:29) the Father's knowledge and care; and disciples are more valuable than sparrows.[222]

Jesus's teaching in Matthew 10 presents rejection as forthcoming and not just a possibility. Peter's concept of God's divine protection cannot mean that believers will be kept from persecutions and sufferings. The verb φρουρέω is commonly used for references to military protection or fortification.[223] What Peter describes is the parallel to Paul's teaching in Rom 8:35–39—nothing "will be able to separate us from the love of God" (δυνήσεται ὑμᾶς χωρίσαι ἀπὸ τῆς ἀγάπης τοῦ θεοῦ, 8:39). There may also be a reference to the restraining power of God that prevents temptations from exceeding beyond what individual believers can bear (cf. 1 Cor 10:13). Schreiner sees a connection to Luke 22:32, specifically that God's power and protection refer to keeping a believer from losing faith. He writes, "God's power protects us because his power is the means by which our faith is sustained."[224] The use of the present participle signifies God's ongoing protection while believers are enduring these trials.[225]

Peter is most concerned with how these believers respond to persecutions and sufferings, something each of the apostles would have been concerned with in discipling younger believers in the faith. For example, when Paul says that Timothy followed his example in persecutions and

---

222. Harink, *1 and 2 Peter*, 46.

223. Schreiner and Caneday, *The Race Set before Us*, 246.

224. Schreiner, *1, 2 Peter, Jude*, 65.

225. Pierce, *Spirits and the Proclamation of Christ*, 233.

sufferings, he does not only mean that Timothy likewise experienced persecutions and sufferings familiar to those of Paul; he means that Timothy viewed them the same and responded in a like manner to how Paul did. Although Peter could mention his own experiences of persecution and suffering, he chooses instead to refer continuously to how Jesus suffered (and why he suffered). Like James, Peter begins by exhorting his audience to rejoice in the midst of their persecutions and sufferings (1 Pet 1:6, 8; 4:13). The following table outlines some of Peter's exhortations:

Exhortations in 1 Peter

1. Prepare themselves (1:13).
2. Act soberly and be on the alert (1:13; 4:8; 5:8).
3. Place their hope completely on the return of Christ (1:13).
4. Not be conformed into their old ways of life (1:14).
5. Be holy, like God, in everything they do (1:15; 2:11–12; 3:16; 4:15).
6. Conduct their lives in fear (1:17).
7. Love one another (1:22).
8. Properly pursue and foster spiritual growth (2:2).
9. Submit to all human authorities (2:13–20).
10. Follow in Christ's example (2:21–25).
11. Live with spouses in honorable ways (3:1–7).
12. Be harmonious, sympathetic, brotherly, kind-hearted, humble, and hospitable (3:8; 4:8–9; 5:6).
13. Not return evil for evil (2:23; 3:9).
14. Always share the gospel (3:15).
15. Have the same purpose that Christ had (4:1).
16. Use the spiritual gifts God has given for the edification of the church (4:10–11).
17. Not be surprised at the trial(s) that is being experienced (4:12).
18. Entrust their souls and their cares to God (4:19; 5:6–7).
19. Resist Satan by faith, mindful that they are not alone in what they are experiencing (5:9).
20. Wait for God's Son and the comfort that will be provided at his return (5:10).

Table 6. Exhortations in 1 Peter.

There are additional exhortations in the NT, such as James's exhortation "Do not complain" (μὴ στενάζετε, Jas 5:7). Each of these commands provides a great understanding for how the apostles instructed disciples to follow in the sufferings they experienced and those they saw in Christ. A couple of these are especially important to consider as they relate to likeness education.

The example in Peter's letter is Christ. The clearest example of this is found in 1 Pet 2:21–25. Peter says believers have been called for this very purpose (εἰς τοῦτο γὰρ ἐκλήθητε).[226] Εἰς τοῦτο with the verb ἐκλήθητε is found twice in 1 Peter (see 1 Pet 3:9). The clause refers back to the suffering Peter describes in 1 Pet 2:19–20, namely suffering that is (1) experienced for no cause and (2) steadfastly endured.[227] At no point in the letter does Peter explicitly discuss what will happen if believers do not follow this example.[228] One can imagine that the degree to which "praise and glory and honor" will be presented at the return of Christ will be affected in some way (1 Pet 1:7). Closer to the context, however, is the idea of pleasing God (τοῦτο χάρις [2x]) in 1 Pet 2:19–20. Why would Peter use Jesus's example? The example is not just a model for how to suffer. It also serves as a model for how God utilizes unjust suffering. Lauri Thurén says Jesus's example shows how unjust suffering serves God's purposes of bringing about positive results.[229] In the case of Christ, God accomplished the forgiveness of sins and the capacity to live to righteousness (1 Pet 2:24). Concerning the "how" of suffering, Peter is concerned with three things in Christ's example: (1) holiness, (2) Jesus's steadfast endurance, and (3) Jesus's choice to not reciprocate actions against him. Concerning the first, Paul has the same purpose in his long list of examples in Hebrews 11.[230] The latter is a practice esteemed in Judaism as wise living[231] and, when seen in Jesus's life, further strengthens the motif that he is the Wisdom of God (Matt 11:19; 12:42). Following Christ's example

---

226. Εἰς τοῦτο is semantically equivalent to the noun πρόθεσις found in 2 Tim 3:10–11a (Bretall, "The Concept of Purpose," 167).

227. Schreiner, *1, 2 Peter, Jude*, 141; McDonald, "The View of Suffering," 187 n.43. The εἰς τοῦτο in 1 Pet 3:9 most likely refers back to this same purpose and description given in 1 Pet 2:19–20 (Jobes, *1 Peter*, 220).

228. Thurén, *Argument and Theology in 1 Peter*, 145.

229. Ibid.

230. Cosby, *The Rhetorical Composition and Function of Hebrews 11*, 89.

231. Zerbe, *Non-Retaliation in Early Jewish and New Testament Texts*, 35–39.

(ὑπογραμμός) is similar to the OT saints following in the way of wisdom, a theme found throughout Proverbs.

The NT regularly appeals to the example of Jesus Christ.[232] He washes the disciples' feet as an example (John 13:15). Jesus's disciples are told to love like they have been loved by Jesus (John 13:34). Paul connects Timothy's "good confession" to Jesus's "good confession" in 1 Tim 6:12–13. Jesus's example of other-centeredness and focus on the only thing that mattered is given to the Philippians (Phil 2:5–11). Luke even presents the chronology of Jesus's ministry as an example for recording Paul's missionary work (Acts 13–28). Even Gary L. Colledge explains what happens with the imitation of Christ's example in his book on Charles Dickens. The imitation of Jesus's example, he says,

> is obviously no simple copying of selective activities. Nor is it mere moralism for its own sake or a superficial religious facade propped up by pious-looking activities. Rather, it is the deeper, more profound sense of having our lives and minds transformed by an encounter with Jesus resulting in our being conformed more and more to the mind of Christ.[233]

The word Peter uses to describe Christ's example is unique, one that conjures up educational imagery. The ὑπογραμμός was an outline tool used for tracing. Similar to what kindergarteners use today, a ὑπογραμμός featured an outline that students would write over (or, trace) in order to learn the technique for replicating an image.[234] A similar idea is found in Paul's letter to the Romans, where he refers to those who "follow in the footprints" (στοιχοῦσιν τοῖς ἴχνεσιν) of Abraham (Rom 4:12).[235] Louw and Nida aptly place it under the domain for "imitate" in their lexicon.[236] There is something about the example that Jesus has given for believers to follow that, as Colledge points out, goes far beyond simply being a moral or how-to guide. The examples that are laid out for believers—all of them whether Paul's or Peter's—are areas that God is at work in conforming Jesus's brothers into his image. The expositions on Christ's mind, humility, sufferings, and death found in Paul and Peter are designed to change and

---

232. Cole, *He Who Gives Life*, 175.

233. Colledge, *God and Charles Dickens*, 51.

234. Kelly, *A Commentary on the Epistles of Peter and of Jude*, 120.

235. Stumpff, "ἴχνος," 402–3.

236. Louw and Nida, *Greek-English Lexicon of the New Testament*, 125.

transform the mind of a believer (Rom 12:2). As the mind is changed, the believer follows more and more in the footsteps of Jesus Christ.

What was Peter's audience to take away from the Jesus's example according to 1 Pet 2:19–25? Andreas J. Köstenberger says Christ is "presented as an example of suffering for what is right."[237] In addition to this, Peter certainly covers how one should act in the midst of suffering. If not, why mention Jesus's refraining from threats? The example is more than just not returning insult for insult as found in 1 Pet 2:23. The first part of Peter's explanation of the example is actually found in 2:22, as well as the verses prior to the εἰς τοῦτο in v. 21. Before any references to Jesus's steadfast endurance or unwillingness to participate in reciprocal verbal blows, Peter mentions Jesus's holiness. Quoting Isa 53:9 (substituting ἁμαρτίαν for ἀνομίαν [LXX]),[238] he stresses the complete innocence of Jesus. He is the only one who ever lived and suffered without having ever committed a single sin. The example of Jesus's suffering without having committed any sin is used to prepare the minds (1 Pet 1:13) of Peter's audience that they should be holy in all their actions (1 Pet 1:15). In 1 Pet 2:20, he emphasizes the importance of suffering for "doing good" (ἀγαθοποιοῦντες) as opposed to "sinning" (ἁμαρτάνοντες).

The Semantic Frame of Likeness Education, Part III

"After being fully trained, each disciple will be like his or her teacher." Romans 8:29–30 shows that ultimately God's eternal end has been to make humans into the likeness of his Son. Every reference to this transformation has eschatological overtones. For example, Paul says that at the return of Jesus Christ, believers will be transformed (Phil 3:21). God does not give believers a completely new body. He uses the body that believers always had and transforms this body into a new one fit for the eternal state. Paul describes its qualities in 1 Cor 15:50–54 as "imperishable" and "immortal." The likeness believers will one day be conformed entirely into is distinct from the likeness experienced by Adam prior to and after the Fall.

237. Köstenberger, "The Use of Scripture," 245.

238. Moyise, "Isaiah in 1 Peter," 182–84. The authors of the NT were especially interested in showing how Isaiah 53 was fulfilled literally in the person of Jesus Christ (see Thomas, *Evangelical Hermeneutics*, 245–46); Wilkins, "Isaiah 53 and the Message of Salvation in the Gospels," 109–32; Stott, *The Cross of Christ*, 144ff.

It is generally agreed that this conformity extends to include one's character, fully aligned to the character of Jesus Christ. Not only is the physical state of a believer completely changed (e.g., body of humility → conformity to → body of Christ's glory, Phil 3:21), but every genuine believer will have his or her character transformed as well (e.g., the character of a believer → conformity to → the character of Jesus Christ, Luke 6:40). This means the eternal state of a believer is one where his or her own character will be reflective of the Lord Jesus Christ (i.e., to look upon the resurrected believer will be similar to looking upon God's own Son). Jesus is described as the exact likeness of his Father (Heb 1:3). He is so exactly like his Father that John, who says no one at any point in human history has seen the Father, says Jesus has fully explained him (ἐξηγήσατο, John 1:18). While a different verb is used in John 14:8, the same idea is conveyed by Philip's request to Jesus: "Lord, show the Father to us" (κύριε, δεῖξον ἡμῖν τὸν πατέρα). Jesus's answer is, "The one who has seen me has also seen the Father" (John 14:9). Another example of Jesus's likeness is seen early in Jesus's ministry. When he tells the Jews that he and the Father are one, they get ready to stone him (John 10:30–31). God's Son is unique, as one of the members of the divine Trinity, and believers are never made into little christs; they are, according to Rom 8:29–30, being made into a familial relationship—brother to brethren. Believers are adoptive children becoming like the Father who adopted them and his one and only Son. Nevertheless, conformity to him includes complete character and physical transformation.

Even though complete transformation into the likeness of God's Son is not reached until the consummation of the ages with the return of Jesus and the eternal state, God's plan includes beginning this process once a believer is saved and working toward that end until the end of one's life (e.g., 2 Cor 3:18; Col 3:9–10).[239] What makes this transformation even possible is the presence of the Holy Spirit in one's life and the new life that accompanies this regeneration. Believers, now undead from their trespasses and sins and the deeds of flesh described in Galatians 5, are able to live from a pure heart and bear spiritual fruit (e.g., love, joy, peace, patience, etc.).

The training of future disciples, after the ascension of Jesus Christ to the right hand of his Father, involved a consistent presentation of the life and person of Jesus Christ. For example, Paul refers to the mind of Christ in Phil 2:5–8 in order to illustrate what it looks like to live for

239. Howard, *Paul, the Community, and Progressive Sanctification*, 68.

others, selflessly and with humility. In Ephesians, he uses the example of Christ as the standard for how husbands should aim to love their wives (Eph 5:25–27), also an example of his selflessness and concern for others. Peter specifically referred to the way Jesus suffered as a ὑπογραμμός (1 Pet 2:21), and he said that believers were specifically called to follow in his footsteps, footsteps that for Jesus led to the cross, his death, and ultimately his glorification.

In addition to Jesus's example, Paul regularly uses supplementary examples. For example, in Philippians Paul uses the following as examples: Jesus (Phil 2:5–8), himself (Phil 2:14–18; 3:4–14), Timothy (Phil 2:19–24), and Epaphroditus (Phil 2:25–30). In Phil 3:17, Paul tells believers in Philippi to follow the example (τύπος) they had seen in him and his missionary partners. He also uses anti-examples to a lesser degree (Phil 3:2, 18–19). Hebrews 11 contains a number of different examples of faith from Israel's history. The example of Jesus is presented as the supreme example. It is into his likeness that believers are being shaped, so it is no surprise that the apostles continually refer to him. It may be surprising to some to see Paul make reference to so many examples other than Christ. However, examples, personal or otherwise, have a powerful rhetorical effect in teaching, whether they are provided in face-to-face instruction or letters, such as found in the New Testament.

Summary

Each of the Gospels is primarily concerned with presenting who Jesus is and recording his teachings, with a heavy concentration on the final week of Jesus's life. Each of the Gospel authors is careful to include sections that explicitly present Jesus as the example for believers to follow after. The apostles continue to appeal to Christian believers to follow in the example of Jesus Christ. When they write their letters, they are writing in response to specific issues. They are not writing general letters, like homilies. Their letters are situation-specific. As such, the appeals to Jesus as example are not exhaustive. In other words, there are more applications about the person and character of Jesus as the example for believers' lives than simply those found in the NT letters. While this chapter has not explored the application of Jesus as example (or other examples) to the entire paradigm of holistic transformation found in 2 Tim 3:10–11a, it has shown the continuity between Jesus's teaching, conduct, love, and the other characteristics Paul identifies.

5

Conclusion

Introduction

This chapter provides an overall survey of the research as well as a synthesis of the exegetical results. After offering a summary of the research, a description of the characteristics of likeness education follows. Beyond this, some recommendations for future research are considered.

Summary of Research

Chapter 1 identifies the need for an analysis of Luke 6:40. Using content analysis methodology, Luke 6:40, one of the keystone passages in Christian education literature, serves as the starting point for mining out the theme of likeness education in the New Testament. Jesus says, "A disciple is not above his or her teacher; but each one, after being fully trained, will be like his or her teacher" (Luke 6:40). The study consists of three concentric areas of investigation: (1) Luke 6:40 and its immediate context, (2) Luke-Acts, and (3) the NT corpus. Luke 6:40 serves as the common core of this investigation. The research questions are as follows:

1. What is likeness education according to Luke 6:40 and its immediate context?

2. What is likeness education according to Luke-Acts?

3. What is likeness education according to the New Testament corpus?

Into what likeness, or, better stated, into whose likeness, should a believer's life be made? And, what does this sort of discipleship involve through the lenses of Jesus's teachings and actions and the remainder of the New Testament?

Chapter 2 contains an analysis of Luke 6:40 in its immediate context. It consists of four parts using a top-down methodology. First is an analysis of the structure of Luke 6:40 and its context from macro- to micro-structure. Second is a lexical analysis of the use of παραβολή in Luke 6:39, which has been the subject of much debate in the conclusion of the SOP and has dumbfounded many as to what it refers. Next, there is an analysis of Luke 6:39b–45 and its four proverbial units followed by an analysis of the final unit in the sermon's conclusion (Luke 6:46–49). This analysis concludes with the development of a semantic frame, by which the rest of the Luke-Acts and the NT was analyzed looking for material relevant to likeness education.

Chapter 3 considers likeness education in Luke-Acts as a whole. Before conducting the analysis, a supplementary semantic frame is provided based on 2 Tim 3:10–11a. Paul tells Timothy, "Now you followed my teaching, conduct, purpose, faithfulness, patience, love, perseverance, persecutions, and sufferings" (2 Tim 3:10–11a). In order to have a grid by which to analyze the Gospels and Acts, it is helpful to use these characteristics found in 2 Tim 3:10–11a as a supplementary code. Before moving into the Gospel and Acts, a brief lexical analysis for each of these words is provided. Then, the codes are applied to the Gospel of Luke and Acts. This is followed by a revised framing code and summary thus concluding the chapter.

Chapter 4 is a survey of these characteristics of likeness education in the writings of the NT, particularly the writings of Paul. What sort of conduct does the NT present as exemplary, conduct that is becoming of a participant of the New Covenant? What is the type of love that Timothy would have learned from Paul? How were believers to view persecutions and sufferings? All of these are important questions for determining what likeness education is in the NT and what sort of continuity exists between the life and person of Jesus to future disciples. In addition to this, the following analysis considers what the NT says about who believers will be like after they are fully trained.

Likeness Education in the New Testament

The foundational text for this study is Luke 6:40. Jesus said, "A disciple is not above his or her teacher; but each one, after being fully trained, will be like his or her teacher" (Luke 6:40). The saying is not a parable or part of a parable as far as genre is concerned. The use of παραβολή in Luke 6:39a refers to the end of the SOP (Luke 6:47–49); its use so early is intentional, allowing Luke to mark 6:39–49 as a discourse unit. With the distinct, straight-forward content in Luke 6:39b–45 and the fact that Matthew does not refer to the similar content as παραβολή, there is no strong support to view Luke's use as a collective singular. That he intends for his readers to think about vv. 46–49 in light of vv. 39b–45 is clear by his narrative insertion in v. 39a.[1]

The material found in Luke 6:39b–45 is wisdom material.[2] When Jesus speaks in Luke 6:40, he speaks as a sage providing wise counsel (i.e., proverb).[3] After all, he is the wisdom of God incarnate (Proverbs 8; Col

---

1. Luke could have placed the introduction (εἶπεν δὲ καὶ παραβολὴν αὐτοῖς) immediately before 6:46, however this would not have isolated and marked vv. 39–49 as the conclusion to the Sermon on the Plain. The end of the SOP, therefore, consists of four proverbial units: (1) 6:39b, (2) 6:40, (3) 6:41–42, and (4) 6:43–45. Verses 46–49 contain the climax of the Sermon on the Plain. The parable found in 6:47–49 is a twofold comparison of who someone that comes to Jesus (ὁ ἐρχόμενος πρός με), hears his words (ἀκούων μου τῶν λόγων), and acts on them (ποιῶν αὐτούς) is and is not like. The parable is illustrative, designed to reinforce the importance of coming, hearing, and acting. It does not have a concealing-revealing aspect to it like parables following the day Jesus was rejected. On the use of maxims in introducing mainline material, see Ramsaran, "Living and Dying," 330ff.; Ramsaran, "Paul and Maxims," 432.

2. Bernard Brandon Scott writes:

> "Unlike the Hebrew Bible, the New Testament does not include a collection of wisdom books. . . . Wisdom material is embedded within other genres. At one extreme, the Sermon on the Mount is a wisdom sermon functioning as a single unit within the narrative genre of a gospel. At the other extreme, proverbs are frequently embedded within dialogues" ("Jesus as Sage," 399).

Alan P. Winton, for example, discusses how Luke 6:45 is proverbial and how it is used rhetorically in Luke (*The Proverbs of Jesus*, 136). See also Stein, "The Genre of the Parables," 42; Piper, *Wisdom in the Q-Tradition*; Perkins, *Jesus as Teacher*, 38–61; Evans, *Jesus and His Contemporaries*, 269ff.

3. Stein defines a proverb as "a terse pithy saying that contains in a striking manner a memorable statement" (*The Method and Message of Jesus's Teachings*, 17). For an extra-biblical discussion on proverbs and pragmatics, see Moreno and Pastor, "A Contrastive Discourse Analysis," 357–70. Jesus's familiarity with wisdom sayings, or

1:15–17), the wisdom who is vindicated by works (Matt 11:7–19), and the wisdom who is greater than Solomon (Matt 12:42).[4] While there may be a hint of critique for the disciples or the crowds who are listening,[5] it is not necessary to understand the teachings in this manner. The material in Luke 6:39b–45 is not particularly new or controversial. Alan P. Winton writes:

> Many of the sayings attributed to Jesus within the Synoptics are simply uncontroversial. They show Jesus as standing within a tradition of wisdom piety, which few of his contemporaries would have found objectionable. . . . It needs saying again and again that Jesus is present as standing in continuity with many religious ideas current in the different forms of Judaism in first-century Palestine.[6]

The proverb in Luke 6:40 is likewise uncontroversial and unobjectionable. The way in which the SOP concludes is, however, rather unique and highly controversial. He tells everyone to come to him, to listen to his words, and to do the things that he says.

With proverbs, the goal is to state a general principle that communicates something that is true (even common) but not universal. They are basically warnings designed to lead someone to wise living. Luke 6:40 is not a universal principle. A student or disciple could be under the training of a teacher and not become like him or her, for example, in all the areas Paul identifies in 2 Tim 3:10–11a. The goal in a μαθητής-διδάσκαλος relationship is no less than the likeness between student and teacher. Proverbs have a sort of innate flexibility. Speakers and authors who utilize them clearly have an intended meaning; however, Luke 6:40 can easily be understood negatively as well as positively. The negative aspect fits with the context. Teaching and training by evil teachers will culminate in the reproduction of evil students. Likewise, teaching and training by good teachers culminates with good students on par with their teachers in content and character.

The following list represents some of the characteristics of likeness education gleaned from Luke 6:40:

maxims, came through everyday life and familiarity with his own culture in addition to being the very wisdom of God incarnate (see Luke 2:52).

4. Longman III, *How to Read Proverbs*, 106–9; Bowman Jr. and Komoszewski, *Putting Jesus in His Place*, 103; Ortlund Jr., "The Deity of Christ and the Old Testament," 42–44.

5. Winton, *The Proverbs of Jesus: Issues of History and Rhetoric*, 137.

6. Ibid., 166.

1. Likeness education involves at least one student/disciple and at least one teacher. In the first century, one or more apprentice was placed under the direction of a single teacher due to the sociological construct of the time period.

2. Becoming like one's teacher is contingent upon a certain amount of training (κατηρτισμένος). The proverb offers no indication about the content of this training or the amount of time needed to complete it.

3. A student is the recipient of the training as indicated by the passive voice (κατηρτισμένος). The teacher, therefore, is the one who provides the training.

4. A student does not possess a superior amount or quality of knowledge than his or her teacher (ὑπὲρ τὸν διδάσκαλον).[7]

5. A student does not have authority over his or her teacher (ὑπὲρ τὸν διδάσκαλον).[8]

6. A student, if under the instruction of a bad teacher, will be like (ἔσται ὡς) that teacher in negative ways. In other words, the negative character of a bad teacher will have an impact on the character of a student in some ways. In some ways a bystander could look at the student and see some resemblance of the teacher.[9]

7. Reiling and Swellengrebel, *Translator's Handbook on the Gospel of Luke*, 282. They also suggest that the phrase means "not more important than" (ibid., 282).

8. Witherington III, *Jesus the Sage: The Pilgrimage of Wisdom*, 179. This idea is not explicit in the proverb found in Luke, but it is very apparent when one compares the μαθητής-διδάσκαλος and δοῦλος-κυριός relationships joined side-by-side in Matthew's account (Matt 10:24–25).

9. Not everyone believes the proverb is neutral. For example, Kirk writes:

> "In striking contrast to the deluded fools of verse 39, verse 40 profiles the true sage and the model of correction which produces wisdom. The two verses are antithetically parallel: both have one person leading/educating another; both entail a result, one disastrous, the other successful, one a fall, the other an elevation. The importance of the positive portrayal of the sage-disciple relationship is secured by its placement in the center of the composition." (*Sayings Source*, 170)

Kirk believes that the rhetorical questions in v. 39 are negative, showing the dangers that of a bad teacher-student relationship. Luke 6:40, on the other hand, shows how a good teacher can have a positive impact on a disciple. Nevertheless, nothing in the text provides concrete evidence for reading one as negative and one as positive. Most likely, the proverb is general allowing for the broadest application possible. Arndt says

7. A student, if under the instruction of a good teacher, will be like (ἔσται ὡς) that teacher in positive ways. In other words, the positive character of a good teacher will have an impact on the character of a student in some ways. Again, in some ways a bystander could look at the student and see some resemblance of the teacher.

8. Likeness education is generally true, not universally true. When proverbs provide a result or outcome, be it in connection to a certain lifestyle practice or relationship, that result is generally true, not universally true. Blomberg writes, "In today's forms of education this can prove patently false, but in a context where the teacher remained the constant guide it makes sense."[10] Education in the twenty-first century usually consists of multiple teachers, consisting of shorter periods of time for the student to be exposed to an individual teacher. Even more, education in the twenty-first century tends to isolate the teacher's lifestyle from the instruction (whether intentionally or not). Education has become synonymous with what is heard in the classroom from the teacher and has thus divorced its pedagogical complement, namely what is seen outside the classroom. While the idea of a classroom is not entirely foreign to Jesus's disciples (e.g., the synagogue), or any first-century Jewish or Greek person, teaching took place in the midst of life and not vice versa (i.e., life in the midst of teaching).

---

the text, taken in consideration of v. 39, shows great care must be taken because teachers of poor quality will undoubtedly result in disciples of poor quality. The following quotation is provided to illustrate his point:

> "This verse has caused commentators a good deal of trouble. In unfolding the meaning one may begin by saying that v. 40 teaches the same truth as v. 39. Don't presume to be a teacher of morality if you because of wickedness are not qualified for it. What a tragedy if one undertakes to teach and has no knowledge that can be taught. What will become of the pupil? Will he be benefited? If the teacher is ignorant, so will be the pupil. If the teacher is morally unworthy, the pupil will have the same characteristic. The thought has been expressed that the disciples of Jesus are here admonished not to consider themselves higher than Jesus (Hauck, Z.). This, however, brings in a thought that is not in keeping with the context.—In v. 40b the subject is πᾶς; the context compels us to make it stand for 'every pupil.' Every pupil, when he has really finished the course, will be like his teacher, and not something higher. How important, then, that the teacher be of the right kind!" (Arndt, *Luke*, 197)

10. Blomberg, *Interpreting the Parables*, 404.

9. Likeness education and its characteristics are equally true for both genders. In other words, the proverb makes no distinction about being more or less true for males or females.

10. The proverb is universally applicable, which means that it is true across social, cultural, class, and ethnic lines found throughout the world.

11. A student should carefully consider the character of the one he or she has as a teacher. It is a choice, one that must be approached wisely and with serious consideration.[11] Like a blind person who allows another blind person to guide him into peril (Luke 6:39), like a student who does not first consider the character of a teacher before becoming like him (Luke 6:40), and like people who go to pick fruit without first considering the source (Luke 6:43–45),[12] the second builder in the parable found in Luke 6:47–49 does not consider the importance of looking below the surface of the ground and securing his own structure.[13]

12. Likewise, a teacher should carefully consider those who he or she invites to be a student. In Luke 6:39–49, Jesus does not describe how a student and teacher come to be in a μαθητής-διδάσκαλος relationship. However, the context leading up to the SOP sheds much light on the subject. Jesus spends a whole evening in prayer to God prior to making his selection of twelve apostles known

11. MacArthur says our "wills are prominent in the disciple/teacher relationship—we choose to learn under the direction of the teacher" (MacArthur Jr., *The Power of Suffering*, 105).

12. In the same way that people do not foolishly attempt to gather figs or grapes from sources that obviously do not produce them, people should not look for guidance from those who lack sight or teachers who lack what it is that they truly need.

13. Bock writes:

> "To solidify the warning, Jesus turns to the importance of choosing an instructor, given that the pupil is like the teacher. In our day, the expression 'like parent, like child' portrays what one encounters in this passage: 'like teacher, like student.' In a context where the potential of following a blind teacher is raised (6:39), a point of the passage is to be careful whom you follow." (Bock, *Luke: Volume 1 [1:1–9:50]*, 609)

Elsewhere, Bock writes: "Jesus does not explain the remark or develop the picture, but he is warning us to watch which teacher we follow. If we follow someone who takes in no light, we will stumble. So we are to consider carefully who our teacher is" (Bock, *Luke*, IVP, 128).

(Luke 6:12–16). Each of these men are identified and personally invited by Jesus to leave their affairs to follow him (cf. Luke 5:27; John 15:16). None of the twelve apostles asked Jesus for his permission to follow him, to be his disciple, or to be an apostle. The initiation came entirely from Jesus.

13. Jesus is the teacher into whose likeness his disciples will be like (see Luke 6:46–49).[14] Christian discipleship has at its foundation a direct relationship between an individual and Jesus Christ as the διδάσκαλος.[15] Rossé writes, "Gesu stesso rimane il modello di comportamento insuperabile al quale il discepolo cerca di avvicinarsi nel suo proprio agire."[16] Any intermediary teacher in a Christian relationship should bear the likeness of Jesus so that the student, after being fully trained, will ultimately be like him.

14. Likeness education begins with a disciple coming to Jesus (πᾶς ὁ ἐρχόμενος πρός με, Luke 6:47) and hearing his words (καὶ ἀκούων μου τῶν λόγων, Luke 6:47). The person and the teaching of Jesus are critical in likeness education (John 6:63, 68), even for disciples saved long after Jesus's death and resurrection. He is still the object of every disciple's faith.

15. Likeness education necessitates a teacher who is not spiritually blind. As Jesus said, blindness renders someone unqualified to guide others (Luke 6:39b). If Luke 6:40 is considered closely in light of its preceding verse, according to Craddock, "the message is a warning about that leadership which presumes to guide others in matters that the leader has not personally understood, believed, or appropriated."[17] If considered in light of Luke 6:39b and 6:47, then, as Tiede correctly points out, "the point seems clear that Jesus is the authoritative teacher who will not lead into a pit."[18]

14. Marrow, "Introducing Spiritual Formation," 43.
15. Reiling and Swellengrebel, *Translator's Handbook on the Gospel of Luke*, 282.
16. Rossé, *Il Vangelo di Luca*, 237.
17. Craddock, *Luke*, 92.
18. Tiede, *Luke*, 145. Hartsock adds:

> "The Sermon on the Plain has been concerned with ethics through the transformation of one's character. Here, the transformed character can serve as the light to others, but the untransformed character will serve only to mislead. The untransformed character, then, is labeled as one that is 'blind,' and the one whose character is blind and whose

16. Likeness education involves a spiritual capacity to do the things Jesus commands (καὶ ποιῶν αὐτούς, Luke 6:47). In Luke 6:45, Jesus speaks of a good person who does that which is good and a bad person who does that which is evil. The connection for each of them, according to v. 45b, is the correlation of their heart to their works. Jesus does not elaborate here on how someone acquires a heart that is filled with good. The beginning to this process is always the forgiveness of sins, which there is an account of before the SOP and after (Luke 5:18–26; 7:40–50).

Paul told Timothy he had followed him in nine different areas. They are: teaching, conduct, purpose, faithfulness, patience, love, perseverance, persecutions, and sufferings (2 Tim 3:10–11a). Each of these areas is important and constitutes, at least for the apostle Paul, a holistic development of a disciple.

1. *Teaching* refers to the theological instruction in the broadest sense. It includes instruction given in one-to-one settings, small groups, and larger venues.

2. *Conduct* is the desired effect of teaching. When teaching is successful, it becomes incorporated into the way a person leads his or her life.

3. *Purpose* refers to the inward motivations, or resolve, that governs a person's life.

4. *Faithfulness* is one's responsible commitment to the mission and resources that God gives a person.

---

spiritual eyes are not yet open cannot serve as the much-needed guide to others." (*Sight and Blindness*, 180)

Likewise, Fonck writes:

"The Israelites in the Old Testament manifested the utmost solicitude for the blind (Lev. 19, 14; Deut. 27, 18; Job, 29, 15; Is. 42, 16). But he who would lead the blind, must be able, above all things, to see the way himself. Foolish and disastrous to the last degree for all would be the conduct of a blind man who undertook to act as a leader to his companions in misfortune. . . . In cities and in villages, gutters and ditches, receptacles for all kinds of rubbish, or some badly-covered cistern might prove a source of danger." (*The Parables of the Gospel*, 267)

5. *Patience* (i.e., longsuffering) refers to a person's extended, active patience toward individuals or groups that are hostile toward him or her.

6. *Love* is a part of the fruit of the Holy Spirit, the result of a transformed heart toward fellow-believers as well as enemies of the cross of Christ.

7. *Perseverance* refers to one's unwavering resolve to holiness and active submission to the sovereignty of God in pursuing one's purpose in Christ.

8. *Persecutions* refer to the acts of ill-will or hostility toward others, often for religious reasons.

9. *Sufferings* refer to the effects of persecutions.

Taken as a whole, they represent the clearest explanation of what likeness education entails. When Jesus says a disciple will be like his or her teacher, it can mean nothing less than he or she will follow after the teacher's teaching, conduct, purpose, faithfulness, patience, love, perseverance, persecutions, and sufferings.

Teaching is extremely important in likeness education. In fact, the importance of teaching is evident just by the order of the characteristics found in 2 Tim 3:10–11a. Διδασκαλία is first among the rest. Its importance cannot be minimized. Jesus, in the conclusion to the SOP, mentions coming to him, hearing his words, and doing the things that he says (Luke 6:47). At times in Jesus's ministry mention is made to the works that he did. John the Baptist, for example, heard about Jesus's works (ἀκούσας τὰ ἔργα τοῦ Χριστοῦ, Matt 11:2). John, the Gospel author, makes specific reference to Jesus's works more than any other (e.g., John 5:20, 36; 6:28; 7:3; 9:3, 4; 10:25, 32, 37–38; 14:10–12; 15:24). These most often refer to miraculous works; imbedded within them are evidences of Jesus's character out of which the works were performed. Only once does Jesus specifically refer to giving his disciples an example for them to follow (John 13:15). Jesus's works usually (if not always) are accompanied by verbal instruction. Teaching is essential to likeness education. Having the example of Jesus alone would be insufficient for God to accomplish his purpose. The purpose of God in likeness education miserably fails apart from teaching that is traced back to the apostles and prophets (i.e., those who are given for the foundation of the church, Eph 2:19–22) and ultimately to Jesus himself.

There is another element to likeness education—imitation. Craddock writes:

> In our culture it is argued that a leader's personal life be kept separate from his or her professional life, but in Luke's culture, modeling behavior, especially by a teacher, was a primary responsibility. Example was a major factor in pedagogy, and imitation of one's teacher was the basic mode of learning. Many New Testament texts support this understanding of the teacher-disciple relationship (Acts 20:17–35; I Cor. 4:15–17; 11:1; Phil 3:17; Titus 2:7). And it is fair to say that most congregations do not separate behavior in a leader from skills for leadership.[19]

When Paul identified the nine areas Timothy followed him in, he acknowledged that his life served as an example to Timothy in each one. Paul regularly alluded to his own personal example, as Craddock indicates above. Paul desired for individuals that he was personally training, like Timothy and Titus, to imitate his example (Titus 2:7). He wanted elders that he had identified to view his life as a model for them to follow (Acts 20:17–35). He also wanted churches as a whole to see his example and copy that sort of lifestyle (1 Cor 11:1; Phil 3:17).

Recognizing the importance a living-example can have in likeness education, Paul exhorted two of his closest disciples, Timothy and Titus, to be sure they likewise presented their lives as examples in and around Ephesus and Crete. Paul tells Timothy, "Do not let people disregard you on account of your young age, but instead prove to be an example (ἀλλὰ τύπος γίνου) in the areas of speech, conduct, love, faithfulness, and purity to those who believe" (1 Tim 4:12). To Titus Paul says:

> In absolutely everything, present yourself as an example (σεαυτὸν παρεχόμενος τύπον) of good works, with sound teaching, acting as one ought to act, using healthy words, so that the one who acts out of opposition might be put to shame, having nothing bad to say about us (Tit. 2:7–8).

Given the former exhortation, a person could rightly be discounted if his lifestyle was not appropriate—especially for a young person. Three of the areas Paul mentions to Timothy are areas he identifies Timothy followed him in—conduct, faithfulness, and love (2 Tim 3:10–11a). Nolland

19. Craddock, *Luke*, 92.

writes, "The teacher does not merely impart a body of information but rather teaches the disciple to be as a person what the teacher already is. Only Jesus himself is finally adequate as teacher."[20]

Conclusion

This study offers a unique paradigm for assessing Christian education using Luke 6:40 and 2 Tim 3:10–11a. The temptation in Christian circles is to associate the mental acquisition of content with successful instruction.[21] Rote memorization is far from the holistic transformation that God intends for Christian believers. That is called intellectualism. God's plan since before the creation of the world is to make believers into the image of his Son (Rom 8:29). But has a discussion about in what ways a believer's person should bear the likeness of God's Son been neglected? Moreover, has one of the most important areas of Christian discipleship been neglected—modeling and mentoring? I wonder if Christian discipleship can really take place apart from a more mature believer shepherding a less mature believer in the Christian life. Somehow it appears as if teaching (i.e., verbal instruction) has become synonymous with Christian education. It is important; after all, Paul includes it first in his list to Timothy in 2 Tim 3:10–11a. However, Daryl Eldridge says, "Listening is not learning and telling is not teaching."[22] He adds, "Imitation requires seeing the behavior and then practicing it. Learning is putting feet to ideas. It is trying out faith in the real world. It is being obedient to the commands of our Lord."[23]

So what about this μαθητής-διδάσκαλος relationship? Köstenberger writes:

> Paul and Timothy provide a well-known biblical example of this dynamic: 'You, however, have followed my teaching, my conduct, my aim in life, my faith, my patience, my love, my steadfastness, my persecutions and sufferings that happened to me' (2 Tim 3:10–11). Just as Paul called God's people to be imitators of God as his beloved children (Eph. 5:1), he also

20. Nolland, *Luke 1–9:20*, 310.

21. Malina and Neyrey, *Portraits of Paul*, 27 and 93; Bock, *Luke: Volume 1 (1:1–9:50)*, 612.

22. Eldridge, "The Disciple," 82.

23. Ibid., 83.

wrote, 'Be imitators of me, as I am of Christ' (1 Cor. 11:1). The pattern of imitation is thus to proceed from God to Christ to the mentor and to the mentee."[24]

Likeness education involves seeing and hearing the person of Jesus Christ. This takes place through the faithful exposition of the word of God, both his words and works. It also includes the faithful modeling of Christ-like character, specifically the embodiment of his teachings and his actions. For believers since the ascension of Jesus Christ until his return, the promise is this: When the faithful exposition of the word of God is matched by the faithful embodiment of Jesus's teachings and actions, believers will continue to grow into the likeness of God's Son (2 Pet 3:18). Ultimately, when a believer dies or the Son of God returns and believers are called up to meet him in the sky—in the twinkling of an eye—he or she will be entirely changed and will be like Christ, having a body conformed to the body of his glory (Phil 3:21; 1 Cor 15:50–58) and having a character just like the one so evident in the Gospels.

24. Köstenberger, *Excellence*, 40–41.

Appendix 1

Outline of Acts

The following divisions (not the chart) are provided by Thomas D. Lea and David Alan Black in *The New Testament: Its Background and Message*, 2nd ed. (Nashville, TN: B&H Academic, 2003), 291–328:

Major Divisions	Episode Divisions	
	I.	The Ascension of Jesus (1:1–11)
	II.	The Choice of Matthias (1:12–26)
	III.	The Day of Pentecost (2:1–47)
	IV.	The Healing of the Lame Man and the Arrest of Peter and John (3:1–4:31)
	V.	Generosity and Hypocrisy in the Early Church (4:32—5:42)
Witness in Jewish Culture	VI.	The Appointment of the Seven (6:1–7)
	VII.	Stephen's Sermon and Martyrdom (6:8—8:4)
	VIII.	The Widespread Ministry of Philip (8:5–40)
	IX.	The Conversion and Early Preaching of Paul (9:1–31)
	X.	The Miracles, Vision and Preaching of Peter (9:32—11:18)
	XI.	The Gospel in Antioch (11:19–30; 12:25)
	XII.	Persecution by Herod Agrippa I (12:1–23)

Major Divisions	Episode Divisions	
	XIII.	Beginning of Paul's First Missionary Journey, Antioch in Syria (13:1–3)
	XIV.	Ministry in Cyprus (13:4–13)
	XV.	Paul in Pisidian Antioch (13:14–52)
	XVI.	Ministry in Iconium, Lystra, Derbe, and Return to Antioch (14:1–28)
	XVII.	The Jerusalem Council (15:1–35)
	XVIII.	Beginning of Paul's Second Missionary Journey (15:36–41)
	XIX.	Ministry in Philippi (16:1–40)
	XX.	Ministry in Thessalonica and Berea (17:1–15)
Witness in Gentile Culture	XXI.	Ministry in Athens (17:16–34)
	XXII.	Ministry in Corinth (18:1–22)
	XXIII.	Beginning of Paul's Third Missionary Journey, Ministry in Ephesus (19:1—20:1)
	XXIV.	Ministry in Greece and Back to Jerusalem (20:2—21:16)
	XXV.	Arrest and Imprisonment in Jerusalem (21:17—23:35)
	XXVI.	Paul's Appearance before Felix (24:1–27)
	XXVII.	Paul before Festus (25:1–12)
	XXVIII.	Paul before Festus and Herod Agrippa II (25:13—26:32)
	XXIX.	The Voyage to Rome (27:1—28:16)
	XXX.	Paul's Ministry in Rome (28:17–31)

Appendix 2

Jesus's Prayers in John

John 17 is not the first prayer of Jesus found in the Johannine discourse. It is actually the third. The two other prayers are found in John 11:41–42 and 12:27–30. Preceding both of these, John includes the account of Jesus feeding the multitudes and that Jesus prayed prior to distributing the bread and fish (John 6:11). This act of prayer is mentioned only in passing as part of the narrative. The accounts in John 11 and 12 contain the actual words of Jesus as he prayed (i.e., direct discourse), just as is found in John 17. The similarities between the prayers (i.e., the introduction and the concluding purpose statement) are extremely important.

Each of the Gospels concentrates a majority of its narrative on the events surrounding the last week of the life of Christ. Concerning the event known as "The Lord's Supper," John far exceeds the amount of information provided by the synoptic authors. Where Matthew has only thirteen verses about Jesus's Passover meal with his disciples and Mark and Luke both have fourteen, John, on the other hand, has a whopping 155 verses.

The importance of this account, known more recently as the "Farewell Cycle," is marked by its direct proximity to the Isaiah 6 passage in John 12. In fact, in this regard, John actually parallels the synoptic authors. Matthew and Mark both associate this verse at the tragic account of the nation of Israel's rejection of their Messiah (Matt 12:22–37; 13:14–15; Mark 3:20–30; 4:12). The difference between the two is (1) when during the life of Jesus the Isa. 6:9–10 passage is quoted and (2) by whom it is quoted. In the Synoptic Gospels, the reference to Isaiah is made by Jesus on the same day, according to Matthew, that Jesus's power was attributed to the power of Satan. In the Synoptics, the tragic decision on the part of the nation is marked by Jesus's initiation of the use of parables in his teaching. In John, however, the reference to Isaiah is made as an authorial insertion by John. Jesus had entered Jerusalem willingly approaching his hour. He prayed that God would glorify his name. The Father audibly responded by saying that he had done so and would do so again. As John records, Jesus at this point spoke about his approaching death. The crowd was disbelieving. The latter part of John 12:36 sums it up—"These things Jesus spoke, and he went away and hid himself from them." It is here that John inserts his quotation of Isa. 6:10. Chapter 13 is introduced in light of this and with the first recognition that the ὥρα that had been anticipated throughout the narrative had finally arrived.

The relationship between John 17 and its four preceding chapters is important. Black says John 17 "forms a unit of its own, but one that obviously is inseparable from its larger context."[1] The account of the Lord's Supper with the disciples on the eve that Jesus was betrayed and handed over to be crucified is actually found in chapters 13–17. What has now been identified as the Farewell Discourse actually begins at John 13:31. The preceding thirty verses continue John's narrative. As L. Scott Kellum writes, "[T]he content of 13:31–38 should be understood as introducing the following discourse."[2] The new discourse unit is marked in John 13:1 with the temporal clause πρὸ δὲ τῆς ἑορτῆς τοῦ πάσχα. The temporal element is narrowed down even further in John 13:2 with the clause καὶ δείπνου γινομένου. Within this part of the narrative, John includes many key events essential to his narrative. As previously mentioned, this is the first identification in the narrative that the hour, which the audience had been anticipating, had finally arrived from the perspective of Jesus. Because of this, John 13:2–30 is essential in demonstrating for the audience what actually brings about the events that take place in John 18:12–19:42 and following. In John 13:2, John identifies the spiritual realm that is at work in bringing Jesus to the cross (see Luke 22:53). John records the account of Jesus cleaning the disciples' feet, including Judas's feet. And with total control, Jesus predicts and identifies the one who will betray him. Forming an *inclusio* to this section of the narrative, Satan then enters into Judas and Judas departs from the supper with the permission of Jesus (John 13:27).

1. Black, "On the Style and Significance of John 17," 143.
2. Kellum, *The Unity of the Farewell Discourse*, 151.

It is at John 13:31 that Jesus begins his discourse with the disciples dining with him, and the teaching does not end until 16:33. Kellum writes:

> The speech is . . . naturally divided from the beginning and concluding episodes, forming a self-contained unit. The boundaries of the speech are clearly marked by the departure of Judas (13:30) and the beginning of the prayer (17:1).[3]

The great majority of the discourse is Jesus speaking to his disciples. There is some dialogue within the unit, however. There are five sub-audiences within the section with whom Jesus interacts: (1) Jesus and Peter (John 13:36–38), (2) Jesus and Thomas (John 14:5), (3) Jesus and Philip (John 14:8), (4) Jesus and Judas (not Iscariot) (John 14:22), and (5) Jesus and the disciples collectively (John 16:30). Each of these interactions, with the exception of the fifth, begins with a request or question by the disciple and launches into a teaching segment. The final interaction is a confession by the disciples of the omniscience of Jesus and that he came from God. The latter actually plays an integral role in the prayer recorded in John 17.

The prayer of Jesus in John 11:41–42 takes place immediately prior to the raising of Lazarus from the dead (John 11:1–57). Generally speaking, the prayer falls at the end of the discourse unit. Instead of ending it, the prayer is followed by a response of the Jews that is contrasted with a collective decision by the chief priests and Pharisees to kill Jesus (John 11:53). In this manner, John 17 is quite distinct. That prayer provokes no response; after all, the hour had finally come. No response is recorded from any audience except the disciples after John 17. And the only invitation to respond, inserted by John, is found after the entire trial and crucifixion—"And he who has seen has testified, and his testimony is true; and he knows that he is telling the truth, so that you also may believe" (John 19:35). John identifies three character groups: Lazarus and his family, Martha and Mary (John 11:1–45), the disciples with special attention on Thomas (John 11:7-14), and the Jews (John 11:19, 36-37). The prayer is introduced in the exact same fashion as the prayer in John 17: ἦρεν τοὺς ὀφθαλμοὺς ἄνω καὶ εἶπεν (John 11:41). There are only two differences between the introduction in John 11 and John 17. First, the verb is different. John uses the base verb αἴρω in the first prayer whereas the same verb is used with the prefixed preposition ἐπί- (ἐπαίρω) in the

3. Kellum, *The Unity of the Farewell Discourse*, 3.

final prayer. Second, John adds an additional prepositional phrase εἰς τὸν οὐρανὸν in the second (John 17:1).[4] In both prayers, Jesus addressed God as πάτερ. The prayer in John 11 emphasizes the access that the Son has to the Father. Jesus specifically gave thanks because the Father hears him (εὐχαριστῶ σοι ὅτι ἤκουσάς μου), and he added that the Father always hears him (πάντοτέ μου ἀκούεις). While the word ἀκούω never appears in John 17, the focus is intensified around oneness. Jesus's prayer in John 11 concludes with a content clause wrapped up in a purpose clause. Both are extremely common in John 17. The purpose clause is marked by the ἵνα, and the content clause is marked by the ὅτι. Moreover, the actual content of both clauses are found in both prayers of Jesus. The concept of Jesus being sent by the Father becomes critical in the final prayer (John 17:8, 18, and 21).

The prayer in John 12:28 takes place after Jesus had raised Lazarus from the dead yet prior to the Farewell Discourse. This prayer is very brief, only five words. It actually shares similarities with John 11:41–42 and John 17:1–26. Like John 11, this prayer evokes a response. In this case, the responses are from the Father and from the crowd standing around. No such response is found in John 17. Also, both John 11:42 (διὰ τὸν ὄχλον τὸν περιεστῶτα) and 12:29 (ὄχλος ὁ ἑστὼς καὶ ἀκούσας) draw attention to the crowd in relation to the prayer. In John 11, the crowd is the subject of the purpose clause. Jesus prays so that they will respond. In John 12, the crowd responds to the response of the Father. The content of the prayer of John 12 is extremely important to the prayer of John 17. Jesus prayed, "Father, glorify your name" (John 12:28). In the final prayer, Jesus prayed twice, "Father, glorify your Son" (John 17:1). The two prayers are lexical and syntactical siblings. Both requests are related to the glory and glorifying power of God. And both follow the same syntax: verb + genitive pronoun + article + predicate noun.

4. Some have supposed, unconvincingly, that this additional phrase signifies that Jesus, in some special and supernatural way, was looking "into" heaven. There is no good reason to understand this prepositional phrase in this manner.

Bibliography

Abasciano, Brian J. *Paul's Use of the Old Testament in Romans 9.10–18: An Intertextual and Theological Exegesis.* Library of New Testament Studies. New York: T. & T. Clark International, 2011.

Abbott-Smith, G. *A Manual Greek Lexicon of the New Testament.* New York: Charles Scribner's Sons, 1922.

Achterberg, Cheryl L., and Susan W. Arendt. "The Philosophy, Role, and Methods of Qualitative Inquiry in Research. In *Research: Successful Approaches*, 3rd ed., edited by Elaine R. Monsen and Linda Van Horn, 65–78. Chicago, IL: Diana Faulhaber, 2008.

Adams, Jay E. *How to Help People Change: The Four-Step Biblical Process.* Grand Rapids: Zondervan, 1986.

Adeyẹmi, Fẹmi. *The New Covenant Torah in Jeremiah and the Law of Christ in Paul.* Studies in Biblical Literature 94. New York: Peter Lang, 2007.

Adler, Emily Stier, and Roger Clark. *An Invitation to Social Research: How It's Done.* 4th ed. Belmont, CA: Wadsworth, 2011.

Adoyo, Priscilla Anyango. "The Application of Biblical Principles of Conflict Transformation in Ethno-Religious Situations in Jos and Kaduna, Nigeria." D.Miss. diss., Fuller Theological Seminary, December 2007.

Alday, Salvador Carrillo. *El Evangelio según Lucas.* Navarra, Spain: Verbo Divino, 2009.

Aldrich, Joe. *Lifestyle Evangelism: Learning to Open Your Life to Those around You.* Colorado Springs, CO: Multnomah Books, 1993.

Alikin, Valeriy A. *The Earliest History of the Christian Gathering: Origin, Development and Content of the Christian Gathering in the First to Third Centuries.* Supplements to Vigiliae Christianae. Leiden: Brill, 2010.

Allen, David L. *Hebrews.* NAC. Nashville, TN: B&H, 2010.

Allen, Ronald J. "The Story of Jesus according to 'Luke': The Gospel of Luke." In *Chalice Introduction to the New Testament*, edited by Dennis E. Smith, 175–97. Atlanta, GA: Chalice, 2004.

Allison Jr., Dale C. *Studies in Matthew: Interpretation Past and Present.* Grand Rapids: Baker Academic, 2005.

———. *The Historical Christ and the Theological Jesus.* Grand Rapids: Eerdmans, 2009.

Andersen, Margaret, and Howard F. Taylor. *Sociology: Understanding a Diverse Society.* 4th ed. Belmont, CA: Wadsworth, 2008.

Andria, Solomon. *Romans.* Africa Bible Commentary Series. Grand Rapids: Zondervan [HippoBooks], 2012.

Antonakos, John. *The Greek Handbook: A Compendium of the Greek Language in Chart Form.* Bloomington, IN: AuthorHouse, 2012.

Apperson, George L. *Dictionary of Proverbs.* 2nd ed. Ware, England: Wordsworth, 2006.

Arens, Eduardo. *Los Evangelios Ayer y Hoy: Una Introducción Hermenéutica*. Lima, Peru: Editorial Paulinas, 2006.

Arichea Jr., Daniel C. "Reading Romans in Southeast Asia: Righteousness and its Implications for the Christian Community and Other Faith Communities." In *Navigating Romans through Cultures: Challenging Readings by Charting a New Course*, edited by Yeo Khiok-khng, 205–24. Romans through History and Culture Series. New York: T. & T. Clark International, 2004.

Arndt, William F. *Luke*. Concordia Classic Commentary Series. St. Louis, MO: Concordia Publishing House, 1956.

Arnold, Bill T., and John H. Choi. *A Guide to Biblical Hebrew Syntax*. New York: Cambridge University, 2003.

Arnold, Clinton E. *Ephesians*. ZECNT. Edited by Clinton E. Arnold. Grand Rapids: Zondervan, 2010.

Ashcraft, Morris. "Apostle/Apostleship." In *Mercer Dictionary of the Bible*, edited by Watson E. Mills, 47–48. Macon, GA: Mercer University Press, 1991.

Atkins, E. M. "Cicero." In *The Cambridge History of Greek and Roman Political Thought*, edited by Christopher Rowe and Malcolm Schofield, 477–516. New York: Cambridge University Press, 2000.

Attridge, H. W. *The Epistle to the Hebrews*. Hermeneia. Minneapolis, MN: Fortress, 1989.

Avalos, Hector. "Blindness." Page 193 in *Eerdmans Dictionary of the Bible*. Edited by David Noel Freedman. Grand Rapids: Eerdmans, 2000.

Babbie, Earl. *The Practice of Social Research*. 12th ed. Belmont, CA: Wadsworth, 2010.

Badcock, Gary D. *The Way of Life: A Theology of Christian Vocation*. Grand Rapids: Eerdmans, 1998.

Báez, Juan, and Pérez de Tudela. *Investigación Cualitativa*. 2nd ed. Madrid, Spain: ESIC, 2009.

Bailey, Kenneth D. *Methods of Social Research*. 4th ed. New York: The Free Press, 1994.

Bailey, Kenneth E. *Jacob and the Prodigal: How Jesus Retold Israel's Story*. Downers Grove, IL: InterVarsity, 2003.

———. *Jesus through Middle Eastern Eyes: Cultural Studies in the Gospels*. Downers Grove, IL: InterVarsity, 2008.

———. *Paul through Mediterranean Eyes: Cultural Studies in 1 Corinthians*. Downers Grove, IL: InterVarsity, 2011.

Baird, J. Arthur. "Content Analysis and the Computer: A Case Study of the Scientific Method to Biblical Research." *JBL* 95:2 (1976) 255–76.

———. "Content Analysis, Computers and the Scientific Method in Biblical Studies," *Perspectives in Religious Studies* 4:2 (1977) 109–36.

———. *Holy Word: The Paradigm of New Testament Formation*. New York: Sheffield Academic, 2002.

Balz, Horst, and Gerhard Schneider, eds. "καταρτίζω." *EDNT* 2:268. Grand Rapids: William B. Eerdmans, 1991.

Barnett, Paul. *Jesus and the Rise of Early Christianity: A History of New Testament Times*. Downers Grove, IL: InterVarsity, 1999.

Barrio, Mario López. *El Amor en la Primera Carta de San Juan*. Mexico City: Universidad Iberoamericana, 2007.

Barton, Bruce B., et al. *Luke*. Life Application Bible Commentary. Edited by Grant Osborne and Philip Comfort. Carol Stream, IL: Tyndale, 1997.

Baucham Jr., Voddie. *Family Driven Faith: Doing What It Takes to Raise Sons and Daughters Who Walk With God*. Wheaton, IL: Crossway, 2007.

Bauer, W. *A Greek-English Lexicon of the New Testament and other Early Christian Literature*. Translated and edited by W. F. Arndt and F. W. Gingrich. Chicago, IL: The University of Chicago, 1957.

Beale, G. K. *1–2 Thessalonians*. The IVP New Testament Commentary Series. Edited byGrant R. Osborne. Downers Grove, IL: InterVarsity, 2003.

Beaudean Jr., John William. *Paul's Theology of Preaching*. Dissertation Series 6. Edited by James Wm. McClendon Jr. Macon, GA: Mercer University Press, 1988.

Beck, James R. *Jesus and Personality Theory: Exploring the Five-Factor Model*. Downers Grove, IL: InterVarsity, 1999.

Bell, Richard H. *Provoked to Jealousy: The Origin and Purpose of the Jealousy Motif in Romans 9–11*. Wissenschaftliche Untersuchungen zum Neuen Testament 2.Reihe 63. Tübingen: Mohr Siebeck, 1994.

Belli, Filippo. *Argumentation and Use of Scripture in Romans 9–11*. Analecta Biblica 183. Rome: Gregorian & Biblical Press, 2010.

Belleville, Linda L. *2 Corinthians*. The IVP New Testament Commentary Series. Edited by Grant R. Osborne. Downers Grove, IL: InterVarsity, 1996.

Berkhof, Louis. *Systematic Theology*. Combined ed. Grand Rapids: Eerdmans, 1996.

Bernard, H. Russell. *Research Methods in Anthropology: Qualitative and Quantitative Approaches*. 4th ed. Lanham, MD: AltaMira, 2006.

———. *Social Research Methods: Qualitative and Quantitative Approaches*. Thousand Oaks: Sage, 2000.

Bernard, H. Russell, and Gery W. Ryan. *Analyzing Qualitative Data: Systematic Approaches*. Thousand Oaks: Sage, 2010.

Bertram, Georg. "στρέφω, ἀναστρέφω, ἀναστροφή, καταστρέφω, καταστροφή, διαστρέφω, ἀποστρέφω, ἐπιστρέφω, ἐπιστροφή, μεταστρέφω." In *TDNT* 7: 714–29, edited by Gerhard Friedrich, translated and edited by Geoffrey W. Bromiley. Grand Rapids: Eerdmans, 1968.

Best, E. *Ephesians*. ICC. New York: T. & T. Clark International, 1998.

Betz, Hans Deiter. *Galatians: A Commentary on Paul's Letter to the Churches in Galatia*. Hermeneia. Philadelphia, PA: Fortress, 1979.

Bird, Michael F. *Jesus and the Origins of the Gentile Mission*. New York: T. & T. Clark International, 2006.

Birley, Graham, and Neil Moreland. *A Practical Guide to Academic Research*. London: Kogan Page, 1998.

Black, C. Clifton. "John Mark in the Acts of the Apostles." In *Literary Studies in Luke-Acts: Essays in Honor of Joseph B. Tyson*, edited by Richard P. Thompson and Thomas E. Phillips, 101–20. Macon, GA: Mercer University Press, 1998.

———. *Mark: Images of an Apostolic Interpreter*. Minneapolis, MN: Augsburg Fortress, 2001.

Black, David Alan. "El Camino para Auto-Apoyo según Tesalonicenses." Translated by Thomas W. Hudgins and Lesly J. Hudgins. *Daveblackonline.com* (April 8, 2010). Online: http://daveblackonline.com/el%20camino.htm.

———. *It's Still Greek to Me: An Easy-to-Understand Guide to Intermediate Greek*. Grand Rapids: Baker Academic, 1998.

———. *Learn to Read New Testament Greek*. 3rd ed. Nashville, TN: B&H, 2009.

————. *Linguistics for Students of New Testament Greek: A Survey of Basic Concepts and Applications.* 2nd ed. Grand Rapids: Baker, 1995.

————. "On the Style and Significance of John 17." *CTR* 3:1 (1988) 141–59.

————. "On the Pauline Authorship of Hebrews (Part 1): Overlooked Affinities between Hebrews and Paul." *Faith and Mission* 16 (1999) 32–51.

————. "On the Pauline Authorship of Hebrews (Part 2): The External Evidence Reconsidered." *Faith and Mission* 16 (1999) 78–86.

————. *Paul, Apostle of Weakness: Astheneia and Its Cognates in the Pauline Literature.* Rev. ed. Eugene, OR: Pickwick, 2012.

————. *The Authorship of Hebrews: The Case for Paul.* Topical Line Drives, vol. 1. Gonzalez, FL: Energion, 2013.

————. "The Thessalonian Road to Self-Support." *Daveblackonline.com* (April 8, 2010). Online: http://daveblackonline.com/thessalonian_road_to_selfsu.htm.

————. *Using New Testament Greek in Ministry: A Practical Guide for Students and Pastors.* Grand Rapids: Baker, 1993.

————. *Why Four Gospels? The Historical Origins of the Gospels.* 2nd ed. Gonzalez, FL: Energion, 2010.

Black, David Alan, and Thomas W. Hudgins. "Jesus on Anger (Matt 5,22a): A History of Recent Scholarship." In *Greeks, Jews, and Christians: Historical, Religious, and Philological Studies in Honor of Jesús Peláez del Rosal*, edited by L. Roig Lanzillotta and I. Muñoz Gallarte, 91–104. Cordoba: El Almendro, 2013.

Black, Mark C. *Luke.* The College Press NIV Commentary. Joplin, MO: College Press, 1996.

Blanchard, Ken, and Phil Hodges. *Lead Like Jesus: Lessons from the Greatest Leadership Role Model of All Time.* Nashville, TN: Thomas Nelson, 2005.

Blass, Friedrich. *Grammar of New Testament Greek.* Translated by Henry St. John Thackeray. 2nd rev. ed. New York: The MacMillan Company, 1905.

Blomberg, Craig L. *Interpreting the Parables.* 2nd ed. Downers Grove, IL: InterVarsity, 2012.

————. *Jesus and the Gospels: An Introduction and Survey.* 2nd ed. Nashville, TN: B&H, 2009.

————. *Neither Poverty nor Riches: A Biblical Theology of Possessions.* NSBT. Edited by D. A. Carson. Downers Grove, IL: InterVarsity, 1999.

Blomberg, Craig L., and Mariam J. Kamell. *James.* ZECNT. Edited by Clinton E. Arnold. Grand Rapids: Zondervan, 2008.

Blue, Brad. "The Influence of Jewish Worship on Luke's Presentation of the Early Church." In *Witness to the Gospel: The Theology of Acts*, edited by I. Howard Marshall and David Peterson, 473–98. Grand Rapids: William B. Eerdmans, 1998.

Bock, Darrell L. *Acts.* BECNT. Grand Rapids: Baker Academic, 2007.

————. *Luke.* The IVP New Testament Commentary Series. Edited by Grant R. Osborne. Downers Grove, IL: InterVarsity, 1994.

————. *Luke: Volume 1 (1:1–9:50).* BECNT. Edited by Moisés Silva. Grand Rapids: Baker Books, 1994.

Bockmuehl, Markus. *The Epistle to the Philippians.* Black's New Testament Commentaries. London: A&C Black, 1997.

Bøe, Sverre. *Cross-Bearing in Luke.* Wissenschaftliche Untersuchungen zum Neuen Testament 2.Reihe 278. Tübingen, Germany: Mohr Siebeck, 2010.

Boles, Kenneth L. *Galatians and Ephesians.* The College Press NIV Commentary. Joplin, MO: College Press, 1993.

Bolton, Barbara, and Charles Smith. *Creative Bible Learning for Children Grades 1–6.* Glendale, CA: International Center for Learning, 1977.

Borchert, Gerald L. *Worship in the New Testament: Divine Mystery and Human Response.* St. Louis, MO: Chalice Press, 2008.

Borg, Marcus J. *Conflict, Holiness, and Politics in the Teachings of Jesus.* New York: Continuum International, 1998.

Boring, M. Eugene. *Mark: A Commentary.* The New Testament Library. Louisville, KY: Westminster John Knox, 2006.

Boring, M. Eugene, and Fred B. Craddock. *The People's New Testament Commentary.* Louisville, KY: Westminster John Knox, 2004.

Borland, James A. "Woman in the Life and Teachings of Jesus." In *Recovering Biblical Manhood and Womanhood: A Response to Evangelical Feminism,* 2nd ed., edited by John Piper and Wayne Grudem, 113–23. Wheaton, IL: Crossway, 2006.

Bosch, David J. *Transforming Mission: Paradigm Shifts in Theology of Mission.* Rev. ed. Maryknoll, NY: Orbis, 2011.

Bowman, John. *The Gospel of Mark: The New Christian Jewish Passover Haggadah.* Leiden: E. J. Brill, 1965.

Bowman Jr., Robert M., and J. Ed Komoszewski. *Putting Jesus in His Place: The Case for the Deity of Christ.* Grand Rapids: Kregel, 2007.

Boyatzis, Richard E. *Transforming Qualitative Information: Thematic Analysis and Code Development.* Thousand Oaks: Sage, 1998.

Branick, Vincent P. *Understanding the New Testament and Its Message: An Introduction.* Mahway, NJ: Paulist, 1998.

Brawley, Robert L. *Text to Text Pours Forth Speech: Voices of Scripture in Luke-Acts.* Bloomington, IN: Indiana University Press, 1995.

Bretall, Robert. "The Concept of Purpose in Reformation Thought." In *Religion and Human Purpose: A Cross Disciplinary Approach,* edited by William Horosz and Tad Clements, 165–95. Studies in Philosophy and Religion 6. Dordrecht: Martinus Nijhoff, 1987.

Brodie, Thomas L. *Genesis as Dialogue: A Literary, Historical, and Theological Commentary.* New York: Oxford University Press, 2001.

———. *The Gospel according to John: A Literary and Theological Commentary.* New York: Oxford University, 1993.

Brooks, James A., and Carlton L. Winbery. *Syntax of New Testament Greek.* Lanham, MD: University Press of America, 1979.

Brown, Schuyler. *Apostasy and Perseverance in the Theology of Luke.* Analecta Biblica 36. Rome: Pontifical Biblical Institute, 1969.

Bruce, Alexander B. *The Synoptic Gospels.* The Expositor's Greek Testament. Vol. 3. Edited by W. Robertson Nicoll. Grand Rapids: Eerdmans, 1951.

———. *The Training of the Twelve: Timeless Principles for Leadership Development.* Grand Rapids: Kregel, 1988.

Bruce, F. F. *The Epistle to the Galatians: A Commentary on the Greek Text.* NIGTC. Exeter, England: Paternoster Press, 1982.

———. *The Epistle to the Hebrews.* NICNT. Rev. ed. Grand Rapids: Eerdmans, 1990.

Brueggemann, Walter, et al. *Texts for Preaching: A Lectionary Commentary Based on the NRSV—Year B.* Louisville, KY: Westminster John Knox, 1993.

Bruner, Frederick Dale. *Matthew, A Commentary: The Churchbook: Matthew 13–28.* Rev. ed. Grand Rapids: Eerdmans, 2004.

Bryant, Beauford H., and Mark S. Krause. *John.* The College Press NIV Commentary. Joplin, MO: College Press, 1998.

Buckwalter, H. Douglas. *The Character and Purpose of Luke's Christology.* Society for New Testament Studies Monograph Series 89. New York: Cambridge University Press, 1996.

Bullinger, E. W. *A Critical Lexicon and Concordance to the English and Greek New Testament Together with an Index of Greek Words and Several Appendices.* London: Longmans, Green, & Co.,1895.

————. *Foundations of Dispensational Truth.* New York: Cosimo, 2009.

Burke, Trevor J. "Pauline Paternity in 1 Thessalonians." *Tyndale Bulletin* 51:1 (2000) 59–80.

Burkett, Delbert. *An Introduction to the New Testament and the Origins of Christianity.* Cambridge, UK: Cambridge University, 2002.

Burridge, Richard A. *Imitating Jesus: An Inclusive Approach to New Testament Ethics.* Grand Rapids: Eerdmans, 2007.

Burton, E. D. *A Critical and Exegetical Commentary on the Epistle to the Galatians.* ICC. Edinburgh: T. & T. Clark, 1921.

Buttman, Alexander. *A Grammar of the New Testament Greek.* Andober: Warren F. Draper, 1981.

Byrne, Brendan. *Lifting the Burden: Reading Matthew's Gospel in the Church Today.* Collegeville, MN: The Liturgical Press, 2004.

————. *Romans.* Sacra Pagina. Edited by Daniel J. Harrington. Collegeville, MN: Liturgical Press, 1996.

Cachia, Nicholas. *The Image of the Good Shepherd as a Source for the Spirituality of the Ministerial Priesthood.* Tesi Gregoriana Serie Spiritualità 4. Rome: Editrice Pontificia Università Gregoriana, 1997.

Cahalan, Kathleen A. *Introducing the Practice of Ministry.* Collegeville, MN: The Liturgical Press, 2010.

Calhoun, Adele Ahlberg. *Spiritual Disciplines Handbook: Practices that Transform Us.* Downers Grove, IL: InterVarsity, 2005.

Calvert-Koyzis, Nancy. *Paul, Monotheism, and the People of God: The Significance of Abraham Traditions for Early Judaism and Christianity.* New York: T. & T. Clark International, 2004.

Carlson, Kent, and Mike Lueken. *Renovation of the Church: What Happens When a Seeker Church Discovers Spiritual Formation.* Downers Grove, IL: InterVarsity, 2011.

Carson, D. A. *Love in Hard Places.* Wheaton, IL: Crossway, 2002.

————. *The Gospel according to John.* The Pillar New Testament Commentary. Grand Rapids: Eerdmans, 1991.

Carson, D. A., and Douglas J. Moo. *An Introduction to the New Testament.* Grand Rapids: Zondervan, 2005.

Carter, Warren. *Matthew and the Margins: A Socio-Political and Religious Reading.* New York: T. & T. Clark International, 2000.

Cassidy, Richard J. *Paul in Chains: Roman Imprisonment and the Letters of St. Paul.* New York: Crossroad, 2001.

Castelli, Elizabeth A. *Imitating Paul: A Discourse of Power*. Literary Currents in Biblical Interpretation. Louisville, KY: Westminster John Knox, 1991.

Cerone, Jacob N. "The Use of γράφω and Its Compounds in Eusebius: Origen and Pauline Authorship of Hebrews?" www.jacobcerone.com (August 19, 2013). Online: http://jacobcerone.com/2013/08/19/the-use-of-%ce%b3%cf%81%ce%ac%cf%86%cf%89-and-its-compounds-in-eusebius-origen-and-pauline-authorship-of-hebrews/.

Chafer, Lewis Sperry. *Systematic Theology: Volumes 5 and 6*. Grand Rapids: Kregel, 1976.

Chalke, Steve, with Joanna Wyld. *Apprentice: Walking the Way of Christ*. Grand Rapids: Zondervan, 2009.

Chance, J. Bradley. "Luke 15: Seeking the Outsiders." *Review and Expositor* 94 (1997) 249–257.

Chandler, Christopher N. "Love Your Enemies as Yourself (Leviticus 19:18B) in Early Jewish-Christian Exegetic Practice and Missional Formulation." In *'What Does the Scripture Say?' Studies in the Function of Scripture in Early Judaism and Christianity*, vol. 1: The Synoptic Gospels, edited by Mark Goodacre, 12–56. Studies in Scripture and Early Judaism and Christianity. Library of New Testament Studies 469. New York: T. & T. Clark International, 2012.

Chandra, Soti Shivendra, and Rajendra K. Sharma. *Research in Education*. New Delhi, India: Atlantic, 2007.

Charlesworth, James H. "Introduction: Why Evaluate Twenty-Five Years of Jesus Research?" In *Jesus Research, an International Perspective: The Proceedings of the Biennial Princeton-Prague Symposium on the Current State of Studies on the Historical Jesus*, edited by J. H. Charlesworth and Petr Pokorný, 1–15. Grand Rapids: Eerdmans, 2009.

Chilton, Bruce. "The Trial of Jesus Reconsidered." In *Jesus in Context: Temple, Purity, and Restoration*, edited by Bruce Chilton and Craig A. Evans, 481–500. Leiden: Brill, 1997.

Chomsky, Noam. *Lectures on Government and Binding: The Pisa Lectures*. 7th ed. Berlin: Walter de Gruyter, 1993.

Ciampa, Roy E., and Brian S. Rosner. *The First Letter to the Corinthians*. The Pillar New Testament Commentary. Grand Rapids: Eerdmans, 2010.

Clarke, Andrew D. *A Pauline Theology of Church Leadership*. Library of New Testament Studies. New York: T. & T. Clark, 2008.

———. *Secular and Christian Leadership in Corinth: A Socio-Historical and Exegetical Study of 1 Corinthians 1–6*. Leiden: E. J. Brill, 1993.

———. "The Role of the Apostles." In *Witness to the Gospel: The Theology of Acts*, edited by I. Howard Marshall and David Peterson, 169–90. Grand Rapids: William B. Eerdmans, 1998.

Closson, Don. "Public, Private, or Home Education." In *Kids, Classrooms, and Contemporary Education: Probing the Headlines that Impact Your Family*, edited by Don Closson, 118–128. Grand Rapids: Kregel, 2000.

Coffey, Amanda, and Paul Atkinson. *Making Sense of Qualitative Data: Complementary Research Strategies*. Thousand Oaks: Sage, 1996.

Cohen, Daniel Ronnie. "Subject and Object in Biblical Aramaic: A Functional Approach Based on Form-Content Analysis." *Afroasiatic Linguistics* 2:1 (1975) 1–23.

Cohen, Louis, et. al. *Research Methods in Education*. 5th ed. New York: RoutledgeFalmer, 2000.

Cole, Graham A. *He Who Gives Life: The Doctrine of the Holy Spirit*. Foundations of Evangelical Theology. Edited by John S. Feinberg. Wheaton, IL: Crossway, 2007.

Cole, R. Alan. *Galatians*. The Tyndale New Testament Commentaries. 2nd ed. Grand Rapids: Eerdmans, 1989.

———. *Mark*. 2nd ed. The Tyndale New Testament Commentaries. Grand Rapids: Eerdmans, 1989.

Colledge, Gary L. *God and Charles Dickens: Recovering the Christian Voice of a Classic Author*. Grand Rapids: Brazos, 2012.

Collins, Raymond F. *The Power of Images in Paul*. Collegeville, MN: Liturgical Press, 2008.

———. *1 Corinthians*. Sacra Pagina. Edited by Daniel J. Harrington. Collegeville, MN: The Liturgical Press, 1999.

———. *1 & 2 Timothy and Titus*. The New Testament Library. Louisville, KY: Westminster John Knox, 2002.

Cook III, William F. "Principles of Spiritual Warfare in Light of Jesus' Temptations." *Theological Educator* 54 (Fall 1996) 13–19.

Cosby, Michael R. *The Rhetorical Composition and Function of Hebrews 11: In Light of Example Lists in Antiquity*. Macon, GA: Mercer University Press, 1988.

Cosgrove, Charles H. *The Cross and the Spirit: A Study in the Argument and Theology of Galatians*. Mercer Classroom Series. Macon, GA: Mercer University Press, 1988.

Costa, Alfredo Sampaio. "Compasión." In *Diccionario de Espiritualidad Ignaciana*, vol. 1, 2nd ed., 356–59. Madrid: Compañía de Jesús, 2007.

Cottrell, Jack. *Romans*. The College Press NIV Commentary. Joplin, MO: College Press, 2005.

Cousar, Charles B. *An Introduction to the New Testament: Witnesses to God's New Work*. Louisville, KY: Westminster John Knox, 2006.

Cousins, Don. "Overseeing Staff." In *Mastering Church Management* 137–150, edited by Don Cousins, et. al. Portland, OR: Multnomah, 1990.

Craddock, Fred B. *Luke*. Interpretation. Louisville, KY: John Knox, 1990.

Crawford, Sidnie White. *The Temple Scroll and Related Texts*. Companion to the Qumran Scrolls. Sheffield, England: Sheffield Academic, 2000.

Crump, David. *Knocking on Heaven's Door: A New Testament Theology of Petitionary Prayer*. Grand Rapids: Baker Academic, 2006.

Culpepper, Robert H. "The Humanity of Jesus: An Overview." *FM* 5:2 (Spring 1988) 14–26.

Cunningham, David S. *Christian Ethics: The End of the Law*. New York: Routledge, 2008.

Dahl, Nils A. "Paul and the Church at Corinth." In *Christianity at Corinth: The Quest for the Pauline Church*, edited by Edward Adams and David G. Horrell, 85–97. Louisville, KY: Westminster John Knox, 2004.

Dana, H. E., and Julius R. Mantey. *A Manual Grammar of the Greek New Testament*. Upper Saddle River, NJ: Prentice Hall, 1927.

Danker, Frederick W. *A Greek-English Lexicon of the New Testament and Other Early Christian Literature*. 3rd ed. Based on Walter Bauer's *Griechisch-deutsches Worterbuch zu den Schriften des Neuen Testaments und der fruhchristlichen Literatur*, 6th ed., ed. Kurt Aland and Barbara Aland, with Viktor Reichmann, and on previous English editions by W. F. Arndt, F. W. Gingrich, and F. W. Danker. Chicago: The University of Chicago Press, 2000.

Danker, Frederick William, and Kathryn Krug. *The Concise Greek-English Lexicon of the New Testament.* Chicago, IL: The University of Chicago, 2009.

Dawsey, James M. *The Lukan Voice: Confusion and Irony in the Gospel of Luke.* Macon, GA: Mercer University, 1986.

De Boer, Martinus C. *Galatians: A Commentary.* The New Testament Library. Louisville, KY: Westminster John Knox, 2011.

De Gasperis, Francesco Rossi. *Sentieri di Vita: La Dinamica degli Esercizi Ignaziani nell'itinerario delle Scritture.* Part 2. Milan, Italy: Paoline, 2007.

Demarest, Bruce. *The Cross and Salvation: The Doctrine of Salvation.* Foundations of Evangelical Theology. Edited by John S. Feinberg. Wheaton, IL: Crossway, 1997.

DeMoss, Matthew S. *Pocket Dictionary for the Study of New Testament Greek.* Downers Grove, IL: InterVarsity, 2001.

Denaux, Adelbert. *Studies in the Gospel of Luke: Structure, Language and Theology.* Tilburg Theological Studies. Berlin: LIT, 2010.

DeSilva, David A. *An Introduction to the New Testament: Contexts, Methods and Ministry Formation.* Downers Grove, IL: InterVarsity, 2004.

———. *The Jewish Teachers of Jesus, James, and Jude: What Earliest Christianity Learned from the Apocrypha and Pseudepigrapha.* New York: Oxford University Press, 2012.

Díaz, José Manuel. *El Santo Evangelio Según San Lucas: Traducción y Comentario.* Bogotá: Editorial El Catolicismo, 1961.

Dillersberger, John. *The Gospel of Saint Luke.* Westminster, MD: The Newman Press, 1958.

Dodd, C. H. *More New Testament Studies.* Manchester, England: The University Press, 1968.

Donahue, Bill, and Greg Bowman. *Coaching Life-Changing Small Group Leaders: A Practical Guide for Those Who Lead and Shepherd Small Group Leaders.* Grand Rapids: Zondervan, 2006.

Donahue, John R., and Daniel J. Harrington. *The Gospel of Mark.* Sacra Pagina. Edited by Daniel J. Harrington. Collegeville, MN: The Liturgical Press, 2002.

Donelson, Lewis R. *I & II Peter and Jude: A Commentary.* The New Testament Library. Louisville, KY: Westminster John Knox, 2010.

Donfried, Karl P., and I. Howard Marshall. *The Theology of the Shorter Pauline Letters.* New York: Cambridge University Press, 1993.

Doriani, Daniel M. "A Redemptive-Historical Model." In *Four Views on Moving Beyond the Bible to Theology,* edited by Stanley N. Gundry and Gary T. Meadors, 75–120. Grand Rapids: Zondervan, 2009.

Doyle, G. Wright. *Jesus: The Complete Man.* Bloomington, IN: AuthorHouse, 2008.

Dupont, Jacques. *Les Béatitudes.* Vol. 1. Paris : Gabalda, 1969.

Drane, John. *Introducing the New Testament.* Minneapolis, MN: Fortress Press, 2001.

Dunn, James D. G. *The Theology of Paul the Apostle.* Grand Rapids: Eerdmans, 1998.

———. *1 Corinthians.* T. & T. Clark Study Guides. New York: T. & T. Clark International, 1999.

Dvorjetski, Estee. *Leisure, Pleasure and Healing: Spa Culture and Medicine in Ancient Eastern Mediterranean.* Supplements to the Journal for the Study of Judaism 116. Leiden: Brill, 2007.

Dysinger, Luke. "Endurance." Page 486 in *The Westminster Dictionary of Christian Spirituality*. Edited by Philip Sheldrake. Louisville, KY: Westminster John Knox, 2005.

Edwards, Richard A. "Narrative Implications of Gar in Matthew." *CBQ* 52:4 (1990) 636–55.

Eisenbaum, Pamela. "The Virtue of Suffering, the Necessity of Discipline, and the Pursuit of Perfection in Hebrews." In *Asceticism in the New Testament*, edited by Leif E. Vaage and Vincent L. Wimbush, 331–354. New York: Routledge, 1999.

Eldridge, Daryl. "The Disciple: Called to Learn." In *The Teaching Ministry of the Church: Integrating Biblical Truth with Contemporary Application*, edited by Daryl Eldridge, 75–88. Nashville, TN: B&H, 1995.

Ellicott, Charles J. *A Critical and Grammatical Commentary on the Pastoral Epistles*. Eugene, OR: Wipf & Stock, 1998.

Elwell, Walter A., and Philip W. Comfort. "Apostle, Apostleship." In *Tyndale Bible Dictionary*, 95–96. Wheaton, IL: Tyndale, 2001.

Erickson, Millard J. *Christian Theology*. 2nd ed. Grand Rapids: Baker, 1998.

———. *Introducing Christian Doctrine*. Edited by L. Arnold Hustad. 2nd ed. Grand Rapids: Baker Academic, 2001.

Estep Jr., James Riley. "It's All Greek to Me! Education in Greek Culture." In *C.E.: The Heritage of Christian Education*, edited by James Riley Estep Jr., 4.1–4.22. Joplin, MO: College Press, 2003.

Estes, Douglas. *The Questions of Jesus in John: Logic, Rhetoric and Persuasive Discourse*. Leiden: Brill, 2012.

Evans, Craig A. *Jesus and His Contemporaries: Comparative Studies*. Leiden: E. J. Brill, 1995.

Evans, C. F. *Saint Luke*. TPI New Testament Commentaries. Philadelphia, PA: Trinity Press International, 1990.

Evans, Tony. *Our God is Awesome: Encountering the Greatness of Our God*. The Understanding God Series. Chicago, IL: Moody, 1994.

Fagbemi, Stephen Ayodeji A. *Who Are the Elect in 1 Peter? A Study in Biblical Exegesis and Its Application to the Anglican Church of Nigeria*. Studies in Biblical Literature 104. New York: Peter Lang, 2007.

Fantin, Joseph D. *The Greek Imperative Mood in the New Testament: A Cognitive and Communicative Approach*. Studies in Biblical Greek. New York: Peter Lang, 2010.

Farnell, F. David. "When Will the Gift of Prophecy Cease?" *BibSac* 150 (April-June 1993) 171–202.

Fee, Gordon D. *To What End Exegesis: Essays Textual, Exegetical and Theological*. Grand Rapids: Eerdmans, 2001.

Feinberg, John S. *No One Like Him: The Doctrine of God*. Foundations of Evangelical Theology. Edited by John S. Feinberg. Wheaton, IL: Crossway, 2001.

Fillion, Louis Claude. *Vida de Nuestro Señor Jesucristo II: Vida Pública*. Translated by R. P. Victoriano and M. Larrainzar. Madrid: RIALP, 2000.

Finlan, Stephen. *The Apostle Paul and the Pauline Tradition*. Collegeville, MN: Liturgical Press, 2008.

Fisher, N. R. E. *Slavery in Classical Greece*. London: Bristol Classic Press, 1993.

Fitzmyer, Joseph A. *To Advance the Gospel: New Testament Studies*. The Biblical Resource Series. 2nd ed. Grand Rapids: Eerdmans, 1998.

———. *First Corinthians*. New Haven, CT: Yale University Press, 2008.

Flichy, Odile. *La Obra de Lucas: El Evangelio y los Hechos de los Apóstoles*. Navarra, Spain: Verbo Divino.

Flick, Uwe. *An Introduction to Qualitative Research*. 4th ed. Thousand Oaks: Sage, 2009.

———. *Introducing Research Methodology: A Beginner's Guide to Doing a Research Project*. Thousand Oaks: Sage, 2011.

Foley, Toshikazu S. *Biblical Translation in Chinese and Greek: Verbal Aspect in Theory and Practice*. Linguistic Biblical Studies 1. Leiden: Brill, 2009.

Fonck, Leopold. *The Parables of the Gospel: An Exegetical and Practical Explanation*. Translated by E. Leahy. Edited by George O'Neill. New York: Frederick Pustet Co., Inc., 1915.

Forlines, F. Leroy. *Romans*. The Randall House Bible Commentary. Edited by Robert E. Picirilli. Nashville, TN: Randall House, 1987.

———. *The Quest for Truth: Answering Life's Inescapable Questions*. Nashville, TN: Randall House, 2001.

Foster, Ruth Ann, and William D. Shiell. "The Parable of the Sower and the Seed in Luke 8:1–10: Jesus' Parable of Parables." *Review and Expositor* 94 (1997) 259–267.

Fowl, Stephen E. "A Metaphor in Distress: A Reading of ΝΗΠΙΟΙ in 1 Thessalonians 2:7." *NTS* 36:3 (1990) 469–473.

———. *Ephesians: A Commentary*. The New Testament Library. Louisville, KY: Westminster John Knox, 2012.

France, R. T. *The Gospel of Matthew*. NICNT. Grand Rapids: Eerdmans, 2007.

Fredriksen, Paula. *Jesus of Nazareth: King of the Jews*. New York: Vintage Books, 1999.

Freed, Edwin D. *The Apostle Paul and His Letters*. Oakville, CT: DBBC, 2005.

Friberg, Timothy, et. al. *Analytical Lexicon of the Greek New Testament*. Victoria, Canada: Trafford, 2005.

Friedrich, Carsten. *Das Neue Testament: Überblick, Hintergrund und Erklärungen*. Kassel, Germany: Born-Verlag, 2009.

Frye, John W. *Jesus the Pastor: Leading Others in the Character and Power of Christ*. Grand Rapids: Zondervan, 2000.

Fung, Ronald Y. K. *The Epistle to the Galatians*. NICNT. Grand Rapids: Eerdmans, 1988.

Furnish, Victor Paul. *1 Thessalonians, 2 Thessalonians*. ANTC. Nashville, TN: Abingdon, 2007.

Garland, David E. *Luke*. ZECNT. Vol. 3. Edited by Clinton E. Arnold. Grand Rapids: Zondervan, 2011.

———. *1 Corinthians*. BECNT. Grand Rapids: Baker Academic, 2003.

Garlington, Don B. "Jesus, the Unique Son of God: Tested and Faithful." *BibSac* 150 (July-September 1994) 284–308.

Geldenhuys, Norval. *Commentary on the Gospel of Luke*. Grand Rapids: Eerdmans, 1954.

Getz, Gene. *Elders and Leaders: God's Plan for Leading the Church*. Chicago, IL: Moody, 2003.

———. *Loving One Another*. One Another Series. 3rd ed. Colorado Springs, CO: Victor, 2002.

Gingrich, F. Wilbur. *Shorter Lexicon of the Greek New Testament*. Chicago, IL: The University of Chicago, 1965.

Glenny, W. Edward. "1 Peter 2:2a: Nourishment for Growth in Faith and Love." In *Interpreting the New Testament Text: Introduction to the Art and Science of Exegesis*, edited by Darrell L. Bock and Buist M. Fanning, 441–448. Wheaton, IL: Crossway, 2006.

Golden, Mark. "Slavery and Homosexuality at Athens." In *Studies in Homosexuality*, vol. 1: Homosexuality in the Ancient World, edited by Wayne R. Dynes and Stephen Donaldson, 162–178. New York: Garland, 1992.

Goldenberg, Robert. "Religious Formation in Ancient Judaism." In *Educating People of Faith: Exploring the History of Jewish and Christian Communities*, edited by John Van Engen, 29–47. Grand Rapids: Eerdmans, 2004.

González, Justo L. *Essential Theological Terms*. Louisville, KY: Westminster John Knox, 2005.

———. *Luke*. Belief. Louisville, KY: Westminster John Knox, 2010.

Gourgues, Michel. *Luc, de l'Exégèse à la Prédication: Carême, Pâques, Année C.* Montreal, Canada: Fides, 1994.

Grassmick, John D. "Galatians." In *The Bible Knowledge Word Study: Acts-Ephesians*, edited by Darrell L. Bock, 367–420. The Bible Knowledge Series. Colorado Springs, CO: Victor, 2006.

Green, Gene L. *The Letters to the Thessalonians*. The Pillar New Testament Commentary. Grand Rapids: Eerdmans, 2002.

Green, Joel B. "Context." In *Dictionary for Theological Interpretation of the Bible*, edited by Kevin J. Vanhoozer, 130–133. Grand Rapids: Baker Academic, 2005.

———. *The Gospel of Luke*. NICNT. Grand Rapids: Eerdmans, 1997.

———. *1 Peter*. The Two Horizons New Testament Commentary. Grand Rapids: Eerdmans, 2007.

Greenlee, J. Harold. *A Concise Exegetical Grammar of New Testament Greek*. 5th ed. Grand Rapids: William B. Eerdmans, 1986.

Grenz, Stanley J. *The Social God and the Relational Self: A Trinitarian Theology of the Imago Dei*. The Matrix of Christian Theology. Louisville, KY: Westminster John Knox, 2001.

Grbich, Carol. *Qualitative Data Analysis: An Introduction*. Thousand Oaks: Sage, 2007.

Griffin, William Paul. *The God of the Prophets: An Analysis of Divine Action*. Sheffield: Sheffield Academic, 1997.

Grinnell Jr., Richard M., and Yvonne A. Unrau. *Social Work Research and Evaluation: Foundations of Evidence-Based Practiced*. 9th ed. New York: Oxford University, 2011.

Guest, Greg, et al. *Applied Thematic Analysis*. Thousand Oaks: Sage, 2012.

Guthrie, Donald. *Hebrews*. The Tyndale New Testament Commentaries. Grand Rapids: Eerdmans, 1983.

———. *New Testament Introduction*. 4th rev. ed. Downers Grove, IL: InterVarsity, 1990.

———. *The Pastoral Epistles: Introduction and Commentary*. The Tyndale New Testament Commentaries. 2nd ed. Grand Rapids: Eerdmans, 1990.

Guthrie, George H. *The Structure of Hebrews: A Text-Linguistic Analysis*. Leiden: E. J. Brill, 1994.

Guy, H. A. *The Gospel of Luke*. New York: St. Martin's Press, 1972.

Habermas, Ronald T. *Introduction to Christian Education and Formation: A Lifelong Plan for Christ-Centered Restoration*. Grand Rapids: Zondervan, 2008.

Hagner, Donald A. *Hebrews*. Understanding the Bible Commentary Series. 2nd ed. Grand Rapids: Baker, 2011.

————. *The Use of the Old and New Testaments in Clement of Rome.* Leiden: E. J. Brill, 1973.

Hall, Douglas John. *Imaging God: Dominion as Stewardship.* Grand Rapids: Eerdmans, 1986.

Hall, Randy. "For to This You Have Been Called: The Cross and Suffering in 1 Peter." *Restoration Quarterly* 19:3 (1976) 137–147.

Hamilton, Hollister Adelbert. *The Negative Compounds in Greek.* Baltimore, MD: John Murphy Company, 1899.

Hanson, Anthony T. "The Origin of Paul's Use of ΠΑΙΔΑΓΩΓΟΣ for the Law." *JSNT* 34 (October 1988) 71–76.

Hare, Douglas R. A. *Matthew.* Interpretation. 9th ed. Louisville, KY: Westminster John Knox, 2009.

Harink, Douglas. *1 and 2 Peter.* Brazos Theological Commentary on the Bible. Grand Rapids: Brazos, 2009.

Harrington, Wilfrid J. *The Gospel according to St. Luke: A Commentary.* Westminster, MD: Newman Press, 1967.

Harris, William V. *Restraining Rage: The Ideology of Anger Control in Classical Antiquity.* Cambridge, MA: Harvard University Press, 2001.

Harrison, E. F. "Apostle." In *Evangelical Dictionary of Theology,* 2nd ed., edited by Walter A. Elwell, 85–87. Grand Rapids: Baker, 2001.

Hartin, Patrick J. *James.* Sacra Pagina. Edited by Daniel J. Harrington. Rev. ed. Collegeville, MN: Liturgical Press, 2009.

————. *James, First Peter, Jude, Second Peter.* New Collegeville Bible Commentary. Collegeville, MN: Liturgical Press, 2006.

Hartsock, Chad. *Sight and Blindness in Luke-Acts: The Use of Physical Features in Characterization.* Leiden: Brill, 2008.

Hauck, F. "ménō." In *TDNT,* abr. ed., edited by Gerhard Kittel and Gerhard Friedrich, translated and edited by Geoffrey W. Bromiley, 581–584. Grand Rapids: William B. Eerdmans, 1985.

Hawthorne, Gerald F. *Philippians.* WBC. Vol. 43. Edited by Bruce M. Metzger, et. al. Waco, TX: Word, 1983.

Hayes, John H. and Carl R. Holladay. *Biblical Exegesis: A Beginner's Handbook.* Rev. ed. Louisville, KY: Westminster John Knox, 1987.

Hays, Christopher M. *Luke's Wealth Ethics.* Wissenschaftliche Untersuchungen zum Neuen Testament 2.Reihe 275. Tübingen: Mohr Siebeck, 2010.

Hays, Richard B. *First Corinthians.* Interpretation. Louisville, KY: Westminster John Knox, 1997.

Heim, John Paul. *Ephesians: Empowerment to Walk in Love for the Unity of All in Christ.* Studies in Biblical Literature. Atlanta: SBL, 2007.

Heliso, Desta. *Pistis and the Righteous One.* Wissenschaftliche Untersuchungen zum Neuen Testament 2.Reihe 235. Tübingen: Mohr Siebeck, 2007.

Hendricks, Howard. *Teaching to Change Lives: Seven Proven Ways to Make Your Teaching Come Alive.* Rev. ed. Colorado Springs, CO: Multnomah, 1987.

Hersey, Paul H., et. al. *Management of Organizational Behavior: Leading Human Resources.* 10th ed. Upper Saddle River, NJ: Prentice Hall, 2012.

Hester, David C. "Luke 4:1–13." *Interpretation* 31:2 (January 1977) 53–59.

Hesse-Biber, Sharlene Nagy, and Patricia Leavy. *The Practice of Qualitative Research.* 2nd ed. Thousand Oaks: Sage, 2011.

Heywood, David. *Divine Revelation and Human Learning: A Christian Theory of Knowledge.* Burlington, VT: Ashgate, 2004.

Hirsch, Alan, and Dave Ferguson. *On the Verge: A Journey into the Apostolic Future of the Church.* Exponential Series. Grand Rapids: Zondervan, 2011.

Hobbs, Herschel H. *An Exposition of Luke.* Grand Rapids: Baker, 1966.

Hock, Ronald F. "Paul and Greco-Roman Education." In *Paul in the Greco-Roman World: A Handbook,* edited by J. Paul Sampley, 198–227. Harrisburg, PA: Trinity Press International, 2003.

———. "Paul's Tentmaking and the Problem of His Social Class." In *Tentmaking: Perspectives on Self-Supporting Ministry,* edited by James M. M. Francis and Leslie J. Francis, 4–13. Christian Perspectives. Herefordshire, England: Gracewing, 1998.

———. *The Social Context of Paul's Ministry: Tentmaking and Apostleship.* Minneapolis, MN: Fortress, 1980.

Hoehner, Harold W. *Ephesians: An Exegetical Commentary.* Grand Rapids: Baker Academic, 2002.

Hoekema, Anthony A. "The Reformed Persepctive." In *Five Views on Sanctification,* edited by Stanley N. Gundry, 59–90. Grand Rapids: Zondervan, 1987.

Holleran, J. Warren. *The Synoptic Gethsemene: A Critical Study.* Analecta Gregoriana 191. Rome: Università Gregoriana Editrice, 1973.

Holmas, Geir O. *Prayer and Vindication in Luke-Acts: The Theme of Prayer within the Context of the Legitimating and Edifying Objective of the Lukan Narrative.* Library of New Testament Studies. New York: T. & T. Clark International, 2011.

Holmes, Arthur F. *Building the Christian Academy.* Grand Rapids: Eerdmans, 2001.

Hooker, Morna D. "John's Baptism: A Prophetic Sign." In *The Holy Spirit and Christian Origins: Essays in Honor of James D. G. Dunn,* edited by Graham N. Stanton, et. al., 22–40. Grand Rapids: Eerdmans, 2004.

Hooper, Duane. *Christian School Teacher: Ministry of Caring for Kids.* League City, TX: Xulon, 2008.

Horn, Cornelia B., and John W. Martens. *"Let the Little Children Come to Me": Childhood and Children in Early Christianity.* Washington, D.C.: Catholic University of America, 2009.

Howard, C. D. C. "Blindness and Deafness." In *Dictionary of Jesus and the Gospels: A Compendium of Contemporary Biblical Scholarship,* edited by Joel B. Green, et. al., 81–82. Downers Grove, IL: InterVarsity, 1992.

Howard, James M. *Paul, the Community, and Progressive Sanctification: An Exploration into Community-Based Transformation within Pauline Theology.* Studies in Biblical Literature 90. New York: Peter Lang, 2007.

Hübner, Hans. *Law in Paul's Thought: A Contribution to the Development of Pauline Theology.* Translated by James C. G. Greig. New York: T. & T. Clark International, 1984.

Hudgins, Thomas W. "An Application of Discourse Analysis Methodology in the Exegesis of John 17." *Eleutheria* 2:1 (2012) 24–57. Online: http://digitalcommons. liberty.edu/eleu/vol2/iss1/4.

Hughes, John A. "Why Christian Education and Not Secular Indoctrination?" In *Think Biblically: Recovering a Christian Worldview,* edited by John MacArthur, 239–258. Wheaton, IL: Crossway, 2003.

Hughes, Philip Edgcumbe. *A Commentary on the Epistle to the Hebrews.* Grand Rapids: Eerdmans, 1977.

Hughes, Richard A. *Lament, Death, and Destiny*. Studies in Biblical Literature 68. New York: Peter Lang, 2004.

Hultgren, Arland J. *The Parables of Jesus: A Commentary*. Grand Rapids: Eerdmans, 2000.

Hume, Douglas A. *The Early Christian Community*. Wissenschaftliche Untersuchungen zum Neuen Testament 2.Reihe 298. Tübingen: Mohr Siebeck, 2011.

Humphreys, Fisher. *I Have Called You Friends: New Testament Images that Challenge Us to Live as Christ Followers*. Birmingham, AL: New Hope Publishers, 2005.

Hunter, Archibald M. *Introducing the New Testament*. 3rd rev. ed. Philadelphia, PA: The Westminster Press, 1972.

Hurtado, Larry W. *Lord Jesus Christ: Devotion to Jesus in Earliest Christianity*. Grand Rapids: Eerdmans, 2003.

Ibáñez Moreno, Ana, and Ana Ortigosa Pastor. "A Contrastive Discourse Analysis of Proverbs in English and Spanish: The Discovery of How Much Can Be Communicated through So Little." In *Linguistic Perspectives from the Classroom: Language Teaching in a Multicultural Europe*, edited by JoDee Anderson, et.al., 357–370. Galicia, Spain: Universidad de Santiago de Compostela, 2004.

Icenogle, Gareth Weldon. *Biblical Foundations for Small Group Ministry: An Integrational Approach*. Downers Grove, IL: InterVarsity, 1994.

Ireland, Dennis J. *Stewardship and the Kingdom of God: An Historical, Exegetical, and Contextual Study of the Parable of the Unjust Steward in Luke 16:1–13*. Leiden: E. J. Brill, 1992.

Issler, Klaus. "Jesus' Example: Prototype of the Dependent, Spirit-Filled Life." In *Jesus in Trinitarian Perspective: An Introductory Christology*, edited by Fred Sanders and Klaus Issler, 189–225. Nashville, TN: B&H, 2007.

———. "Philosophy of Education." In *Faith and Learning: A Handbook for Christian Higher Education*, edited by David S. Dockery, 97–121. Nashville, TN: B&H, 2012.

Iwe, John Chijioke. *Jesus in the Synagogue of Capernaum: The Pericope and its Programmatic Character for the Gospel of Mark, An Exegetico-Theological Study of Mk 1:21–28*. Tesi Gregoriana Serie Teologia 57. Rome: Editrice Pontificia Universatà Gregoriana, 1999.

Jansma, Theodore J. "The Temptation of Jesus." *WTJ* 5:2 (May 1943) 166–181.

Jao, Greg. "Honor and Obey." In *Following Jesus without Dishonoring Your Parents*, edited by Jeanette Yep, 43–56. Downers Grove, IL: InterVarsity, 1998.

Jeffers, James S. *The Greco-Roman World of the New Testament Era: Exploring the Background of Early Christianity*. Downers Grove, IL: InterVarsity, 1999.

Jeffrey, David Lyle. *Luke*. Brazos Theological Commentary on the Bible. Grand Rapids: Brazos Press, 2012.

Jervis, L. Ann. *Galatians*. Understanding the Bible Commentary Series. Grand Rapids: Baker, 1999.

Jobes, Karen H. *1 Peter*. BECNT. Grand Rapids: Baker Academic, 2005.

Johnson, Alan F. *1 Corinthians*. The IVP New Testament Commentary Series. Edited by Grant R. Osborne. Downers Grove, IL: InterVarsity, 2004.

Johnson, Luke Timothy. *Prophetic Jesus, Prophetic Church: The Challenge of Luke-Acts to Contemporary Christians*. Grand Rapids: Eerdmans, 2011.

———. *The Gospel of Luke*. Sacra Pagina. Vol. 3. Edited by Daniel J. Harrington. Collegeville, MN: The Liturgical Press, 1991.

———. *The Writings of the New Testament: An Interpretation*. Philadelphia, PA: Fortress Press, 1986.

Johnson Jr., Earl S. *Hebrews*. Interpretation Bible Studies. Louisville, KY: Westminster John Knox, 2008.

Johnson Jr., S. Lewis. "Divine Love in Recent Theology." *TrinJ* 5 (1984) 175–187.

Jones, David C. "Love: The Impelling Motive of the Christian Life." *Presbyterion* 12:2 (Fall 1986) 65–92.

Judge, E. A. *The First Christians in the Roman World*. Wissenschaftliche Untersuchungen zum Neuen Testament 229. Tübingen: Mohr Siebeck, 2008.

Juel, Donald. *Luke-Acts: The Promise of History*. Atlanta, GA: John Knox, 1983.

Julien, Heidi. "Content Analysis." In *The SAGE Encyclopedia of Qualitative Research Methods*, vol. 2, edited by Lisa M. Given, 120–121. Thousand Oaks: Sage, 2008.

Just Jr., Arthur A. *Luke 1:1–9:50*. Concordia Commentary. St. Louis, MO: Concordia Publishing House, 1996.

———. *The Ongoing Feast: Table Fellowship and Eschatology at Emmaus*. Collegeville, MN: The Liturgical Press, 1993.

Karrer, Martin. *Jesus Christus im Neuen Testament*. NTD Ergänzungsreihe 11. Göttingen: Vandenhoeck und Ruprecht, 1998.

Keating, Daniel. *First and Second Peter, Jude*. Catholic Commentary on Sacred Scripture. Grand Rapids: Baker Academic, 2011.

Kee, Howard Clark. "Sociological Insights into the Development of Christian Leadership Roles and Community Formation." In *Handbook of Early Christianity: Social Science Approaches*, edited by Anthony J. Blasi, et. al., 337–360. Walnut Creek, CA: AltaMira, 2002.

Keener, Craig S. *A Commentary on the Gospel of Matthew*. Grand Rapids: Eerdmans, 1999.

———. *Matthew*. The IVP New Testament Commentary Series. Edited by Grant R. Osborne. Downers Grove, IL: InterVarsity, 1997.

Kellum, L. Scott. *The Unity of the Farewell Discourse: The Literary Integrity of John 13.31–16.33*. JSNTSS 256. New York: Continuum, 2004.

Kelly, J. N. D. *A Commentary on the Epistles of Peter and of Jude*. Black's New Testament Commentaries. London: A&C Black, 1969.

Kent, Keri Wyatt. *Deeper into the Word: Reflections on 100 Words from the New Testament*. Bloomington, MN: Bethany House, 2011.

Kie, John, and Su Vining. "Disciple Them, Keep Them: Family Discipleship and the Great Commission." In *The Great Commission Connection*, edited by Raymond F. Culpepper, 401–412. Cleveland, TN: Pathway Press, 2011.

Kilgallen, John J. *Twenty Parables of Jesus in the Gospel of Luke*. Subsidia Biblica 32. Rome: Pontificio Istituto Biblico, 2008.

Kim, Yung Suk. *Christ's Body in Corinth: The Politics of a Metaphor*. Paul in Critical Contexts. Minneapolis, MN: Fortress, 2008.

Kingsbury, Jack Dean. *Conflict in Luke: Jesus, Authorities, and Disciples*. Minneapolis, MN: Augsburg Fortress, 1991.

Kirk, Alan. *The Composition of the Sayings Source: Genre, Synchrony, and Wisdom Redaction in Q*. Leiden: Brill, 1998.

Klauck, Hans-Josef. *Ancient Letters and the New Testament: A Guide to Context and Exegesis*. Translated and edited by Daniel P. Bailey. Waco, TX: Baylor University Press, 2006.

———. *The Apocryphal Gospels: An Introduction*. New York: T. & T. Clark, 2003.

Klenke, Karin. *Qualitative Research in the Study of Leadership*. Bingley, England: Emerald Group, 2008.

Klein, George. "Christian Love according to 1 Cor 13." *Concordia Theological Monthly* 30:6 (June 1959) 432–445.

Klein, Hans. *Das Lukasevangelium*. Meyers Kritisch-Exegetischer Kommentar Über das Neue Testament. Göttingen: Vandenhoeck & Ruprecht, 2006.

Klein, William W. *Become What You Are: Spiritual Formation according to the Sermon on the Mount*. Tyrone, GA: Authentic Media, 2006.

Knight III, George W. *The Pastoral Epistles: A Commentary on the Greek Text*. NIGTC. Grand Rapids: Eerdmans, 1992.

Koet, Bart J. "Isaiah in Luke-Acts." In *Dreams and Scripture in Luke-Acts: Collected Essays*, 51–80. Contributions to Biblical Exegesis and Theology 42. Leuven, Belgium: Peeters, 2006.

Konczyk, R. J. *Melchizedek and the Temple: The Promise of the Ages*. Bloomington, IN: AuthorHouse, 2008.

Köstenberger, Andreas J. *A Theology of John's Gospel and Letters: The Word, the Christ, the Son of God*. Biblical Theology of the New Testament. Edited by Andreas J. Köstenberger. Grand Rapids: Zondervan, 2009.

———. *Excellence: The Character of God and the Pursuit of Scholarly Virtue*. Wheaton, IL: Crossway, 2011.

———. "The Use of Scripture in the Pastoral and General Epistles and the Book of Revelation." In *Hearing the Old Testament in the New*, edited by Stanley E. Porter, 230–254. Grand Rapids: Eerdmans, 2006.

Köstenberger, Andreas J., et al. *The Cradle, the Cross, and the Crown: An Introduction to the New Testament*. Nashville, TN: B&H, 2009.

Köstenberger, Andreas J., and Peter T. O'Brien. *Salvation to the Ends of the Earth: A Biblical Theology of Mission*. Edited by D. A. Carson. Downers Grove, IL: InterVarsity, 2001.

Köstenberger, Margaret Elizabeth. *Jesus and the Feminists: Who Do They Say That He Is?* Wheaton, IL: Crossway, 2008.

Köster, Helmut. *Introduction to the New Testament, Volume 2: History and Literature of Early Christianity*. 2nd ed. Berlin: Walter de Gruyter, 2000.

Kremer, J. "πάθημα." In *EDNT* 3:1–2, edited by Horst Balz and Gerhard Schneider. Grand Rapids: William B. Eerdmans, 1993.

Krippendorff, Klaus. *Content Analysis: An Introduction to Its Methodology*. 2nd ed. Thousand Oaks: Sage, 2004.

Kroeker, Greta Grace. *Erasmus in the Footsteps of Paul*. Toronto: University of Toronto Press, 2011.

Kruse, Colin G. "Apostle." In *Dictionary of Jesus and the Gospels: A Compendium of Contemporary Biblical Scholarship*, edited by Joel B. Green, et. al., 27–33. Downers Grove, IL: InterVarsity, 1992.

———. *John*. The Tyndale New Testament Commentaries. Grand Rapids: Eerdmans, 2003.

Kuhli, Horst. "εἰκών." In *EDNT* 1:388–391, edited by Horst Balz and Gerhard Schneider. Grand Rapids: William B. Eerdmans, 1990.

Kümmel, Werner Georg. *Introduction to the New Testament*. Rev. ed. Translated by Howard Clark Fee. Nashville, TN: Abingdon, 1975.

Kurz, William S. *Reading Luke-Acts: Dynamics of Biblical Narrative.* Louisville, KY: Westminster John Knox, 1993.

LaCelle-Peterson, Kristina. *Liberating Tradition: Women's Identity and Vocation in Christian Perspective.* Grand Rapids: Baker Academic, 2008.

Lachs, Samuel Tobias. *A Rabbinic Commentary on the New Testament: The Gospels of Matthew, Mark and Luke.* Hoboken, NJ: KTAV, 1987.

Ladd, George Eldon. *A Theology of the New Testament.* Rev. ed. Grand Rapids: Eerdmans, 1993.

Lai, Patrick. *Tentmaking: The Life and Work of Business as Missions.* Crownhill, England: Authentic Media, 2005.

Lamb, David T. *God Behaving Badly: Is the God of the Old Testament Angry, Sexist and Racist?* Downers Grove, IL: InterVarsity, 2011.

Lancaster, Jane C. "Timothy." Page 1313 in *Eerdmans Dictionary of the Bible.* Edited by David Noel Freedman. Grand Rapids: Eerdmans, 2000.

Laverdiere, Eugene. *Dining in the Kingdom of God: The Origins of the Eucharist according to Luke.* Chicago, IL: Liturgy Training Publications, 1994.

Lazaridis, Nikolaos. *Wisdom in Loose Form: The Language of Egyptian and Greek Proverbs in Collections of the Hellenistic and Roman Periods.* Mnemosyne Supplementa: Monographs on Greek and Roman Language and Literature. Leiden: Brill, 2007.

Lea, Thomas D., and David Alan Black. *The New Testament: Its Background and Message.* 2nd ed. Nashville, TN: B&H, 2003.

Lee, Jae Hyun. *Paul's Gospel in Romans: A Discourse Analysis of Rom 1:16–8:39.* Linguistic Biblical Studies 3. Leiden: Brill, 2010.

Lee, Witness. *The Divine Dispensing of the Divine Trinity.* Anaheim, CA: Living Stream Ministry, 1983.

Lenski, R. C. H. *The Interpretation of St. Luke's Gospel.* Vol. 1. Columbus, OH: The Wartburg Press, 1946.

———. *The Interpretation of St. Luke's Gospel.* Vol. 1. Minneapolis, MN: Augsburg Fortress, 2008.

Lester, Andrew D. *The Angry Christian: A Theology for Care and Counseling.* Louisville, KY: Westminster John Knox, 2003.

Letterman, Mary. "Public Education, Christian Schools, and Homeschooling." In *Introducing Christian Education: Foundations for the Twenty-First Century,* edited by Michael J. Anthony, 276–282. Grand Rapids, Baker Academic, 2001.

Levinsohn, Stephen H. *Some Notes on the Information Structure and Discourse Features of Luke 22 and 6:20–49.* Dallas, TX: SIL International, 2009.

Lewis, Donald M. *With Heart, Mind, and Strength: The Best of Crux—1979–1989.* Vol. 1. Langley, British Columbia: CREDO, 1990.

Lichtenberger, Hermann. "Messianic Expectations and Messianic Figures during the Second Temple Period." In *Qumran-Messianism: Studies on the Messianic Expectations in the Dead Sea Scroll,* edited by James H. Charlesworth, et. al., 9–20. Tübingen: Mohr Siebeck, 1998.

Liddell, Henry G., and Robert Scott. *An Intermediate Greek-English Lexicon.* Oxford: Clarendon, 1900.

Liefeld, Walter L. *Ephesians.* The IVP New Testament Commentaries. Edited by Grant R. Osborne. Downers Grove, IL: InterVarsity, 1997.

———. *1 and 2 Timothy, Titus.* The NIV Application Commentary. Grand Rapids: Zondervan, 1999.

Lieu, Judith. *The Gospel of Luke.* Peterborough, England: Epworth, 1997.

Lim, Kar Yong. *'The Sufferings of Christ Are Abundant in Us': A Narrative Dynamics Investigation of Paul's Sufferings in 2 Corinthians.* New York: T. & T. Clark International, 2009.

Limburg, James. *Psalms.* Westminster Bible Companion. Louisville, KY: Westminster John Knox, 2000.

Lincoln, Andrew. *The Gospel according to St. John,* Black's New Testament Commentaries. New York: Continuum, 2005.

Lindars, Barnabas. "Paul and the Law in Romans 5–8: An Actantial Analysis." In *Law and Religion: Essays on the Place of the Law in Israel and Early Christianity,* edited by Barnabas Lindars, 126–140. Cambridge: James Clark & Co., 1988.

———. *The Theology of the Letter to the Hebrews.* New York: Cambridge University Press, 1991.

Lioy, Dan. *The Decalogue in the Sermon on the Mount.* Studies in Biblical Literature 66. New York: Peter Lang, 2004.

Litfin, Duane. *Conceiving the Christian College.* Grand Rapids: Eerdmans, 2004.

Little, Christopher R. *Mission in the Way of Paul: Biblical Mission for the Church in the Twenty-First Century.* Studies in Biblical Literature 80. New York: Peter Lang, 2005.

Litwak, Kenneth D. "A Coat of Many Colors: The Role of the Scriptures of Israel in Luke 2." In *Biblical Interpretation in Early Christian Gospels: Volume 3: The Gospel of Luke,* edited by Thomas R. Hatina, 114–132. Library of New Testament Studies. New York: T. & T. Clark International, 2010.

Loader, William. "What Happened to 'Good News for the Poor'? On the Trail of Hope beyond Jesus." In *Reflections on the Early Christian History of Religion,* edited by Cilliers Breytenbach and Jörg Frey, 233–266. Ancient Judaism and Early Christianity 81. Leiden: Brill, 2013.

Long, Thomas G. *Matthew.* WBC. Louisville, KY: Westminster John Knox, 1997.

Longenecker, Richard N. *Galatians.* WBC. Dallas, TX: Word, 1990.

———. Introduction to *Patterns of Discipleship in the New Testament,* 1–7. Grand Rapids: Eerdmans, 1996.

———. "The Pedagogical Nature of the Law in Galatians 3:19–4:7." *JETS* 25 (1982) 53–61.

Longman III, Tremper. *How to Read Proverbs.* Downers Grove, IL: InterVarsity, 2002.

Lopez, Davina C. *Apostle to the Conquered: Reimagining Paul's Mission.* Minneapolis, MN: Fortress, 2008.

Louw, Johannes P. "Macro levels of Meaning in Lk 7:36–50." In *A SouthAfrican Perspective on the New Testament: Essays by South African New Testament Scholars Presented to Bruce Manning Metzger during his Visit to South Africa in 1985,* edited by J. H. Petzer and P. J. Martin, 128–135. Leiden: E. J. Brill, 1986.

Louw, Johannes P., and Eugene A. Nida. *Greek-English Lexicon of the New Testament Based on Semantic Domains.* Vol. 1. 2nd ed. New York: UBS, 1989.

———. *Greek-English Lexicon of the New Testament Based on Semantic Domains.* Vol. 2. 2nd ed. New York: UBS, 1996.

Love, Patrick. "Document Analysis." In *Research in the College Context: Approaches and Methods,* edited by Frances K. Stage and Kathleen Manning, 93–96. New York: Brunner-Routledge, 2003.

Luck, G. Coleman. *Luke: The Gospel of the Son of Man.* Chicago, IL: Moody, 1960.

Lull, David J. "'The Law Was Our Pedagogue': A Study in Galatians 3:19, 25." *JBL* 105 (1986) 489–95.

Luschnig, C. A. E. *An Introduction to Ancient Greek: A Literary Approach*. 2nd ed. Revised by C. A. E. Luschnig and Deborah Mitchell. Indianapolis, IN: Hackett, 2007.

MacArthur Jr., John F. *Ashamed of the Gospel: When the Church Becomes Like the World*. Wheaton, IL: Crossway, 1993.

———. *Charismatic Chaos*. Grand Rapids: Zondervan, 1992.

———. *The Power of Suffering: Strengthening Your Faith in the Refiner's Fire*. Colorado Springs, CO: David C. Cook, 1995.

MacDonald, Margaret Y. *Colossians and Ephesians*. Sacra Pagina. Edited by Daniel J. Harrington. Rev. ed. Collegeville, MN: Liturgical Press, 2008.

MacGorman, J. W. "The Law as Paidagogos: A Study in Pauline Analogy." In *New Testament Studies: Essays in Honor of Ray Summers*, edited by Huber L. Drumwright and Curtis Vaughan, 99–111. Waco, TX: Markahm Press Fund, 1975.

Major, H. D. A., et al. *The Mission and Message of Jesus: An Exposition of the Gospels in the Light of Modern Research*. London: Ivor Nicholson and Watson, 1937.

Malherbe, Abraham. "'Gentle as a Nurse': The Cynic Background to I Thess ii." *NovT* 12 (1970) 203–217.

Malina, Bruce J. *Timothy: Paul's Closest Associate*. Paul's Social Network: Brothers and Sisters in Faith. Collegeville, MN: Liturgical Press, 2008.

Malina, Bruce J., and Jerome H. Neyrey. *Portraits of Paul: An Archaeology of Ancient Personality*. Louisville, KY: Westminster John Knox, 1996.

Manser, Martin H. *The Facts on File Dictionary of Proverbs: Meanings and Origins of More Than 1,700 Popular Sayings*. Facts on File Library of Language and Literature. 2nd ed. New York: Facts on File, 2007.

Mappes, David A. "What Is the Meaning of 'Faith' in Luke 18:8?" *BibSac* 167 (July–September 2010) 292–306.

Marrow, Jonathan. "Introducing Spiritual Formation." In *Foundations of Spiritual Formation: A Community Approach to Becoming Like Christ*, edited by Paul Pettit, 31–50. Grand Rapids, MI: Kregel Publications, 2008.

Marshall, I. Howard. *The Gospel of Luke: A Commentary on the Greek Text*. NIGTC. Grand Rapids: William B. Eerdmans, 1978.

———. "Holiness in the Book of Acts." In *Holiness and Ecclesiology in the New Testament*, edited by Kent E. Brower and Andy Johnson, 114–128. Grand Rapids: Eerdmans, 2007.

———. "Jesus—Example and Teacher of Prayer in the Synoptic Gospels." In *God's Presence: Prayer in the New Testament*, edited by Richard N. Longenecker, 113–121. Grand Rapids: Eerdmans, 2001.

———. *The Pastoral Epistles*. ICC. New York: T. & T. Clark, 1999.

Marshall, I. Howard, et. al. *Exploring the New Testament: A Guide to the Letters and Revelation*. Vol. 2. 2nd ed. Downers Grove, IL: InterVarsity, 2011.

Mateos, Juan. *El Aspecto Verbal en el Nuevo Testamento*. Estudios de Nuevo Testamento I. Madrid: Ediciones Cristiandad, 1977.

Matera, Frank J. *Galatians*. Sacra Pagina. Edited by Daniel J. Harrington. Collegeville, MN: Liturgical Press.

———. *New Testament Ethics: The Legacies of Jesus and Paul*. Louisville, KY: Westminster John Knox, 1996.

————. *New Testament Theology: Exploring Diversity and Unity*. Louisville, KY: Westminster John Knox, 2007.

————. *Romans*. ΠΑΙΔΕΙΑ Commentaries on the New Testament. Grand Rapids: Baker Academic, 2010.

Matthews, Christopher R. "Disciple." In *The Westminster Theological Wordbook of the Bible*, edited by Donald G. Gowan, 107–110. Louisville, KY: Westminster John Knox, 2003.

Matthews, Kenneth A. *Genesis 1–11:26*. NAC. Vol. 1A. Nashville, TN: B&H, 1996.

Mays, James Luther. *Hosea*. The Old Testament Library. Philadelphia, PA: The Westminster Press, 1969.

McBurney, Donald H., and Theresa L. White. *Research Methods*. 8th ed. Belmont, CA: Wadsworth, 2010.

McCartney, Dan G. *James*. BECNT. Grand Rapids: Baker Academic, 2009.

McDonald, J. Ian H. "Questioning and Discernment in Gospel Discourse: Communicative Strategy in Matthew 11:2–9." In *Authenticating the Words of Jesus*, edited by Bruce Chilton and Craig A. Evans, 333–362. Leiden: Brill, 1999.

————. *The Crucible of Christian Morality: Religion in the First Christian Centuries*. New York: Routledge, 1998.

McDonald, Lee Martin, and Stanley E. Porter. *Early Christianity and its Sacred Literature*. Peabody, MA: Hendrickson, 2000.

McDonald, Patricia M. "The View of Suffering Held by the Author of 1 Peter." In *The Bible on Suffering: Social and Political Implications*, edited by Anthony J. Tambasco, 165–187. Mahwah, NJ: Paulist Press, 2001.

McKenzie, John L. *Dictionary of the Bible*. New York: Touchstone, 1965.

McKeown, James. *Genesis*. The Two Horizons Old Testament Commentary. Grand Rapids: Eerdmans, 2008.

McLean, B. H. *New Testament Greek: An Introduction*. New York: Cambridge University Press, 2011.

McNichol, Allan J. *Jesus' Directions for the Future: A Source and Redaction-History Study of the Use of the Eschatological Traditions in Paul and in the Synoptic Accounts of Jesus' Last Eschatological Discourse*. New Gospel Studies 9. Macon, GA: Mercer University, 1996.

Meadows, Lynn M., and Diane M. Dodendorf. "Data Management and Interpretation Using Computers to Assist." In *Doing Qualitative Research*, 2nd ed., edited by Benjamin F. Crabtree and William L. Miller, 195–220. Thousand Oaks: Sage, 1999.

Melchert, Charles F. *Wise Teaching: Biblical Wisdom and Educational Ministry*. Harrisburg, PA: Trinity Press International, 1998.

Melick Jr., Richard R. *Philippians, Colossians, Philemon*. NAC. Vol. 32. Nashville, TN: B&H, 1991.

Melick Jr., Richard R., and Shera Melick. *Teaching that Transforms: Facilitating Life Change through Adult Bible Teaching*. Nashville, TN: B&H, 2010.

Merriam, Sharan B. *Qualitative Research: A Guide to Design and Implementation*. San Francisco, CA: Jossey-Bass, 2009.

Meye, R. P. "Disciple." In *ISBE* 1: 947–948, rev. ed. Grand Rapids: Eerdmans, 1979.

Meyer, Jason C. *The End of the Law: Mosaic Covenant in Pauline Theology*. NAC Studies in Bible and Theology. Edited by E. Ray Clendenen. Nashville, TN: B&H, 2009.

Meynet, Roland. *Treatise on Biblical Rhetoric*. International Studies in the History of Rhetoric. Translated by Leo Arnold, et. al. Leiden: Brill, 2012.

Michaelis, Wilhelm. "πάσχω, παθητός, προπάσχω, συμπάσχω, πάθος, πάθημα, συμπαθής, συμπαθέω, κακοπαθέω, συγκακοπαθέω, κακοπάθεια, μετριοπαθέω, ὁμοιοπαθής, πραϋπάθεια." In *TDNT* 5:904–939, edited by Gerhard Friedrich, translated and edited by Geoffrey W. Bromiley. Grand Rapids: Eerdmans, 1967.

———. "πήρα." In *TDNT* 6:119–121. Edited by Gerhard Friedrich. Translated and edited by Geoffrey W. Bromiley. Grand Rapids: Eerdmans, 1968.

Middleton, J. Richard. *The Liberating Image: The Imago Dei in Genesis 1*. Grand Rapids: Brazos, 2005.

Mihaila, Corin. *The Paul-Apollos Relationship and Paul's Stance toward Greco-Roman Rhetoric*. Library of New Testament Studies. New York: T. & T. Clark International, 2009.

Miller, John B. F. *Convinced that God had Called Us: Dreams, Visions, and the Perception of God's Will in Luke-Acts*. Leiden: Brill, 2007.

Mitchell, Margaret M. "Concerning *peri de* in 1 Corinthians." *NovT* 31 (1989) 229–256.

Mitchell, Michael R. *Leading, Teaching, and Making Disciples: World-Class Christian Education in the Church, School, and Home*. Bloomington, IN: CrossBooks, 2010.

Moessner, David P. "'The Christ Must Suffer': New Light on Jesus-Peter, Stephen, Paul Parallels in Luke-Acts." In *The Composition of Luke's Gospel: Selected Studies from Novum Testamentum*, 117–153.Leiden: Brill, 1999.

Moffitt, David M. *Atonement and the Logic of Resurrection in the Epistle to the Hebrews*. Supplement to Novum Testamentum 141. Leiden: Brill, 2011.

Moloney, Francis J. *The Gospel of John*. Sacra Pagina. Edited by Daniel J. Harrington. Collegeville, MN: The Liturgical Press, 1998.

Moo, Douglas. *The Letter of James*. The Pillar New Testament Commentary. Grand Rapids: Eerdmans, 2000.

———. *The Epistle to the Romans*, NICNT. Grand Rapids: Eerdmans, 1996.

Moon, Jongyoon. *Mark as Contributive Amanuensis of 1 Peter?* Berlin: Lit Verlag, 2009.

Morris, Leon. *Luke*. The Tyndale New Testament Commentaries. 2nd ed. Grand Rapids: Eerdmans, 1988.

———. *New Testament Theology*. Grand Rapids: Zondervan, 1986.

———. *The Cross in the New Testament*. Grand Rapids: Eerdmans, 1965.

———. *The Gospel according to Matthew*, The Pillar New Testament Commentary. Grand Rapids: Eerdmans, 1992.

———. *The First and Second Epistles to the Thessalonians*. NICNT. Rev. ed. Grand Rapids: Eerdmans, 1991.

Moule, C. F. D. *The Origin of Christology*. New York: Cambridge University Press, 1977.

Moulton, Harold K., ed. *The Analytical Greek Lexicon Revised*. Grand Rapids: Zondervan, 1978.

Mounce, William D. *The Morphology of Biblical Greek: A Companion to Basics of Biblical Greek and the Analytical Lexicon to the Greek New Testament*. Grand Rapids: Zondervan, 1994.

Moxnes, Halvor. *Putting Jesus in His Place: A Radical Vision of Household and Kingdom*. Louisville, KY: Westminster John Knox, 2003.

Moyise, Steve. "Isaiah in 1 Peter." In *Isaiah in the New Testament*, edited by Steve Moyise and Maarten J. J. Menken, 175–188. New York: T. & T. Clark, 2005.

Muddiman, John. *The Epistle to the Ephesians*. Black's New Testament Commentaries. New York: Continuum, 2001.

Mussies, Gerard. *Dio Chysostom and the New Testament: Collected Parallels.* Leiden: E. J. Brill, 1972.

Navarro, Luis Sánchez. "Agápē en El Evangelio de Juan." *Scripta Theologica* 39 (2007) 171–184.

Navarro, Pablo, and Capitolina Díaz. "Análisis de Contenido." In *Métodos y Técnicas Cualitativas de Investigación en Ciencias Sociales,* edited by Juan Manuel Delgado and Juan Gutiérrez, 177–224. Madrid: Síntesis, 1994.

Nave Jr., Guy D. *The Role and Function of Repentance in Luke-Acts.* Leiden: Brill, 2002.

Navone, John. *Themes of St. Luke.* Rome: Gregorian University, 1970.

Neuendorf, Kimberly A. *The Content Analysis Guidebook.* Thousand Oaks: Sage, 2002.

Neusner, Jacob. *Theological Dictionary of Rabbinic Judaism: Principle Theological Categories.* Lanham, MD: University Press of America, 2005.

Niang, Aliou Cissé. *Faith and Freedom in Galatia and Senegal: The Apostle Paul, Colonists and Sending Gods.* Leiden: Brill, 2009.

Nickle, Keith F. *Preaching the Gospel of Luke: Proclaiming God's Royal Rule.* Louisville, KY: Westminster John Knox, 2000.

Nida, E. A., et al. *Style and Discourse.* Cape Town, South Africa: Bible Society, 1983.

Nienhuis, David R. *Not by Paul Alone: The Formation of the Catholic Epistle Collection and the Christian Canon.* Waco, TX: Baylor University Press, 2007.

Nolland, John. "Classical and Rabbinic Parallels to 'Physician, Heal Yourself,' (Lk. IV 23)." *NovT* 21 (1979) 193–209.

———. *Luke 1–9:20.* WBC. Vol. 35a. Edited by David A. Hubbard, et. al. Dallas, TX: Word Books, 1989.

Northouse, Peter G. *Leadership: Theory and Practice.* 6th ed. Thousand Oaks, CA: Sage, 2013.

Novaković, Lidija. *Messiah, the Healer of the Sick.* Wissenschaftliche Untersuchungen zum Neuen Testament 2.Reihe 170. Tübingen: Mohr Siebeck, 2003.

Nun, Mendel. "Cast Your Net upon the Waters: Fish and Fisherman in Jesus' Time." *BAR* 19:6 (November-December 1993) 46–56.

———. "Ports of Galilee: Modern Drought Reveals Harbors from Jesus' Time." *BAR* 25:4 (July-August 1999) 18–31, 64.

O'Brien, Peter Thomas. *Introductory Thanksgivings in the Letters of Paul.* Leiden: E. J. Brill, 1977.

———. *The Letter to the Ephesians.* The Pillar New Testament Commentary. Grand Rapids: Eerdmans, 1999.

———. *The Letter to the Hebrews.* The Pillar New Testament Commentary. Grand Rapids: Eerdmans, 2010.

O'Toole, Robert F. *Luke's Presentation of Jesus: A Christology.* Subsidia Biblica 25. Rome: Editrice Pontificio Istituto Biblico, 2004.

———. *The Christological Climax of Paul's Defense.* Analecta Biblica 78. Rome: Biblical Institute Press, 1978.

———. "What Role Does Jesus' Saying in Acts 20:35 Play in Paul's Address to the Ephesian Elders?" *Biblica* 75 (1994) 329–349.

Ó Fearghail, Fearghus. *The Introduction to Luke-Acts: A Study of the Role of Lk 1,1–4,44 in the Composition of Luke's Two-Volume Work.* Analecta Biblica 126. Rome: Pontificio Istituto Biblico, 1991.

Oden, Thomas C. *First and Second Timothy and Titus,* Interpretation. Louisville, KY: Westminster John Knox, 1989.

Ogden, Greg. *Discipleship Essentials: A Guide to Building Your Life in Christ*. Expanded ed. Downers Grove, IL: InterVarsity, 2007.

Olyan, Saul M. *Disability in the Hebrew Bible: Interpreting Mental and Physical Differences*. New York: Cambridge University Press, 2008.

Ortlund Jr., Raymond C. "The Deity of Christ and the Old Testament." In *The Deity of Christ*, edited by Christopher W. Morgan and Robert A. Peterson, 39–60. Theology in Community. Wheaton, IL: Crossway, 2011.

Osborne, Grant R. *The Hermeneutical Spiral: A Comprehensive Introduction to Biblical Interpretation*. Rev. ed. Downers Grove, IL: InterVarsity, 2006.

Oster Jr., Richard E. *1 Corinthians*. The College Press NIV Commentary. Joplin, MO: College Press, 1995.

Palachuvattil, Mathew. *"The One Who Does the Will of the Father," Distinguishing Character of Disciples according to Matthew: An Exegetical Study*. Tesi Gregoriani 154. Rome: Pontificia Università Gregoriana, 2007.

Pascuzzi, Maria. *Ethics, Ecclesiology and Church Discipline: A Rhetorical Analysis of 1 Corinthians 5*. Tesi Gregoriana Serie Teologia 32. Rome: Editrice Pontificia Università Gregoriana, 1997.

Pao, David W., and Eckhard J. Schnabel. "Luke." In *Commentary on the New Testament Use of the Old Testament*, edited by G. K. Beale and D. A. Carson, 251–414. Grand Rapids: Baker Academic, 2007.

Park, Yoon-Man. *Mark's Memory Resources and the Controversy Stories (Mark 2:1–3:6): An Application of the Frame Theory of Cognitive Science to the Markan Oral-Aural Narrative*. Leiden: Brill, 2010.

Parsons, Mikeal C. *Luke: Storyteller, Interpreter, Evangelist*. Peabody, MA: Hendrickson Publishers, 2007.

Patella, Michael F. *The Gospel according to Luke*. New Collegeville Bible Commentary. Collegeville, MN: Liturgical Press, 2005.

Patterson, Paige. "The Meaning of Authority in the Local Church." In *Recovering Biblical Manhood and Womanhood: A Response to Evangelical Feminism*, edited by John Piper and Wayne Grudem, 248–260. Wheaton, IL: Crossway, 2006.

Patton, Michael Quinn. *Qualitative Research and Evaluation Methods*. 3rd ed. Thousand Oaks: Sage, 2002.

Pazmiño, Robert W. *Foundational Issues in Christian Education: An Introduction in Evangelical Perspective*. 3rd ed. Grand Rapids: Baker Academic, 2008.

Pentecost, J. Dwight *The Words and Works of Jesus Christ: A Study of the Life of Christ*. Grand Rapids: Zondervan, 1981.

Perkins, Pheme. *Jesus as Teacher*. Understanding Jesus Today. New York: Cambridge, 1990.

———. *Reading the New Testament*. 3rd rev. ed. Mahway, NJ: Paulist, 2012.

———. "1 and 2 Thessalonians." In *HarperCollins Bible Commentary*, 2nd ed., edited by James L. Mays, 1131–1136. New York: HarperCollins, 2000.

Perrin, Norman, and Dennis C. Duling. *The New Testament: An Introduction*. 2nd ed. Edited by Robert Ferm. New York: Harcourt Brace Jovanovich, 1982.

Peters, Ted. *God, the World's Future: Systematic Theological for a New Era*. 2nd ed. Minneapolis, MN: Augsburg Fortress, 2000.

Peterson, David. "The Worship of the New Community." In *Witness to the Gospel: The Theology of Acts*, edited by I. Howard Marshall and David Peterson, 373–396. Grand Rapids: William B. Eerdmans, 1998.

Picirilli, Robert E. *The Gospel of Mark*. The Randall House Bible Commentary. Edited by Robert E. Picirilli. Nashville, TN: Randall House, 2003.

———. "1 Thessalonians." In *Randall House Bible Commentary: 1 Thessalonians through Philemon*, edited by Robert E. Picirilli, 1–97. Nasvhille, TN: Randall House, 1990.

Pickett, Raymond. *The Cross in Corinth: The Social Significance of the Death of Jesus*. Sheffield, England: Sheffield Academic Press, 1997.

Pickup, Martin. "Matthew's and Mark's Pharisees." In *In Quest of the Historical Pharisees*, edited by Jacob Neusner and Bruce D. Chilton, 67–112. Waco, TX: Baylor University Press, 2007.

Pierce, Chad T. *Spirits and the Proclamation of Christ*. Wissenschaftliche Untesuchungen zum Neuen Testament 2.Reihe 305. Tübingen: Mohr Siebeck, 2011.

Piñero, Antonio. *Literatura Judía de Época Helenística en Lengua Griega: Desde la Versión de la Biblia al Griego hasta el Nuevo Testamento*. Historia de la Literatura Universal. Madrid, Spain: Síntesis, 2006.

Piper, R. A. *Wisdom in the Q-Tradition: The Aphoristic Teaching of Jesus*. Society for New Testament Studies Monograph Series 61. New York: Cambridge, 1989.

Plummer, Alfred. *A Critical and Exegetical Commentary on the Gospel of S. Luke*. ICC. 5th ed. Edinburgh: T. & T. Clark, 1922.

Poggemeyer, Joseph. *The Dialectic of Knowing God in the Cross and Creation: An Exegetico-Theological Study of 1 Corinthians 1,18–25 and Romans 1,18–23*. Tesi Gregoriana Serie Teologia 127. Rome: Editrice Pontificia Università Gregoriana, 2005.

Poirier, John C. "The Meaning of Πίστις in Philippians 1:27." *The Expository Times* 123:7 (Apr 2012) 334–337.

———. "The Measure of Stewardship: Πίστις in Romans 12:3." *Tyndale Bulletin* 59:1 (2008) 145–152.

Pollock, John. *The Apostle: A Life of Paul*. 2nd ed. Colorado Springs, CO: David C. Cook, 2012.

Porter, Stanley E., et al. *Fundamentals of New Testament Greek*. Grand Rapids: William B. Eerdmans, 2010.

Powell, Ivor. *Luke's Thrilling Gospel*. Grand Rapids: Kregel, 1984.

Powell, Mark Allan. *Introducing the New Testament: A Historical, Literary, and Theological Survey*. Grand Rapids: Baker Academic, 2009.

Quinn, Arthur, and Lyon Rathbun. "Anadiplosis." Page 9 in *Encyclopedia of Rhetoric and Composition: Communication from Ancient Times to the Information Age*. Edited by Theresa Enos. New York: Garland, 1996.

Quinn, Jerome D., and William C. Wacker. *The First and Second Letters to Timothy*. Eerdmans Critical Commentary. Grand Rapids: Eerdmans, 2000.

Ramsaran, Rollin A. "Living and Dying, Living Is Dying (Philippians 1:21): Paul's Maxim and Exemplary Argumentation in Philippians." In *Rhetorical Argumentation in Biblical Texts*, edited by Anders Eriksson, et. al., 325–338. Emory Studies in Early Christianity. Harrisburg, PA: Trinity Press International, 2002.

———. "Paul and Maxims." In *Paul in the Greco-Roman World: A Handbook*, edited by J. Paul Sampley, 429–456. Harrisburg, PA: Trinity Press International, 2003.

Rapske, Brian. *The Book of Acts in its First Century Settings*. Vol. 3, *Paul in Roman Custody*. Grand Rapids: Eerdmans, 1994.

Rausch, Thomas P. *Who is Jesus? An Introduction to Christology*. Collegeville, MN: Liturgical Press, 2003.

Ray, Daniel Lee. "A Content Analysis of Jesus' Teaching Methods in Comparison With Current Differentiated Teaching." Ed.D.diss., Southeastern Baptist Theological Seminary, September 2011.

Reich, Keith A. *Figuring Jesus: The Power of Rhetorical Figures of Speech in the Gospel of Luke*. Leiden: Brill, 2011.

Reiling, J., and J. L. Swellengrebel. *A Translator's Handbook on the Gospel of Luke: Helps for Translator's Prepared under the Auspices of the United Bible Societies*. Leiden: E. J. Brill, 1971.

Rengstorf, K. H. "μαθητής." In *TDNT* 4:415–461, edited by Gerhard Kittel, translated and edited by Geoffrey W. Bromiley. Grand Rapids: Eerdmans, 1967.

Rhein, Francis Bayard. *An Analytical Approach to the New Testament*. Woodbury, NY: Barron's Educational Series, 1966.

Richard, Earl J. *First and Second Thessalonians*. Sacra Pagina. Edited by Daniel J. Harrington. Collegeville, MN: Liturgical Press, 2007.

―――. *Reading 1 Peter, Jude, and 2 Peter: A Literary and Theological Commentary*. Macon, GA: Smyth & Helwys, 2000.

Richards, Lawrence O. *Christian Education: Seeking to Become Like Jesus Christ*. Grand Rapids: Zondervan, 1975.

Richardson, Peter. "Corinthians, First Letter to the." In *Eerdmans Dictionary of the Bible*, edited by David Noel Freedman, 281–283. Grand Rapids: Eerdmans, 2000.

Ridderbos, Herman. *Paul: An Outline of His Theology*. Grand Rapids: Eerdmans, 1975.

Riesenfeld, Harald. "ὑπέρ." In *TDNT* 8:507–516, edited by Gerhard Friedrich, translated and edited by Geoffrey W. Bromiley. Grand Rapids: Eerdmans, 1972.

Rindoš, Jaroslav. *He of Whom It Is Written: John the Baptist and Elijah in Luke*. Österreichiesche Biblische Studien 38. Frankfurt, Germany: Peter Lang, 2010.

Ringe, Sharon H. *Luke*. Westminster Bible Companion. Louisville, KY: Westminster John Knox, 1995.

Robertson, A. T. *A Grammar of the Greek New Testament in Light of Historical Research*. Nashville, TN: Broadman Press, 1934.

―――. *The Gospel according to Luke*. Word Pictures of the New Testament. Vol. 2. Revised and updated by Wesley J. Perschbacher. Grand Rapids: Kregel, 2005.

Robinson, Maurice A., and Mark A. House. *Analytical Lexicon of New Testament Greek*. Rev. ed. Peabody, MA: Hendrickson, 2012.

Roetzel, Calvin J. *The Letters of Paul: Conversations in Context*. 5th ed. Louisville, KY: Westminster John Knox, 2009.

Rossé, Gérard. *Il Vangelo di Luca: Commento Esegetico e Teologico*. 4th ed. Rome: Città Nuova, 2006.

Rothschild, Clare K. *Hebrews as Pseudepigraphon*. Wissenschaftliche Untersuchungen zum Neuen Testament 235. Tübingen: Mohr Siebeck, 2009.

―――. *Luke-Acts and the Rhetoric of History*. Wissenschaftliche Untersuchungen zum Neuen Testament 2.Reihe 175. Tübingen: Mohr Siebeck, 2004.

Rousseau, John J., and Rami Arav. "Machaerus (Hebrew, *Makhwar*)." In *Jesus and His World: An Archaeological and Cultural Dictionary*, 187–189. Minneapolis, MN: Augsburg Fortress, 1995.

Royalty Jr., Robert M. *The Origin of Heresy: A History of Discourse in Second Temple Judaism and Early Christianity*. Routledge Studies in Religion. New York: Routledge, 2013.

Rowland, Christopher, and Christopher R. A. Morray-Jones. *The Mystery of God: Early Jewish Mysticism and the New Testament*. Compendia Rerum Iudaicarum ad Novum Testamentum 12. Leiden: Brill, 2009.

Rubio, Gonzalo. "Semitic Influence in the History of Latin Syntax." In *New Perspectives on Historical Latin Syntax: Syntax of the Sentence*, edited by Philip Baldi and Pierluigi Cuzzolin, 195–240. Trends in Linguistics Studies and Monographs. Berlin: Walter de Gruyter, 2009.

Ruis-Camps, Josep, and Jenny Read-Heimerdinger, ed. *The Message of Acts in Codex Bezae: A Comparison with the Alexandrian Tradition*. Vol. 2. New York: T. & T. Clark, 2006.

Ruiz Olabuénaga, José Ignacio. *Metodología de la Investigación Cualitativa*. 5th ed. Social Science Series 15. Bilbao, Spain: 2012.

Runge, Steven E. *Discourse Grammar of the Greek New Testament: A Practical Introduction for Teaching and Exegesis*. Peabody, MA: Hendrickson, 2010.

Rusam, Dietrich. "Das Lukasevangelium." In *Einleitung in das Neue Testament*, edited by Martin Ebner and Stefan Schreiber, 184–207. Stuttgart, Germany: W. Kohlhammer, 2008.

Ryan, G., and H. Bernard. "Techniques to Identify Themes." *Field Methods* 15:1 (2003) 85–109.

Ryken, Leland, et. al., eds. "Blind, Blindness." In *Dictionary of Biblical Imagery*, 99. Downers Grove: IL: InterVarsity, 1998.

———. "Gold." In *Dictionary of Biblical Imagery*, 340–341. Downers Grove, IL: InterVarsity, 1998.

———. "Human Authority." In *Dictionary of Biblical Imagery*, 59–63. Downers Grove, IL: InterVarsity, 1998.

———. "Mercy." In *Dictionary of Biblical Imagery*, 547–548. Downers Grove, IL: InterVarsity, 1998.

Ryrie, Charles C. *First and Second Thessalonians*. Everyman's Bible Commentary. 3rd ed. Chicago, IL: Moody, 2001.

———. "Perspectives on Social Ethics, Part IV: Apostolic Perspectives on Social Ethics." *BibSac* 134 (October-December 1977) 314–328.

Sabourin, Léopold. *L'Évangile de Luc: Introduction et Commentaire*. Rome: Pontificia Università Gregoriana, 1992.

Sakharov, Nicholas V. *I Love, There I Am: The Theological Legacy of Archimandrite Sophrony*. New York: St. Vladimir's Seminary Press, 2002.

Saldarini, Anthony J. *The Fathers according to Rabbi Nathan: A Translation and Commentary*. Leiden: E. J. Brill, 1975.

Salevao, Iutisone. *Legitimation in the Letter to the Hebrews: The Construction and Maintenance of a Symbolic Universe*. New York: Sheffield Academic, 2002.

Sam, L. R. Arul. *The Love Commandment of Jesus Christ and Its Implication in the Indian Context*. New Delhi: ISPCK, 2008.

Saussy, Carroll. *The Gift of Anger: A Call to Faithful Action*. Louisville, KY: Westminster John Knox, 1995.

Schenck, Kenneth. *Understanding the Book of Hebrews: The Story behind the Sermon*. Louisville, KY: Westminster John Knox, 2003.

Schmidt, Karl Ludwig. "ἀγωγή, παράγω, προάγω, προσάγω, προσαγωγή." In *TDNT* 1: 128–134, edited by Gerhard Kittel, translated and edited by Geoffrey W. Bromiley. Grand Rapids: Eerdmans, 1964.

Schnackenburg, Rudolf. *Epistle to the Ephesians: A Commentary*. Edinburgh, Scotland: T. & T. Clark, 1991.

Schneider, Gerhard. "ἀγάπη." In *EDNT* 1:8–12, edited by Horst Balz and Gerhard Schneider. Grand Rapids: William B. Eerdmans, 1990.

Schnelle, Udo. *Theology of the New Testament*. Translated by M. Eugene Boring. Grand Rapids: Baker, 2009.

Scholz, Daniel J. *Jesus in the Gospels and Acts: Introducing the New Testament*. Winona, MN: St. Mary's, 2009.

Schrage, W. "τυφλός, τυφλόω." In *TDNT* 8:270–294, edited by Gerhard Friedrich, translated and edited by Geoffrey W. Bromiley. Grand Rapids: Eerdmans, 1972.

Schreier, Margrit. *Qualitative Content Analysis in Practice*. Thousand Oaks: Sage, 2012.

Schreiner, Thomas R. *Galatians*. ZECNT. Edited by Clinton E. Arnold. Grand Rapids: Zondervan, 2010.

———. *1, 2 Peter, Jude*. NAC. Vol. 37. Grand Rapids: B&H, 2003.

Schreiner, Thomas R., and Ardel B. Caneday. *The Race Set before Us: A Biblical Theology of Perseverance and Assurance*. Downers Grove, IL: InterVarsity, 2001.

Scott, Bernard Brandon. "Jesus as Sage: An Innovating Voice in Common Wisdom." In *The Sage in Israel and the Ancient Near East*, edited by John G. Gammie and Leo G. Perdue, 399–416. Winona Lake, IN: Eisenbrauns, 1990.

Scott, David, and Marlene Morrison. *Key Ideas in Educational Research*. New York: Continuum International, 2006.

Seals, Thomas L. *Proverbs: Wisdom for All Ages*. Abilene, TX: Quality Publications, 1982.

Sedlacek, Tomas. *Economics of Good and Evil: The Quest for Economic Meaning from Gilgamesh to Wall Street*. New York: Oxford University Press, 2011.

Senior, Donald P. *1 Peter*. Sacra Pagina. Edited by Daniel J. Harrington. 2nd ed. Collegeville, MN: Liturgical Press, 2008.

Serrano, Andrés García. *The Presentation in the Temple: The Narrative Function of Lk 2:22–39 in Luke-Acts*. Analecta Biblica 197. Rome: Gregorian and Biblical Press, 2012.

Sharma, A. P. *Development of Western Education Thoughts*. New Delhi: Concept Publishing, 1997.

Shkul, Minna. *Reading Ephesians: Exploring Social Entrepreneurship in the Text*. Library of New Testament Studies. New York: T. & T. Clark International, 2009.

Sider, John W. "Proportional Analogy in the Gospel Parables." *NTS* 31 (1985) 1–23.

Silverman, David, ed. *Qualitative Research: Theory, Method and Practice*. 2nd ed. Thousand Oaks: Sage, 2004.

Skreslet, Stanley H. *Picturing Christian Witness: New Testament Images of Disciples in Mission*. Grand Rapids: Eerdmans, 2006.

Sleeman, Matthew. *Geography and the Ascension Narrative in Acts*. Society for New Testament Studies Monograph Series 146. New York: Cambridge University, 2009.

Smith, Kevin G. "A Grammatical Exposition of 2 Timothy 3:16–17." *Conspectus: The Journal of the South African Theological Seminary* 9 (March 2010) 95–105.

Smith, Michael J. "The Role of the Pedagogue in Galatians." *BibSac* 163:650 (April-June 2006) 197–214.

Spivey, Robert A., and D. Moody Smith. *Anatomy of the New Testament: A Guide to Its Structure and Meaning*. 3rd ed. New York: MacMillan, 1982.

Stagg, Frank. "Luke's Theological Use of Parables." *Review and Expositor* 94 (1997) 215–229.

Stanton, G. N. *Jesus of Nazareth in New Testament Preaching.* Society for New Testament Studies Monograph Series 27. New York: Cambridge University Press, 1974.

———. "Sermon on the Mount/Plain." In *Dictionary of Jesus and the Gospels: A Compendium of Contemporary Biblical Scholarship,* edited by Joel B. Green, et. al., 735–744. Downers Grove, IL: InterVarsity, 1992.

Stegemann, Ekkehard W., and Wolfgang Stegemann. *The Jesus Movement: A Social History of its First Century.* Translated by O. C. Dean Jr. Minneapolis, MN: Fortress, 1999.

Stein, Robert H. *Jesus the Messiah: A Survey of the Life of Christ.* Downers Grove, IL: InterVarsity, 1996.

———. *Luke.* NAC. Vol. 24. Edited by David S. Dockery. Nashville, TN: B&H, 1992.

———. *Mark.* BECNT. Grand Rapids: Baker Academic, 2008.

———. "The Genre of the Parables." In *The Challenge of Jesus' Parables,* edited by Richard N. Longenecker, 30–50. Grand Rapids: Eerdmans, 2000.

———. *The Method and Message of Jesus' Teachings.* Rev. ed. Louisville, KY: Westminster John Knox, 1994.

Stevens, Gerald L. *New Testament Greek Primer.* Eugene, OR: Cascade Books, 2004.

Storms, Sam. *Chosen for Life: The Case for Divine Election.* Wheaton, IL: Crossway, 2007.

Stott, John. *The Cross of Christ.* 20th ann. ed. Downers Grove, IL: InterVarsity, 2006.

———. *The Story of the New Testament.* Revised by Stephen Motyer. Grand Rapids: Baker, 2001.

Stumpff, Albrecht. "ἴχνος." In *TDNT* 3: 402–407, edited by Gerhard Friedrich, translated and edited by Geoffrey W. Bromiley. Grand Rapids: Eerdmans, 1965.

Summers, Ray. *Jesus, the Universal Savior: Commentary on Luke.* Waco, TX: Word, 1972.

Sumney, Jerry L. *Colossians: A Commentary.* The New Testament Library. Louisville, KY: Westminster John Knox, 2008.

Sweetland, Dennis M. "Following Jesus: Discipleship in Luke-Acts." In *New Views on Luke and Acts,* edited by Earl Richard, 109–123. Collegeville, MN: The Liturgical Press, 1990.

———. "Luke the Christian." In *New Views on Luke and Acts,* edited by Earl Richard, 48–63. Collegeville, MN: The Liturgical Press, 1990.

Swetnam, James. *Introduction to the Study of New Testament Greek: Part 1, Morphology.* Subsidia Biblica 16:1. 2nd rev. ed. Rome: Pontificio Istituto Biblico, 1998.

Talbert, Charles H. *Learning through Suffering: The Educational Value of Suffering in the New Testament and in Its Milieu.* Zacchaeus Studies: New Testament. Collegeville, MN: The Liturgical Press, 1991.

———. *Reading Acts: A Literary and Theological Commentary on the Acts of the Apostles.* Rev. ed. Macon, GA: Smyth & Helwys, 2005.

———. *Reading Luke: A Literary and Theological Commentary on the Third Gospel.* Rev. ed. Macon, GA: Smyth & Helwys, 2002.

Tannehill, Robert C. *Luke.* ANTC. Edited by Victor Paul Furnish. Nashville, TN: Abingdon, 1996.

———. *The Narrative Unity of Luke-Acts: A Literary Interpretation.* Vol. 2. Minneapolis, MN: Augsburg Fortress, 1990.

Tenney, Merrill C. *New Testament Survey*. Revised by Walter M. Dunnett. Grand Rapids: Eerdmans, 1985.

Tepedino, Ana Maria. *Las Discípulas de Jesús*. Translated by Pablo Manzano. Madrid: Narcea, 1995.

Tesch, Renata. *Qualitative Research Analysis Types and Software Tools*. Philadelphia, PA: RoutledgeFalmer, Taylor & Francis, 1990.

Thielman, Frank. *Paul and the Law: A Contextual Approach*. Downers Grove, IL: InterVarsity, 1994.

Thiselton, Anthony C. *The First Epistle to the Corinthians: A Commentary on the Greek Text*. NIGTC. Grand Rapids: Eerdmans, 2000.

———. *The Hermeneutics of Doctrine*. Grand Rapids: Eerdmans, 2007.

———. *The Living Paul: An Introduction to the Apostle's Life and Thought*. Downers Grove, IL: InterVarsity, 2009.

———. *1 Corinthians: A Shorter Exegetical and Pastoral Commentary*. Grand Rapids: Eerdmans, 2006.

Thomas, Robert L. *Evangelical Hermeneutics: The New Versus the Old*. Grand Rapids: Kregel, 2002.

———. *Understanding Spiritual Gifts: A Verse-by-Verse Study of 1 Corinthians 12–14*. Rev. ed. Grand Rapids: Kregel, 1999.

Thomas, Robert L., and Stanley N. Gundry. *A Harmony of the Gospels*. New York: HarperCollins, 1978.

Thompson, Alan. *One Lord, One People: The Unity of the Church in Acts in its Literary Setting*. Library of New Testament Studies. New York: T. & T. Clark, 2008.

Thompson, James W. *Moral Formation according to Paul: The Context and Coherence of Pauline Ethics*. Grand Rapids: Baker Academic, 2011.

———. *Pastoral Ministry according to Paul: A Biblical Vision*. Grand Rapids: Baker Academic, 2006.

Thurén, Lauri. *Argument and Theology in 1 Peter*. Sheffield: Sheffield Academic, 1995.

Tiede, David L. *Luke*. ACNT. Minneapolis, MN: Augsburg, 1988.

Tiegreen, Chris. *Feeling Like God: The Emotional Side of Discipleship—and Why You Can't Fully Follow Jesus Without It*. Carol Stream, IL: Tyndale, 2008.

Titscher, Stefan, et al. *Methods of Text and Discourse Analysis*. Thousand Oaks: Sage, 2000.

Tomlinson, F. Alan. "The Purpose and Stewardship Theme within the Pastoral Epistles." In *Entrusted with the Gospel: Paul's Theology in the Pastoral Epistles*, edited by Andreas J. Köstenberger and Terry L. Wilder, 52–83. Nashville, TN: B&H, 2010.

Totelin, Laurence M.V. *Hippocratic Recipes: Oral and Written Transmission of Pharmacological Knowledge in Fifth- and Fourth-Century Greece*. Leiden: Brill, 2009.

Towner, Philip H. *The Letters to Timothy and Titus*. NICNT. Grand Rapids: Eerdmans, 2006.

Towner, W. Sibley. *Genesis*. WBC. Louisville, KY: Westminster John Knox, 2001.

Trenchard, Warren C. *Complete Vocabulary Guide to the Greek New Testament*. Rev. ed. Grand Rapids: Zondervan, 1998.

Tropper, Amram. *Wisdom, Politics, and Historiography: Tractate Avot in the Context of the Graeco-Roman Near East*. Oxford Oriental Monographs. Oxford: Oxford University, 2004.

Trost, Travis D. *Who Should Be King in Israel? A Study on Roman Imperial Politics, the Dead Sea Scrolls, and the Fourth Gospel.* Studies in Biblical Literature 139. New York: Peter Lang, 2010.

Tso, Marcus K. M. *Ethics in the Qumran Community.* Wissenschaftliche Untersuchungen zum Neuen Testament 2.Reihe 292. Tübingen: Mohr Siebeck, 2010.

Tuggy, Alfred E. *Léxico Griego-Español del Nuevo Testamento.* El Paso, TX: Mundo Hispano, 1996.

Turner, David L. *Matthew.* BECNT. Grand Rapids: Baker Academic, 2008.

Twelftree, Graham H. *People of the Spirit: Exploring Luke's View of the Church.* Grand Rapids: Baker Academic, 2009.

Van Cangh, Jean-Marie. "Did Jesus Call Himself 'Son' and 'Son of Man'?" In *Jesus Christ Today: Studies of Christology in Various Contexts,* edited by Stuart George Hall, 3–26. Berlin: Walter de Gruyter, 2009.

Van Voorst, Robert E. *Jesus Outside the New Testament: An Introduction to the Ancient Evidence.* Grand Rapids: Eerdmans, 2000.

Verhey, Allen, and Joseph S. Harvard. *Ephesians.* Belief. Louisville, KY: Westminster John Knox, 2011.

Volf, Judith M. Gundry. *Paul and Perseverance: Staying In and Falling Away.* Tübingen: Mohr Siebeck, 1990.

Voorwinde, Stephen. *Jesus' Emotions in the Gospels.* New York: T. & T. Clark International, 2011.

Vorster, Willem S. "The Structure of Matthew 13." In *Speaking of Jesus: Essays on Biblical Language, Gospel Narrative and the Historical Jesus,* edited by J. Eugene Botha, 139–148. Leiden: Brill, 1999.

Wachsmann, Shelley. *The Sea of Galilee Boat.* College Station, TX: First Texas A&M University Press, 2009.

Wagner, Walter H. *Christianity in the Second Century: After the Apostles.* Minneapolis: MN: Augsburg Fortress, 1994.

Walker, Peter. *In the Steps of Saint Paul: An Illustrated Guide to Paul's Journeys.* 2nd ed. Oxford: Lion Hudson, 2011.

Wall, Robert W. *Community of the Wise: The Letter of James.* The New Testament in Context. Valley Forge, PA: Trinity Press International, 1997.

Wallace, A. J., and R. D. Dusk, *Moral Transformation: The Original Christian Paradigm of Salvation.* New Zealand: Bridghead, 2011.

Wallace, Daniel B. *Greek Grammar, Beyond the Basics: An Exegetical Syntax of the New Testament.* Grand Rapids: Zondervan, 1996.

Wallen, Norman E., and Jack R. Fraenkel. *Educational Research: A Guide to the Process.* 2nd ed. Mahwah, NJ: Lawrence Erlbaum Associates, 2011.

Wallis, Ian G. *The Faith of Jesus Christ in Early Christian Traditions.* Society for New Testament Studies Monograph Series 84. New York: Cambridge University Press, 1995.

Wanamaker, Charles A. *The Epistles to the Thessalonians.* NIGTC. Grand Rapids: Eerdmans, 1990.

Ware, Bruce A. *The Man Christ Jesus: Theological Reflections on the Humanity of Christ.* Wheaton, IL: Crossway, 2013.

Warrington, Keith. *The Message of the Holy Spirit.* Bible Themes Series. Edited by Derek Tidball. Downers Grove, IL: InterVarsity, 2009.

Weaver, John B. "The Noble and Good Heart: Καλοκἀγαθία in Luke's Parable of the Sower." In *Scripture and Traditions: Essays on Early Judaism and Christianity in Honor of Carl R. Holladay*, edited by Patrick Gray and Gail R. O'Day, 151–172. Supplement to Novum Testamentum 129. Leiden: Brill, 2008.

Weima, Jeffrey A. D. "The Function of 1 Thessalonians 2:1–12 and the Use of Rhetorical Criticism: A Response to Otto Merk." In *The Thessalonians Debate: Methodological Discord or Methodological Synthesis?*, edited by Karl F. Donfried and Johannes Beutler, 114–131. Grand Rapids: Eerdmans, 2000.

Weiss, H. F. "διδασκαλία." In *EDNT* 1: 316–317, edited by Horst Balz and Gerhard Schneider. Grand Rapids: William B. Eerdmans, 1990.

Wendel, Susan. *Scriptural Interpretation and Community Self-Designation in Luke-Acts and the Writings of Justin Martyr*. Supplement to Novum Testamentum 139. Leiden: Brill, 2011.

Wenham, David. *Paul: Follower of Jesus or Founder of Christianity?* Grand Rapids: Eerdmans, 1995.

Weren, Wim J. C. "The Ideal Community according to Matthew, James, and the Didache." In *Matthew, James, and Didache: Three Related Documents in Their Jewish and Christian Settings*, edited by Huub van de Sandt and Jürgen K. Zangenberg, 177–200. Atlanta, GA: SBL, 2008.

White, Newport J. D. "The First and Second Epistles to Timothy." In *The Expositor's Greek Testament*. Vol. 4. Edited by W. Robertson Nicoll. New York: Dodd, Mead and Co., 1910.

Wierzbicka, Anna. *What Did Jesus Mean? Explaining the Sermon on the Mount and the Parables in Simple and Universal Human Concepts*. New York: Oxford University, 2001.

Wilkins, Micheal J. "Disciples." In *Dictionary of Jesus and the Gospels: A Compendium of Contemporary Biblical Scholarship* 176–182, edited by Joel B. Green, et. al. Downers Grove, IL: InterVarsity, 1992.

———. *Following the Master: A Biblical Theology of Discipleship*. Grand Rapids: Zondervan, 1992.

———. "Isaiah 53 and the Message of Salvation in the Gospels." In *The Gospel according to Isaiah 53: Encountering the Suffering Servant in Jewish and Christian Theology*, edited by Darrell L. Bock and Mitch Glaser, 109–132. Grand Rapids: Kregel, 2012.

———. *Matthew*. The NIV Application Commentary. Grand Rapids: Zondervan, 2004.

Wilkinson, David, and Peter Birmingham. *Using Research Instruments: A Guide for Researchers*. New York: RoutledgeFalmer, 2003.

Williams, David J. *1 and 2 Thessalonians*. Understanding the Bible Commentary Series. 2nd ed. Grand Rapids: Baker, 2011. E-book accessed on March 9, 2013, from Google Books.

Williamson, Clark M., and Ronald J. Allen. *The Teaching Minister*. Louisville, KY: Westminster John Knox, 1991.

Williamson, Peter S. *Ephesians*. Grand Rapids: Baker Academic, 2009.

Willis, Wendell. "Agape." In *Eerdmans Dictionary of the Bible*, edited by David Noel Freedman, 27–28. Grand Rapids: Eerdmans, 2000.

Wink, Walter. "Neither Passivity nor Violence: Jesus' Third Way (Matt. 5:38–42 par.)." In *The Love of Enemy and Nonretaliation in the New Testament*, edited by Willard M. Swartley, 102–125. Louisville, KY: Westminster John Knox, 1992.

Winston, George, and Dora Winston. *Recovering Biblical Ministry by Women: An Exegetical Response to Traditionalism and Feminism.* Longwood, FL: Xulon, 2003.

Winton, Alan P. *The Proverbs of Jesus: Issues of History and Rhetoric.* Sheffield, England: JSOT, 1990.

Witherington III, Ben. *Grace in Galatia: A Commentary on Paul's Letter to the Galatians.* New York: T. & T. Clark International, 2004.

———. *Jesus the Sage: The Pilgrimage of Wisdom.* Minneapolis, MN: Augsburg Fortress, 1994.

———. *Letters and Homilies for Hellenized Christians, Volume 1: A Socio-Rhetorical Commentary on Titus, 1-2 Timothy and 1-3 John.* Downers Grove, IL: InterVarsity, 2006.

———. *Paul's Narrative Thought World: The Tapestry of Tragedy and Triumph.* Louisville, KY: Westminster John Knox, 1994.

———. *The Acts of the Apostles: A Socio-Rhetorical Commentary.* Grand Rapids: Eerdmans, 1998.

———. *The Indelible Image: The Theological and Ethical Thought World of the New Testament.* Vol. 1: The Individual Witnesses. Downers Grove, IL: InterVarsity, 2009.

———. *Women in the Ministry of Jesus.* New York: Cambridge University Press, 1984.

———. *1 and 2 Thessalonians: A Socio-Rhetorical Commentary.* Grand Rapids: Eerdmans, 2006.

Wolcott, L. Thompson. "Satyāgratha and Makrothumia." *Encounter* 60:1 (Winter 1999) 37–54.

Wood, Booby R. *A Passion for His Passion: A Devotional Commentary on the Book of Acts.* Bloomington, IN: CrossBooks, 2012.

Woodruff, Larry. *The Proclamation of Jesus: Meditations on Jesus and His Message according to Matthew, Mark, Luke, and John.* Bloomington, IN: Xlibris, 2009.

Wright, N. T. "Faith, Virtue, Justification, and the Journey to Freedom." In *The Word Leaps the Gap: Essays on Scripture and Theology in Honor of Richard B. Hays,* edited by J. Ross Wagner, et. al., 472–497. Grand Rapids: Eerdmans, 2008.

———. *Luke for Everyone.* London: Society for Promoting Christian Knowledge, 2001.

Xenophon. *The Education of Cyrus.* Translated and annotated by Wayne Ambler. New York: Cornell University, 2001.

Yen, Maria Do Thi. *The Lucan Journey: A Study of Luke 9:28–36 and Acts 1:6–11 as an Architectural Pair.* Bern, Switzerland: Peter Lange, 2010.

Young, Norman H. "*PAIDAGOGOS*: The Social Setting of a Pauline Metaphor." *NovT* 29:2 (April 1987) 150–176.

———. "The Figure of the *Paidagōgos* in Art and Literature." *Biblical Archaeologist* 53:2 (June 1990) 80–86.

Young, Richard A. *Intermediate New Testament Greek: A Linguistic and Exegetical Approach.* Nashville, TN: B&H, 1994.

Yount, William R. *Created to Learn: A Christian Teacher's Introduction to Educational Psychology.* 2nd ed. Nashville, TN: B&H, 2010.

Zerbe, Gordon M. *Non-Retaliation in Early Jewish and New Testament Texts: Ethical Themes in Social Contexts.* Sheffield: JSOT, 1993.

Zerwick, Maximilian. *Biblical Greek: Illustrated by Examples.* Translated by Joseph Smith. Rome: Pontificio Istituto Biblico, 1963.

Zodhiates, Spiros. *The Complete Word Study Dictionary: New Testament.* Iowa Falls, IA: World, 1992.

Author Index

Scripture Index

OLD TESTAMENT

Acts (*cont.*)